BRUM ROCKED ON!

Laurie Hornsby

Edited by
Mike Lavender

*S*pecial thanks to: Bob Adams, Rod Allen, Harvey Andrews, Graham Ashford, Mick Atkins, George Asbury, Geoff Bache, Micky Bakewell, Maurice Barnes, Tim Bellamy, Brenda Bosworth, Chuck Botfield, Mike Brassington, Ray Bridger, Denis Brown, Mike Burney, Danny Burns, Alan Burrows, Trevor Burton, Rob Caiger, Hartley Cain, Andy Cameron, Johnny Carroll, Mike Carroll, Phil Cash, Dave Challinor, Albert Chapman, Pete Chatfield, Carl Chinn, Alan Clee, Paul Cole, Andy Coleman, Norman Crandles, Dave Cunnington, Tony Dalloway, Mick Davis, Gerry Day, Mel Day, Honri Edouarde, Malc Edwards, Dave Evans, Keith Evans, John Ford, Mal Ford, Les Fortnam, Gerry Freeman, Raymond Froggatt, Ken Fryer, Danny Gallagher, Steve Gibbons, Kex Gorin, Trevor Greaves, Peter Green, Johnny Haines, Norman Haines, Lenny Hall, Brian Harbison, Les Hemming, Jeff Hibbard, John Holman, Martin Hone, Johnny Jones, Reg Jones, Ace Kefford, Mike Kellie, Stasia Kennedy, Roy Kent, Grant Kierney, Danny King, John Landon, Gordon Lee, Gerry Levene, Don McGinty, Laurie Mansfield, Carol Marson, Greg Masters, Terry Matthews, Trisha May, Rob Moore, Johnny Neal, Tony Newman, Brian Nichols, Roger Ottley, Bev Pegg, Dave Pegg, Phil Pearce, Jimmy Powell, Keith Powell, Maurice Preece, Rick Price, Arthur Ray, Mal Ritter, Charlie Robinson, John Rooney, Euan Rose, John Rowlands, Derry Ryan, John Ryan, Phil Savage, Mike Sheridan, Rob Sheward, John Singer, Keith Smart, John Smith, Pete Smith, Ronny Smith, Frankie Spencer, Roger Spencer, Richard Terry, Bobby Thomson, Ray Trilloe, Geoff Turton, Ken Underhill, Doug Vallander, Roy Vears, Terry Wallace, Tim Ward, Clint Warwick, Bob Watkins, Carl Wayne, Pat Wayne, Trevor Westwood, Alan Williams, Tony Withers & Colin Wood.

*E*xtra special thanks to: Tony Brown for invaluable assistance and input. Visit Tony's website, www.themoodyblues.co.uk for more on the MBs. Further resources of particular interest to readers of Brum Rocked On! — Higher and Higher at www.moodies-magazine.com , www.brumbeat.net and, for anything related to ELO, Face the Music at www.ftmusic.com

At the time of going to press, the 'prequel' to this book, Brum Rocked! — the story of rock 'n' roll in Birmingham through the 1950s up to 1963, is sold out. If you would like to be notified in the event of a re-print or the release of a CD ROM version, please register your interest, with a contact address, at: info@brumrock.co.uk or TGM Ltd, Four Ashes Road, Solihull, B93 8NE, UK.

Laurie Hornsby   *Facing: Keith Powell & the Valets at Digbeth Civic Hall 1964*

WE'LL BE RIGHT IN SEVENTH HEAVEN

I t was the Romans' belief that should you disturb a reflected image of yourself, perhaps with a stone cast upon a pool of water, then your soul would be damaged and your life would take seven years to renew itself. That mystical number seven came into its own with the Christian interpretation of the Creation which stated that the world was created in seven days and that seven days would be the duration of its week.

When the clock strikes five, six and seven . . . Bobby Thomson, with Bill Haley

In 1949, the first spark to pop music's creation — the 45rpm single — went almost un-noticed on this side of the Atlantic, but seven years later, in the spring of 1956, the wonderful world of the young found itself in a state of ecstasy, in fact, some would say in seventh heaven. As if the revolving circle of time had finally discovered the very purpose of the little black (seven inch!) disc, it paused to deliver into their midst the hip swinging, hillbilly cat, Elvis Presley, whose recordings of 'Heartbreak Hotel' and 'Blue Suede Shoes' duly leaped into the top ten of the nation's hit parade.

In Britain it seemed every mature adult that held a strong moral view had already been struggling to come to terms with a middle-aged, kiss-curled, singing guitarist by the name of Bill Haley. This man, along with his outfit, the Comets, had preached the joys of putting on 'glad rags' and having fun until the unearthly hour of one in the morning!

To the horror of supposedly good and proper folk, rock 'n' roll music didn't die. Instead it grew with such power. A power that was aided and abetted by two deeply religious men, who, when at the piano, radiated a force so strong as to cause a wounding musical rift between parents and their teenaged offspring. It was to be a rift that would never heal.

Little Richard

Richard Penniman, or to give him his professional title, Little Richard, went totally 'over the top' as his screeching voice proclaimed the splendiferous delights that were to be had 'up the alley' with the goodtime gal, Long Tall Sally, because she, you see, had everything that uncle John could ever wish for.

If Little Richard went over the top, then Jerry Lee Lewis went positively into orbit. Here was a man who had received the call from above to preach the Good Word to those who had strayed and yet, booting the piano stool into touch, proceeded to inform everyone of a secretly located barn where there was a 'Whole lotta shakin' goin' on.'

And only those who had strayed knew anything about the shakin' that Jerry Lee referred to.

Jerry Lee Lewis

Chuck Berry

Back up in the woods among the evergreens stood a rock 'n' roll poet by the name of Chuck Berry. This was the man who had dared to advise dear Ludwig van Beethoven to kindly roll over and get out of the way 'cause the bandstands were rockin' all over Chuck's hometown of St Louis, down to New Orleans then back up to Boston.

In Lubbock, Texas, Buddy Holly was pickin' and singin' the praises of a painted up lady by the name of Annie, who worked The Midnight Shift. With hair worn so high and a red dress so tightly fitted, Annie would happily show her gratitude for that extra-special lift.

By 1959, in the space of two years, Buddy Holly had graced the Top Ten of our charts half a dozen times with songs (in the main self-penned) which would prove so inspirational to the pioneers of contemporary music over the coming years.

*Buddy Holly & the Crickets
visit Longbridge*

Eddie Cochran & Gene Vincent at Coventry Theatre

The British charts were first published on November 14th, 1952 when the New Musical Express declared the Al Martino recording, 'Here in my Heart' to be the number one best selling single record of that particular week.

Buddy Holly perished in a plane crash in the early hours of 3rd February, 1959. A morning that has since been referred to as the day the music died.

Just a year on, in April of 1960, two rebels without causes were taking their rock 'n' roll music to the people of Great Britain with a nation wide theatre tour.

With the successful tour nearing completion, a taxi carrying the 'Be Bop A Lula' and 'Blue Jean Bop' man, Gene Vincent and his rock 'n' roll compadre, Eddie Cochran, hit a kerb and overturned.

In the early hours of a spring morning, in the still of the Wiltshire countryside, Eddie Cochran, the American singer, songwriter and guitarist, whose brief catalogue consisted of such rock 'n' roll gems as 'Summertime Blues', 'C'Mon Everybody' and 'Somethin' Else' lay dead.

John Gibbins was twenty-one years old in 1956 and, as a fine trumpet player, was a prominent member of the Birmingham music scene of that time. He also organised the **Swing Shift**, a jazz club that met at the **Old Stone Cross**, Dale End, Birmingham and had witnessed, first hand, the rock 'n' roll invasion that was responsible for the collapse of the Big Band set up.

John Gibbins at the Swing Shift

The West End, Suffolk Street

"Trombones was the first to cop it, and it was all down to that rock 'n' roll stuff," snapped John.

"I remember seeing trombonists crying on the streets. If you played trombone it was goodnight nurse." said John, shaking his head.

"I used to do a bit with the **Fred Brinklow Band** at the **West End** in Suffolk Street. Fred reckoned he could combat the rock 'n' roll revolution with a burst of his showbiz skills, which he'd honed whilst working as a Butlins' holiday camp entertainer. Fred would emerge from the wings wearing a pith helmet, khaki shorts and clutching a French horn. He'd then blast into 'The Post Horn Gallop' until his lungs could take no more."

John Gibbins paused, winced, topped up his morning cuppa with a drop of 'mothers' ruin' and, for a few seconds, in his mind, John was back on the West End bandstand.

"Poor Fred," he sighed, sipping his tea from the saucer, "The teddy boys just buried him."

The Birmingham teddy boys did not, however, bury the likes of Danny King and the Royals, the Modernaires or Gerry Levene and the Avengers. Mike Sheridan and the Nightriders, El Riot and the Rebels and Pat Wayne and the Rockin' Jaymen all escaped unscathed. As did Keith Powell plus Carl Wayne with the Vikings. The Dominettes, Johnny Neal and the Starliners and the Olympics were perfectly safe. Danny Burns and the Phantoms, Lee Stevens and the Satellites, the Rockin' Berries, Carl and the Cheetahs, Peter Green and the Beachcombers and Denny Laine and the Diplomats may have suffered some form of verbal bruising along the way but, with youth on their side, they emerged as winners. As did Mark Stuart and the Crestas, Gerry Day and the Dukes and quite a few more outfits like them.

Trombone sales were on the slide, and the writing was on the wall for George Clay's Accordion Centre, but the Bingo Boys' favourite amusement arcade was flourishing

All were embraced as heroes by the crepe soled, greasy haired teds, some referred to as 'Bingo Boys' because their place of worship was the amusement arcade next to the Grand Casino ball-room, in Corporation Street.

There, these young purveyors of rock 'n' roll music, in their drape coats and drainpipes or fifty-bob suits, were un-knowingly selecting which musical styles would prosper in the brave new 1960s, and which would fall by the wayside.

Snappy suit or drape coat & drainpipes – the first port of call for the teds would be the Fifty Shilling Tailors

So, seven years after the emergence of Elvis the Pelvis, the carousel revolved once more, and off it stepped the Beatles; firing waves of creativity, inspiration and ambition into the soul of the youth of the land and tempting teenagers to join the new extravaganza of the rock 'n' the circus. A circus which lost one of its star attractions when, following a seven-year itch, the High Courts were asked to set about granting the Beatles their decree absolute.

But what a seven year period it was for Brumbeat. The Applejacks, the Rockin' Berries, the Fortunes, Spencer Davis Group, the Move, Locomotive, and the Moody Blues all achieved top ten chart positions on the national hit parade, waving the flag for the city of Birmingham.

Seven acts. There's that number again. Moving on seven years to 1977, as we here in Britain danced in the streets, celebrating our Queen's Silver Jubilee, word filtered through from Memphis, Tennessee that the King had boarded his Mystery Train and was bound for the Promised Land where he would take his place in that mansion in the sky to rest, peaceful in the knowledge that the circle remained unbroken.

Have you heard the news? No, it ain't 'Good Rockin' Tonight'. . . Elvis just threw a seven.

Chapter One

HEY BABY WON'T YOU TAKE A CHANCE

In 1956, as a result of the output of American rock 'n' roll and rhythm and blues artistes, musical seeds were scattered in youthful abandon around the city of Birmingham in the hope that someday these seeds would produce a harvest of sorts.

From the most humble and primitive beginnings came **Vikings** armed with battered acoustic guitars, a washboard and a tea-chest bass. Roaming the streets of Nechells, this band of young Vikings seemed the friendly type, performing songs that told of activities upon the 'American Deep South Railroad.'

The Vikings' first rehearsal at Nechells Green Community Centre

By 1961 the Vikings had welcomed into their camp, from the Castle Bromwich fjords, a new leader in the shape of **Carl Wayne**. The distinct image and outstanding vocal ability of their new leader would give the Vikings the necessary strength required in their quest to find the elusive dream.

The objective of the Erdington Methodists was to embrace saints and sinners alike. With this task completed, joyous skiffle sessions were held at the **Apollo** cinema, Tyburn Road, resulting in these **Saints and Sinners**

Saints & Sinners 1958

taking an excursion along to the Navigation pub, where they won three suitcases in a talent contest. How these spoils were divided is unknown, but by 1959, their tea-chest bassman, **Ray Thomas**, had packed his bags and set off to join in with a band of **Rebels**, claiming the role of **El Riot** for himself in the process.

Rainbow Boys

Grasshoppers at Blakenhall School

Somewhere over the rainbow, way up Lozells Road, was a place that never warranted a mention in lullabies. It was the assembly room above the Birmingham Co-Operative store. Here, the **Rainbow Boys**, in all their splendour, would strum merrily away on their guitars in the belief that if happy little bluebirds could fly over the rainbow, then why couldn't they.

As far as the Small Heath neighbourhood was concerned, the **Noisy Boys**, a bunch of skifflers, were just that until, with the arrival of amplifiers, they became even more noisy as the **Rockin' Modernaires** and headed south, on the A45, to take up residence at the **Swan** pub at Yardley.

East of Yardley lies the suburb of Garrett's Green where teddy boys and their girlfriends would be hoppin' and a-boppin' at the **Blakenhale High School** Hop to the earthy sounds that **Grasshoppers** were making.

A band of **Dukes**, in the late fifties, were holding court in the Newtown area. These Dukes served Danny, their King, well, and Danny King was well pleased.

A closer examination of the ranks revealed the presence of a former Rainbow Boy, **Albert Eccles**. Albert by now, was being addressed as **Clint Warwick**.

When Mr King broke ranks to serve with the **Royals**, **Gerry Day**, a former boxer and street corner do-whop performer, who had been crooning with the **Del Saints**, found himself keeping company with Dukes.

Keeping company with **Counts** was **Bobby Earl** of Warstock. In reality 'Bobby' was **Reg Jones** whose younger brother **Chris** was, in 1961, rehearsing up his own outfit, the **Chantelles**, at the **Warstock** pub in Yardley Wood, with his fourteen year old nephew **Chris Kefford**. The two Chris's would scrape up any money they could to buy obscure recordings by instrumental groups like the Ventures, the Hunters and the Packabeats. From these sources, the Chantelles would draw their material; material that could be enhanced by the addition of an electronic keyboard player to their company.

Danny King & Clint Warwick

Del Saints at the Red House, Wheeler Street

Henry, from Shirley, was the proud owner an electric organ that Sooty would have probably disowned, and Henry had been blessed with the ability to play the Tornados instrumental hit of August 1962, 'Telstar',

Tony Withers

backwards. Unfortunately Henry made a poor job of playing it forwards and so his days as a Chantelle were numbered from the start.

In the mid 1950s, the Jackie Cooper School of Dance, based at 60, Shirley Road, Acocks Green, had put together a pantomime troupe that performed at factory Christmas parties in and around Birmingham. In its chorus was a young lad with gymnastic skills, **Brian Hines**. As rock 'n' roll songs began to figure prominently on the pop music charts, so Jackie Cooper, the troupe's pianist, encouraged young Brian Hines to 'do a couple with the ol' catarrh'.

By the summer of 1959, Brian had teamed up with **Tony Withers**, who played guitar with the Acocks Green outfit, the **Buccaneers**. Together Brian and Tony were the **Hepcats**, on the prowl in search of an audience. On finding such an audience at the **Dogpool** pub in Stirchley, Brian Hines was immediately ordered from the premises for appearing to be under the legally required age of fourteen years. The same judgement was handed down to him at the **Warstock** pub but, with grim determination, the Hepcats were finally allowed to perform at the **Valley** pub, Yardley Wood, on condition that Brian didn't stray from the sanctuary of the far corner of the bar room.

The Buccaneers with Peter Green & the Beachcombers

When Brian eventually did stray it was to become **Johnny Dean**, leader of a bunch of rockers that took their name from a model of Norton motorcycle, the **Dominators**.

As a boy, **Peter Green** had marvelled at the way his grandfather, seated at the upright piano, would entertain the Camden Street neighbourhood with a little ditty, 'Shimmies and Shirts', a novelty song that told of the Monday morning ritual of boiling the family wash in the courtyard brewhouse.

'We mangle shirts, shimmies and sheets and things to cover your bum,' would be the comical lyric dancing around in Peter's head as his young mind drifted into golden slumbers.

Yardleys

The geography and construction of the popular song always held a fascina-tion for the inquisitive Peter Green; how the song would paint a picture in the listener's mind; how there would be a phrase somewhere in the layout that would trigger a reaction, prompting people to sing along with the performer.

By 1960 Peter Green had formed a musical partnership with **Dezi Vyse**, another young lad with rock 'n' roll aspirations, and the two guitarists built on early experiences of free-and-easy performances to form the **Beachcomb-ers**.

Progressing from **St Patrick's Church Hall**, across from Dudley Road Hospital, to the hallowed **Plaza**, Rookery Road, Handsworth, Peter Green

Bobby Coral with the Beachcombers

was prompted to invest 140 guineas in a pink Fender Strato-caster guitar from **Yardleys** music shop on Constitution Hill.

A second vocalist, **John Ship**, professionally known as **Bobby Coral**, was then brought in to augment the Beachcomber line-up.

Bobby Coral became the subject of heavy investment by the Beachcombers when a stage suit was purchased for him. This suit would always be referred to as Bobby's dinner suit, allegedly due to the gravy spillage down its front!

The Grand Hotel

Never spilling a drop of gravy during their course of their duties as silver service waiters at the Grand Hotel, Colmore Row, were a group of lads, who, when off duty, flew high as the **Deltas**, with vocalist **Pat Wayne** acting as their musical maitre d'.

By 1962 Pat had hung up his black and whites to make the journey from the Grand Hotel to the **Crown** pub, in Hill Street, where he served most admirably as vocalist with the **Rockin' Jaymen**.

Pat Wayne & the Deltas

Las Vegas (the coffee bar)

Ronny Smith, Phil Ackrill, and Bev Bevan were, in 1960, unenthusiastic pupils at Moseley Grammar School. The only effort the young Bev seemed to make at school was the coiffeuring of his 'Bobby Rydell' hairstyle. All other efforts went into furthering their progress as **Ronny and the Renegades**, who made their debut as would-be pop stars at the **Las Vegas** coffee bar on Summer Row, a place that was already frequented by real-life renegades!

It followed that pretty soon the Renegades took amnesty to become **Senators**.

Ronny Smith and Bev Bevan had managed, despite being under-age, to gain admission to the **Adelphi Ballroom**, West Bromwich, where they witnessed the American legend, Gene Vincent, in action. As their leather clad hero swung his leg over the microphone stand one last time, the two schoolboys ran for the exit doors with Bev managing to purloin the show's advertising poster as he did so. This poster hung on his bedroom wall throughout the remainder of the decade. Beneath the name Gene Vincent, in bold letters, was the name of that evening's supporting artiste — **Don Arden**. Every morning when Bev Bevan awoke, the first thing his eyes would focus on was the name of the man that would turn his dream of rock 'n' roll stardom into reality, with or without the Bobby Rydell hairstyle.

Taking employment at Zissmans', the gents outfitters in Sparkbrook, Ronny Smith passed away his time by creating names for fictitious pop groups. Zissmans' were, in late 1961, promoting a trendy new line in shirts, the Daylin Diplomat. Ronny's imagination was triggered. Taking a pencil from behind his ear and dabbing the lead tip on his tongue he began doodling on the back of the cardboard shirt box. As Ronny Smith doodled, so the Daylin Diplomat evolved into **Denny Laine and the Diplomats**.

Ronny & the Renagades

Gene Vincent

By early 1962, Senators Phil Ackerill and Bev Bevan had entered into an ambitious project with Dominators **Dave 'Wongy' Wheeland** and **Brian Hines**. It was the formation of a travelling band with Messrs Ackerill, Bevan, Wheeland and Hines now enjoying professional status. When it came to naming the new outfit, Ronny Smith's wordplay resurfaced. Doodle became reality. Denny Laine and the Diplomats were born.

The **Dominettes** could be confined no more. From the steam of the **Sicilio** coffee bar on Five Ways, they broke free of their shackles to demonstrate, via their charismatic front man **Steve Gibbons**, a genuine feel for rock and blues. Come the early sixties and with four years experience of the music biz under their belts, the Dominettes were very aware of the importance of image. Drummer **Jim Holden** shrewdly observed that the band weren't exactly smooth operators when it came to persuasive conversation with members of the opposite sex. In fact, compared to the booted and suited clientele of the Sicilio, the Dominettes were just a bunch of **Uglys**.

Sicilio Coffee Bar

Initially with **Billy King** at the helm, **Mike Sheridan** and his **Nightriders** rode a path of determination to become one of Birmingham's most popular attractions. This popularity was borne out when, in January of 1962, they were awarded first place over Cliff Ward and the Cruisers in the **Locarno** beat group contest. That night Mike Sheridan had chosen to make his appearance in front of the two-thousand punters, posing in menacing stance, on top of the grand piano.

As the stage revolved to reveal the Nightriders, Mike Sheridan growled the lines of Johnny Kidd's tried and tested opening routine.

"I can tell by the way that you look at me!"

Little ladies, some close to fainting, screamed out heart felt feelings.

Mike, making eye contact, let his backbone slip and provocatively pursed his lips.

"I can tell pretty momma and it's plain to s-"

"Oy! Get down!" interrupted the Locarno odd-job man, climbing onto the stage.

Gesturing franticly, the brown cow-gowned, flat-capped old chap continued shouting his orders.

"Get orf that pee-anna! Now!"

Mike Sheridan, understandably distracted, struggled on.

"I can tell by the way that hold my-"

"I said ooorf!" yelled the old man, tugging at Mr Sheridan's tapered flannels.

Night Owls

Sundowners

The packed ballroom descended into chilling silence as Mike, in respect of his elder, dutifully obeyed.

"D'you do that at 'ome?" asked the odd job man, cuffing the young punk's ear.

Perhaps the wise old man of the Locarno needed the tranquillity of the countryside to ease his troubled mind. Indeed he would have been welcome to spend his weekend summer nights on Cannock Chase in company with the **Night Owls**, a Druid-style bunch of jolly Castle Bromwich folk.

Those aptly named **Sundowners**, from Acocks Green, provided the jigs and reels for the gibberish-chanting Night Owls as they pranced around the campfire until the twittering of the birds heralded a brand new dawn.

The dawn couldn't come too quickly for **Mick Atkins**, the Sundowners' lead guitarist. With a repertoire that was extremely limited to say the least, every other tune he played was 'Guitar Boogie Shuffle'.

Maybe guitarist **Martin Baggott** and his combo, the **Crestas**, knew a few more tunes. Martin, along with rhythm guitarist **Phil Cash** (whose guitar was bigger than him) and drummer **Gerry Freeman**, were bob-a-job Boy Scouts of the 1st Olton Company and had initially formed the group to 'ride along on the crest of a wave' at a couple of Gang Shows. Helped out by Gerry's fiancé, **Megan Davies**, who managed to sing a song or two, the Crestas progressed to paid gigs at **Solihull Council House**, with Megan now finding her way around a bass guitar.

Fellow Boy Scout, **Don Gould** soon augmented their line up as pianist, and with it came a new name. The Crestas became the **Jaguars**.

The Crestas

There was also a band of **Jaguars** running loose around the Worcestershire countryside. These Jaguars had a guitarist, **Dave Mason** and a drummer with a moody image by the name of **Jim Capaldi**, who hailed from the town of Evesham. However Evesham, in 1963, was a fair journey from Solihull, so it would have been highly unlikely that the paths of these Jaguars would cross.

The Jaguars

Spencer Davis

Crossing the leafy paths of Birmingham University in early 1962 was a young gentleman from Swansea, intent on studying German. However, once the student grant had been obtained, the first thing that **Spencer Davis** did was to purchase a twelve-string guitar in order to perform skiffle songs with the **Excelsior Jazz Band**.

In the autumn of that year, the Excelsior jazzers, being charitable lads, offered their services at a concert that took place at **Digbeth Civic Hall** in aid of Oxfam.

Sharing that bill was the **Muff Woody Jazz Band**. They had first seen the light of day at **Great Barr Comprehensive School** as the **Suburban Stompers** and were led by bass player **Muff Winwood**, with his young brother **Steve** along on piano and guitar.

Digbeth Civic Hall

The thing that the Excelsior and Muff Woody jazzers had in common in those days was the drummer that they shared — **Pete York** — a Nottingham lad who was apprenticed at the firm of Guest, Keen and Nettlefolds in Winson Green.

During the Oxfam benefit concert, Spencer Davis was joined for an impromptu session of blues and skiffle by Pete York and the Winwood brothers.

Hill Street blues at the Golden Eagle

Six months later, in the spring of 1963, and with the demand for rhythm and blues music growing stronger by the day, Spencer Davis telephoned the Winwood brothers and Pete York. Their pleasure was requested at the **Golden Eagle** pub in Hill Street to make up the **Rhythm and Blues Quartet**

It was a call that made pop music history because it bought to the attention of the Birmingham public the incredible talents of pianist, guitarist and possessor of quite the most unique set of vocal pipes around when it came to black blues songs, Stevie Winwood.

These talents were demonstrated in no uncertain terms by stunning versions of Hogey Carmichael's 'Georgia', Leiber and Stoller's 'Searchin'' or perhaps some Howlin' Wolf, Lightnin'' Hopkins, Willy Dixon or a couple of Muddy Waters numbers that were included for good measure.

A good measure of Chuck Berry material was always guaranteed in the performances of Longbridge's **Rockin' Berries** — hence their name.

The Rockin' Berries had started out in 1959 as the **Bobcats**, a skiffle band at Moseley Art School, where pupils would marvel at the ability of guitarist **Brian 'Chuck' Botfield**. Here was a lad who could strum the chords to 'Diana' without once looking at his fingers!

The Rockin' Berries had spent a fair amount of 1961 and 1962 in Germany, honing their performing skills. On their return home, these skills were demonstrated by soulful renditions of the Coasters' 'Along Came Jones' or 'Western Movies'. During these performances, the Rockin' Berries would all don ten-gallon cowboy hats to bring a little 'prairie dust' into the proceedings.

During their early German days, the Rockin' Berries had been fronted by the man billed as 'Mr Dynamite', the rhythm and blues artiste, **Jimmy Powell**. On leaving the Rockin' Berries, Jimmy Powell went on record as the first Brumbeat artiste with a commercial release — 'Sugar Babe', produced by Jack Good for the Decca Record Company.

The Rockin' Berries at Rubery Social Club

O n the morning of January 1st, 1962, the Decca Record Company put four young hopefuls from Liverpool through their paces. The outcome of that recording test was that the head of Artistes and Repertoire at Decca Records, Dick Rowe (and that was his name, not his address) advised the enthusiastic manager of these four young men that they should forget any hopes of a musical career. Guitar groups were, in his professional opinion, on the way out!

Chapter Two

ONE – TWO – THREE – FOUR!

A simple count in was all it took to ignite a musical revolution that rolled on for a decade and will never ever be experienced again. Paul McCartney's count-in, in March 1963, not only cued in the world to the first ever Beatles' album 'Please Please Me', it generated a kick start into a way of life that would for many a youth be the warmest and most special of grooves.

The Beatles had been in Birmingham on Sunday, the 13th of January. Interrupting a tour of Scottish ballrooms, they had travelled to the **ATV Studios** in Aston, to mime to their newly released second single, 'Please Please Me'.

ATV's Television Theatre and studios in Aston

This was the Beatles' network television debut, their contribution to the

'Thank Your Lucky Stars' pop show, which went out to the nation on the following Saturday evening.

What the viewers witnessed on that transmission was the launch of the swinging sixties in music, fashion and attitude.

Here was a pop act, the like of which had never been seen before. No moody facial expressions for these boys. Instead, like Cheshire cats, these Beatles grinned so cheekily into the cameras, punching out their very own lyrics in gritty and strangely melodic voices. Voices that would suddenly and quite unexpectedly break into wild falsetto, and when that falsetto line, "Whoa yeah!" came hollering out, these Beatles would be shaking their busby style fringes around, inciting screams of uncontrollable adulation from the studio audience.

This group didn't dance in step or aim their guitars menacingly to choreographed movements. This group moved as they felt. Be it on or off the beat. Who cared? And through it all, came the message loud and clear, " Hey, you out there! You too can do this as well if you really want to."

On the evening of the transmission, the Beatles appeared at the **Old Hill Plaza**. They were booked to appear at the **Ritz** in Kings Heath immediately afterwards but with snow falling so heavily, the date was re-arranged for early February.

As the youth of Great Britain lay shell shocked in their beds on the morning of Sunday, 20th January 1963, as a result of the first sightings of the Fab Four, the **Vikings**, like so many bands of Vikings before them, were crossing the English Channel. These Vikings, **Carl Wayne**, **Terry Wallace**, **Johnny Mann**, **Barry Harbor** and **Dave Hollis** were bound for the Rio Bar, Stuttgart, Germany where they were to perform from 7:30pm until 3:00am, seven nights a week. Also squeezed into the van and gasping for air was **Alan Wooldridge**, a capable vocalist, who was along to lend a hand should Carl Wayne's vocal chords surrender to such rigorous demands.

All smiles & Fenders – Carl Wayne & the Vikings

Danny Burns could confirm the extent of those demands. Following an engagement with his band of Phantoms at the Storyville club, Frankfurt, he had returned to his Erdington roots that very same week.

"I'd been singing rock stuff flat out every evening from seven at night until four in the morning," said Danny, who in reality was the highly conservative **Peter Worrall**. "I told the Vikings to watch out. Them Germans want your blood!"

Shortly after commencing work at the Rio Bar, the Vikings went for broke and acquired Fender guitars and amplifiers.

"We already had the grey suits," explained Terry.

The **Chantelles** couldn't afford grey suits but their guitarist **Chris Jones** did manage to push the boat out and purchase an echo chamber.

"We were doing the **Warstock** pub every other Friday," said **Chris Kefford**, "But we needed a singer. My uncle Reg put us on to **Johnny Fincham**, who knew a few songs. Then the Counts packed up and suddenly **Reg Jones** was available. Johnny was coming good so we had two singers."

Discarding the stage name '**Bobby Earl**' for the cooler sounding '**Steve Farren**', the experienced Reg Jones was able to introduce the Chantelles into the big wide world of the Birmingham music scene.

"I introduced the Chantelles to the 'Whispering Giant' who took us from the Warstock and the Haven pubs in Yardley Wood to the pleasures that awaited at the **Wharf Hotel,** Holt Fleet." said Reg, rather proudly. The Whispering Giant in question was the agent, **John Saint**.

R eg **Calvert**, the agent and promoter, didn't have a nickname, but good fortune entered his life by way of the **Strollers**.

Whilst pupils at Moseley Grammar School in 1960, **Rod Bainbridge** and **Barry Pritchard** had begun strumming together, and with the addition of drummer **Mee Clark**, the Strollers struck a blow for freedom at **Wythall Village Hall**. "No bass in those days," said Rod.

Finally, with the addition of **Mick Tomlinson** on bass, the Strollers took a stroll over Highters Heath to arrive at **Shirley Institute**. After a few successful performances at the Institute, the Strollers were engaged to provide accompaniment at **Billesley Community Centre**, for a young gentleman, originally from Coventry, but now sporting an Australian accent and a genuine suntan — Frank Ifield.

Cliftones — Rod Allen, Barry Prichard & Glen Dale

Come 1963, the Strollers were a proficient group and making regular appearances for Reg Calvert at the **BRS Club** on Bromford Lane, Erdington and **Nuneaton Co-op Hall**.

Rod Bainbridge takes up the story, "Reg Calvert saw something in myself and Barry. He suggested we turn full-time professional. The other two lads didn't fancy the idea anyway, but Barry and I went willingly. I was working for the Co-op Insurance at the time, so what had I got to lose?"

Chez Calvert — Clifton Hall

Coming under the guidance of Reg Calvert entailed taking up residence at the Calvert household, Clifton Hall, Rugby, where Rod Bainbridge, now using the professional name of **Rod Allen**, and Barry Pritchard, shared accommodation with other Calvert discoveries, **Buddy Brittain**, **Danny Storme**, **Glen Dale** and **Mike West**.

Discovering that their voices married perfectly together with Glen Dale, who originally hailed from Ashford, Kent, Rod and Barry pooled their efforts to become the **Cliftones**, taking aboard guitarist **Dave Carr** and drummer **Andy Brown** in the process.

Mike West was, as most Cockneys are, a born showman. When Reg Calvert suggested that he become **Robbie Hood**, a pop singer with a band of merry men in support, Mike West headed for the forest immediately.

"Please don't ask," pleaded Rod Bainbridge, dropping his head into his hands. "Yes, we did it! Tights and all! Just for a while we were the **Merrimen**!"

Cliftones with Ketty 'Love Letters' Lester

Although the Cliftones didn't know it at the time, their association with Mike West would lead them to a change of fortunes.

Good fortune had already prevailed three year previously for the **Modernaires** when **Joe Regan** had paid them a visit at the **Swan** pub at Yardley. Joe immediately engaged the Modernaires for three nights a week at his **Ritz Ballroom** in Kings Heath and one night a week at his **Handsworth** and **Old Hill Plazas**. With their two night residency at the Swan, the Modernaires, as semi-professionals, were living the life of Riley.

Looking out for the kind of break that would lead *them* to the life of Riley were a bunch of young hopefuls from the Shard End area of the city. At fourteen years of age, **Kex Gorin**, of Brownfield Road, was still a pupil at Alderlea secondary school, but had very little interest in anything else but hammering his drums. Every spare moment was spent with a couple of

Modernaires at the Swan, Yardley

fellow school pupils, guitarists **Jeff Lynne** from Shard End Crescent, and **Dave Watson**, who lived over the road from Jeff, next to the good doctor Dean's surgery.

"We'd practice all the Del Shannon songs and whatever we could pick up from the Beatles, for hours on end," explained Kex .

It was this study of lyrical and melodic construction that was to prove so wondrously inspirational for Jeff Lynne in the years to come.

Initially toying with the name the Rockin' Hellcats, they finally settled on the 'Andicapps, their first public appearance being the **Shard End Social Club**, in Brookbank Avenue. So successful were the 'Andicapps in their interpretation of the hit songs of the day that their services were called for at **Aylesford Hall** on Packington Avenue and **Moorfield Hall** on Hartshill Road, just off the Heathway.

Returning from Aylesford Hall one evening, their van pulled up outside the Lynne household with such a jolt that the back doors flew open and the drum cases rolled away down Shard End Crescent!

"Jeff was not amused and grabbed his amplifier, his red Burns guitar and struggled off up the pathway. For some reason, probably temper, he accidentally left his guitar out on the path overnight," recalled Kex Gorin. "It rained during the night and rusted all the magnetic pick-ups."

Shaking, but not with temper was **Roy Vears**, the lead singer of Kings Norton's **Strangers**. Every Tuesday evening the youth of the Pool Farm estate would descend upon **Greaves Hall** to witness the strange events that occurred during the electrifying guitar break in the band's rendition of Johnny Kidd's 'Shakin' All Over'.

"Roy would freeze every nerve in his body then—bingo!" exclaimed rhythm guitarist **Dave 'Effram' Evans**. "His arms, legs, fingers, in fact his whole body, would start shaking as if he'd stuck his thumb into the light bulb socket!"

Roy and Dave, with lead guitarist **Tony Lawrence**, had begun their rock 'n' roll sessions at Greaves Hall back in 1962, when the extent of their equipment was a 15 watt Watkins Dominator amplifier and a ten-bob tape recorder microphone.

Strangers & friends

With the addition of bass guitarist **Ian White** who, according to Dave Evans, 'could pull the birds', and drummer **Roger Spencer**, who had done the rounds of the pubs with his pianist father, the Strangers impressed **Joe Regan** enough to obtain bookings at the **Ritz**, Kings Heath.

One evening, as the Strangers tootled home from the Ritz, they chanced upon a broken down vehicle on Parsons Hill, Kings Norton. Stopping to lend a hand, the boys were astonished to recognise the grubby face that emerged from beneath the bonnet of the vehicle. It was none other than the swashbuckling cockney himself, **Fred Heath**, alias **Johnny Kidd** (minus his eyepatch).

With Brummie hospitality in full flow, Johnny Kidd, chilled to the bone and hands caked in muck and oil, was ushered to the Spencer household where hot tea was in abundance.

As Johnny Kidd gulped his tea, the furniture was rearranged to create enough space in the far corner of the lounge for Roy Vears, who was in the hallway psyching himself up, to demonstrate his 'Shakin' All Over' routine for the man himself.

The Teenscenes

"Credit where its due, Roy's shaking took some beating that night," said Dave Evans. "We was proud of him."

Johnny Kidd, obviously impressed, looked up and yawned, "Great. Yeah. Any more tea in the pot?"

The **Three Gs** from Smethwick, comprising of **Dennis Horsley**, **Roger Francis** and **Colin Cooper**, decided to board the rock 'n' roll wagon by joining forces with drummer **Johnny Turton** and guitarist **Trevor Greaves**, who had both seen service with Ladywood's **Teenscenes**. Making their base at the **Birmid Club** in Smethwick, the boys rehearsed solidly before confidently hitting the road as the **Crescendos**.

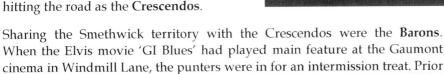

Crescendos at the Birmid Club

Barons at the Farcroft

Sharing the Smethwick territory with the Crescendos were the **Barons**. When the Elvis movie 'GI Blues' had played main feature at the Gaumont cinema in Windmill Lane, the punters were in for an intermission treat. Prior to the 'Pearl and Dean' commercial slot the Barons performed their signature tune, 'Baron Beat', and another original of theirs 'Drinka Pinta Milka Day', both numbers composed by their guitarist **Ken Underhill**. Completing the line up were **Al Hawkins** on guitar, **Maurice Hayward** on bass, drummer **Brian Hughes** with **Keith Armstrong**, alias **Jerry Noble**, out front as the 'vocalist with the showmanship.'

Word of the 'Baronbeat' travelled fast. Billy Elliot, a former West Bromwich Albion footballer, was now licensee of the **Farcroft**

*Fred Hall's alter ego –
Billy Yukon*

Hotel, Rookery Road in Handsworth. Billy was quick to contact **Fred Hall**, manager of the Barons. Soon the boys were part of the fixtures and fittings at the Farcroft.

Most evenings **Fred Hall** would drive the Barons to their engagements. He'd help unload the equipment before setting off for the Delishia, formerly a cinema, on Gosta Green, or the Embassy Rink in Sparkhill where, on arrival, he would change into navy blue woollen swimming trunks. With the house tannoy broadcasting a fanfare of trumpets, courtesy of a crackling 78rpm record, Fred Hall would mount the splintered wooden steps and hop confidently through the ropes and into the wrestling ring. Rinsing his mouth with water from a Tizer pop bottle, Fred would be bending and stretching whilst acknowledging the vicious looking character facing him in the opposite corner. The master of ceremonies, gesturing to Fred, would then announce, in such grand manner, "Ladeez and Genteelmen! Direct from the Norf West Frontier! The former scalp-hunter, **Billy Yukon**!"

Billy Yukon and the Barons, were well aware of a bunch of renegades on the loose in the Perry Barr area. These **Renegades**, guitarists **Denis Gibson**, **Kim Brown** and **Ian Mallett** with **Graham Johnson** on drums, were on friendly terms with a band of **Cimarrons** who roamed the south-westerly plains of the Longbridge and Rednal areas of Birmingham. Guitarists **Rick Price** and **Alan Hicks** initially had **John Shepherd** on tom-toms before **Dave Spillsbury** started beating out the messages. **Maurice Preece** was the peace-seeking bass player.

"We always referred to Dave as 'Spanner'," explained Maurice. "Something to do with his nuts!"

*Lee Zenith & the
Cimarrons*

An extremely wild 'medicine man' sort of chap in a yellow suit led these Cimarrons. At night he bore the name of **Lee Zenith**; by day he was **Ray Hyde**, a subdued apprentice electrician from Stechford.

"He was a Zenith and Hyde character," observed a wise Maurice Preece.

Lee Zenith and the Cimarrons had cut their teeth with a weekly session in the school hall of Harborne Juniors in Station Road, before moving into the big league of licensed premises.

WSJM was a big promotions set-up around Birmingham in early 1963, booking such haunts as the **Hen and Chickens** at Langley, the **Golden Cross** at Harborne, the **White Lion** at Portway and **The Clock** at Bickenhill. Lee Zenith and the Cimarrons visited them all.

AB **Promotions** was another company that was keen to be seen as friendly to the likes of Renegades, Cimarrons, Barons and anyone else that could whack out a tune. The 'A' was **Bob Anthony** and the 'B' was **Bob Bradley**, lead guitarist with **Danny Ray and the Rayvons**.

Cliff Ward & the Cruisers

The two Bobs stuck on the rock 'n' roll entertainment at the **Black Horse**, in Northfield, the **Selly Oak Institute**, the **Tarde-bigge** at Finstall near Bromsgrove, and **Droitwich Winter Gardens** where Lee Zenith and the Cimarrons would alternate their appearances with **Cliff Ward and the Cruisers**.

"Droitwich was something else crowd-wise," said Maurice Preece. "Lee Zenith, or Ray, if you like, would holler out rock 'n' roll all night, jumping on the tables and all over the place!"

At the **Masonic Hall** on **Bordeseley Green East**, Lee Zenith was in no mood to take prisoners. He would always close with 'Kansas City', using the old Red Indian ploy of lulling his prey into a false sense of security. With the crowd yelling back the chorus, "Hey, hey, hey, hey!" Lee Zenith and the Cimarrons were not allowed to depart without an encore. So fired up was Lee Zenith that he threw himself into the Little Richard barnstormer, 'Long Tall Sally'. As the yellow suited Lee screamed "We're gonna have some fun tonight!" he leapt high into the air. On landing, one of his legs went straight through the wooden boards of the stage!

Lee Stevens & the Satellites

There was some fun to be had at **Alex Hooper's** ballroom, especially on a Friday, when the attraction was **Lee Stevens and the Satellites**, who were 'guaranteed,' as it said on the posters, 'to put you into orbit'. The Satellites were guitarists **Paul Brunt**, **Roger Gauntlett** and **Mike Clifford**, who doubled on what he described as a mouth harp. Sixteen-year-old **Malcolm Priddey** hammered his drums solidly at the back of the stage. Lee Stevens was actually an Alum Rock youth — **Norman Crandles**.

"By day I had been working at the

Gerry Levene

Beatles with Gerry Day at Maney Hall

Southalls factory. We were in the female hygiene business," Norman explained, coughing with slight embarrassment. "Then the Satellites took off and we were working six nights a week — so I threw the towel in."

It was backstage at the **Adelphi Ballroom**, West Bromwich, when the young Satellite Malc Priddey experienced his first taste of pop star adulation from an infatuated fan. As young master Priddey climbed down from the drum riser on the revolved stage, a voluptuous woman lay in wait. Manoeuvring him to a nearby cubbyhole, she started to kiss and cuddle the boy who was not long out of short trousers.

"They said she'd been with half the men in West Bromwich — but in those days it was only a small place," said Malcolm, in defence of his reputation.

"Suddenly there was a torch shining in my eyes," he explained a little shame faced. "It was the bouncers — I'd been leaning on the master light switch and plunged the whole ballroom into darkness!"

With their single 'Please Please Me' riding high on the nation's best selling charts, the Beatles were fast becoming Britain's number-one live attraction. **Gerry Levene**, who with his band the **Avengers**, had supported the Beatles quite a few times around Merseyside spoke of the close affinity the Beatles had with their army of fans.

"Ken Smith had booked them at **Maney Hall**, Sutton Coldfield, way before the release of 'Please Please Me' for a fee of fifty quid. Brian Epstein could

have demanded four or five times that amount but they were intent on fulfilling all bookings at the agreed fee where possible."

Gerry Day of the Dukes picks up the tale, "At Maney Hall, myself and the Dukes always closed the show. Ken Smith introduced me to the Beatles and asked if I'd mind opening for them. I said it was okay with me as long as it didn't affect the dough. After all, twelve quid was twelve quid!"

Phil King & the Couriers at Elmdon Heath Village Hall

Keith Williams was, at that time, a member of Phil King and the Couriers and one of the privileged present to witness the Beatles at Maney Hall.

"The Beatles were an absolute powerhouse of energy," recalled Keith. "What they generated that night was fantastic. From their opener, Little Richard's 'Oh Ma Soul' right through to their last song, 'Roll Over Beethoven', which Ringo played standing up!"

Keith Williams' band, the Couriers had commenced life in 1960 at Bushmoore Hall, Hall Green. With Keith on bass, the Couriers had Brian Ennis on drums, with Dave Castle and Roy Quilliam on guitars. Eventually Phil Jones, from Pype Hayes had joined the fold as vocalist. Stealing everything Bobby Vee had going for him Phil and the boys hit the road as Phil King and the Couriers. A road that led them to the Royal Oak at Kingsbury, where, for a fee of five pounds, they appeared every Sunday evening.

Frock 'n' roll – the Sabres with Christine Hill. . .

. . . and without

A couple of days after Maney Hall, the Beatles played the re-arranged date at the Ritz, Kings Heath. Supporting them on that memorable evening were the Sabres, from Smethwick. Originally formed at Holly Lodge Grammar School, they had cut their teeth at the Uplands Youth Club before progressing to the Gay Tower Ballroom in Edgbaston. Having a glamorous rhythm guitarist in Christine Hill was certainly no handicap but by the time the Sabres had made the big time of the Regan venues, Christine had found pastures new on the working mens' club circuit, and had been replaced by pianist John Gordon.

Guitarist Bob Watkins recalls the evening the Sabres supported the Beatles, "We had half an hour to play before the Beatles got on stage," said Bob. "The crowd was packing in solidly around the stage and there were Vox amps and drums being passed over people's heads. As we struggled off the stage the Beatles arrived at the top of the stairs, surrounded by the bouncers with

Ronny & the Senators at Alex Hoopers —

— featuring Tony & Ronny on piano

Joe Regan shouting for everyone to "Git out off der way!" Mr Regan was a happy man. He had re-arranged the snowed off date at the same fee that he'd negotiated with Brian Epstein three months previously!"

Still working for the same fees but without complaint, especially at **Alex Hooper's**, was **Ronny Smith**. Having made showbiz history by surviving the touch and go merchants at the **Las Vegas Coffee Bar**, Ronny, with the **Senators**, appeared most Saturdays at Alex Hooper's. The Senators now comprised of **Tony Withers** and **John Starkey** on guitars, **Tony Lewis** was on bass with **Alan Bennet**, formerly of the **Avengers**, at the drum kit.

Ronny Smith, always the showman, would climb onto the grand piano, and with the audience egging him on, and much to the management's distain, he would dance the twist and then leap from the piano and into the audience. The management's only pleasure came when Ronny would slip and fall off the highly polished Steinway.

A big song for the Senators back in the Spring of 1963 was Joey Dee's 'Peppermint Twist'. Ronny Smith tells the tale, "John Starkey's stage suit previously belonged to a bloke called Jumbo, who was enormous and the

trousers were like barrage balloons. John was a mere five feet three inches and weighed eight stones soaking. When we did 'Peppermint Twist' John would be twisting like a lunatic, but the trousers never moved!"

Hi Cards at Weoley Castle Community Centre

Moving very nicely around **Weoley Castle**, first at the **Community Centre** and then the **California** pub were **Frankie Williams** and the **Hi Cards**, who were **Ray Sheldon**, and **Colin Brookes** on guitars, **Jim Bevan** on bass and on drums, **Dave Parker**. Frankie Williams was from the old school," said **Johnny Neal**, (not exactly a newcomer to the scene himself!)

Neither was **Gerry Levene**. What he and his band, the **Avengers**, needed was a hit record. Indeed he and the band — guitarists **'Sprike' Hopkins** and **Alan Watson**, bass player **Jimmy Onslow** and drummer **Graeme Edge** — had been promised by their main employer, **Ma Regan**, that when the appropriate moment came, she would have a word with the people from Decca Records. After all, she was giving Decca artists plenty of engagements at her ballrooms.

Holding up the bar of the **California** pub on a regular basis was local teddy boy **John Ryan**. In his midnight blue drape, tailored especially for him by Hedley James of Cotteridge, John Ryan was a true reflection of the youth of the day.

Hi Cards — Frankie Williams takes the mic

"I also had a spare drape made which was stardust and so Hedley James put a pair of blue suede shoes in the bag for nothing. He said the soles was crepe — but they seemed okay to me." admitted John in total honesty. Being a regular at the California, John Ryan had witnessed, first hand, the emergence onto the rock and blues scene of 'Mr Dynamite' him-

self — **Jimmy Powell**, firstly with the **Rockin' Berries**, then the **Detours** and the **Jumpin' Jacks**.

"Jimmy would insist on the Jumpin' Jacks jumpin' to the beat as they played," John Ryan continued. "Half way through a song he'd glance over his shoulder to make sure they was still jumpin'!"

Sombreros at the Acorn

Mexican folk, it is said, jump on their sombreros. At the King George V pub, Northfield, the local Gardeners' Association were holding their annual bash and much preferred to dance *to* these **Sombreros**, passing the hat around at the evening's conclusion.

The Sombreros, who hailed from the Northfield neck of the woods — vocalist **Pete Smith**, guitarists **Grant Kearney** and **Stan Homer** with **Brian Bardell** on drums — were making their show business debut.

"We never had a bass player in the early days," said Grant, "But we were happy." They were happier still when they found bass guitarist **Rick Williams**.

The boys had already cut their teeth at the **Downbeat Club**, which met at the **Acorn** in Wheeler Street, Hockley and the **Glebe** pub, in Kitts Green where it was said that if you had two ears, you were a stranger. The Sombreros had proved their worth. Their only problem was transport.

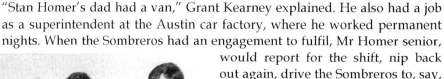

William & the Conquerors at Hopwood Caravan Club

"Stan Homer's dad had a van," Grant Kearney explained. He also had a job as a superintendent at the Austin car factory, where he worked permanent nights. When the Sombreros had an engagement to fulfil, Mr Homer senior, would report for the shift, nip back out again, drive the Sombreros to, say, the **Meadway** pub at Kitts Green, where they had a regular Friday night residency, and then sneak back into the factory.

At ten o'clock, Mr Homer would again go absent without leave and pick up the boys from the Meadway, before smuggling himself back into Britain's biggest factory having made sure that the Sombreros were tucked up safely in their beds.

The Spanish term for cowboys is Vaqueros. These **Vaqueros** rode the high Sierras of Yardley Wood, calling in at the **Christ Church Youth**

Club where **Brian Harbison**, **Mick Webley** and **Bob Adams** would swig a little cactus juice and strum their Futurama guitars whilst percussionist **Bryan Miles** would rattle his maracas.

Realising that the way forward was to have a singer handy, **Mick Fisher**, who hung out at the **Holy Cross Youth Club**, was shanghaied into the line up. To celebrate the transformation, Brian Harbison purchased a proper bass guitar and the Vaqueros took a step back in time to emerge as **William and the Conquerors**.

Harry 'Al' Jackson

Solihull's **Jaguars** were also hungry to compete in the pop group market but as a purely instrumental outfit they didn't have a prayer. An advertisement in the 'Birmingham Mail' for a vocalist brought **Harry 'Al' Jackson** into the picture. **Phil Cash**, of the Jaguars, popped down to the salon in Olton where Al was a hairdresser.

"Al seemed an okay bloke so I offered him the job. His dad kept the Moonrakers pub, so maybe there was the chance of a few gigs into the bargain!" Phil Cash recalls. Al Jackson and the Jaguars quickly became regulars at the **Hen and Chickens** on the Wolverhampton Road and the **Atlas Ballroom**, Stechford.

As the fragrance of Cadbury's chocolate wafted around Bournville, the youth of that picturesque suburb were twistin' and shakin' to the electrifying sounds of **Johnny and the Alpines** at the **St Francis Church Hall** on Bournville Green.

Johnny & the Alpines

The Alpines journey down the rock 'n' roll highway had commenced twelve months earlier, when **Gordon Lee**, of Selly Oak, having witnessed a **Danny Ray and the Rayvons** rehearsal, sold his bike and bought a guitar.

"My school mate, **Brian Osman**, pulled in **Dave Sambrooks**, who had a bass and **Brian Hall**, who had some drums, which helped, I suppose," said Gordon Lee

'Johnny' was one **John Henderson** and most Saturday nights Johnny and the Alpines would have them swinging from the rafters at the **St Francis Centre** on Bournville Green.

Most probably, swinging from those rafters would have been a young man in his late teens. He would have been urging Gordon to pick out, on his white Fender guitar, the biting introduction to 'That'll Be The Day'. Or perhaps punch out, on muted bass strings, the riff that would cue the Alpines into 'Maybe Baby'. Oh, if only this young man could hear the downward strum of an A to a D chord on that guitar, and join in on the line 'If You Knew Peggy Sue', this young man would return home a happy lad.

Spencer Davis Group

Home for this rafter swinging Buddy Holly fanatic was just across from the church hall, in Beech Road, Bournville. At that time this lad, **Laurie Mansfield**, was gainfully employed as a clerk at the Cadbury factory. Laurie's ambitions however lay far beyond Easter eggs, Flake bars and cocoa based nightcaps. In the coming years Laurie Mansfield would demonstrate, via the most grand and prestigious stages of the world, from the West End to Broadway, just how much a 'Buddy' fan he truly was.

Hardly the most prestigious stage in the world of show business was the stage at the **Golden Eagle** pub. It did however, exhibit to the bulging crowds, through the thick fog of Park Drive fumes and the heady aroma of Ansells Nut Brown ale, the four musicians who had been known as the **Rhythm and Blues Quartet**, but were now parading their good selves as the **Spencer Davis group**.

When Johnny and the Alpines auditioned at the Regan's house in Woodbourne Road, Edgbaston, their leader, Gordon Lee, received the highest compliment **Mrs Regan** could bestow.

Ma Regan

"Gordon," she said in her quaint Irish brogue, "Oy loike de littell band yerr haff dare. Cudd yerr do der Plairtha ferr me on Thaterdee noyt?"

"We did most Saturdays at the **Plaza**," said Gordon, "Well, that's where we'd turn up at, along with a dozen or more other outfits! There'd be Bedford vans all parked in a line blocking up Rookery Road in Handsworth. Ma Regan would then be shouting "You lot over dare! Go to dee udder Plairtha!"

From the Farcroft car park, on Rookery Road, Handsworth, the keen eyes of **Billy Yukon** gazed north. It was in the Yukon blood to seek greener pastures. And so it came to be that **Fred Hall**, alias Billy Yukon, moved the **Barons** to a higher plain. They journeyed from the Farcroft to the next street corner, which was Aylesford Road, to arrive at the Handsworth Plaza. The timing was perfect. Ma Regan was in the market for a resident band. A resident band that would be able to give a professional standard of musical accompaniment to visiting 'name' recording artistes.

"Could der Barons follow der dots?" asked Ma Regan.

"No problem," replied a confident Billy Yukon, sensing employment. "They'll read the music as well if you like."

"I really believed we'd made it, getting the Plaza job — playing alongside outfits like Gerry and the Pacemakers," said Barons guitarist **Ken Underhill**. "They gave a good show, and they were the first band I'd heard in recent years that weren't swimming in echo."

The vacancy had arisen because the previous residents, the **Beachcombers**, had been lured away by the cockney caballero with the gravel voice, from the 'Stars and Garters' television sing-along show, **Tommy Bruce**.

Tommy Bruce & the Bruisers

Peter Green, leader of the Beachcombers, explains: "We'd backed Tommy Bruce a few times and he'd become a mate of ours. At the Plaza, one night, Tommy turned up with **Barry Mason**, the songwriter and general hustler. Barry asked if we fancied moving to London to be with Tommy permanently. He also said he could hustle us a record deal into the bargain."

Peter Green and the Beachcombers, **Bobby Coral**, **Mac McGinty** and **Dave Mountney**, at the mention of a record deal, were in London within a fortnight, sharing a flat in Bayswater with **Troy Dante**, **Jess Conrad** and **Leapy Lee**.

"I knew there and then, London was for me," said Peter Green.

However, London and the whole thing that went with being part of a travelling band wasn't for drummer Dave Mountney, who quit and was immediately replaced by Mac's brother **Don McGinty**.

"My first show with the Bruisers was at Sheffield City Hall," recalled Don. "That winter, at the beginning of 1963 was a killer. I climbed into the Ford Thames van that the Bruisers travelled in. There was no heater. I soon sussed why Dave Mountney had opted out!"

In the shadow of the wall surrounding Winson Green Prison, in Preston Road to be exact, sixteen year old **Norman Haines** had finally come to terms with the techniques of getting a tune out of the guitar he'd acquired a year or so previously. At Handsworth New Road School he'd blasted the cornet in the school band. "But," said Norman, " 'Cathy's Clown' did it for me, so I bought this guitar."

After struggling with minor problems like total bewilderment, his pal, **Terry Dews**, came to his rescue.

"Terry's mom, Isabella, was the honky-tonk pianist at the Engine pub in Park Road, a kind of Winson Green's 'Mrs Mills', so she was a big help," said Norman. "Anyway, she'd slipped Terry the secret of chord formations and we were away as the **Van Dels**, a play on the word 'vandals'."

Gerry Day & the Dukes

Jack Woodroffe's shop, just a makeover away from the grand opening in 1946

John Hancox, whose cousins, Alan and Brian, were in Gerry Day and the Dukes, was a school pal of Norman's.

"John only had a full kit of drums didn't he." said Norman in spiv like fashion.

The first appearance of the Van Dels was at **McKechnies Social Club**, Aldridge, supporting Gerry Day and the Dukes.

Jack Woodroffe had been a professional musician with the Jack Hylton orchestra. From there he had taken the position as piano teacher at Scotchers' music store, 59/61 Corporation Street. In 1946, he founded his own musical instrument shop in John Bright Street. During the school summer recess of 1962, the Jack Woodroffe music shop provided **Dave Pegg** with his first electric guitar.

"It was a second hand Rossetti Lucky 7," recalls Dave, "It cost my dad a fiver, an absolute fortune for him. It had been hand painted. White on the front with black sides."

"**Brian Hines** was a bit of a role model for me as I got more into the idea of being in a beat group," Dave explained, "He had been three years above me at Yardley Grammar School where he was 'King Cat', and by now he had become **Denny Laine**, playing professionally with his **Diplomats**."

"Oh yeah, I got the Bert Weedon 'Play in a Day' book for the chords. I spent six weeks practicing and all I had to show for my efforts was lacerated fingers!"

However, news travelled fast around Acocks Green that young Dave Pegg from Tavistock Road, was really cutting the mustard as a guitarist. A concert was set up for the young master Pegg to demonstrate his newly acquired skills at a youth club that met in a hut at the rear of the Greet pub, in Tyseley.

"Dad gave me a lift down there. We pulled up outside but I got terrific stage fright and bottled it. I wouldn't get out of the car!"

Eventually the **Trespassers**, an outfit from Dave's home ground Acocks Green, invited him into their line up. The Trespassers appeared regularly at **St Michael's Church Hall**, a gig Dave knew well from earlier years when he'd been a choirboy there, with his long time pals from Yardley Grammar, **Maurice Barnes**, and Jaguar-to-be, **Al Jackson**.

Those **Jaguars** were shortly to become those **Applejacks**. **Gerry Freeman**, their drummer, had long admired Tony Meehan's drumming techniques. Tony and bass player Jet Harris, both former Shadows were enjoying a top ten hit with an instrumental 'Applejack'. Hence the change of name and with it, a change of fortune. Noticed by **Les Holmes**, manager of **Solihull Civic Hall**, the Applejacks began what was to become a very successful Monday night residency there. In fact it would shape their lives for the next few years.

Les Holmes' brother-in-law was the London impresario **Joe Brannelly**. Formerly the banjo player in the Ambrose Dance Band, Joe had sole representation of ex-Ambrose vocalist Kathy Kirby. With Kathy's single 'Dance On' showing in the charts, Joe Brannelly was a useful man to have around. **Arthur Smith**, an uncle of Gerry Freeman, was actually managing the Applejacks but welcomed the idea of working with the big boys.

Arthur Smith

When Joe Brannelly viewed the Applejacks he could smell success. They were clean and well-mannered teenagers who played their instruments with the confidence of seasoned professionals. With a 'cheeky chappie' competent pop singer out front and the added attraction of a female presence in the line up, the equation was perfect. Timing would be of the essence.

A story was leaked to local newspapers that Joe Brannelly had offered a contract worth ten thousand pounds to the Applejacks, but with three of them still at school for another year, the offer was politely refused. Whether or not such an offer was ever made is anyone's guess, but the band bathed in the publicity. Solihull Civic Hall was packed to capacity every Monday evening with fans of the Applejacks. All Joe Brannelly had to do was to bide his time.

Biding his time at Scrivens' opticians in Hurst Street was a twenty-five-year-old salesman from Kings Norton, **Mike Carroll**. As a schoolboy, Mike had played trumpet with Fisher and Ludlow's brass band, progressing, in the pre rock 'n' roll days, to Ada Road Schools with the Sid James band. Other times would find him with the **Den Jones** outfit at Kings Heath Baths.

"We had four saxes, three trumpets, a trombone, piano, bass and drums. It was half a crown to get in so work the wages out for yourself," said Mike.

Mike Carroll

The Wal Thomas band at Ada Road Schools

After a spell in Canada, the Channel Island of Jersey was Mike Carroll's next port of call. He became the resident crooner at the Corbiere Hotel, working for a pound a night. By day he was a sales representative for Benson and Hedges cigarettes and Hennessy brandy.

"Eventually the brandy won and I had to come home," Mike confessed in total honesty.

Two camera salesmen at Scrivens' shop were trying their hand at organising a dance night at the **Mackadown** pub in Kitts Green, and invited Mike Carroll to lend a hand at the door.

"The night wasn't that successful," explained Mike. "They hadn't enough money to pay the band so I paid them out of my own pocket and took over the promotion of the Mackadown myself."

Nomads

With the Mackadown came the start of what was to be a rather special relationship between Mike Carroll and the whole of the exploding Brumbeat scene.

Part of this Brumbeat scene were the **Nomads**. Along with **Malc Clarke** on guitar, brothers **Bob and Dick 'Short Trousers' Johnson** made regular appearances at the George pub, Bristol Road South in Northfield. Then, with **Stuart Gargan** and saxophonist **John Robinson** augmenting the line up, they changed their tune and overnight became the **Highwaymen**. In their capes and wellington boots they would stand and deliver to anyone that was willing to accommodate them.

Highwaymen

Every street in Birmingham seemed to be spawning a band. It was unusual for an outfit to consider calling it a day. But that's just what the **Cutaways** did.

Formed three years previously by ex-Saint and Sinner **Mike Brassington**, the personnel of the Cutaways had Mike with **Pete Williams** on guitar, **Vic Moody** on bass and **Ray Walpole** on drums. Since their formation, the Cutaways had been the darlings of **McKechnie's** bop sessions at Aldridge, and they didn't take too kindly to the new interpretation of how beat music should be played.

"The Cutaways were authentic rockers, playing Holly, Vincent, and Cochran material," stated Mike Brassington, "And we had intended to remain authentic rockers, but we couldn't compete in the new mop-top era, so we retired gracefully. I went on to put together a trio which played regularly at the **Delta Metal Social Club** in Holly Lane, Erdington. That was why we came to be known as the **DM Trio**."

Cutaways

Mike Brassington's affinity to 50s rock had been resolved since the morning of 3rd February 1959. Sixteen-year-old Mike had been preparing to set out from his home in Hansons Bridge Road, Pype Hayes to Moseley School of Art where he was a pupil, when the bad news arrived on the door-step. So moved and shocked was he by what he read that he put down his satchel to make an entry in his diary. Then he picked up his guitar to play a few of Buddy's songs to mark his passing.

In the early 70s, Mike Brassington accompanied the Birmingham singer and songwriter **Johnny Killigrew** to Nashville, Tennesse, where Johnny was due to record an album. After a couple of days in Music City, Mike could not resist the temptation to board a Greyhound bus to Lubbock, Texas. There he looked up the number and boldly phoned Buddy Holly's parents. His audacity paid off, and the call led to a meeting with them later that day.

Mike accepted their invitation to stay overnight, and at breakfast the following morning, he recounted to Mr and Mrs Holly the emotional entry he'd made into his diary back in February, 1959.

"Mrs Holly stood and asked to be excused," said Mike, "I thought that I'd upset her."

When she returned to the breakfast room she was holding a white Fender Stratocaster. "This is Buddy's guitar," she whispered, "The one they found in the snow. Will you play it for us?"

Mike, fingers stumbling to form the D chord and dropping to C on the downward strum, sang the Buddy Holly lines, 'Well all right so I'm bein' foolish. It's all right let people know. Well all right! Well all right! Let's live that love with all of our might.'

"Portable cassette recorders had just arrived on the market and by the grace of God I had mine in my pocket," said Mike. "Obviously I'll treasure that tape until I get the call from above."

With the Beatles —
El Riot & the Rebels at
the Riverside Restaurant
(George — don't do that!)

Mop-top mania was fine as far as **El Riot and the Rebels** were concerned. Heading for the **Riverside Restaurant** in Tenbury Wells, deep in the heart of the Worcestershire countryside, they rode into town to find themselves billed as the support band. Not surprising, as the main act that was sitting proudly at number one on the charts with their newly released single, 'From Me to You.'

"Tenbury Wells was, and still is, a very laid back place," commented the drummer with the Rebels, **Rob Sheward**, "But the crowd was going bonkers with just the thought of having the Beatles in the vicinity!"

Rob continues, "As we played our opening song, 'Say Mama', the atmosphere was electric and I was hitting the kit with everything I could muster. Then my bass drum pedal snapped. Just as I was panicking Ringo Starr crawled across the stage and fitted a spare pedal on for me. The Beatles were them kind of blokes."

Grant Harvey, the one time leader of the **Wildcats**, from the tranquil suburb of Bournville, now had a band of **Sundowners** in the way of **Geoff Knowles** and **Mike Dolan** on guitars, **Errol McNeil** on bass and **Denny Washington** driving them quite superbly on drums. Professional dreams came to fruition with the opportunity to spend the summer in the Cornish town of Bude, performing at the Headland Pavilion.

Sundowners

"Errol had a proper job to think of," explained Mike Dolan, "So a lad from Solihull took his place and off we went."

Grant Harvey and the Sundowners settled into this new lifestyle quite easily. Everything was fine until the new lad's parents arrived unannounced on a spying mission. Concluding that a shady lifestyle was not for their privately educated offspring, the lad was immediately removed from the raunchiness and general debauchery of Bude and returned to the sanity of Solihull for his own good.

MEANWHILE ELSEWHERE . . .

1963 - Harold Wilson appointed Labour leader - Profumo/Keeler Scandal - Beeching axes railway branch lines - Martin Luther King gives 'I have a dream' speech - the Great Train Robbery - 'That Was The Week That Was' show pulled - TV - Dr Who - Ready Steady Go! - Cinema - From Russia With Love - The Birds . . .

Mike's younger brother, **Steve Dolan**, was not a bad exponent of the bass guitar. He'd only been out of school for two weeks and had started work at the Cadbury factory when the call came from Bude. The Sundowners were in need of a full-time professional bass guitarist. Steve informed the Cadbury wages office that any holiday pay due to him should be forwarded to him at the Headland Pavilion, Bude.

Four Northfield lads were arriving on the scene as the **Tempests**. Vocalist **Alan Burrows** was ably supported by guitarists **Roy Hopkinson**, **Roger Jack** and **Keith Richards**, with **Albert Carr** at the drums. Wednesday evenings would see the Tempests appearing at the **King George V** pub in Northfield, for a fee of three pounds.

"But we never drew a penny," said Alan most determinedly, "We were saving for a brand new Shure microphone, which we did finally buy."

Alan Burrows continued with more than a hint of mischief, "We also had a fan club secretary and a Vox amplifier that we all went through."

With shoulders back and heads high, the Tempests arrived for their most prestigious engagement to date. It was the **Jewish Club**, Ellis Street, Holloway Head, where it seemed the crème de la crème of Birmingham society made up the audience. With the Tempests hitting the groove of Eddie Cochran's 'C'mon Everybody',

Tempests

Alan Burrows strutted across the stage with the treasured Shure microphone wedged under his armpit. Clapping his hands, willing the audience to love him, the boy was surely blessed.

"Then wallop!" said Alan, "I dropped the microphone. I heard the thud as it landed on the bare boards. The microphone never worked again. And, for a while, neither did the Tempests!"

Still enjoying a healthy worksheet with **Tommy Bruce**, the **Bruisers** were now, with the help of hustler **Barry Mason**, involved in producing demos to promote new songs to established recording artistes.

Bruisers

"Barry kept his word about a record deal," **Peter Green** explained, "**Norrie Paramor** at EMI Columbia had been made aware of us and was showing interest in signing the Bruisers."

Danny King & the Royals in Chamberlain Square

However, when push came to shove, it emerged that Norrie Paramor saw Peter as a solo prospect, even going as far as dreaming up a professional name for him — **Peter Lee Stirling**. When Mr Paramor's enthusiasm waned, Peter was passed over to another EMI producer, **Ron Richards**, who immediately signed the Bruisers as a band. Ron Richards then touted Tin Pan Alley for a suitable song and returned with a Johnny Worth composition entitled 'Blue Girl.' The song was recorded and duly released on the Parlophone label in July of 1963.

Bob Smith was a man with his finger on the pulse of the phenomenon that was to become known as Brumbeat. Operating as an agent from his office in Dale End, Bob acted as the Birmingham representative for the powerful George Cooper Agency of Oxford Street, London. In early June of 1963 Bob Smith put the word out to his bands and artistes that **Norrie Paramor**, head of EMI's Columbia label, was coming to town on a talent spotting mission. The timing could not have been more perfect for **Danny King and the Royals**. They had just made it back from a month-long engagement at the Palette club in Fulda in southern Germany when the EMI auditions were announced.

Rob Pryke's banana kingdom

"Personally, I always found auditions demeaning," said Danny King, "But everybody was on a high so I went along with it all."

The **Moat House Club** was the chosen venue for the auditions. Situated at the bottom of Bradford Street, it had formerly been a factory. Rob 'The Banana King' Pryke, had initially intended to use the premises as part of his fruit and vegetable business, but during the clearing out process he changed his plans. The discovery of ancient oak beams and other interesting old features within the building motivated him to turn it into a pop venue and nightclub.

Norrie Paramor's brief was to seek out and sign groups to his record label and hopefully present a challenge to his colleague at EMI, George Martin, the head of the Parlophone label which had scooped the prized pickings of the Merseybeat artists. Norrie and **Bob Barratt** sat and watched as band after band shuffled on and played two songs as instructed: "A fast one and a ballad please." Finally five outfits, Danny King and the Royals, **Mike Sheridan and the Nighriders**, **Carl and the Cheetahs**, **Pat Wayne and the Rockin' Jaymen** and **Keith Powell and the Valets** were told, "Congratulations. Sign here."

When Pat Wayne and the Rockin' Jaymen signed, it was on the understanding that they change their name, as Decca were endeavouring to promote **Peter Jay the Jaywalkers** and it could all get rather confusing.

"I had a word down Peter Green's ear and he said it was okay with him for us to use his old name, the **Beachcombers**," said Pat.

"The EMI audition? I was late as usual," confessed Danny King, shrugging his shoulders. "Coronation Street was on television and I wasn't gonna miss that for anyone. When I finally arrived at the Moat House I got a standing ovation for just turning up!"

Carl Barron & the Cheetahs with Norrie Paramor

El Riot and the Rebels turned up and, to everyone's amazement, were promptly turned down.

Mick Atkins of Acocks Green's **Sundowners** recalls *their* experience of 'turning up' at the Columbia auditions: "We pulled up outside the Moat House and opened the back doors of the van," said Mick. "This important looking bloke appeared and said "Don't bother, you're too ugly!"

The **Uglies** wouldn't have been too ugly for EMI, but unfortunately they were in

Germany for their first trip abroad. When the German offer came, vocalist **Steve Gibbons** and drummer **Jimmy Holden** immediately surrendered their daytime employment. "The others in the band weren't working anyway," said Steve.

The Uglies would have surely proved a breath of fresh air at the Moat House proceedings with their folk, blues and rock approach. Heavily influenced by Lonnie Donegan, their set would include Lonnie's 'San Miguel' and 'Gambling Man' interspersed with an Ugly brand of humour that had Steve Gibbons announcing "For our next one, we'd like to play a number cut by the Diamonds."

The Uglies

The Sundowners weren't the only ones feeling unhappy at being left out of the EMI auditions. **Carl Wayne and the Vikings** were back from Germany and raving mad with anger at the thought of missing out on the chance of an audience with Norrie Paramor.

"Our first gig back was the **Bournbrook**," said **Terry Wallace**. "We thought we'd pick up where we left off. Did we get a shock!" Such was the pace of change in the six months they had been away, the Vikings' image and repertoire had become totally outdated. To regain their former status as one

Carl Wayne & the Vikings

of Birmingham's major attractions it was back to the drawing board for the Vikings.

Arriving back from Germany at much the same time were the **Rockin' Berries**. When they had departed they were a pretty raw rhythm and blues act that relied heavily on the 'grizzly bear' voice of **Jimmy Powell** and the honkin' sax of **Dennis Ryland**. Oh, how the Rockin' Berries had changed. Their welcome home gig was at the **California** pub in Weoley Castle and drummer **Terry Bond**, following the compere's grand announcement, gave a strong count in. That was the cue for front man **Clive Lea** and rhythm guitarist **Geoff Turton** to pitch perfectly into their microphones the opening line from the Coasters' little gem 'Yakity Yak' — 'Take out the papers and the trash!'

A stunning falsetto performance by Geoff on the Four Seasons' 'Sherry' quite literally brought the house down. When Clive and Geoff amalgamated their talents for a send up of the Paul and Paula novelty 'Hey Paula', it became apparent to everyone that the Rockin' Berries were showing the way when it came to all-round professional entertainment.

"While we were in Germany," said Geoff Turton, "We were aware of the breaking of the Beatles and the whole Merseybeat explosion. We worked damned hard while we were away to make sure that when we got home we would be the best around."

On the 5th July, the Beatles made their final appearance for the Regan's, with the **Old Hill Plaza** playing host to the, by now, 'Fab Four.' Singing and sax playing (although not both at the same time) **Denis Brown** was the resident bandleader at Old Hill and was 'in charge of all things backstage.'

"We'd had the Beatles before so I knew what to expect, or so I thought," said Denis. "If it was pandemonium on their last appearance back in January then God only knows how to

Hey Paula – Berries Clive & Geoff

describe this one. The queue outside began forming at lunchtime. When the doors opened at seven there must have been two thousand kids pushing to get in. The Beatles again arrived over the roof of the George pub, at the rear of the building and, seeing me, John Lennon said, "Aye Cobber! Whisky and cokes all round if you don't mind!"

Nicky James

"The **Strangers** were battling to keep the multitude entertained but there was just this loud constant chant for the Beatles. Finally, I took a deep breath and entered their dressing room. "Lads please!" I called "Time to do it." John Lennon, looked up and said, "Okay then Cobber. Take us to your leader."

As the Beatles played a thirty minute set to a wall of screaming that rendered their performance totally inaudible, **Mike Sheridan and the Nightriders** set up on the back of the revolving stage.

"I could just about make out 'Twist and Shout' recalled **Roger Spencer**, "So I got behind my drums. The Beatles came running off and I pushed a pen into a passing hand. The hand quickly scribbled on my tom-tom, 'Love and kisses, Paul McCartney.' Then the stage whizzed round and all we saw was the backs of our audience. They were all rushing to get out of the place and catch the Beatles leaving!"

As Denny Laine and the Diplomats rushed to get out of Scunthorpe Baths, an Elvis Presley look-alike/sound-alike with a Black Country accent managed to acquire a seat in the Diplomats' van. **Nicky James**, or **Mick Nicholls** as he was known to close friends, had sung a few songs at the baths that evening. So impressed had the Diplomats been with the lad's performance that they'd invited him to join the band as co-frontman with Denny.

Once in Birmingham, Nicky acquired a grey Mark 2 Jaguar and had the name 'Nicky James' professionally written on the sides of this impressive vehicle. Nicky had the whole world at his feet and practically every woman at his beck and call. Here was a man with film star looks, the voice of an angel and now able to name-drop the highly popular Diplomats as his backing band.

"And there lay the problem," said **Tony Withers** of **Ronny Smith and the Senators**. "Denny Laine was not happy about being upstaged."

The Senators, having built up a considerable following and a healthy worksheet, were in a position to talk business with Nicky who was, in their opinion, hotter than Tonto's backside. In the upstairs function room of the Greet pub, the Senators and Nicky James went through their paces. He liked them. They liked him. From now on it would be 'Nicky James with Ronny and the Senators'.

Denny Laine & the Diplomats

Ronny, being nobody's fool, insisted on the first spot, where he could hit the crowd with a great beefy version of the Screamin' Jay Hawkins belter 'Who Do You Love', climbing over any piano that was handy.

As the curtain rose for the second half, the Senators would strike up with the pounding guitar riff of Barratt Strong's 'Money'. The mean and magnificent Nicky James, in red silk jacket, would then step into the pencil spotlight and scream those immortal lines, "The best things in life are free! But you can keep 'em for the birds and bees! Give me money! That's what I want!"

Nicky James & the Senators

"That and your clothes," chipped in Ronny Smith, who was by now using the professional stage name, **Tab Memphis**. "If Nicky was off somewhere after the gig, maybe the Moat House or the Cedar Club, he'd think nothing of 'borrowing' your shirt, jacket or your Chelsea boots from the dressing room without telling you. If he fancied bedding down in town, he'd climb onto the roof of Alex's pie stand and from there, he'd scramble through the window of Bruce Jordan's office where he'd snuggle down on the couch in the reception. With Nicky, nothing was sacred."

Nothing was sacred when it came to lifting the trading name of 'The Cavern', from Ray McFall's Liverpool cellar, which had given birth to the Merseyside rock scene. Jumping onto the Cavern theme were **Phil Peters**, Peter Lee Stirling's uncle, and **Barry Mason**, Tommy Bruce's manager. Taking control of 'Jazzland' a former trad jazz club that operated from a cellar on Summer Row, at the rear of the Hall of Memory, they relaunched the venue as the '**Brum Beat Cavern**.'

The Redcaps

"It was not in any way for the claustrophobic," recalled **Mike Kellie**, the drummer with Solihull based group, the **Phantoms**. "The Black Hole of Calcutta had nothing on that place!"

Not to be outdone, over in Small Heath, **Joe** and **Mary Regan** wasted precious little time in re-naming their Wordsworth Road venue — so the Garryowen Club became the **Brum Kavern**.

With all this pandemonium happening in her ballrooms on a regular basis, Ma Regan was true to her word regarding recording prospects for her artistes and had fixed arrangements for the **Redcaps**, and **Gerry Levene and the Avengers** to record for Decca.

Gerry Levene and the Avengers

In August of 1963, Gerry and his band recorded what was a crowd favourite from their live set, 'Dr Feelgood.' The release date was pencilled for late September

"Then I got a call from Mike Smith at Decca asking me to record with session musicians," explained Gerry Levene.

The song Gerry recorded in a solo capacity had been a minor hit for Conway Twitty entitled 'It's Drivin' Me Wild.' The song's composer, Bert Russell, was flown in from the States to assist Mike Leander with the production.

"Mike Smith made it clear that my solo effort would be the 'A' side with 'Feelgood' relegated to 'B' side status," Gerry continued, "I argued that the Avengers and I were a team and not to be split on any account."

As a result of Gerry's loyalty, Decca Records indefinitely postponed the release of 'Dr Feelgood'.

EMI were counting their blessings that they hadn't separated **Peter Lee Stirling** from the **Bruisers** and had chosen to have the group record 'Blue Girl', because by that steamy summer of 1963, 'Blue Girl' was in the charts at number 37 and rising.

Temporarily separated from **Pat Wayne** for a record release were the newly named **Beachcombers**. Norrie Paramor, impressed by their standards, had allowed the band full blown credit on the instrumental piece, 'Mad Goose.'

The Beachcombers

However Pat Wayne with the Beachcombers were quite successful with their first record release. 'Go Back To Daddy', written by John Chesterton and Bob McNally (who were progress chasers at the Rover factory, Solihull) sold extremely well in Scandinavia, making number 4 on the Swedish chart.

Unfortunately **Danny King and the Royals** soon lost the feelgood factor regarding their relationship with Norrie Paramor and EMI.

"Basically, Columbia hadn't, in my opinion, got a clue about rock 'n' roll," Danny explained. "They never let my band, the Royals, record, and they insisted on me doing cornball stuff like 'Young Blood' and 'Tossin' and Turnin'. It was miles away from rock 'n' roll."

Pat Wayne

Miles away from rock 'n' roll was the grand old city of Cambridge. That's where, in the summer of 1959, the Smart family of Victoria Road, Aston chose to spend a week's holiday.

"It promised to be the most boring week of my childhood," said **Keith Smart**, "But the bloke who kept the pub where we stayed had some drums and I couldn't keep off them!"

Four years later, with the whole of the country, except Cambridge, in the grip of Beatlemania, Mr Smart senior buckled under pressure and bought his lad, Keith, a basic kit to thrash around on.

The Everglades – with interesting wiring

"Me and my mate **Trevor Ireson**, who lived around the corner from me in Whitehouse Street, just burned with the notion of having a band of our own." said Keith Smart.

The notion became reality when Keith and Trevor, who were a regulars at the Summer Hill Ice Rink, palled up with fellow skater **Grenville Williamson**, a Bartley Green lad who was in possession of a 'guaranteed not to split' guitar.

"In the early days Trevor just sang and we'd whack my drums over to Bartley Green on the number 12 bus to practice at Grenville's house with another lad from the ice rink, **Billy Hunter**, who could strum a few chords."

The Everglades at the Reservoir

With **Trevor** now adopting the professional name of **Burton**, the lads called themselves the **Everglades** and first presented themselves to the public at the **Reservoir** pub in Ostler Street, Ladywood. With waistcoats made by Grenville's mother and the acquisition of bass guitarist, **Roger Ball**, the Everglades made good progress to the city centre where promoter **Dougie Thompson** began to use the band on a regular basis at his **Rainbow Suite** venue in High Street. "By now," said Keith Smart, "Trevor Burton was getting into playing guitar."

The Stringbeats

Vernon Perera was another young man getting into playing guitar. Vernon, in 1962, was working as a lathe turner at the Tom Carrington factory in West Bromwich when he was joined on the factory floor by sixteen year old **Austin Griffith**, newly arrived from the sunny Caribbean island of Grenada.

"I'd been buzzin' with music since I was nine," said Austin. "Vernon suggested that we find a couple of players and see what we could make of it."

What Austin (now better known as **Mel Day**) and Vernon came up with was **Steve Sylvester** on the bass, **Lloyd David** on drums and a keyboard player, **Chris Brown**. Spending every available moment in a cold and damp West Bromwich coal cellar, the boys finally emerged into the light of day and headed south, down the Holyhead Road. Arriving at the Soho Road, they knocked on the doors of both the **Continental** and the **Monte Carlo Clubs** to announce themselves as the **Stringbeats**.

Word spread fast and furious across Birmingham about these West Brom wich boys who were managing to create the good-time feel in their shows. So much so, that the Stringbeats soon found themselves being regularly featured at the **Brum Beat Cavern** in Summer Row and **St John's Restaurant** in Digbeth.

Danny King

Danny King was in the market for another band and along came three members of the **Chantelles** — guitarist **Chris Jones**, his nephew, **Chris Kefford** on bass, and drummer **Barry Smith** to become **Danny King and the Jesters**. However, having two Chris's in the line up was so confusing for Danny that he insisted one of them adopt another name.

"There was always this bloke following us around," said Danny. "Everything Chris Kefford did, whether it was his playing or his flash dance movements, this bloke would say, "Yeah, that's ace!" From then on Chris became known as **Ace Kefford**."

"Every time the curtains drew back and the girls caught sight of Ace you'd hear a swoon from them and then they'd gather in mass around the stage, screaming for him," sighed Danny, pausing to light a Park Drive cigarette. "Fortunately for me, there were always one or two girls who would settle for second best!"

As the summer sun began to lose its strength, so Danny began to reveal a weakness. It was becoming an open secret that he was addicted to the television series 'Coronation Street', which meant on certain nights he would only be available to perform at late shows. However, there was a far more serious addiction controlling the fragile frame of Danny King. He couldn't, for the life of him, stay off the pinball machines. **John Butler**, JB to his many pals, and proprietor of the **Last Chance Café** in Aston, was always able to holiday twice a year on the island of Majorca from the proceeds of Danny's financial input to his machine.

"One night, well into the early hours," said JB, "Danny arrived at the Last Chance with the most beautiful girl in the world on his arm. It was three in the morning and Danny was pumping silver into the machine." In the belief that romance was simply a heartbeat away, the girl clung determinedly to Danny's arm. At five-thirty Danny was still playing when she fainted with exhaustion! As the unconscious body collapsed over him, Danny King was screaming in panic for help. "Danny was so concerned so that she'd rock the machine!" said JB.

October 1963 saw the launch of 'Midland Beat', a monthly publication that was edited by the highly respected journalist **Dennis Detheridge**, whose knowledge of the local music scene was second to none. Its aim was to reflect the pop, rock and jazz events that

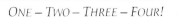

Dennis Detheridge

were happening in and around Birmingham. Holding down the post of advertising manager was the maestro of the cornet, **John Gibbins**.

Of course, the whole concept was borrowed from 'Mersey Beat', a similar magazine that dealt with musical activity in and around Liverpool which was enjoying its third year of publication. Everyone assumed that 'Mersey Beat' founder and editor, Bill Harry, was referring to the beat that bands like the Big Three and Faron's Flamingos hammered out. The truth was that Bill Harry, when planning circulation, had studied a map of Merseyside and imagined a policeman walking his beat — hence 'Mersey Beat.'

Walking the Erdington beat one sunny October afternoon was an inquisitive police sergeant. Riding on the crisp autumn breeze, the sound of a beat group could be heard coming to grips with their very own rendition of 'Surfin' USA', a recent hit for the Beach Boys.

John Rowlands takes up the story, "There was **Billy Dixon** and **Geoff Nicholls** with their guitars, **Pete Webb** on drums and me on bass. We called ourselves the **Boll Weevils**. We'd decided to see how we sounded in Billy's back garden, which was on Gravelly Lane, so we set the gear up on the lawn and let it blast."

The Boll Weevils, even donned their stage attire of black trousers with white shirts for the garden party. As they sang of waxing down their surfboards and of girls with bushy blond hairdos, so the latch rattled on the back gate and the uniformed police sergeant, stepping from the white-washed walled entry and onto the blue bricked patio, announced himself.

"Afternoon all," he said, saluting and bending his knees, "I'm from Wilton Road station and we've 'ad a few phone calls appertaining to what is hoccurrin' wiv you lot and all these 'ere alectic catarrhs."

Boll Weevils at the Navigation, Erdington

When enlightened as to the purpose of the impromptu session, the sergeant sternly informed the four teenaged Boll Weevils that such outdoor events operated strictly under licence. A licence that was granted by Birmingham Magistrates after applications had been vetted and approved by the Fire Brigade following consultation with the St Johns Ambulance Brigade and the local Parish Council.

"So let's 'ave no more of this 'ere boogie woogie palaver or else," warned the sergeant.

While making his exit, he turned once again to the trembling, shame faced boys. "You wouldn't have a card for our social club by any chance?"

Jimmy Powell had a card. A business card that informed the recipient that Jimmy and his band, the **Dimensions**, were 'direct from London.' This was no exaggeration. Jimmy had, through sheer hard graft, established himself at venues like the **Crawdaddy** at Richmond, where the Rolling Stones had previously been in residence, and the **Marquee** in Wardour Street, right in the heart of Soho's action.

When Jimmy Powell played London, he was always aware of a young lad in the audience, matching him word for word on every song. Sometimes this lad would bring along a battered twelve string guitar to strum, or perhaps blow a harmonica.

Thinking it made sense to have a second singer to open the show, who could then announce 'Mr Dynamite' onto the stage, Jimmy Powell took this young disciple under his wing and into the Dimensions came one **Roderick Stewart** or, as he preferred to be known, Rod.

At the **California** pub, in Weoley Castle, the social events were organised, under the banner of the 'Blues' supporters club, by Welshman Vernon Rowlands. Jimmy made his move. The Dimensions, being direct from London, should be engaged immediately at a fee way above the normal fifteen pounds. What Vernon did give Jimmy was a free hand to run a grand raffle in order to boost the fifteen quid and feed the talented but hungry London brigade.

On a cold and bleak November Sunday evening at the California, the Dimensions, in the glow of a coal fire, struck up with a couple of songs before Rod Stewart announced to the crowd "Here he is! With his hit record 'Sugar Babe'! Decca recording artiste! Mr Dynamite himself! Birmingham's very own Jimmy Powell!"

An Englishman, Isaac Flavell, who'd made a nice few quid prospecting for gold in California, had actually built the pub. On the pub car park stood a twenty-foot high granite pillar, on which the pub sign, 'The California' swung. Perched on the top of the pillar was a basket of Californian fruit, fashioned out of marble.

Being the master salesman that he was, Jimmy Powell had managed to sell raffle tickets to half the population of Weoley Castle. At fifteen minutes past ten, the grand draw was announced. From an empty Smith's crisp box, Jimmy drew a ticket that he'd promised would change some innocent person's lifestyle considerably. Would Jimmy lie? Cheers rang out as the beaming claimant made his way to the stage.

"What have I won?" asked the claimant excitedly.

"A basket of fruit for you my son," chirped Jimmy in passable Cockney.

"Where is it then?"

"On top of that pillar on the car park," chuckled Jimmy, pointing to the door, "Help yourself!"

Jimmy Powell & the Dimensions with Rod Stewart

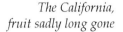

The California, fruit sadly long gone

Rod Stewart

Miracle site — Yeats's

Jimmy and his Dimensions high-tailed it back to London to fulfil their Tuesday night residency at Ken Collier's blues club in Newport Street, but they returned a few weeks later for a gig that would bring the curtain down on Jimmy's association with Rod Stewart and the Dimensions.

At the **59 Club**, in John Bright Street, Rod asked for equal billing. The request was refused on the grounds that no one steals Jimmy Powell's thunder. Rod Stewart didn't steal his thunder; instead he stole his band and took off to accompany Chuck Berry on a nationwide tour of theatres, leaving Jimmy high and dry. He also left an unsolved mystery behind him. Who played the harmonica solo on Millie's March 1964 chart success, 'My Boy Lollipop'?

The story that has carried over through the years is that Rod Stewart was responsible for the work, however Jimmy Powell takes issue.

"Not true!" states Jimmy emphatically. "Chris Blackwell at Island Records booked *me* to do that session, and do it I did!"

In the cellar clubs, pubs and church hall hops around Birmingham, the kids who bluebeated around the dance floors cared little about who actually performed that mouth organ solo. For all they cared, it could have been the poor old blind busker chap from outside C&A's store in Corporation Street. A poor old blind busker who, at one-thirty every lunchtime would be guided across Corporation Street and into Yates' wine lodge, where, after a fair few schooners of South African dry white, his sight would miraculously return.

Sadly, at two-thirty pm, as the licensee urged customers to drink up and vacate the premises, the old chap would once again be plunged into a world of total darkness. Just in time for a late afternoon 'blowing and sucking' session.

Perhaps, in one of his less visually impaired moments, the busker may have noticed a youth, just out of school, sparring with the dummies in the window of C&A, in an effort to come to terms with the art of window dressing — there again, maybe not — **Jeff Lynne** only lasted there half a day.

Agencies were now beginning to play a major role in the local music scene. Miss **Terry Matthews**, a Dubliner by birth had arrived in Birmingham in the late 50s and take up employment as a telephonist at Bosworth, Bailey and Cox, a law firm with offices in Newhall Street. There she found herself working alongside **Tim Bellamy**, the drummer with **Johnny Dean and the Dominators**. Having worked in a semi-professional capacity as a magician's assistant and also attained a high standard as a harmonica player, Terry knew how the entertainment business operated.

After attending rehearsals and being impressed by the Dominators, especially the talents of **Brian 'Johnny Dean' Hines**, Terry arranged for the tailor Alan Fradgley, of Dudley, to make smart band jackets for them, and then she set about filling the gaps in their diary.

"They were mastering the art of driving the girls wild," said Terry, "Especially Brian. It's a little sad now to look back and see the raw deals that the music business had in store for him."

It was a natural progression for Terry to launch the **Terry Matthews Agency**, which traded from an office Lysways Street, Walsall.

Johnny Dean & the Dominators

3JR Promotions, a company based in Sutton Coldfield, had been conceived, in love, **by John Ford**. Following successful nights at the **Royal Hotel**, Sutton Coldfield, John spread his wings to take in promotions at **Tamworth Assembly Rooms** and **Lichfield Guild Hall**.

"It was in the line of duty at Lichfield Guild Hall that I got this 'ooter!" said John, tapping his oddly shaped nose.

Born in Edgbaston in 1937, **John Singer** had started work in the jewellery trade but his involvement in fundraising events for the members of the **Cotton Youth Institute** in Ellis Street, Holloway Head, changed all that.

"My first venture was booking **Johnny Duncan and the Bluegrass Boys**, which was a great success." recalls John.

Madge Whitehouse, secretary of the Midland jazz club asked John to promote another show using the services of Acker Bilk and the Paramount jazz band. This time he went for the **Birmingham Town Hall** as his venue, choosing a Friday evening to present the show.

"Because we'd have overlapped into the Saturday, our Sabbath, I was forced to promote independently," explained John.

As beatniks jived into the early hours, a reporter and photographer from the Sunday Mercury smuggled themselves into the Town Hall and snapped a picture of an unconscious drunk. A courting couple, holding hands were also photographed gazing adoringly at each other.

That weekend the Sunday Mercury carried the headline, 'Does The Second City Need This Debauchery?'

With another late night event booked for the following Friday at the Town Hall, John Singer pleaded with the relevant Birmingham City councillors to visit the show and see first-hand what kind of house was being kept. The Monday after that event the Birmingham Mail headline read, 'Council Gives Go Ahead To All Night Raves.' John Singer

Robbie Hood

Roy Everett

The Blueshounds outside 'The Morgue' at the King's Head, Bearwood

smiled, having booked the Town Hall well in advance for future events.

"It was perfect publicity," said John, I had the front page to myself and it never cost a penny. I could have sold out ten times over."

Robbie Hood and his Merrimen weren't exactly selling out ten fold but were popular enough around the dance halls to give **Reg Calvert** the confidence to approach Decca Records for a contract.

What Reg Calvert hadn't realised was that bows and arrows and Lincoln green tights didn't transfer very well to disc and Decca advised Robbie Hood to surrender himself to the authorities immediately. Decca did, however, like the sound of the Merrimen and, in granting them amnesty, acquired their signatures on a contract.

Not only did the boys commence a relationship with the highly respected producer, **Shel Tarmy**, they also found themselves renamed. At the suggestion of Shel Tarmy, the band of Merrimen became the band of **Fortunes**.

The **Climbers**, formerly the **Dakotas**, were now a howling blues band that featured soulful voice of **Roy Everett** or, as he was known off-duty to his pals, **Roy Taylor**.

Unfortunately for the Climbers, the bass player, **Greg Masters**, decided to seek fame and fortune with **Mike Sheridan and the Nightriders**, whose outgoing bass player, **Brian Cope**, had decided that there was definitely no fortune to be had.

Into Greg's Climbers shoes climbed **Honri Edouarde**.

Honri ("It should have been *Henri* but the bloke wrote Honri on me susstificate") Edouarde had seen action with the **Del Saints** and had since been earning beer money by deputising for **John Lodge** as one of **El Riot's Rebels**.

John Lodge, as part of his apprenticeship with Parkinson Cowan, had been gaining work experience in Paris.

"If you believed that one, you'd believe you can plat fog," said Honri.

"My only problem was," he continued, "John Lodge was a strapping six footer and I was, and still am, five feet three inches. I'd have his El Riot strides pulled up to my chin."

El Riot, alias **Ray Thomas** was still seething about the

failed EMI audition. Ambitious as ever, he decided that if the rock 'n' roll life style was what it would take to knock the Rebels into shape, then Hamburg was the place to take them. Unfortunately, the Rebels weren't feeling that rebellious. Only **Mick Pinder** was willing to share the dream. So, with saddlebags packed Mr Pinder and Mr Thomas bade 'Adios!' to the Brum scene in search of excitement on the erotic Reeperbahn as the **Krew Kuts**.

For Mick Pinder, the transformation into fully professional status meant the surrender of his proper day-job. For a year or so, he'd been employed as a tester for a revolutionary instrument — the Mellotron. Manufactured by Streetly Electronics, a company that was run by John Bradley from a workshop near Walsall, the Mellotron was the predecessor of what the world now knows as the sampler. Pressing the keys on the Mellotron's keyboard would trigger the playback of corresponding pre-recorded tapes deep in the console's vast, mysterious and notoriously unreliable innards. Despite its efforts to mimic real flutes or strings, the Mellotron had its own distinct haunting tone. Time would tell that this was not to be Mick Pinder's final farewell to that unmistakable moody sound.

The mighty Mellotron, driven by Graham Dalley

The **Sundowners**, following their failure to even play the EMI audition, were left high and dry by the departure of their two vocalists. The remaining members answered an advertisement in the Melody Maker placed by a certain **Mike West**, alias **Robbie Hood**. Mr West, having lost his band to Decca, was recruiting new **Merrimen** who would swear allegiance to the cause, although, as **Mick Atkins** said, "We never really did get to find out exactly what cause we were fighting for!"

The Sundowners passed the audition with ease. They couldn't fail. They were the only band that turned up! Their first engagement, having vowed to serve the people, was at the Boston Gliderdrome.

"Robbie Hood spelled it out," said Mick Atkins, "The music was secondary. We got to Boston on the afternoon and Mike West put us through our paces. The emphasis was on showmanship. As soon as the band was announced we were to fight with our swords, swooping through the audience from the back of the room," Mick explained, taking up a fencing stance to drive the story home.

"Once on stage we blasted into the 'Robin Hood' theme. How we got away with it I don't know, but the second gig

Sundowners behind the Scout hut on Spring Road

was in London, at a blues club in the West End. There were three bands on, and we were topping the bill."

As the Merrimen charged through the crowd in that damp cellar club, in their outfits of Lincoln green, or as Mick Atkins described them, 'urinal green', certain elements of the audience ducked in fear of decapitation.

"We eventually got into the song," said Mick, " 'Robin Hood! Robin Hood! Ridin' though the glen!' Mike West fired his arrow across the stage and once again missed the dartboard. He then made his grand entrance, in all his Robin Hood regalia, to absolute silence."

Mick Atkins paused for a while. "We died the most painful death I can ever remember experiencing. Our careers as Robbie's Merrimen finished right there!"

Wild times with the Textones

Harris Dry Cleaners advised folk, in their promotional blurb, to 'have your clothes textoned'. At the works social club, in Perry Barr, the band in residence was, appropriately enough, the **Textones**. **Jim Nicholls**, who played sax and banjo in the band had encouraged his son Brian by showing him a few chords on the guitar.

Initially in search of romantic refreshment at **Billy Pond's Dance School** in Green Lane, Small Heath, **Brian Nicholls** instead befriended **Vic Jarvis**, a lad from Bordesley Green.

"We were there to pull the birds," confessed Brian, "But with the whole country being turned upside down by the Beatles thing, we got stuck into musical chitchat."

Billy Pond's Ballroom & Dance Studios

With Vic Jarvis as bass player, Brian Nicholls formed the **Fleetwoods**. **John Taylor** on guitar, **Wally Onions** on drums with vocal honours falling to **Jeff Jacey**. Now Jeff was a lad who claimed to have dynamite contacts within the

London pop scene. According to him he was on first name terms with top record company executives. Unfortunately these claims proved to be the fantasies of a desperate man. Jeff Jacey was forced to depart with his reputation in shreds.

Not perturbed about being led up the garden path, Brian Nichols sought out the legendary **Big Al Johnson**, who was holding court at the Golden Cross, in Short Heath, and asked for advice on how to play the Duane Eddy piece 'Shazam'.

"Al took me to one side and I felt so privileged," recalls Brian.

"How do you play the fiddly bits?" asked the keen apprentice.

Into an innocent ear, beer soaked lips whispered the secret.

"You just prat about," confided the master.

Brian Nichols winked. Big Al winked back. Big Al knew his secret was safe.

A revamped line up of the Fleetwoods took aboard **Dave Crewdson** and **Pete 'Floss' Britton** on guitars.

"Floss was a tremendous blues guitarist and blew good harmonica into the bargain," said Brian.

With **Ray Green** on drums, the Fleetwoods found themselves at the **Brum Kavern**, Small Heath playing support to the Searchers, and followed up with a gig at **All Saints Youth Club** in Four Oaks for a fee of four pounds. A promise was made to the boys that their fee would be increased two-fold for their next engagement at the youth club, but at the time of writing, the Fleetwoods are still waiting to be re-engaged.

Staying cool – the Fleetwoods

Affter leaving Turves Green Boys' School, four lads — budding guitarists **Phil Pearce**, **Pete White** and **Roger Ottley**, with drummer **Chris McCabe** — spent the summer playing for a few shillings as the **Rockin' Rockets**, backing local heart throb **Roy Brown** at the **Willows** pub in Kings Norton.

Roger Ottley takes up the tale, "I'd got a Hofner bass and had fathomed out how to amplify it through the family radio. I was 'doing a show' in the mirror when someone knocked on the front door. I danced into the hall, still plugged in, and pulled the radio off the sideboard, smashing the valves to bits."

Roger continued, "Phil Pearce's dad, we used to call him 'Mr Beans', was an electronics wizard, so he built us proper amplifiers. I was round his house one day and Fireball XL5 was on the television. Mr Beans nodded at the screen and said, "Course, you know they're not proper actors.'"

Guru – Big Al Johnson

"I used to play 'Saturday Night at the Duckpond' on a Tuesday at the **Dogpool**." declared Phil Pearce, scratching his head in disbelief. He was referring of course to the Cougars interpretation of Tchaikovsky's 'Swan Lake.'

The Rotundas

Smallbrook Ringway, July 1963

Roy **Brown** and the **Rockets** embarked on a grand tour of the Pershore Road public houses, the **Grant**, the **British Oak**, and the **Thee Horseshoes** and finally, the **Dogpool**. There a young man wearing ice blue jeans (that were so tight they'd have made Gandhi look like a teddy boy) asked to be allowed to sing. From beneath a quiff that was struggling to absorb at least four scoops of Brylcream, came the most angelic of voices.

Roger Conway, known to his mates for obvious reasons as '**Twitty**', delivered an emotionally charged version of Red Foley's 'Old Shep.' Later, as handkerchiefs were hung over radiators to dry, two decisions were taken — Twitty the Brylcream boy would replace Roy Brown, and **Roger Ottley**, drawing the short straw, was to be the man to break the bad news to Roy.

"I took him to one side for a quick word," said Roger, "But Roy butted in, 'Before you start, I've just spent my wages on a leather suit. It's cost a fortune but you'll love it.' I thought he was gonna kill me when I gave him the bad news."

Entering a new phase, with a new front man, the Rockets decided it was time to jettison their old identity. They looked for inspiration across the brave new skyline that was forming — and found it in the unique crown of the Smallbrook Ringway development. Forthwith the Rockets would answer only to one name — the **Rotundas**.

Chevrolets were whizzing along Smallbrook Ringway towards Digbeth. In fact **Rockin' Chevrolets**, heading for their regular Saturday night appearance at the **Midland Red Social Club** on the corner of

Allison Street. With other regular nights on their worksheet like the **Bolton Arms**, Small Heath, and on Fridays, the **Dog and Partridge**, Yardley Wood, life was looking good for singer **Neil Cressin**, bass player **Dave Whaddley** and drummer **Pat Pegg**. Newly recruited to the Rockin' Chevrolets from the **Pursuers** (an Aston outfit that featured the 'Fabulous Shaker') came the strictly rhythm guitarist **Alan Meredith** and — on lead guitar, with his party piece the Dakotas' 'Cruel Sea' — **Tony Iommi**.

Things were getting serious, musically that is, with **Dave Pegg**. He was now in the company of **Dave and the Emeralds**. Fronting the Emeralds was **Dave Quedgley**. Brother **Keith Quedgley** hammered the drums whilst **Al Shipton** played bass along to Dave Pegg's guitar playing, which was improving by the day.

Carl Wayne & the Vikings at Handsworth Plaza

O n the morning of Friday 22nd November 1963, **Carl Wayne and the Vikings** parked up their Bedford Dormobile at Manchester airport and boarded a flight to Belfast where they were to provide musical accompaniment for Scottish pop singer, **Johnny Bev**.

The Vikings rehearsed with Johnny all afternoon. As they broke for their evening meal, news was breaking through from Dallas of the Kennedy assassination. Obviously sharing a state of shock and horror with the rest of the world, Carl Wayne and the Vikings nevertheless took to the stage that night with a positive attitude. Their mission was to lift the audience from the grief of the murder of such a well respected Irish American.

Unfortunately Johnny Bev didn't share such professionalism as an entertainer.

Nicky James & the Senators at Kidderminster Town Hall

"It was obvious that he was totally smashed," said **Terry Wallace**. "Johnny reached out for the mic, missed it and fell off the stage. We just carried on regardless. Nobody missed him. It was just one of those nights when nothing seemed to matter anymore."

Like the rest of their generation, the Vikings would remember where they were when they heard the news that day. No doubt it's the same for most other Brum rockers. **Ronny Smith** with **Nicky James and the Senators** were at **Kidderminster Town Hall**. **Cal Denning and the Cimarrons** were above Burton's at the **Star Ballroom**, Sparkhill, whilst **Danny Burns and the Phantoms**

The Rockin' Berries

Carl Barron

struggled through the mist to the **Tardebigge** pub near Bromsgrove. **Dave Lacey and the Corvettes** worked to a stunned and saddened **Old Hill Plaza**. The **Rockin' Berries** were at **Englebach Youth Club**, Turves Green.

Mike Sheridan and the Nightriders tried to put the news to the back of their minds. They were at **Abbey Road** recording their next single for Columbia Records.

"Norrie Paramor gave us a pre-release copy of the album 'With the Beatles'," explained **Roger Spencer**. "We fancied 'All My Lovin'' but Norrie decided to go with 'Please Mr Postman'. Either way it was a waste of time. Without original material, we were doomed to always be one step behind."

One step behind **Carl Barron** were the **Cheetahs**. It was made clear that the band would not be required for the recording of a Bob Barratt song. Only Carl was allowed into the studio, to add his voice to the pre-recorded orchestral backing track of 'This Is Only The Beginning'. The Cheetahs later shuffled in, like schoolboys after a detention, to record the B side, 'Beg, Borrow or Steal.'

With the sessions completed, the boys made their way from the Abbey Road studios to sample the magical mayhem of London's West End. A sign over a Soho doorway advertised the services of a 'Society Clairvoyant'. Curiosity got the better of **Euan Rose** and Carl, and they warily entered the spiritual parlour.

"I was told by the gypsy lady that I would be married twice, which is what has happened," said Euan. "She then told Colin that he would shortly experience a change in lifestyle — he would walk away from all that he'd worked for. The woman then paused, looked me square in the eyes, and warned, 'Don't ever go to South Africa because you won't come back alive.' "

The **Black Cat Club** was held every Friday evening at **Colmore Farm School**, Rubery, and had been the Cheetahs' lair for two years. In November 1963, as the Cheetahs' first spot came to a close, Carl Barron proudly announced to the crowd that they were about to hear the record that "me and Mr Paramor have done, and it's in the shops next week."

Everyone gathered excitedly around the stage as Carl placed his microphone in front of a Dansette record player and out through the public address system crackled 'This Is Only The Beginning.'

"At the end there was this embarrassing silence," said Euan Rose. "Everybody was so bitterly disappointed. Where were the Cheetahs on the record? Whatever had happened to rock 'n' roll? Carl was visibly shaken."

The record was released one week later but Carl Barron had quit the Cheetahs two days previously. Just like the gypsy lady predicted. Colin walked away from everything he'd worked for. A few weeks later he headed for a new life in South Africa.

"Can you imagine how I felt when I heard of his death?" said Euan. "The clairvoyant had delivered her fatal prediction to the wrong man."

Colin Smith, the Cheetahs' Carl Barron, died of a heart attack in Johannesburg, South Africa in 1992 aged forty eight.

The man behind the Barron – Colin Smith

Perhaps **Peter Green** (**Peter Lee Stirling** as he was now known in professional circles) was receiving guidance from the spiritual world, or maybe it was just hard work and effort on his part, either way, perseverance with his song writing was beginning to yield the necessary results.

Peter and his group, the **Bruisers**, were in constant demand at Regent Sound studios, in Denmark Street, the heart of London's Tin Pan Alley. Most working days would see the Bruisers making demonstration recordings of songs for the publishing houses that populated the neighbouring buildings.

One particular morning in late in 1963, found the Bruisers working on a handful of songs brought over for them by **Stuart Reid** of Robbins Music. As engineer Bill Farley prepared to play back the morning's recordings for Stuart Reid's approval, Peter was sat in a corner working on an almost completed song.

Ever-changing 60s landscapes – Birmingham's skyline, and bands like the Senators

"When the night is cold and my arms want someone to hold, I think of you," sang Peter to his acoustic guitar accompaniment. "When the rain is falling, I hear you calling to me. I think of you."

Stuart Reid was all ears. "Spend the afternoon cutting a demo of that song," he instructed the Bruisers, "I'll see if I can pitch it for you."

While Johnny Bev was nursing his hangover in the early hours of the morning after the Kennedy assassination, the **Vikings** had flown out of Belfast to Manchester. Jumping into their van they set off for the **Crown** pub in the centre of Birmingham for a lunchtime show. A quick wash and brush up and then a drive up the Bristol Road saw them at the **Station** pub in Selly Oak for the evening. What a life! What a way to earn a shilling! **Barry Harbor** of the Vikings was not so enthusiastic. He decided that a more stable existence was for him. After taking a shearing at the barbers, Barry successfully applied for a proper job at Wesleyan and General Insurance on Colmore Row, making way for **Tony Lewis**, formerly of **Ronny and the Senators**, to take his place as a Viking. For Tony Lewis, however, it was to be a mere flirtation.

Ke Va HQ – J&C

Vikings welcome Ace Kefford aboard

It was to be a mere flirtation for **Ace Kefford** with **Danny King and the Jesters**. Disillusioned, he left the band, rolled up his sleeves, and started work as a builder's labourer on the construction of the Rotunda in Birmingham centre. During a lunch hour break he wandered along the almost completed Smallbrook Ringway and into Hinckley Street, intending to browse around **Jones and Crossland's** music store.

Jim Powell collared Ace as he came round the corner. Jim, manager of **Keith Powell and the Valets**, had set himself up as an agent operating under the name **Ke Va Entertainments**. Seeing no need for kosher premises, he plied his trade literally from the doorstep of Jones and Crossland's showroom. He probably knew the meaning of being in the 'right place at the right time' better than most of his competitors!

After popping around the corner for two teas from Alex's pie stand, Jim Powell ushered Ace inside the shop. Sitting him down on a second-hand Selmer TruVoice amplifier, he explained his dilemma. Bass player, **John Allseybrooke** was not going to be available for a while and the Valets needed a bass guitarist to help out. Did Ace fancy the part-time appointment?

Terry Wallace continues the tale, "For some reason it never worked out with **Tony Lewis** as a Viking. We were playing at the **Old Hill Plaza** and in the other band was our old singer Keith Powell with his Valets. There was this blonde haired lad moving like a demon, singing like a bird, and twanging his bass like we'd never heard before. Carl said straight away 'He's for us.' "

"I couldn't believe my luck," said Ace, "The one minute I'm shovelling cement on the Rotunda for peanuts. The next minute I'm in **Carl Wayne and the Vikings** and picking up twenty odd quid a week. Okay, it was a little bit 'pat' for me, the Burtons suit and all that, but they were a great bunch of blokes and I like to think I made some good input with my Sam Cooke and Impressions material."

The Phantoms

About to make a big impression was **Joe Brannelly**, the **Applejacks** agent. He now thought that the time was right to approach his friend **Mike Smith** of the Artiste and Repertoire department at Decca Records.

Desperate to regain his company's credibility after the notorious Beatles blunder, Mike Smith made the journey to Solihull to find out what these Applejacks were all about. When he arrived at Solihull Civic Hall he was three hours late. Everyone except the Applejacks had gone home. Even the support band, the **Phantoms**, (guitarist **Mick Lawrence**, bass player **Bob Griffin** and drummer **Mike Kellie**) were back home in Marston Green by the time the man from Decca arrived.

As Mike Smith wandered around the dance floor, playing football with a discarded cigarette packet, the Applejacks rattled off a couple of songs.

"Mike Smith said he'd let us know if he could use us," explained Phil Cash, "And with that, he pushed the fire door open and was gone!"

Ray Bridger made a sudden exit from his home in Northfield when, at the age of fourteen, he ran away to sea. He served a year in the Merchant Navy before returning to Birmingham to commence musical activities with the **Satellites**. Not to be confused with the Lee Stevens mob, these

Satellites at Westcote Hall

Satellites — Ray, along with guitarist **Cliff Southall** and drummer **John Sly** — orbited around **Edgewood Hall** at Rednal, and **Westcote Hall** at Frankley Beeches. Ray then upped and left to become singer and rhythm guitarist with a Stirchley outfit, the **Firebirds**, who were led by guitarist **Terry Hall**.

Amongst the Firebirds' audience at a **Black Cat Club** gig one night were the **Cheetahs**, on the prowl for a replacement for **Carl Barron**. After the show the Cheetahs pounced, offering Ray Bridger a place in the band. Ray resigned his position as a tester at Woolf's, the dummy factory in Selly Oak. Slipping into the famous animal skin outfit, Ray performed for the first time as a Cheetah at the **Atlas Ballroom**, Stechford.

Cheetah skins would have been as welcome as the flowers in May for the ex-Rebels **Ray Thomas** and **Mick Pinder**. They were chilled to the bone as the freezing winds howled around the streets of Hamburg. Living in diabolical squalor, the boys were lucky to be alive after a gunman had opened fire, spraying bullets around the club where they had been appearing. Stony broke and with no prospect whatsoever of any improvement, they decided to walk home to Birmingham. With the frost cracking on the pavement beneath their feet, the boys made it as far as the British Consulate. After threatening to throw a housebrick through the window if financial assistance was not forthcoming, Messrs Thomas and Pinder were given travel tickets and loaned five shillings each.

In no need whatsoever of financial assistance were the **Modernaires**, who were still riding high as one of the most sought after bands in Birmingham. Public taste was demanding powerful vibrations from the stage and the Modernaires gave it good and solid. With their two saxophonists, **Maurice 'Moss' Groves** and **Jimmy Alexandre**, organist **Mo Jones**, and guitarist **Tommy Russell** rocking away like a roaring furnace on the solid groove of bass player **Wilf Clare** and drummer **Tony Finister**, they gave vocalist **Micky Bakewell** everything to play for.

On visits to the Regan ballrooms, professional London based bands could not help but be impressed with the standard of the Modernaires, and one such outfit, Cliff Bennett and the Rebel Rousers made no secret of their admiration for Moss Groves and what they described as his 'sax appeal.'

"We were at the **Silver Beat Club** in Stephenson Street and working with the Rebel Rousers again," recalled Micky Bakewell. "That's when Cliff Bennett made his move for Moss, and all we could do was wish him well on his move to London and the big boys."

The Modernaires replaced Moss with saxophonist **Teddy Gray**. Cliff Bennett and the Rebel Rousers, with the assistance of Moss Groves' driving saxophone licks, hit the top ten soon after with 'One Way Love.'

David Gooch signing the Crestas to Dial Records

An ex-actor, **David Gooch**, who'd actually delivered dialogue at the National Theatre no less, came up with a great idea to market Brum Beat to the record buying public. He formed his own label, **Dial Records**, and following an audition at the **Moat House**, selected fourteen bands for an album to be called — 'Brum Beat.'

The **Hollick and Taylor** studio was booked for Monday, 30th of December 1963, to record the fourteen bands in one session! First on the studio floor, at eight thirty that morning, were the **Cimarrons** who were showcasing their new drummer **Roger Pearson**, and a new face to replace **Lee Zenith**. Following Lee's departure they'd worked for a short while without the obligatory front man, then for a while with a female vocalist, **Paula Livings**, before discovering salesman **John Fletcher** at Nelson House Menswear in Dale End. With a little imagination John Fletcher measured up overnight to become **Cal Denning**, leader of the Cimarrons.

"Christmas is coming and the geese are getting fat. Please put a penny in the old man's hat," sang out an old Oxford Street busker holding out his ragged titfer. It was mid-December and **Peter Lee Stirling** was happy to oblige the old chap with a pocketful of loose change. After all it was the season of goodwill to all men, and Peter Lee Stirling had that peaceful, contented feeling. In late November, the **Bruisers** had played the ballroom on Cleethorpes pier supporting Liverpool's Merseybeats, who were basking the glory of their first release, 'It's Love That Really Counts', making the top thirty.

The Cimarrons' new vocalist — Cal Denning

"We'd included Pete Green's song 'I Think of You' in our set," **Don McGinty**, the Bruisers drummer explained. "Tony Crane, the leader of the Merseybeats demanded to know where we'd got that song from as they'd just recorded it!"

Stuart Reid of Robbins Music had succeeded in placing Peter Green's first professional pitch, 'I Think of You', with the Merseybeats. The recording would soon be showing in Britain's top ten best selling singles.

"As soon as I cut that demo, I knew that I'd acquired the knack of writing a popular song," said Peter. "So that was my New Year's resolution — to write good pop songs."

Chapter Three

1964

BABY USED TO STAY OUT . . .

Lee Lombard at the Adelphi, West Bromwich

Norman Haines' Brum Beats

As the dance floors all over Britain stamped out 1963 and stamped in 1964 to the beat of the Dave Clark 5's 'Glad All Over', the music press informed its readers that they were stamping to the 'Tottenham Beat.'

At the **Adelphi**, in West Bromwich, the **Satellites** played and **Lee Stevens** stamped around, in no mood to take prisoners.

The stage of the Adelphi was edged with coloured glass panels that radiated a glow to enhance the artiste's performance. Stamping harder on every beat, Lee's Cuban-heeled feet eventually smashed through the panels. Visible only from the knees up, like the dance band on the Titanic, Lee Stevens performed until the very end, when the Satellites prized him from the debris and carted him to Hallam hospital with a badly gashed leg.

A more gentle song on the charts in January 1964 was the **Merseybeats'** recording of the **Peter Lee Stirling** composition, 'I Think Of You'.

Norman Haines pitches in, "We were still called the **Van Dels**, but with black American acts like Martha Reeves and the Vandellas about to break, we needed a change to avoid confusion. Every time I put the radio on it seemed I was hearing the name 'Merseybeats' so I thought why not? Let's go for the **Brum Beats**. That's how the name came about."

With the new name came a new recruit — **Trevor Langham** (another old school pal of Norman Haines) on keyboards. "Trevor was classically trained and played prettily. I used to spread his fingers over the keys and tell him to thump it out," said Norman, holding his head in his hands.

The Brum Beats manager, **Vic Wakelin** was a fair pianist and a prominent member of the Musicians' Union. He was also the works manager of Brightside Electro Plating in Summer Lane, and had the use of the firm's J4 minibus, which proved handy for the Brum Beats of an evening. With the help of his contacts in the Musicians' Union, Vic organised a 'Blues Meets Trad' session at the **Hollybush** on Hagley Road, Quinton. **John Gibbins**, the trumpeter, sat in with them for the session, and a good night was had by all.

John Gibbins with the Brum Beats at the Hollybush, Quinton

Doing a fair bit of sitting in at the **Seven Stars Blues Club**, deep in the heart of Stourbridge were three young followers of the rhythm and blues cause. **Stan Webb** played guitar, **Chris Wood** was a mean flautist and **Robert Plant** could howl out the blues with the best of them. Eager to become a part of the honourable profession of music, Stan and Chris, with the help of pianist **Christine Perfect**, became the **Sounds of Blue**. Christine, back in her days at Moseley School of Art, had been a member of **Chuck Botfield's Rockin' Berries**. Robert Plant meanwhile, chose a more pop orientated avenue by joining the **Crawling Kingsnakes**.

Phil King and the Couriers, had spent the last eighteen months whizzing around delivering the goods. With the abdication of Phil King, they made a democratic decision to become the **Congressmen**. Their regular Saturday evening gig at the **Royal Oak**, Hockley Heath, had a special significance for them on 1st of February 1964. That was the release date for the eagerly awaited **Dial Records** album 'Brum Beat', and there, on track 11 were the Congressmen with 'The Shuck'.

Ma Regan had similar ideas for an album of Brum beat bands. An

The Congressmen at the Royal Oak, Hockley Heath

album that would feature the crème de la crème of the outfits she was booking into her ballrooms. Seven groups were eventually invited to the **Old Hill Plaza** for an audition to be held in the presence of the Decca representative, **Les Reed**. One such band was, from Dudley, the **Strangers**.

Tony Dalloway, their rhythm guitarist, takes a deep breath and picks up the story. "Myself, **Jake Elcock, Mike Aston** and **Roy 'Dripper' Kent** had been in the **Marauders**. The Marauders became the Strangers and we had first **Geoff Crewe** and then **Jack Thornton** from Tipton's **Teenbeats** as our singers before **Johnny O'Hara**, who went on to front the **Californians**. In those days the big event for us was Monday nights at **Dudley Liberal Club**. Eventually Dripper became the permanent man up front with **Alan Clee** coming in on lead guitar."

When the Strangers made their way to the Plaza for the Decca audition, they found Les Reed in a no-nonsense mood. Addressing all the young hopefuls, Mr Reed spelled out what he expected, "I don't want to hear 'Johnny B Goode' all night. Anything original — I want to hear it. Okay?"

Getting a reaction — the Strangers

It had to be okay. The Strangers disappeared to the basement toilets where Tony Dalloway strummed out his only effort to date. Although Les Reed didn't care much for the song, he liked the Strangers. A couple of weeks later and the Strangers were in London. They recorded a song which Les Reed had found for them entitled 'Return to Mary' and the Dripper Kent composition, 'What a Way'. That song, with its stomping Dave Clark feel, became the opening track on the Decca 'Brum Beat' album. The Strangers chose a West End Chinese restaurant to celebrate the making of their first record, toasting the future with a crate of Charrington's bottled shandy.

"I've always had a weak bladder," confessed Tony Dalloway, "and when we left the restaurant I'd drunk so much shandy my back teeth were floating."

Seeking the solitude of a darkened alley, in total privacy, Tony hovered over a drain and closed his eyes. With a condition line holding steady at 45 degrees, Tony, in his mind, journeyed through the steamy gates of heavenly bliss to the point of no return.

"That's when Jake and Alan picked me up by the elbows and plonked me down in the middle of Oxford Street!" recalled Tony Dalloway, leaving the rest of the story to the imagination. "I was lucky I never got six months."

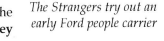

The Strangers try out an early Ford people carrier

Also selected for the Decca Brum Beat project were the **Mountain Kings**, the **Blue Stars,** the **Kavern Four**, with their original song 'I Want To Dance', and **Dave Lacey and the Corvettes**. Dave Lacey and the other Stourbridge lads — guitarists **Winston 'Django' Jones**, and **Roy Pinson**, bass player **John Jauncy** and drummer **Dave Little** — had first seen the light of day as musicians at **Brook Street Youth Club**.

Blue Stars

When they entered the Evening Dispatch sponsored group contest at the **Handsworth Plaza**, Dave and the Corvettes were as surprised as anyone at the end of the evening, when the compere, **Alan Freeman** from Pye Records, declared them the outright winners.

Dave Lacey at Brierley Hill Civic Hall

"We won stage suits from the tailor **Bernard Zissman** and a six month contract for the Regan ballrooms," said Dave.

The six months actually went on for six years as Dave Lacey and the Corvettes proved immensely popular with the Regan clientele.

"We never did the audition for Decca," explained Dave. "We turned up at the studio to find Les Reed had found two country and western songs for us to record. So we just plugged in and stuck 'em down on tape. But the songs were about as far away from our stage act as you could possibly get."

Ricky Graham & the Corvettes at Moor Pool Hall, Harbourne

Not too far away from Stourbridge, as the crow flies, were Rubery's **Corvettes**. These Corvettes, guitarists **Derek Morgan** and **Paul Brunt**, drummer **Bert Humphries** and the player with six strings on his bass guitar, **Pete Allen**, provided excellent accompaniment for singer **Graham Finch** at **Moorpool Hall, Harborne**. Graham, when clad in his gold lame jacket, much preferred to be known as **Ricky Graham**. Personally signed photographs of Ricky and the Corvettes were now gracing many a young Harborne debutante's bedroom wall. Bert Humphries being a particular fave rave.

Roller-skating up the Stratford Road from the Embassy Sportsdrome, Sparkbrook, the British Junior Champion speed skater paused for a moment outside the Mermaid pub. High on speed, in the healthiest possible way, **Danny Gallagher**, from Baker Street, Sparkhill, then thundered on to his destination — the **Star Ballroom**, above Burton's the Tailors. Removing his skates, Danny climbed the stairs to witness a performance by **Johnny Shane and the Solitaires**.

Johhnny Shane & the Solitaires

Knocked out by what he saw, especially the standard of musicianship of drummer **George Mills** and guitarist **Dave Bache**, Danny was determined to work even harder at his own efforts to master the bass guitar.

"Then I saw an advert in the Birmingham Mail for a bass player," recalled Danny. "I showed up and to my amazement it was Johnny Shane and the Solitaires. **Kenny Lowe** was packing in and I got the job!"

With a worksheet bursting at the seams, Danny's visits to the Embassy roller rink became more and more infrequent. Such was the growing popularity of Johnny Shane and the Solitaires, that by mid 1964 Danny had hung up his skates, preferring a rock 'n' roll career to a life of grazed kneecaps and elbows.

Christine Holmes

As a result of their outstanding stage shows, the **Rockin' Berries**, **Keith Powell and the Valets** and Solihull's **Christine Holmes** were all selected to appear in the 'Beat Room' programme on the recently launched

BBC2 television channel. To promote the show, an advertising trailer was filmed in the newly opened Bull Ring Centre, showing Keith and the Valets in full swing amongst the shoppers and traders. It had been planned to also feature **Danny King** in the programme's trailer.

"I rehearsed the camera shots and the film crew started messing me about," said Danny. "I went for an egg and chips in Woolworth's and never bothered to go back!"

Swapping his skates for Chelsea boots – Danny Gallagher with the Solitaires

Bob Barratt, **Norrie Paramor**'s assistant at Columbia, maintained that they really had great belief in Danny's singing talent.

"We had Ivor Raymonde's orchestra set up and waiting to record with Danny at Abbey Road," recalled Bob. "Danny let us down. He never showed."

Danny King made it as far as the **Kardomah** coffee bar, across from Snow Hill Station, where he'd planned to board the London train. He had a coffee and a cigarette and then he had a change of heart.

Kardomah, Colmore Row

"Sure I let Columbia down but they let me down first," said Danny, shrugging his shoulders.

A truce was called between Danny and Norrie Paramor when Columbia agreed to allow Danny to record a song he had found for himself. Always keeping his ears alert for a quality song, Danny had picked up on a number which had been a minor American hit for Vic Dana in 1962. In Danny King's opinion this Dick Glasser composition, 'I Will', was twenty-four carat material.

"At that point," said Danny, "I was willing to take back everything I'd said about Columbia. Then word reached us that **Billy Fury** had recorded the song and Decca were releasing it that very week. So near yet so far away."

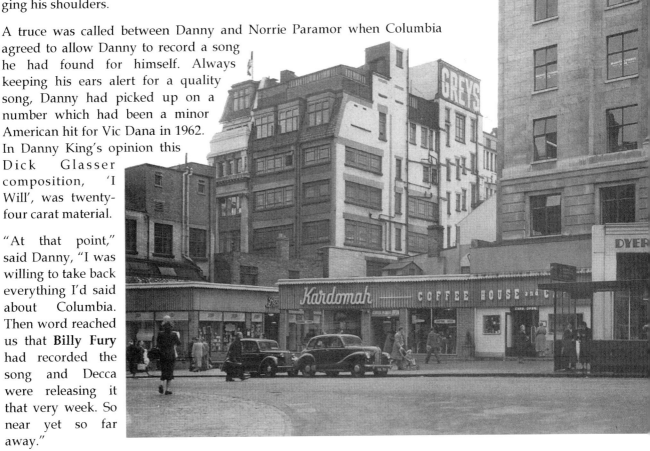

With the catchword 'Brumbeat' now firmly embedded in everyone's minds, it was full steam ahead for **Norman Haines' Brum Beats**.

"The bookings were rolling in," recalled Norman. "We literally couldn't put a foot wrong."

Neither could **Ma Regan**. At the **Handsworth Plaza**, she was now regularly booking a bunch of musical youths — former **Eko**, **Graham Ashford** on vocals, saxist **Paul Carter**, and on drums, ex-**Beachcomber Dave Mountney**. Completing the line-up were guitarist **Roger Hill** and bass player **Graham Gallery** (both late of **Bobby and the Dominators**). They had the pedigree and the talent but, as yet, no name.

Mustering up all of her artistic creativity, Ma Regan gazed at the light blue neon sign that flickered above the entrance doors to the Handsworth Plaza.

"Dat's it boys!" she screamed. "Yurr de **Plazents**!"

The Plazents were so highly rated by Ma Regan that she had a word with the people at Decca. Their response was brief and to the point — "Get another drummer, find a proper name, and you've got a deal!" Dave Mountney was unceremoniously replaced by **Alan 'Bugsy' Eastwood**, leaving Ma Regan to dream up another name for these excellent purveyors of Brumbeat.

"Dat's it!" she again screamed, "Day will be de **Brum Beats**!"

"That's all Birmingham needed," said Norman Haines. "Two Brum Beats! It seemed whenever I turned up for a gig the booker would ask where Roger Hill was and when Roger went anywhere they'd ask where Norman Haines was."

The other Brum Beats

The Plazents/Brum Beats release for Decca, which they promoted with a guest appearance on 'Thank Your Lucky Stars', was entitled, appropriately enough, 'I Don't Understand'.

Gerry Levene and the Avengers didn't understand the poor response to their record, 'Dr Feelgood'. Now some five months old, the feel of the recording was not that of the moment. Despite a prestigious appearance on 'Thank Your Lucky Stars', the band failed to generate public interest and sales were disappointing. So disappointing that enthusiasm within the Avengers began to wane. **Graeme Edge** confided in Gerry Levene that he and **Denny Laine** were thinking of making a fresh start. Was Gerry interested in participating in such a project?

"We arranged an initial rehearsal," said Gerry, "But Graeme and Denny took off for a weekend in London instead without telling me."

Arriving back in Birmingham, Graeme Edge and Denny Laine spoke about a new vibrant scene that was exploding in the Smoke. They reckoned London club audiences were just waiting for someone like Gerry Levene to arrive.

"We had a kitty in the Avengers which, at that time was worth about forty pounds. I then found out that our kitty had financed their London excursion. I had nothing more to do with the project after that," said Gerry.

A bonfire and fireworks party held a couple of months earlier, at **Fulford Hall**, Earlswood, home of the **Pryke** family, had featured Denny Laine with his **Diplomats** and **Danny King** with his **Jesters**.

"Denny took me aside and expressed his ideas about breaking away from the Diplomats to play songs that had more of a blues feel rather than out-and-out pop. Would I be interested in being a part of a new set up?" Danny

Clint Warwick

King explained. "I went a step further and suggested **Clint Warwick** as the bass player."

Clint Warwick, who had served his time with Danny King and **Gerry Day's Dukes** picked up the storyline: "The first name we had was the **Soul Preachers** and we knew, me, Graeme and Denny, that we were sounding pretty good. Then Danny stopped coming to rehearsals and we were left in lumber."

The Soul Preachers' chance encounter at the **Moat House** club with the former Rebel, **Ray Thomas**, alias **El Riot** and his pianist, **Mike Pinder** changed everything. Recently returned from Germany and full of wondrous stories, they'd tracked down the former bandits who'd made up the **Rebels** — **Rob Sheward, John Lodge, Brian Betteridge** and **Micky Heard**. Mr Thomas and Mr Pinder were bubbling with excitement about a proposition made to them through local agent **Ralph Horton**. The brewers, Mitchells and Butlers, had approached Ralph

about the possibility of sponsoring a rhythm and blues band of the kind that played regularly in their pubs around Birmingham. In line with their 'Marvellous Beer' advertising logo, Mitchells and Butlers would expect the combo to be called the **M&B Five** — or four, or whatever.

"I for one, couldn't contemplate the risk of casting everything aside to turn full-time professional as I was married with a family," recalled Rob Sheward, "And John Lodge was intent on completing his apprenticeship as a draughtsman."

At the Moat House club Ray Thomas and Mick Pinder, by chance, met with the boys who were seeking to become Soul Preachers.

"We'd got nothing to lose," said Clint Warwick. "Ralph Horton got us rehearsing every day at the **Carlton** club. If nothing else, we'd be on free beer!"

In actual fact, **Phil Myatt**, who ran the Carlton, had initially made the M&B offer to **Brian Yeates** who fronted the **Crestas** as **Mark Stuart**. Brian Yeates gave the offer some thought, but with him now being a Dial recording artiste replied, "Thanks but no thanks."

"If you weren't in by half past seven you'd have no chance," was **Johnny Carroll**'s way of describing a typical evening at the **Golden Cross** pub, Shortheath, Erdington where his band, the **Olympics**, were in residence. Known in the finest circles as the singing dustman, Johnny maintains that originally he had never thought of carving out a show business career for himself.

Relaxing by the Thames – the Olympics outside the Golden Cross

"I joined the **Dakotas** because they were my mates. The singer left so I became the singer. Then the lead guitarist left so I had to learn to play 'Perfidia' and 'Apache' pretty quick!"

Alongside Johnny in the Olympics were rhythm guitarist **Roger Smith**, bass player **Ron Dickson** and drummer **Steve Price**. Recognising the fact that their standards had to be upped in the instrumental and vocal harmony departments, Roger Smith moved 'upstairs' to take on a managerial role. **Brian Betteridge**, the accomplished guitarist from El Riot's now disbanded Rebels, was brought in to supply the fancy guitar licks that were a little more intricate than Johnny Carroll's efforts.

Brian Betteridge's ability to sing the top harmonies must have impressed **Graham Nash** of the **Hollies**, himself a possessor of a fine set of pipes when it came to hitting the high notes. The Olympics had entered a beat group competition at **Wimbledon Palais**, where the rules stated that they must perform a song of their own. Their effort, 'Think of Me', was good enough for Graham, the contest adjudicator, to place the Olympics second in the Grand Final.

Always keen to be a little different from everything else that was happening, the **Uglys** had been endeavouring to write their own material. **Steve Gibbons** would provide lyrics that would be passed over to drummer **Jimmy Holden** and guitarist **Bob Burlison** to provide the necessary chords and melody. Aware that the growing popularity of the **Rockin' Berries** and **Mike Sheridan and Nightriders** was mainly due to their slapstick comedy routines, the Uglys decided to give it a go in the 'all round entertainment' stakes.

"We'd have a Dansette record player in the wings and the Spike Jones and the City Slickers track

Comedy on tap from the Uglys

'Cocktails for Two' on the turntable," Steve Gibbons explained, "**Johnny Gordon**, our organist, would start up the record and we'd all be in a line, miming to all the daft voices and the sound effects. It was pure music hall."

They also used the spirit of vaudeville as an excuse to sup ale by the jug full. Purely for audience reaction of course, the Uglys installed a flagon of ale in **John Husthwaite**'s bass cabinet. Linked to the flagon, and protruding through the speaker cloth, was a tap.

"During an instrumental break, I used to pull a couple of pints," Steve explained, miming the actions. "The beer was a bit warm but beggars can't be choosers!"

Roy Vears and the Strangers, from Kings Norton, hadn't been reduced to begging but you'd never have guessed that from the look of their stage attire. Their new manager, or to be correct manageress, Mrs **Geri Spencer** (mother of Roger, the band's drummer) was determined to smarten them up.

In the belief that image is of the essence, Mrs Spencer was always clad in a fox fur coat, and for headwear, a red hat that was easily 2'6" in diameter. During a shopping expedition on the Coventry Road, Small Heath, she visited a tailor's shop (that actually doubled as a chapatti joint!) There she purchased the glittering material that was soon to be made into Mexican

The shiny gold Sovereigns

New Strangers —
Pete Knight, Mike Parks,
Malcolm Clarke &
Richard Johnson

styled stage suits for the Strangers. Once seen in their gold lamé costumes, there was nothing else for it, from now on they would be the **Sovereigns**, and all that glittered was gold for a while. A Friday night booking in Coventry, late in the March of 1964 at the **Walsgrave Working Mens' Club**, found them working alongside female impressionist **Billy Brean**, who later found fame as **Larry Grayson.** He was so taken with the band and their superb accompaniment to his rendering of 'My Blue Heaven', that after the show he took them into his confidence. It was the eve of the Grand National and Larry urged the Sovereigns to put all their sovereigns on a horse called 'Team Spirit'.

"I had fifty bob each way on Team Spirit," recalled Dave, "And it won at 18/1. I'd have made forty-five quid if only he'd told me to back it on the nose!"

Unfortunately when Dave had enquired how Larry would be inclined to place the flutter, Mr Grayson shyly pursed his lips and replied, "Well, I'm a bit of an each-way man myself."

The Strangers name change to the Sovereigns left the way clear for a bunch of lads who were also operating out of the Kings Norton area. Previously known as the **Nomads**, they had been found wandering around the salubrious area of Middleton Hall Road by guitarist **Pete 'Hank B'** 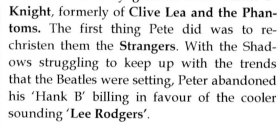 **Knight**, formerly of **Clive Lea and the Phantoms.** The first thing Pete did was to rechristen them the **Strangers**. With the Shadows struggling to keep up with the trends that the Beatles were setting, Peter abandoned his 'Hank B' billing in favour of the cooler sounding '**Lee Rodgers'**.

Decca Records finally fancied the **Applejacks'** chances. The band was asked to attend an initial recording session. **Arthur Smith** and **Joe Brannelly** cupped their hands in prayer. Out of a short-list of half a dozen songs, a **Troy Dante** and the **Bruisers** demo of the Les Reed and **Geoff Stevens'** song 'Tell Me When' was the song selected. When **Tony Hall**, head of promotions at Decca, heard the Applejacks recording, which leant heavily on **Don Gould's** weird and wonderful piano sound, he knew for certain that it was top ten bound. Released on Valentines Day, 'Tell Me When' was still hot from the presses when a copy landed on disc jockey **Jimmy Saville**'s desk. Jimmy agreed with Tony Hall's prediction and gave the record regular airplay on Radio Luxembourg's 'Teen and Twenty Disc Club'. By March of 1964, the record had reached number seven on the charts. While the music press was proclaiming a major advance in the progress of Brumbeat, the national newspapers were asking the headline question, 'Will **Phil Cash, Martin Baggott** and **Don Gould** now leave school?'

Phil Cash laughs at the recollection of his school leaving. "It was total chaos and it was wonderful. All the press and TV were at the school gates as we came out for the last time. Next thing we were on 'Juke Box Jury' then up to Manchester for 'Top of the Pops'. I was just sixteen."

The Applejacks – hard collar

Gerry Freeman quit his job with the Eagle Star Insurance. **Megan Davis** resigned her post as a radiographer at All Saints Hospital, and **Al Jackson** hung up his barber's clippers, happy at the prospect that he would never again have to ask the question, "Anything for the weekend sir?" Even their manager, Arthur Smith, handed in his notice at the Post Office to operate his management affairs from an office at 602, Stratford Road. Sparkhill. He didn't see it as a career gamble as he had a healthy works pension to look forward to. Unfortunately the Post Office didn't see it that way. Arthur Smith, by quitting, had forsaken his pension.

"I suppose Arthur was the original rock 'n' roll victim," sighed Phil Cash.

Perhaps Arthur Smith should have recruited the services of **Johnny Neal** to sort 'em out. At the **Coventry Flying Club**, Johnny and his **Starliners**, along with **Cal Denning and the Cimarrons** had sweat blood in the name of rock 'n' roll. As the two bands were packing away their equipment Cal Denning broke the bad news that the management were not prepared to pay for the evening's entertainment. Johnny sent a Starliner into the office with a polite request for the 'rock of ages', the wages.

"They're stickin' the knock on," was the message relayed back to Johnny Neal from his scout.

Johnny Neal and the Starliners

With Starliners and Cimarrons a noticeable distance behind him, Johnny burst into a smoky back room where, sat at a table, the manager of the establishment was dealing cards in a poker game. Johnny Neal leaned across the table and shoved his fist under the welcher's chin.

"Johnny had some bottle — five minutes later we were whacking up the money on the car park!" a relieved **Maurice Preece** recalled.

Albert Chapman was a lad who could whack it out with the best of them. Always keen amateur boxer, Albert had been a member of the church choir at **St John's**, Perry Barr, sharing ecclesiastical duties with **Muff and Stevie Winwood**, but eventually found all the spiritual fulfillment he needed via his mits. At the tender age of seventeen in search of employment as a doorman, Albert, passing himself off as a twenty-one year old, presented himself to **Albert Archer**, the manager of the Hurst Street **Locarno**.

"Albert Archer was impressed enough to give me job," Albert explained. "He told me to start the next Monday at thirty-bob a night."

Immediately Albert Chapman journeyed to the Handsworth Plaza to seek out **Joe Regan**. He told Joe that he was employed by the Locarno at the rate of thirty shillings an evening. Mr Regan, catching sight of Albert's clenched fists, was convinced that the man had 'muscles in his spit' and cried "Oi'll giff yer two pounds a noight!"

Six pounds for working three nights on the door at the Handsworth Plaza was fine for the lad who already worked by day as a butcher at the Co-op for three pounds and twelve shillings a week!

"Old Joe Regan was so eccentric," chuckled Albert, "He'd wear odd shoes. The night we had **Little Stevie Wonder** at the Plaza, Joe had a carpet slipper on one foot and a welly on the other!"

Big Albert Chapman

The welly behind **Keith Powell and the Valets'** new Columbia single, 'Tore Up' was provided by a bunch of pop fans who probably never actually saw the group! It had loads of screaming and whoopin' and a hollerin' in the background as the track thundered along.

"All the screams on that record were actually for Cliff Richard," explained **Colin Wood**, the Valets' guitarist, "Norrie Paramor had recorded a live session with Cliff, complete with an audience that sounded like his entire fan club. So the crowd reaction was filtered onto our track. It was a nice thought to imagine the birds were going barmy for us."

On the strength of that record, a London agent, **Ossie Newman** of General Artistes, booked Keith and the Valets onto a major national tour with the Rolling Stones. The Stones were currently enjoying their first top ten hit,

'Not Fade Away'. When the tour was completed, the Valets returned to Birmingham to await payment. They waited and waited but the promised payment never arrived.

"There was only thing for it," said **Mal Ford,** organist with the Valets. "The band were broke, the diary was all but empty, and with no sign of us getting our tour money we needed to generate an 'alternative income'."

Keith Powell came up with the bright idea of cleaning windows. There was nothing to it. All that was needed was a ladder, a bucket and a couple of window leathers. Shard End was their chosen patch. So one spring morning in 1964, five aptly named Valets traipsed down Heath Way. Two carried a ladder, one carried a

Keith Powell & the Valets at Digbeth Civic Hall

bucket and Mal, being the smallest, was entrusted with the window leathers. Keith, being the salesman, wore his stage suit and, forcing a grin, rang a doorbell. Receiving a positive response from the gullible householder, the ladder was positioned up to a bedroom window. A leather was then plunged into the bucket of warm soapy water and solemnly handed to Mal Ford. Mal was a strange choice for button boy. Here was a man who, by his own admission, suffered vertigo walking on a deep pile carpet. Still, despite his inner fears, Mal's little legs began their ascent to the top of the ladder. He'd often witnessed window cleaners slap their wet leather on to a window pane before starting to wipe with a circular motion. With confidence at an all time high, Mal Ford hurled the soaking leather at the bedroom window.

"The leather hit the glass and went straight through!" said Mal.

Keith Powell took immediate command of the rapidly deteriorating situation. "'Op it quick!" (or words to that effect) he ordered, and five pairs of legs sprinted off down Heath Way!

Maybe tales of the Valets' swift retreat were the inspiration fo⸱ ⸱eter Lee Stirling's song 'Don't Turn Around'. Then again, maybe not.

"There's no story behind the song," said Peter. "I was a professional song-writer and I wrote what I considered to be an ideal musical vehicle for the Merseybeats' image."

'Don't Turn Around' was the perfect follow up to 'I Think Of You'. Plenty of warm sixth and major seventh chords and even an augmented chord for good measure to give vocalist Tony Crane a chance to shake his shoulder length locks around. By April of 1964 'Don't Turn Around' had become another top twenty hit to add to Peter Lee Stirling's CV. Peter's imagination was then put to the ultimate test when **Stuart Reid**, of Robbins Music, asked him to write a song with the 'Dance On' and 'Secret Love' lady, **Kathy Kirby**, in mind. The result was 'I Belong' and it became Britain's entry for the 1964 Eurovision Song Contest, which was held in Naples. 'I Belong' achieved second place, enhancing Peter Lee Stirling's growing reputation in Tin Pan Alley.

John Singer had ideas for enhancing the back room of the **Kings Head** pub on Hagley Road. Already established in the Bearwood area for some twelve months, John had been presenting the cream of Birmingham and Black Country beat groups at **Thimblemill Baths**, taking over from the extremely capable **Ronnie Hancox** and his Orchestra. It was Ronnie Hancox who had introduced Thimblemill Baths to the delightful **Susan Maughan**, a young lady from Greenway Street, Small Heath. In October of 1962, Susan had made number three on the charts with 'Bobby's Girl', a cover of Marcie Blane's American top ten hit. The Kings Head was just a stone's throw from Thimblemill Baths.

King's Head, Bearwood

"That's why all the windows were broke!" quipped John Singer. "The walls were bare brick, the whole place was so gloomy and fusty. I stuck a couple of plastic skeletons on the walls, dimmed the lights way down low and opened it for business as **The Morgue**. I had **Spencer Davis** there as a regular attraction on Mondays."

John Singer had previously promoted a very successful jazz festival at Fulford Hall, Earls-wood, and had an idea to bring a similar attraction to Bearwood. "Across from the Kings Head is Lightwoods Park," explained John. "I'd realised that the park would be ace to stage a similar festival. It had loads of open space, and was well served by bus routes. It couldn't fail. So I approached Birmingham Council and laid out my plans to them. I was turned down flat." John said with just a slight hint of bitterness. "They laughed me out of the Council House. And what happened? A year later the Birmingham Council put a jazz festival on that was so successful it was untrue. At Lightwoods Park!"

Andy Hamilton at Lightwoods Park, 1964

With or without the stolen festival, John Singer's career as an agent continued to flourish when he amalgamated his showbiz interests with **Ralph Horton**. By day Ralph was a butcher with a shop on Vicarage Road, Kings Heath. By night he was head cook and bottle washer of Ralph Horton Enterprises. The amalgamation of Ralph and John was to be called, appropriately enough, the **Ralph Johns Agency**.

A s Brumbeat gathered strength, so **Tony Withers,** guitarist with **Ronny and the Senators**, could sense his enthusiasm for the bright lights diminishing. Carpet slippers, a mug of hot cocoa and the glow of a two-bar electric fire seemed more appealing than Chelsea boots, a cup of stewed tea and an hour's posing in drizzling rain around **Alex's Pie Stand**. Fortunately for the Senators, Gerry Levene's young guitarist was in search of new horizons, and stepped into the breach.

"The only thing I remember about **Roy Wood** taking over

Alex's Pie Stand

from me," said Tony Withers, "Was that he inherited my Binson echo. We'd been at Moseley Art School at the same time and perhaps the 'old school tie' bit touched my emotions, because I let him have my Binson echo for nothing!"

Prior to Gerry Levene's Avengers, Roy Wood had served a musical apprenticeship with a group of lads from the Lea Hall, Kitts Green area of Birmingham. Roy, together with **Dennis Hunt**, **Brian Alderd**, **Dave Green** and **Billy Martin** were collectively the **Falcons** and were transported around by **Mick Davis** in his old Morris van. The Falcons played the **Ravenscroft Club** in Grange Road, Small Heath, the **Windmill Club** in Queens Road Yardley, and **Lea Hall British Legion**, where Roy's mother pulled the pints, but their biggest engagement was the **Mackadown** pub in Kitts Green.

Roy Wood with the Falcons at the Mackadown

"Roy's party piece in them days was the theme from 'the Dambusters'." recalled Mick Davis. "The barman used to flash the lights as if it was last orders while Roy plucked out the tune!"

The Cheetahs were struggling as a result of the retirement of **Carl Barron**. "Our power to pull a crowd was plummeting, and consequently so were our fees," said **Euan Rose**. "Something had to be done."

Straying temporarily to the Southwest Coast, the Cheetahs promoted their own dances until they were finally back up to scratch and ready to face the discerning Birmingham scene once more.

"We'd do the **Ritz**, Kings Heath and one of the Plazas before moving on to the **Cedar Club**," recalled **Ray Bridger**. "We'd fall out of there and on to the **Café de Paris**."

The Café de Paris was actually the all night pie stand that was sited at the front entrance of Snow Hill Station. Just like Alex's pie stand, which by now had moved from Hill Street to Hurst Street, their pies were soft bottomed with the crusts hand raised.

"Hand raised? Mmm. As they used to say in the Navy," sighed Ray Bridger, himself an ex-mariner.

Cheetahs – spotted on the Southwest Coast

Fraternizing with members of the Merchant Navy in August of 1964 were the Worcester based **Hellions**. **Jim Capaldi** and **Dave Mason**, previously with the **Jaguars** had put in with bass player **Tony Hill** and guitarist **Gordon Jackson**. Impressing the powers that be, the Hellions had won a contract to play the famous **Star Club**, in the German port of Hamburg. The booking agency had insisted on a female presence in the personnel and so for the German trip the Hellions had the vivacious **Tanya Day**, from Aldridge, as their vocalist. In Germany to promote their first single 'Dimples', the **Spencer Davis Group** made a guest appearance at the Star Club one evening. Stevie Winwood, impressed with the talent that Jim Capaldi and Dave Mason were showing, was making mental notes for future reference.

The Spencer Davis Group

Burton's Corporation Street – suited Big Al

Ronny Smith, feeling overworked, underpaid and chronically depressed, quit his position as a Senator. Just as he left, the **Senators** received an offer that would elevate **Nicky James** into the big time. Pye Records had had a mild rethink about Nicky James being 'too Elvis' and, back in the autumn of 1963, released a single, 'My Colour is Blue'. Sales were, at best, disappointing, but Nicky James had not gone unnoticed. The offer was for him to tour with the Senators, as support for the superstar–in–waiting, **Tom Jones**.

"Tom's band was also called the **Senators** so Nicky came up with the name of the **Wild Cherries**," explained Tony Withers. "Something to do with the state of their noses! The tour opened and the Wild Cherries were an absolute smash. Nicky had so much sex appeal. And that's where the trouble started. Tom Jones, not yet the star he was to become twelve months later, had his work cut out to follow Nicky's performance. Next thing was, the Wild Cherries were pulled from the tour and that was that."

With the demise of the Wild Cherries, the pop world's loss was **Mike Sheridan**'s gain. Despite lack of success on the recording front, the **Night-riders** were burning with ambition to succeed nationwide. Well not quite all the band, as **Big Al Johnson**, their ace guitarist was perfectly happy in his role as manager of the Corporation Street tailors, Burton's. By mutual consent, a replacement was sought.

"I'll never forget the first time my mother laid her eyes on **Roy Wood**," recalls Nightrider **Greg Masters**. "My parents were then keeping the **Anchor** pub in Digbeth. It was a Saturday morning and Roy came to the pub. He looked a bit wacky even in those days. 'Where the hell did you dig him up from?' my mother asked."

Itching to get back into the Brum scene were two former members of **El Riot**'s gang, the **Rebels**, drummer **Rob Sheward** and bass player **John Lodge**. Big Al Johnson was snapped up immediately and, because of the advent of the Animals, **Malc Bourne**, along with his Vox Continental organ, was also summoned.

Al's pal – Gene Vincent

"Big Al was a close pal of **Gene Vincent**," explained Rob Sheward. "When Gene was in town, he'd always be Big Al's guest."

The man who gave the world 'Be Bop A Lula' was in town and at ATV studios to record a piece for 'Thank Your Lucky Stars'. Once his effort was done and dusted, Gene Vincent telephoned Big Al to "get me outa here." Al Johnson and Rob Sheward met Gene at the stage door and the three of them drove to a back-street Aston pub. Gene Vincent settled down at a corner table, engrossed in a paperback. When the beer arrived, Gene raised his glass. "Hey Al. Here's to your new band. How's it workin' out?" he asked, before taking a sip. Al mentioned the fact that they still hadn't thought of a name. Gene Vincent held out the cover of the paperback and pointed to the title.

"There's your name!" he declared. The book Gene Vincent was reading was entitled the **Carpetbaggers**.

One of the bands featured on the Dial 'Brum Beat' album, the **Crescendos**, were enjoying the feeling of having the Midas touch. At a social club in Northfield, the Crescendos had, to quote guitarist **Trevor Greaves**, "paralysed 'em". Having packed away the equipment into their Dormobile, the boys were invited to 'have one for the ditch' with the club's steward.

"Unfortunately this chap had a terrible hump on his back," said Trevor remorsefully. "It was a real Charlie Laughton. As he pulled the pints he asked if we'd been re-booked and I told him we'd be back soon. 'Great!' the poor hunchback replied. 'Next time we'll have a right ol' ding dong.' You can't buy lines like that."

Ding dongs weren't enough however, to keep the Crescendos intact. **Colin Cooper** and **Dennis Horsley** departed to form the **Colin Dennis Duo**. When that venture had run its time, Colin embarked on a successful career as a stand up comedian, keeping the professional name of **Colin Dennis**. Meanwhile the remaining Crescendos, troopers that they were, carried on regardless.

The Hunters Moon pub, pre-war, pre-development

Trevor Greaves, shrugged his shoulders. "As it happened, we were playing the **Hunters Moon** over Shard End way. In the audience was **Gordon Andrews** with his wife **Janet Anne**. They'd just wound up their showband, the **Unsquare Men**. We had a chat and they teamed up with us."

So well did the blending of Gordon and Janet with the Crescendos work that more cabaret style bookings began to appear in the diary. **Garrington's Works Social Club** at Bromsgrove was such an example. One comedy routine, which Gordon Andrews had honed to perfection, called for him to dress as a Zulu warrior. Then Gordon would perform a ritual war dance as the Crescendos played the instrumental 'Zulu Stomp'!

Crescendos at the California

'Zulu Stomp' had in fact been written and recorded by **Roy Everett and the Climbers**. Changing their name to the **Brand**, their composition 'Zulu Stomp' appeared as the B side of their single release on the Piccadilly label, 'Lover Not a Fighter'.

Honri Edouarde tells the story behind 'Zulu Stomp'.

"Nothin' to tell really." said Honri. "We done it at **Hollick and Taylor's** studio. We set down a 'Bo Diddley' groove and old man Taylor turned the tape on. Roy Everett blowed and sucked some pretty wild notes on his harmonica. He nearly ruptured himself, but the recording sounded great on playback."

At Garrington's, as the Crescendos picked up the exciting jungle rhythm, so Gordon struggled into his grass skirt, blacked his face, stuck an imitation bone through his nose and leapt out into the audience, scaring the daylights out of everyone by repeatedly banging his shield with a spear. It was a one-man re-enactment of the Zulu massacre at Yorke's Rift.

"Grown men and women ran screaming for cover as this Zulu warrior charged around the ballroom, threatening everything in his path," Trevor Greaves recalled, indulging in a swift King Kong impression. "It was that wild. The atmosphere became more intense and we kept up the groove until we could see Gordon emerging from the mayhem. As he made it back to the stage we could see that the rear of his grass skirt was smouldering. Someone had set it on fire. By the time Gordon made the dressing room there were flames licking his backside!"

The Brand

The **Dragoon** pub, in the Aston Fields area of Bromsgrove, was a hot spot for bands like the **Cellarmen**. The Cellarmen comprised of guitarists **Dave Joynes** and **Kevin Fryer**, with **John Collins** on bass, drums in the capable hands of **Dave Simpson** and **Phil Hobbis** singing and blowing harmonica.

Eddie Stride, Graham Read, Martin Webley, Pete Tansell, Phil Dawson and **Brian Maguire** would often wander down to the Dragoon as the **Nomads**; as would **Cliff Ward with his Cruisers** and **Terry Webb**, in his gold lame jacket; and the **Spiders**, who always wore purple, could be guaranteed to pack the function room. The Spiders did, however, incur problems when their drummer, **John Bonham**, refused to acknowledge requests from the audience to play quieter. **Johnny and the Alpines** however, incurred no such problem — no one turned up for them!

Cellarmen

The **Terry Matthews Agency** was, at this time, going great guns and venturing into promotions at the likes of **Wednesbury Youth Centre**, the **Forum** at Pensett and **Walsall Town Hall**.

"I'd do a lot of business with the **Terry Blood Agency** in Stoke," explained Terry, "And we'd buy in acts like **Little Richard** and **Gerry and the Pacemakers**. A chap by the name of **Mike Lloyd** was full-time booker for the Blood Agency. Mike played rhythm guitar for Wednesbury's **Mark Allan Group**, and he ended up with owning record shops and the theatre up in Stoke under the banner of Mike Lloyd Music."

It was whilst 'working the door' at Wednesbury Youth Centre that Terry Mathews noticed a Commer van, coated in lipstick messages, drive onto the car park.

*Pat Wayne &
the Beachcombers*

"I had the **Rockin' Berries** all set up and ready to play so my curiosity was aroused," Terry Matthews recalled. "**Alan Clarke** of the **Hollies** leaned out of this van and asked if they were working for me that night. 'Not to my knowledge.' was my reply. The response that came back is not repeatable! The van turned round, tyres smoking, and zoomed off down the A41!"

Whilst rehearsing their performance for 'Thank Your Lucy Stars', the **Beachcombers' Pat Wayne** was aware that **Brian Epstein** was watching his every move from the across the studio. Never slow in coming forward, Pat Wayne went over and asked the most powerful man in British show business what the chances were of NEMS Enterprises representing the Beachcombers.

"He eyed me up and down a couple of times and then looked away, turning his nose up as he did so," said Pat, "Not a word but I thought, 'Well, he ain't said no.' "

The floor manager reminded drummer **Brian Sharp** that although the band was miming, studio microphones were 'open' for audience reaction. "Go easy on the drum kit," pleaded the floor manager. As the cameras rolled, the Beachcombers gave their all.

"I could feel Epstein's eyes burning into me and I thought, "Aye up, nearly 'ome and dry." recalled Pat Wayne. "Then I heard some clattering and banging and a roar went up from the audience. I looked round to see Brian Sharp land on his backside, his drums and cymbals raining down on him before bouncing around on the studio floor. In his enthusiasm, Brian had toppled from the rostrum, pulling his kit with him. That's when I saw Epstein scurrying away into the darkness and I called out 'I'll leave our card at the desk!' But we never heard anything."

The Crescendos

After hearing that the **Gay Tower** in Edgbaston had the audacity to present little-known London bands, the **Crescendos** complained bitterly to **Mr Baocchi,** the manager of the ballroom. To their astonishment, their demands for bookings fell on sympathetic ears.

"We invested in 'Dr Zhivago' shirts from **Nelson House** in Dale End," **Trevor Greaves** explained. "When the revolving stage at the Tower whizzed us round to face the crowd, I thought 'This is it mate! This is what it's all about!' "

For Gerry Levene and steed, the Avengers were nowhere to be seen

S urvival was what it was all about for **Gerry Levene**. His **Avengers** were now defunct and he had bookings to honour.

"**Reg Calvert** kept me going. I'd got a good following at his places like the **Co-op Ballroom** in Nuneaton and the **BRS Club** on Bromford Road," recalled Gerry. "**Joe Dignam** and **Tommy Owen** from Danny King's band became the Avengers for a while until I put in with a Coventry group, the **Chicanes**."

The new Avengers? Gerry Levene & the Chicanes

W ith **Jimmy Onslow** and **Sprike Hopkins** installed in the **Diplomats** as a two-man replacement for **Denny Laine**, life again seemed rosy for the 'Dips'.

"I'd always been a bass player but **Stevie Horton** was a perfectly capable player," explained Jimmy Onslow. "So, for the first time in my life I was out front. Songs like 'Fortune Teller' and 'Got My Mojo Workin'' got me wigglin' my backside like Mick Jagger. It certainly pulled the birds. No complaints!"

W hether or not the **D'fenders**, from Bordesley Green were pulling the birds, we can only surmise, but they were driving the little girls crazy every week at the **Shard End Community Centre** on Packington Avenue. With **Jimmy Hill** on drums, **Gordon Davis** on bass and **Tony Steele** on rhythm, vocalist **Maurice King** would yell, "For goodness sake!" before twitching his whole system as he merrily chirped "Ooooh! The hippy hippy shake!"

Lead guitarist **Lenny Hall** picked out the instrumental riff of the Swingin' Blue Jeans version of the Chan Romero classic, note perfect.

"It had to be note perfect," said Lenny. "Every week there was a young kid watching my every move. I found out later he was in the **Andicapps**, it was **Jeff Lynne**."

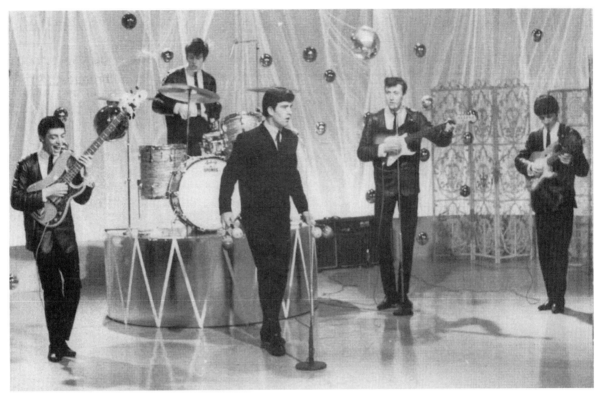

Jimmy Onslow's friendship with **Graeme Edge** proved to be invaluable for the **Moody Blues** in their formative days. With Gerry Levene's Avengers disbanded, Jimmy's Commer van became surplus to requirements as he was now being chauffeured around in the **Diplomats**' famous Ford Thames. The **M&B Five**, poor things, didn't have wheels of any description.

The Diplomats, June 1964

Jimmy Onslow picks up on the storyline: "**Graeme Edge** laid it on me about my van. We struck a deal whereby the M&B Five simply took over the hire-purchase payments," explained Jimmy, cringing at the recollection. "A little voice inside was warning me of a crying match, but we shook hands and I handed them the payments book."

The next day the name 'The M&B Five' was painted on the sides of the van. The next port of call was the **Mackadown**, where promoter **Mike Carroll**, always the gentleman, could be found in the reception area.

"These young lads wandered in and introduced themselves as the M&B Five," said Mike. "They mentioned something about sponsorship from Mitchells and Butlers brewery which, at the Mackadown, meant nothing because it was an Ansells pub!"

Mike Carroll granted the M&B Five their wish to perform during the interval before the main attraction of the evening, **Pete Tierney and the Nighthawks.**

"The M&B Five were fine and I gave them a tenner for their expenses," Mike recalled. "The next I heard about them was they were being billed as the Moody Blues."

The Moody Blues "5"

RYTHM AND BLUES AT ITS BEST.

* * * * *

SOLE REPRESENTATION & MANAGEMENT:—

Midland Top Ten Agency

During an M&B Five rehearsal at the **Carlton Club**, the man from the M&B brewery had put his head round the door. What that man didn't know about beer wasn't worth knowing. Unfortunately, he knew precious little about rock 'n' roll music.

"He made it clear that he didn't rate us and that as far as sponsorship was concerned, all bets were off," said Clint Warwick. "We were too far down the line to turn it in, so we came up with the Moody Blues name from the M and the B and kicked off on our own without the brewery backing."

On the 2nd May 1964, the Carlton Club presented to its members, for the first time, the Moody Blues Five.

Shortly after their debut appearance the Moody Blues Five played the **Ambassadors** club, on the corner of Augustus Road, where it meets Norfolk Road. On the guest list, courtesy of **Clint Warwick** was **Gerry Day**.

"It was all a bit too much for me," Gerry winced, "all that 'Woke up this mornin' business!"

Following the **Robbie Hood** fiasco, the **Sundowners** felt the need to bury their former identities to become the **Chads**. A change of name meant a change of repertoire. Investing in a pile of imported R&B records from the **Diskery** in Hurst Street, and after spending hours painfully deciphering the 'jive talk' lyrics, the Chads were able to perform a programme of blues material that would elevate them on to the growing university circuit. **Vince Martin** of **Friars** agency in Coventry was also impressed. He got them an engagement to entertain at an American airforce base at Toul in France. The contract stipulated that a female vocalist must front the band, so **Pauline Shepherd**, a young lady from the Kingstanding area of Birmingham, duly obliged. Following their arrival by ferry at Calais, a ten-hour drive lay ahead of them.

The Chads

"The van broke down after about six hours, and then so did we!" said **Mick Atkins**.

The **Fortunes**, another bunch of former **Merrimen**, weren't breaking down but were a little disheartened by the fact that their first release on the Decca label, 'Summertime. Summertime', hadn't been a chart success, but in truth, it hadn't fared too badly.

"**Shel Tarmy**, our producer, had found us the song." said **Rod Allen**. "It had been a radio hit in the States for the Jamies but didn't quite make it over here."

Realising that the strength of the Fortunes lay in their vocal performances, Shel Tarmy delved into the catalogue of the **Ivy League's John Carter** and **Ken Lewis**. There, in that hallowed treasure chest, he discovered a song that he believed, with a bit of push and shove, would place the Fortunes up where they belonged. The song was entitled 'Caroline'.

It would have been the old story of another record that just disappeared into the still of the night but for the growing demand for pop music, especially on the airwaves. With the BBC still the 'only show in town' for pop music, with its Light Programme, it was inevitable that the 'pirates' would emerge. On Easter Sunday, 1964, from the good ship 'Caroline' that was bobbing about in the Thames estuary, onto the air came **Radio Caroline**. The station's presenters were in desperate need of a record to use for promotional and link up situations. The Fortunes' 'Caroline', with Rod Allen's distinct vocal tone, slotted in perfectly. As the working city that it was, Birmingham had been a great attraction for the Irish immigrant over the years and consequently a strong social club scene had developed to serve the Irish community. **Martin Gaffney**, in the late fifties, had launched the **Auto Club** in Coleshill Street to cater for the needs of the Irish working man. If the men were 'rained off' from the building sites of the inner city, plentiful supplies of Guinness would be available to help while away the dark clouds.

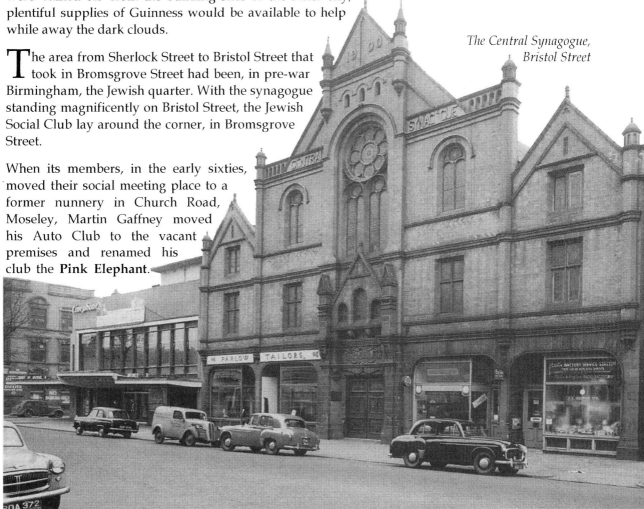

The Central Synagogue, Bristol Street

The area from Sherlock Street to Bristol Street that took in Bromsgrove Street had been, in pre-war Birmingham, the Jewish quarter. With the synagogue standing magnificently on Bristol Street, the Jewish Social Club lay around the corner, in Bromsgrove Street.

When its members, in the early sixties, moved their social meeting place to a former nunnery in Church Road, Moseley, Martin Gaffney moved his Auto Club to the vacant premises and renamed his club the **Pink Elephant**.

Just around the corner, in Hurst Street was the **Shamrock Club** and, in Sparkhill, on Walford Road facing the Embassy Sportsdrome, was the **Harp Club**. The **Burns** brothers, **Matty, Tom, John** and **Mick**, who also had interests in the Irish club scene of North London, owned both the Shamrock and the Harp. With Brumbeat at 'full steam ahead', the **Rooney Brothers** were the popular attraction at both of these venues. Made up of guitarists John and Mike Rooney, drummer **Mike Nash**, bassist **Billy Gilbert**, saxophonist **Dermot Ryan** and **Des Ryan** on piano, the Rooneys proved more than capable of satisfying the musical needs of the Burns brothers' venues. In 1964 the most essential ingredient for success at the Shamrock and Harp clubs was stamina.

The Rooney Brothers

The Boulevards

At the Shamrock Club, the resident combo, the **Matt Flannagan** band, were coming under pressure to display the same stamina as the youthful rock 'n' roll outfits.

"Dare will now be a break as de band are startin' to sober up!" Matt Flannagan announced on more than one occasion.

A chance to get wrecked would have been a fine thing for four budding rock musicians who were calling themselves the **Boulevards**. Whilst still attending Alderlea secondary school, **Tony Clarkin** had whiled away evenings on the car park of the **Harlequin** pub, Shard End, listening to the bands of the day thumping out that good ol' rock 'n' roll.

"Whenever Pat Wayne and the Beachcombers played the Harlequin," said Tony Clarkin, "I'd be hanging round the door watching every guitar lick **Geoff Roberts** ever put down."

The Boulevards had started up in early '64, blatantly stealing the name from the American recording artistes Jill and the Boulevards. With Tony Clarkin was fellow pupil from Alderlea, **Kenny Picket** on rhythm and, on bass, **Kenny Hepworth**. Scouting around, they found a great soulful vocalist in **Geoff Greaves** and a drummer with a good feel in **Antonino Piovesana**. Their first public appearance was at the Alderlea school hop, supporting **Carl Wayne and the Vikings**.

"After the gig," recalled Tony Clarkin, "**Dave Hollis**, the Vikings' drummer, went into great detail about the antics of a professional band on the road. I told the lads there and then that I'd got to have some of that no matter what!"

The **Sovereigns** were about to get up to some of the antics of a professional travelling band. Their chance came about when the mother of guitarist **Dave Evans** wrote to **Jimmy Young** at the BBC, informing 'The Man From Laramie' of the musical talents of these Kings Norton lads, and of the shaking abilities of their vocalist Roy Vears. By return of post came a letter telling the Sovereigns to report to the **Wimbledon Theatre** to participate in a grand shop window of talent. Showcasing their party piece 'Shakin' All Over', the Wimbledon adventure proved a resounding success.

"On the show there was a strong-man, and a boy-and-girl act that did a routine – 'The Waiter, the Porter and the Upstairs Maid'," Dave Evans explained, "The Sovereigns were the only beat group there."

Holiday camp mogul **Fred Pontin** was in the audience and immediately offered the Sovereigns a full summer season at the 'adults only' **Osmington Bay** complex. Twenty pounds a week each, including keep. Okay? Of course it was okay. The Sovereigns spokeswoman, Mrs Spencer, bent forward to shake Fred Pontin's hand and nearly took his eye out with her wide brimmed hat!

On the Easter weekend of 1964, the Sovereigns reported for duty at Osmington Bay with new bass player **Ray Taylor**, formerly of the **Swingin' Chimes** (Geoff Turton's old band, who were still recovering from the indignity of once being billed as the Swingin' *Chimps*). The Sovereigns were also informed that their Ford Thames minibus would be commandeered to meet the new arrivals at Weymouth railway station every Saturday morning.

Tony Lawrence and Dave Evans immediately volunteered their services for the Saturday morning trips, and, in keeping with the time honoured tradition of Hi De Hi Land, totally ignored the frail and elderly to give preference to unaccompanied teenaged girls.

"Tony reckoned we was entitled to first crack at the talent," confessed Dave, lowering his eyeline with immeasurable guilt.

In the spring of 1964 **Phil Pearce**, the lead guitarist with the **Rotundas**, went careering over the handlebars of his motorbike. He had to be replaced, be it only temporarily, but by whom? **Roger Ottley** of the Rotundas recalled being impressed by

Hi de Hi – the Sovereigns, giving holiday camps a bad name

an enthusiastic young guitarist at the **Rainbow Suite** a few weeks previously.

"We played the **Everglades** at cricket in the Co-op arcade beneath the Rainbow Suite," recalled Roger Ottley. "**Trevor Burton** used his Burns guitar as a bat. He walloped one for six but the neck of his guitar went one way and the body went the other!"

Trevor Burton somehow got hold of a Fender Stratocaster and his first gig with the Rotundas was **Church Gresley Memorial Hall**. It was the first time the good folk of Church Gresley had witnessed someone pointing an electric guitar menacingly at speaker cabinet to coax it into howling feedback.

Roger Ottley continued, "Trevor could see what was round the corner and he was gonna be a part of it."

Alan Burrows and his band, the **Tempests**, were doing nicely and wanted in on whatever was happening. Pushing the boat out they took a deep breath and purchased Fender guitars. They reckoned that this upgrade of equipment called for a change of name. To complement their newly acquired Fender guitars they became the **D'Fenders**, with Alan taking the name **Buzz Allen**. Of course Buzz and the boys chose to ignore the existence of Bordesley Green's **Defenders**, or **Max Griffiths' D'Fenders** (who were guitarist Max, **Bob Green** on organ, **Barry Dawes** was the bass player, drummer **Ted Powell** and **Ricky Terry** handling the vocal duties). For Buzz Allen and the D'Fenders, venues such as the **Wharf** at Holt Fleet and **St John Fisher** at West Heath became regular entries in their pocket diaries.

Max Griffiths' D'Fenders

The fact that Lulu and the Luvvers were lingering around in the top ten with their recording of the Isley Brothers 'Shout' was not going down well with **Ma Regan**'s boys, the **Redcaps**.

Fronted by the twins **Mick** and **Dave Walker**, the other Redcaps were sax player **Mac Broadhurst**, guitarist **Roy Brown** and drummer **Alan Morley**. Six months earlier they had seen their far more exciting cut of 'Shout' vanish without trace, even though it had been a huge favourite with fans at their live performances. Unfortunately their next single, **Chuck Berry's** 'Talkin' 'Bout You' fared no better, but with a new lead guitarist, **Mick Blythe**, in their line up,

The Redcaps

their hopes were raised for a third push for the charts. Mick Bythe, formerly of Wolverhampton's **Tremors**, was not a bad songwriter and had come up with a song that had the perfect groove for the period on which a well plotted lyric sat cozily. 'Funny Things', which also contained the by now essential harmonica break managed to sneak in at number fifty for the Redcaps after receiving plenty of national radio play.

Ma Regan rode on what minimal success the Redcaps had achieved by then throwing the **Modernaires'** hat into the Decca Records ring.

Pat Campbell, an American who worked as an artiste and repertoire manager for Decca was sent up from London to the Regan's **Brum Kavern** in Small Heath to take in a typical Modernaires' performance.

"Pat Campbell liked the Mods but asked us if we had any original songs." **Micky Bakewell**, the Modernaires' singer explained.

"I'd had a go and written 'Something On My Mind'. Our guitarist, **Tommy Russell**, had put the chords to it. Pat Campbell thought it was okay and asked me to write another song for a possible B-side, should we get to make a record."

In his head, imagining musical parts for the **Modernaires** brass section, Micky Bakewell came up with 'You're Makin' Me Blue' and again, Tommy Russell added chords and was awarded a writing credit for doing so. At the next Modernaires engagement, the **Ritz**, Kings Heath, the two original songs were included in their set. With a more than happy Pat Campbell in the audience, it was confirmed that the Modernaires were about to become recording artistes. At their first Decca studio session the Modernaires

Wheelie cool –
the Modernaires

learned the hard way that live performances and recording sessions are two different kettles of fish.

"It took nine hours of numerous takes and different arrangements of 'Something On My Mind' before the Decca people were happy," Micky Bakewell sighed. "I thought my head had caved in. Fortunately, we just thundered through 'You're Makin' Me Blue' and, listening to it now, I wish that had been the A-side."

When 'Something On My Mind' came out, it appeared on Decca's American label, RCA Victor.

"We were all stunned with pride," said Micky. "There we were, the Modernaires, on Elvis's record label!"

The Applejacks' affairs were positively thriving as they did the rounds of Britain's top television shows. Pre-recording a slot for BBC's 'Crackerjack', they met with the Beatles, who were there for exactly the same reason. After the recording the Applejacks joined the fab four for drinks at London's celebrated **Ad Lib** club.

"The round was a bottle of Mateus Rosé wine at twenty-five pounds a time and we all paid our corner," recalled Phil Cash. "When we left the Ad Lib we started crying."

Shortly after the boozy session with John Lennon and Paul McCartney, stories were appearing in the music press that the world's most prolific songwriting team was working on a song especially for the Applejacks. The song, 'Like Dreamers Do', had in fact been written three years previously. **Mike Smith** at Decca was well aware of the song long before the Cracker-jack meeting as 'Like Dreamers Do' had been one of the few original songs the Beatles had performed at their failed Decca audition.

Although not as instant a song as 'Tell Me When', 'Like Dreamers Do' nevertheless made number twenty on the charts in June of 1964. It lingered on the airwaves long enough to keep the Applejacks in the public eye until September 19th, when drummer Gerry Freeman and bassist Megan Davies got married at St Alphege Church in Solihull.

"The whole publicity machine was engaged and the press had a field day, but it was never *our* day." said Gerry, with a hint of resentment.

Immediately after the speeches, the Applejacks sped off to the BBC in London for a 'Juke Box Jury' appearance followed by a gig in Bletchley. Pathé News did record the event for cinema outlets and **Bob Danvers Walker**, voice-over artiste supreme, commented on how local bands the

Phantoms and the **Concords** had formed a guard of honour with their guitars. As the camera panned the crowds that surrounded the church, Mr Danvers Walker delivered his famous line "And don't the kids love it".

"Yeah!" Gerry Freeman sighed. "All three thousand of them!"

Although the **Cheetahs** weren't exactly making the Pathé News, affairs were on track. Impressed by their efforts in his studio, **John Taylor**, of **Hollick and Taylor** introduced the lads to **Johnny Franz** of Philips Records. When Johnny Franz discovered that the Cheetahs hadn't figured in EMI's plans, **Carl Barron** being the only one contracted by Norrie Paramor, he

The spot prize once again goes to the Cheetahs

made plans to release 'Mecca', a Gene Pitney song that they had recorded at John Taylor's studio. Enter **Ma Regan** into the ring. She now had sole representation of the Cheetahs. With a record release pending, she paid John Taylor three hundred pounds for the master tapes of 'Mecca' and a cover of a Shirelles hit, 'Soldier Boy'. In October of 1964, 'Mecca' crept up to number 36 on the charts.

Not quite making the top forty but selling with distinction were, from Dudley, the **Congressmen**. Their re-cording, released on the Phillips label, of a Les Reed song, 'Spare a Thought', featured vocalist **Johnny Hounslow**. Looking to American politics for inspiration, Johnny became known as **George E Washington**. His fellow con-gressmen were **Tony Tipper** on drums, **Doug Perry** on rhythm guitar, **Doug Walker** on bass, and on lead guitar, the highly rated **Arthur Ray**. Arthur had caught the music bug as a young boy at his father's pub, the **Market Tavern** in Bilston, watching honky-tonk pianist **Tommy Burton**, who was a regular feature there.

"I would never go to bed before I'd heard Tommy play 'Tiger Rag'," said Arthur.

Dudley didn't have a White House so George and his Congressmen made do with the town's Hippodrome, which, fortunately for them, was owned by their manager and bankroller, **Vic Kendrick**. With its days of variety long gone, the **Dudley Hippodrome** now operated as a bingo hall.

"We'd sleep on studio couches backstage," Arthur Ray recalls. "Rehearsals would be from ten in the morning until five with an hour for lunch, which was a tomato dip in the café opposite. As we were loading up the van so the bingo crowds would start arriving."

The crowds were arriving to line the route of the Solihull Carnival procession in that heady summer of 1964. Young **Les Hemming**, in his own words "a country bumpkin from the village of Umberslade", and his band, the **Casemakers**, climbed aboard the 'Reed's Corrugated Cardboard Cases' float to participate in the grand parade.

"My dad worked at Reed's, on Cranmore Boulevard in Shirley," said Les, "And he talked them into sponsoring my outfit. Reed's made cardboard boxes, hence the name, the Casemakers."

The sponsorship deal was that Reed's bought the band a truly fabulous Guild amplifier from **Studio Musica** in Shirley, and the band would perform during the procession. Then, on arrival in the grand arena, the Casemakers would be free to rock 'n' roll away the glorious July afternoon. The power supply for the Guild amplifier, which fired up the guitars of **Dave Jinks** and **Lenny Jay** and also the microphone for vocalist **Johnny Jinks**, was a fully charged car battery. Les Hemming (if a bumpkin then a posh one) had his own Futurama amplifier for his Burns Trisonic bass, but was not too proud to tap into the car battery along with the rest.

The Casemakers at the Solihull Carnival

Johnny Jinks turned on his charms and, as the wagons rolled, began waving to the crowds, singing out his big number of the day, Billy J Kramer's 'Little Children'.

"We were in seventh heaven," sighed Les, "Once inside the arena we were really gonna let it rock."

Unfortunately, by the time the float carrying the Casemakers arrived at the arena, the car battery was drained of all life. But the Casemakers weren't in any way drained. They still had plenty to give. Reed's Corrugated Cardboard Cases had made sure that the lads, and their amplifier from the sponsorship arrangement, made an appearance at the Grand Carnival Ball that very evening, at the Solihull Civic Hall. Once the **Norman Dovey Big Band** had created the party atmosphere, room was made on the stage for the Casemakers to bring on their amplifier in order to 'let it rock'.

The board and management of Reed's Corrugated Cardboard Cases gathered proudly at the front of the stage as Norman Dovey announced "A twist and twitch session with the Casemakers!" But half way through 'Little Children' the crowd turned nasty and demanded that the Casemakers 'tone it down'. The Casemakers had been thwarted again!

The **Modernaires** were not to be thwarted. Their record 'Something On My Mind' had not faired that badly, picking up sales in the Midlands thanks to their regular personal appearances. To crack the national market meant taking their product to the people. 'Something On My Mind' had received plenty of spins on Radio Luxembourg and the Modernaires had been featured on such national television shows as 'Gazette' and 'Thank Your Lucky Stars', but feelings in the band were mixed on the issue of taking on more 'distance' gigs. Their new London based manager, **Phil Solomons**, however, had a more serious professional attitude. The pressure was on!

Micky Bakewell tells the story. "Phil was pushing us to hit the road. But he was also aware that we had responsibilities at home."

It was agreed that should 'Something On My Mind' show in the national top ten, the Modernaires would take to their Bedford van and join the convoy of hungry musicians that were chasing rainbows up and down the M1 motorway.

"I was at the Drews Lane factory in Washwood Heath as a skilled toolmaker," explained Micky Bakewell. "It was unheard of to walk out of there. When our record never made the charts I didn't know whether to laugh or cry. The decision was made for me."

In September '64 **Brian Nicholls** of the **Fleetwoods** took up an invitation to join the **Shanes,** who were the singing guitarist **Mick Lawson**, whose brother Chris was in the **Grasshoppers**, **Roy Jones** of Sheldon on bass, **Rod Lilley** on lead and **Ken Horden**, late of the **Lawmen**, on drums. "Me and Mick Lawson always blew our earnings on beer," said Brian. "The others were social climbers. Ken Horden was working as a petrol tanker driver but his fiancé used to tell everyone that he was 'in oil'!"

The **Moody Blues** were still waiting to strike oil, and it wasn't for the want of trying. Along with

The Shanes

The Whiskey a Go-go, above Chetwyns, the Man's Shop

other pioneers of the Brum rhythm and blues scene, like the Spencer Davis Group and the King Bees, the Moody Blues could be seen regularly at the **Whiskey a Go-go**, formerly **Laura Dixon's** dance studio in Navigation Street, over, the gents' outfitters. The Whiskey was the place to be, and its promoters, **Chris Griffen** and **Steve Healey**, were fearless when it came to presenting the famous American blues stars such as **John Lee Hooker**, **Memphis Slim** or **Sonny Boy Williamson**. With the Moody Blues still whizzing up and down the M1 motorway in **Jimmy Onslow**'s Commer van, and London bookers hustling provincial promoters for business, it was inevitable that the paths of the Moody Blues and the success-hungry hustler, **Tony Secunda,** would eventually cross.

"We took to Tony and he saw something in us," explained Clint Warwick, the Moody Blues' bass guitarist at the time. "What little money came in, Tony put back into us. He'd take us round the 'in' places and make sure we met the right people. We were starving but we kept at it. We figured if we kept knocking on the door, someone would answer eventually."

Moodies at the Moathouse

When Jimmy Onslow answered the knock on *his* door he came face to face with the bailiffs. "My dad had signed as guarantor on the Commer van that I'd trusted the Moodies with," said Jimmy "The bailiffs were demanding repossession."

Next morning Jimmy Onslow caught the London train. On arrival in the capitol, he began making discreet enquiries about the whereabouts of five Brummies posing as pop stars. A tip-off led Jimmy to a West End side street where he found the Commer van parked. Peeping through the windscreen he saw the five Moody Blues huddled together, fast asleep.

"They'd been living in the van," Jimmy recalled with a smile. "It was knee deep in chip paper!"

Jimmy Onslow coaxed the van back to Birmingham and to the offices of the finance company on Hagley Road. Still daubed on all sides with adoring messages in every shade of lipstick, the van coughed and spluttered its way onto the car park, and into a parking space in front of the building. Secretaries, clerks, tea ladies and all were hanging out of windows to ascertain what exactly had landed. Jimmy switched off the asthmatic engine and hopped out of the cab. The engine, after a few moments of combustive indecision, gave its customary back-fire and stopped.

"I could see a number eight bus coming and I heard some Herbert shout, 'I say! You there! Yes, you with all the hair!' " Jimmy recalled. "I shouted back over my shoulder as I broke into a sprint, 'The keys are in the ignition!' and 'opped onto the number eight!"

Coaxing the **Olympics'** Commer van onto the forecourt of **Dennis Caney's** petrol station on Pershore Road, Stirchley was dustman **Johnny Carroll**. He'd just finished his shift at the Lifford Lane refuse dis-

Star transport — Steve Gibbons with Jim Onslow's Moodymobile

posal site, hung up his hat and gloves, had a stripped down swill and, after topping up the tank, would be off to yet another engagement.

As the forecourt attendant did the necessaries, Johnny Carroll was his usual jovial self. With the number 41 bus stationary in the rush hour jam, Johnny called to the conductress who was idly lazing on the platform

"Hey love! D'ya know the difference between sex and dancin'? Come and have a cha-cha with me then!"

The passengers fell about. It was a typically harmless Johnny Carroll one-liner. It also amused **Dennis Caney**. Dennis was a fan of the Olympics. He was also the chairman of Northfield Divisional Liberals and the proprietor of both the Universal Travel Company and Den Caney Coaches. In other words, Dennis Caney was, compared to most other men, extremely influential and fairly heavy on the hip.

"Dennis asked me there and then, on the garage forecourt, if we would fancy him becoming manager the Olympics. He offered to put a few quid into the band so, on behalf of the others, especially at the mention of money, I readily agreed," said Johnny Carroll.

Johnny and the others also decided to commit the name Olympics to the history books. So, dedicated followers of fashion that they were fast becoming, they became the **Vogues**.

Johnny Carroll – clearly unimpressed by the labour-saving possibilities of the new fangled dustbin trolley

As the Vogues they found themselves back at Wimbledon Palais competing in 'Ready Steady Win'. This contest was judged by record producer **Micky Most**, **Manfred Mann**, whose hit song '5-4-3-2-1' was the theme tune for the TV show 'Ready Steady Go', and finally the man Johnny Carroll admitted to 'worshipping the ground he walked on', **Bill Haley**.

"I thought we'd made it just being in the same room as Bill Haley!" said Johnny.

The Vogues made a good enough impression to be granted a track on the live album of the show, which was produced by Micky Most and titled, appropriately enough, 'Ready Steady Win'.

"Did we receive any royalties? None at all," said Johnny, answering his own question. "But did it matter? Nah!"

"When I started the Mackadown I was lucky to pull a hundred in," said **Mike Carroll**. " Within a couple of months I'd got one of the hottest venues around. Come eight o'clock the 'Full House' board would be up."

Perhaps the success of the Mackadown was aided by

Mike's cleverly worded newspaper advertisements. They always carried the phrase 'But like the man said, please don't be late'. With confidence at an all-time high, Mike looked to the **Black Horse** at Northfield, a magnificent looking 'old coach house' style of inn. The first Thursday of October saw Mike Carroll present the **Rockin' Berries** with the **Memphis Sounds** playing support. The Gods were with him. Agreeing a fee of twenty-five pounds with the Rockin' Berries six weeks previously, both parties were unaware that a rush release of the Berries version of a song by the husband and wife team, **Goffin** and **King**, would result in chart action. That evening, the Black Horse audience witnessed a stunning performance of the Four Seasons' 'Rag Doll' which demonstrated the incredible falsetto abilities of **Geoff Turton** before **Clive Lea** did his razor sharp celebrity impressions that were woven into the **Benny Hill** ditty 'My Baby's Got a Transistor Radio'. The Berries were then able to proudly announce to a packed function room, "We'd like to carry on with our current record that is presently at number 19 on the hit parade, 'He's in Town'."

The Memphis Sounds also played that night in and around the hearth of the coal burning stone fireplace that was the focal point of the Black Horse function room. As their vocalist **Brian Thompson** stood in front of the roaring flames, begging for 'long distance information to give him Memphis Tennessee', he could smell and sense the heat singeing his cavalry twills. Such was the determination to succeed. A determination that had begun at the Austin motor works where **Dave Challinor** had met **Clive** and Brian Thompson, brothers of **Dougie Thompson**, formerly of the Rockin' Berries. An introduction to **Jimmy Powell** resulted in Dave and Clive accompanying Jimmy to his London engagements at **Ken Collyer's** jazz club and Eel Pie Island. There, on hearing **Rod Stewart** with Jimmy's **Dimensions**, they fell in love with the Memphis feel of rhythm and blues, hence the name of their band.

The Black Horse in a bygone age

"But the **Searchers** and the Beatles were the groups to sound like back in Birmingham," said Dave Challinor, "So we practiced up all their songs. By the time we learned the songs, the public mood had changed to Memphis style rhythm and blues, so we had to start over again."

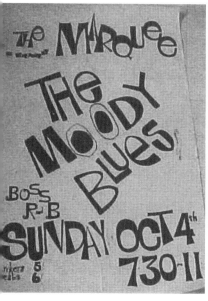

The Moody Blues were used to starting over again. Perseverance was slowly paying off and lady luck smiled on them. On the morning of Thursday, 24th September 1964, Tony Secunda received a telephone call from the **Marquee club**, in London. **Paul Jones**, vocalist with the Manfred Mann group had laryngitis and was unable to perform that evening. Could the Moody Blues make the gig? Not only did the Moody Blues successfully deputise, they were offered, and accepted, a weekly residency at the Marquee.

With the prestige that came with such an engagement, their manager Tony Secunda was able to report back to them that Decca Records had agreed a contract. The Moody Blues were now signed to a major international label. Within weeks, their first recording 'Loose Your Money' was in the shops.

"Unfortunately that's exactly what Decca did!" said Clint Warwick.

Around this time **Dave Pegg** had entered the working world to commence gainful employment at Royal Exchange Insurance in Temple Street.

"All the blokes I worked with were Spencer Davis freaks, and I was no exception," said Dave. "We'd see them at the **Golden Eagle**, the Whiskey in Navigation Street and Digbeth Civic Hall. Spencer and the boys were getting huge. I got the chance to put in with the **Crawdaddies** and I jumped at it."

The Crawdaddies

The Crawdaddies were a regular feature at the **Silver Beat Club**, under the **Exchange** pub in Navigation Street, and the **59 Club**, which was a cellar opposite the **Alexandra Theatre** in John Bright Street. More likely than not, the Crawdaddies would then move on to Bromsgrove Street to play into the early hours at the **Garden of Eden** club, previously known as the **Pink Elephant**. The personnel of the Crawdaddies were Dave Pegg and **Micky Herd** on guitars. **Dave Peace**, who worked in the music section at Rackhams department store, played piano, and on drums was **Don Turner**.

"Don was a drayman for Ansells brewery," explained Dave "For him, it was a five o'clock start. Don would go straight from the Garden

of Eden club to meet the dray wagon."

Dave Pegg continues the story, "The Crawdaddies were doing six nights a week. It was a ball, but total madness. We came out of the Garden of Eden one night and there was a drunk collapsed around a lamp post in Hurst Street. This was about two in the morning. I went home, had a kip and then caught the bus back into town. The drunk was still there, clinging to the lamp post. He'd been there for six hours!"

The Applejacks had been household names for six months and had worked consistently on the strength of their two top twenty records. Survival in the big league rested on maintaining their chart status. 'Three Little Words', written by **Gordon Mills**, was their third release.

"We needed to make the top ten with 'Three Little Words' but it just about scraped into the top thirty," said Phil Cash. "Although we were still kids, we knew that if we didn't pull it round pretty quick, something would have to give."

Something had to give for **Carl Wayne and the Vikings**. They badly needed someone who could get them a recording contract to further their careers. Enter city-centre solicitor **Howard Wynschenk**.

Ace Kefford explains, "Mr Wynschenk set everything in order for us to record for Pye. Our debut single was a cover of the Timmy Yuro song 'What's a Matter Baby', which was recorded at Hollick and Taylor's studio."

Being a respected member of the legal profession, Howard Wynschenk's advice and guidance was invaluable. Here comes the catch. Ace Kefford continues, "Mr Wynschenk, under the name of **Robert Romain**, also wrote songs and stipulated that he wrote our B-sides. When I tell you that his best effort for us was 'Shimmy Shammy Shingle', you'll follow my drift."

Carl Wayne & the Vikings at the Carlton

With a recording contract in his pocket, Carl Wayne had no qualms when it came to singing such an exquisite line as 'Shimmy Shammy Shingle. Make my body tingle!'

About to make the listener's body tingle was **Denny Laine** of the Moody Blues. Although the boys couldn't get arrested with their first release, Decca were not slow in coming forward with the chance of a second pitch at he charts for them. **Clint Warwick** recalls that period in their career.

"We were so full of belief in ourselves that when 'Lose Your Money' did nothing we somehow knew the second one was a bit special."

Clint and the rest of the band were absolutely justified in their belief. The song, 'Go Now', had been presented to them for consideration. Written by the black American **Larry Banks**, the demo was simply his sister, **Bessie**, crooning away to Larry's minimal accompaniment on piano. **Mike Pinder** went to work, fattening out the piano part so that when Denny Laine's broke and busted interpretation of the line "We've already said . . ." cued the band into that waltzy groove, the end result was, to quote Clint Warwick, "somethin' else."

The Moody Blues walked tall out of the **Advision** studios that evening in the belief that they had an immediate smash on their hands.

"But nothing happened," said Clint. "For a few weeks 'Go Now' did nothing and I thought, "Oh, here we go again."

The Rockin' Berries were elated with the success of 'He's In Town' but they were learning the hard way the perils of signing fixed-fee contracts of engagement. In early November of 1964, the Berries were booked for a week of ballroom appearances around Scotland.

"As we took to the high road we got the word that our record was number three on the national chart and number one in Scotland," recalled Chuck Botfield, "And we were playing for thirty quid a night gross!"

MEANWHILE ELSEWHERE . . .

1964 - Fanny Hill banned - Cassius Clay becomes world heavyweight champion - Radio Caroline goes on air - topless dresses - seaside clashes for Mods & Rockers - Nelson Mandela sentenced to life - Labour gains power, Wilson becomes PM - TV - The Man From U.N.C.L.E. - launch of BBC2 - Cinema - A Hard Day's Night - Goldfinger . . .

With promoters determined to cash in on the good fortune of having the number one attraction working for them at rates arranged three months previously, the Berries only consolation was to halve the duration of their performance.

Chuck Botfield explains how it worked. "I'd say to Geoff Turton and Clive Lea, 'Stick 'He's In Town' in after twenty minutes.' As soon as the crowd heard the introduction to the song, they'd go wild and invade the stage. End of play! Bring on the support band!"

The **Diplomats**, Denny Laine's old outfit were still working for the same run of the mill fees and, being fully professional, were experiencing problems when it came to the 'whack up'.

"Being five handed made a big difference to your take home pay," Jimmy Onslow commented rather cautiously. "It was a shame because we'd been using two bass guitars firing at the same time. Great for me 'cause I never 'ad to shake me maracas anymore. Steve Horton would play what he always stuck down and I'd play the same bass line, but I'd use a very trebly, twangy top sound. With **Bev Bevan** hammering away at the back, you can imagine the drive that we generated. But in the end, the money situation won and Steve Horton departed from the Diplomats, leaving me, Bev, Sprike and Phil to soldier on, which we did for a couple of months before turnin' it in completely. It sounds clichéd now, but we were all looking for something more to life."

The **Citizens** of Northfield were also using two bass guitarists although, it has to be said, not at the same time, or even on the same evening.

Drummer **Doug Vallender** explains: "**Tony Garry** and **Dennis Greaves**'s 'proper' jobs alternated between day and night shifts 'a fortnight about'. So when Tony was on nights, Dennis would play bass, and vice-versa."

The other good members of the Citizens were **Doug Clarke** on lead guitar, **Pete Snape** at the piano and out front, keeping order amongst the citizens of Birmingham, vocalist **Dave 'Trink' Atkins**.

The Citizens

Bob **Watkins**, late of Smethwick's **Sabres**, had happily hung up his sword, but was quick to answer the call to pick guitar as a **Wild Cherry** for **Nicky James**. The world was Bob Watkins' oyster.

"To actually stand alongside Nicky onstage and feel a little of the adulation

Wild Cherries

Phil Ackrill's daytime destination

come your way was quite an experience," recalls Bob.

"Then I turned up at the **Moat House** one night and Mrs Pryke informed me that Nicky was 'not available'. Something to do with maintenance payments. . . or lack of them!"

Agent **John Singer** immediately saw to the settlement but two members, rhythm guitarist **Tony Clarkson** and drummer **Alan Bennett** quit the Wild Cherries in search of a less stressful existence.

"**Bev Bevan** and **Phil Ackrill** were just winding down the **Diplomats**, so for a while there we were as the Wild Cherries. With Nicky on best behaviour!"

Phil Ackrill had already decided to explore new horizons and entered the travel agency business, working as an accountant for Doug Ellis at Ellis Travel situated in Needless Alley, whereas Bev Bevan sought daytime solace as a salesman at Lee Longlands, the furniture shop on Broad Street.

The **Prospectors** from Aston were prospecting for the big time on a once a week basis at **Nechells Green Community Centre**. The personnel consisted of the **Phillips** brothers — **Alan**, who sang, and **Jimmy**, who strummed his guitar, **Len Ablethorpe** on drums and, at the age of fifteen, showing an outstanding talent on guitar, **Stanley Hartley Cain**, from Mansfield Road. Dropping the Stanley for his professional name, Hartley Cain was known to his mates simply as 'H'.

"I got music from my dad," said H. "In the early fifties he'd played accordion in a band. Then along came rock 'n' roll and he got squeezed out. **Jim Phillips**, Al and Jim's dad, was our manager."

H continues, "At Nechells Green we'd share the bill with a band called the **Interns** who had a Maltese chap on drums, **Charlie Grima**. Charlie, in the 70s, found fame with Roy Wood's **Wizzard.** Anyway, every Saturday morning the Prospectors would make it over to Bridgnorth to play three songs for the kids' matinee at the town's picture house. In the audience every week was a lad, same age as us and always enthusiastic about how and what we played. At the time we didn't have a bass player and this chap vowed to get a bass and come up to Birmingham to join us — and **Louis Clarke** was true to his word."

The **Andicapps** were also muscling in on the Saturday morning matinee scene. **Jeff Lynne**, **Kex Gorin**, **John Kerton**, **Johnnie** and **Willie Watson** and **Dave Merrick** would make the weekly pilgrimage to Handsworth, where at the junction of Booth Street and Holyhead Road, the magnificent **Regal Cinema** stood. There, during the fifteen minute interval that followed the Disney cartoons and the Flash Gordon serial, the Andicapps would take the stage to play a three song set as the usherettes did battle with the hooligans of Handsworth and Smethwick. Having dodged the Kia-Ora cartons and empty ice cream tubs, the Andicapps would be publicly thanked for their efforts by the manager of the Regal, Mr **Vic Sims**, before making way for the main feature, which nine times out of ten was a Tarzan adventure. Vic Sims, a jovial Cockney, meant every word of his praise. For the next two years, Vic would personally manage the Andicapps.

The Regal Cinema, Handsworth

When **Trevor Langham** deserted the **Brum Beats** for the prestige of being **Pat Wayne**'s keyboard player in the **Beachcombers**, **Terry Dews** decided to demonstrate his own skills on the ivories and invested in a Farfisa organ.

"That Farfisa thing sounded alright 'til you flicked the vibrato on," chuckled **Norman Haines**. "In the finish we pushed the boat out and got a Vox Continental. The Animals were having big hits by then so we were, as they say, in the groove."

Tornados – Heinz, George Bellamy and Alan Caddy at the Handsworth Plaza

An appearance at the **Moat House** in Bradford Street resulted in the **Crescendos** taking a place in the social history of the sleepy town of Evesham, on the banks of the river Avon.

Mrs Pryke, wife of the Moat House proprietor Bob Pryke, topped up their pint pots, swishing the ale around in the glasses in order to produce a foamy head on the beer. An introduction was then made to a Worcestershire entrepreneur.

"We ended up booked to play the opening night at the **Marine Ballroom** at Evesham, with the comedian Bob Monkhouse," said Trevor Greaves. "Those 'Dr Zhivago' shirts paid for themselves time and again!"

Heinz Burt, a young and handsome German lad, who had formerly served in the **Tornados**, was now cutting it on his own as a solo performer. Apart from his looks, the one thing he had going for him was a hit record. 'Just Like Eddie' was a tribute to the late Eddie Cochran. Unfortunately, working against him was his name. Wherever Heinz appeared, sometime during his act, baked beans would be hurled at him, courtesy of the local hooligan brigade. The **Marine Ballroom** engaged Mr Burt's services, doubling up on security and booking the **Crescendos** to support.

"We did a stormer," said **Trevor Greaves**, " The crowd was going berserk so we encored with 'C'mon Everybody'. We came off to find Heinz wanting to kill us. We'd closed with his opening song!"

Steve Newman was a man with a mission to become a country and western singer. 'Welcome To My World' was a song riding high for Jim Reeves at the time, and Steve was to perform this beautifully crafted work in the presence of the Grand Almighty, **Hughie Green**, in an effort to secure inclusion on the television talent show, 'Opportunity Knocks'. Steve took his place in the queue that wound up the staircase of the Midland Hotel in New Street. Standing alongside a juggler with the 'machine gunners,' and a bird impressionist from Digbeth, Steve was well prepared. Earlier that day he'd paid a visit to **Jerome's** studio in the Great Western Arcade, Colmore Row, where he'd posed for a publicity photograph. Life, it seemed, was about to bare fruit for this young man, born in Bordesley Green, raised in Kingstanding, and who had commenced working life for the grocery retailers, 'George Mason' at a wage of three pounds per week. When confined to hospital for quite a few years at Romsley Hill, Clent, suffering with tuberculosis of the kidneys, he discovered artistic leanings within himself. To his amazement he found that he was gifted with words and had begun to write poetry. It also seemed a far better way of expressing emotions than whacking opponents in

The Jungle Coffee Bar

bloody fisticuffs at the **Jungle** coffee bar on Snow Hill, which is how he'd spent his formative years.

A red nosed comedian wound up his act with the old chestnut about Hughie Green falling over his own wallet and Steve Newman entered the 'Opportunity Knocks' arena. After a brief word in the pianist's ear, he took stance in front of the Great One. Nervously, the opening lines, "Welcome to my world, won't you come on in?" stumbled from Steve's lips. Rapidly gaining confidence however, Steve faced his jury. By the time the middle eight bars arrived he was in full flight. Singing out the line "Knock and the door will open," the young Mr Newman went totally thespian and pointed to the door he'd just entered through.

"No thanks!" was the abrupt interruption from Hughie Green

So determined was Steve Newman in his bid for fame that he carried on regardless into the next line. Shading his eyes with the palm of his hand he sang "Seek and ye shall find," only to receive the gut wrenching opinion from 'Uncle Hughie', " Son you're no country and western singer!"

The young man that 'Uncle Hughie' dismissed so flippantly that day, would just four years later be writing and performing his own million selling songs, and in the process become quite a character in and around the Birmingham rock music scene.

Raymond Froggatt tells how it all came about, "I'd invented this geezer, half Steve McQueen, half Paul Newman, in an effort to impress that Hughie Green bloke. All that survives of Steve Newman is the Jerome's photo!"

For Steve Newman — opportunity flops

It was eight o'clock on a freezing cold November evening and pacing up and down the car park of the **Black Horse** in Northfield was promoter **Mike Carroll**.

"I'd booked **Jimmy Powell** and he hadn't arrived. No phone calls. No nothing and I had a full house," recalled Mike.

Jimmy and his band, the **Cock a Hoops** — **Mike** and **Steve Dolan** and **Paul Cullen** on guitars, **Keith Baker** on drums with **Frankie Spencer** on piano — used an old ambulance for transport. Mike Carroll's ears were straining to listen for the sound of the emergency bell.

The Cock a Hoops

"Then onto the car park spluttered an open backed coal wagon," said Mike. "Amongst the sacks of coal, knee deep in slack and looking like the Black and White Minstrels were the Cock a Hoops with their equipment. From out of the passenger door of the cab jumped Jimmy Powell shouting, 'Sorry Mike but the ambulance broke down!' "

"That was Jimmy," said Mike Carroll, "Jimmy Powell never once let me down."

The Astonaires

Trevor Burton

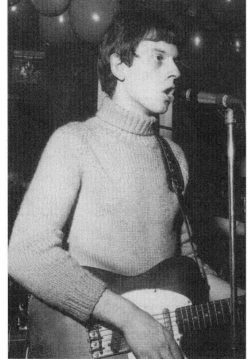

Feeling a bit let down was **Danny Burns**. Along with his group, the **Phantoms**, he was once again back in Birmingham after another German excursion, this time he'd played the **Hit Club** in Hamburg.

"Once home, the Phantoms disappeared into thin air," explained Danny. "My agent, Dougie Thompson, had already arranged more work for me in Dortmond, Germany, but I needed a band from somewhere."

In a workers' café that was situated on Six Ways, Aston, around a Formica top table that was swimming in cold tea, Danny Burns sat with his raw but enthusiastic recruits. Resisting the temptation to grab a crafty lick of the congealed brown sauce from the neck of its bottle, Danny spelled out his plan of action to the starry eyed rock 'n' roll apprentices, who were **John Lee**, a Tipton lad, on drums; on bass, from the **Astonaires**, **Graham Franklin**; on rhythm guitar came **Billy Hunter** from the Everglades; with the lead guitar duties falling into the more than capable hands of Billy's cocky pal, also from the Everglades, **Trevor Burton**. Put them together and what have you got? **Danny Burns and the Burnettes**!

"Then Trevor's mother stepped in and said Trevor was too young to make the trip," Danny explained, and Trevor's mother was absolutely correct because Trevor was still a fifteen year old pupil at Upper Thomas Street School.

Trevor Burton picks up the thread, "So I knew the bass

player in **Danny King's Jesters**, **Pete Allen**. Everybody called him Bone 'cause that's all he was — a walking washboard. But he got me into Danny King's band."

Trevor Burton's father worked as a furnace man at the Amach Steelworks on Tyburn Road. A week's hard graft would see him rewarded with six pounds. His schoolboy son, as a member of Danny King and the Jesters was making double that!

"I was earning more than my teachers in those days!" chuckled Trevor.

No one knew what fee **Jerry Lee Lewis** was on at Birmingham Town Hall on the Monday evening of 7th December 1964, when, supported by Brum's very own **Uglys**, Jerry rocked the joint in aid of the Birmingham Youth Elijah. This was a fund raising event that had been organised by **John Singer**, on behalf of the Jewish Club in Ellis Street.

"We'd heard all these tales about how difficult Jerry Lee could be, but he turned it on for the kids that night," recalled **Steve Gibbons**.

John Singer had arranged an after-show Christmas party at the Ellis Street club and invited the wild man of rock 'n' roll to grace the club with his presence, never believing for one moment that Jerry Lee would attend.

"We were all just hangin' out, drinking and munching when the door opened and in stepped the Killer." Steve continued. "He made a beeline for the upright piano and proceeded to hammer the daylights out of it until the early hours. It was an incredible party. Me and the rest of the Uglys were standing round the piano, with Jerry Lee leading the sing-song."

As the Christmas carol singers sang of goodwill to all men of peace during the damp and miserable closing weeks of 1964, **Mick Atkins**, guitarist with the **Chads**, was not really feeling in a festive mood at all.

The Chads with Jeff Lynne

"Really, I was sick of the whole lot," said Mick, screwing his face up.

An advertisement was placed in the Birmingham Mail for an experienced guitarist. Auditions were held at the scout hut in Spring Road, Acocks Green, the following Saturday afternoon. Every applicant would have been capable of handling the job but there was just one remaining candidate who had yet

to arrive. After waiting almost an hour, the Chads called it a day and were breaking down their equipment when the young enthusiast came through the doors, soaked to the skin and clutching his guitar, which was in a plastic bag.

"The rain had bucketed down all day and this poor kid had been hopping on and off buses all the way from Shard End," said Mick Atkins. "When he pleaded for a chance to play, how could we refuse? As it happened, the lad was an absolute natural. That's how **Jeff Lynne** became a Chad."

Danny Burns and the Burnettes were bound for Germany with a Shrewsbury lad, **Barry Udey**, stepping in for the 'far too young' **Trevor Burton**.

"We never stopped singing all the way to Dortmond," recalled **Danny Burns**. "This was going to be a Christmas to remember for the rest of our lives."

How prophetic. When Danny and the Burnettes arrived in Dortmond late on Christmas Eve they found the whole town closed for the holiday period.

Danny Burns continues the woeful tale, "The only food we could get was milk and biscuits from a nearby vending machine."

The lads spent the whole of Christmas Day huddled together in a freezing Ford Thames van, sipping milk and chewing stale biscuits.

George E Washington and his Congressmen were very much into the festive spirit indulging in 'fab' nights out. On the run up to the yuletide holiday they had been part of a travelling roadshow set up and promoted by the teenage magazine 'Fab'. A 'name' act would always be featured and when, a few days prior to Christmas, the roadshow arrived at the Dorchester Hotel, in London's West End, the Congressmen found themselves in the company of the **Moody Blues**.

Arthur Ray of the Congressmen tells the tale, "I was only fifteen and to be in London at the Dorchester was incredible. After our spot we headed for the hospitality room. We could hear the Moodies playing 'Go Now' downstairs in the ballroom."

Fifteen minutes later the Moody Blues, dressed in their blue stage suits, entered the hospitality room to be greeted by the Fab promotions staff.

"It was the one and only time in my life that I'd experienced smoked salmon," said Arthur.

With Brummie accents flying thick and heavy around the room, the promotions people were beginning to feel a little out of things when a butler, complete with a silver tray and a few bottles of champagne, entered the room.

Arthur continued, "The butler handed **Ray Thomas** of the Moodys a telegram to be read aloud. The telegram said: "Congratulations from all at Decca. 'Go Now' in top twenty."

*Ready to go now —
the Moody Blues*

Chapter Four

1965

GOTTA SWIM OR SINK LIKE A STONE

Bev Bevan had been in a bad way that Christmas, according to his old pal **Ronny Smith**. "**Denny Laine** had cracked it with 'Go Now'. It was Christmas Day and there was Denny with the **Moody Blues** on 'Top of the Pops'. It's his famous quote now but the poor kid was nearly at breaking point. Nodding at the television screen, Bev muttered, 'All I've got to look forward to is the January sales.' "

It was while the Lee Longlands sale was taking place that the challenge of the drum stool with **Carl Wayne's Vikings** came his way.

"**Dave Hollis** called it a day and we advertised in the Birmingham Mail," explained **Terry Wallace**. "Bev didn't answer but somehow found his way to the audition which was in the church hall on Bromford Lane, by Carl Wayne's house."

With Bev now a Viking, the band once again left Birmingham for the peace and tranquility of the Storyville club, Duisburg, Germany, where they were now building a concentrated repertoire of black material, 'Duke of Earl' being a particular favourite with the German audiences.

"Trouble was, the Germans could never figure out exactly what a 'Dook' was!" chuckled Terry.

Lee Longlands loss was the Vikings' gain

Lording it like a duke around the **Rainbow Suite** was drummer **Keith Smart**, formerly of the **Everglades**. Following **Trevor Burton's** departure the band fell apart and Keith filled in by working for **Dougie Thompson** as stage manager at the Rainbow Suite and head cook and bottle washer at Dougie's office in Dale End. The stage management part of the job rarely presented problems for Keith, because Dougie Thompson would always 'accidentally' overbook and have a couple of bands drowning their sorrows in the bar after unsuccessfully trying to argue the toss over a supposedly agreed booking.

"On the babby's life," Dougie Thompson would tell them, cupping his hands as if in prayer, "You ain't in the diary."

Only then would the humanitarian aspect of Dougie Thompson's character reveal itself and he'd kindly allow one of the bands to play an hour set for a fiver.

"If nothing else, it'll pay for the petrol," he'd say, offering his handkerchief.

Then, in mid January of 1965, disaster struck. Not one band turned up. With an empty stage and a Rainbow Suite that was bursting at the seams with punters, Keith Smart's ingenuity was put to the test. He knew there was a concert taking place at **Gosta Green College of Technology** featuring **Spencer Davis**, the **Rockin' Berries** and, from Wolverhampton, the **Montanas**. A phone call to the college social secretary quickly established that he would not be able to poach any of the renowned local bands. But he was informed that the band up from Wales, who had opened the show, was already packed and about to leave. Calling across to one of them, the social secretary handed over to the phone.

Dougie Thompson

"I've got twelve quid," Keith Smart informed the band's vocalist.

"That'll do boyo. We'll be there in ten minutes," was the reply.

"To say that **Tom Jones** was awesome that evening would be quite an understatement," said Keith. "Tom and the Squires humped their gear up the stairs and onto the stage. When the curtains drew back it was every man for himself. The energy that was generated by Tom just had to be seen to be believed!"

Tom Jones returned to Birmingham the following week to record his input for 'Thank Your Lucky Stars' at ATV studios in Aston. It was to be the first airing of 'It's Not Unusual', which was about to become his first smash hit.

"Part of my duties was to stick the posters on the walls around town advertising forthcoming attractions at the Rainbow Suite," Keith Smart explained. "Dougie would loan me his clapped out mini car. There were no brakes. I used to drag my foot along the pavement to slow the thing down!"

Fortunately for Keith, **Trevor Burton** had spoken highly of him to **Danny** *Danny King & the Jesters*
King. Keith was invited to become one of the **Jesters** and his inauguration was at the **Turf** pub on Monument Road where Danny and the **Jesters** held court every Sunday lunchtime.

"**Norrie Paramor** got in touch," said **Pat Wayne**. "He was so excited. He'd found the song that would definitely crack it for me."

The song that Norrie Paramor had in mind for Pat was a powerful ballad that American singer Frankie Laine had charted with back in August '54, entitled 'My Friend'.

Pat's master cut on 'My Friend', recorded in studio 1 at EMI's world famous Abbey Road studios was an absolute gem. With the Ivor Raymonde Orchestra interpreting Norrie Paramor's sensitive arrangement superbly, the round vocal tones that Pat Wayne delivered on that session were a credit to him. Emotion spilled from the former Oratory educated choirboy as he sang — "My friend, the King of all Kings, who walks beside me and is always there to guide me. At the end of that long and lonely road, who will it be to welcome me? My friend."

For the listener it was a highly charged experience. Quite spiritually moving. And there lay the problem that would kill any chance of sales and consequent chart success. The BBC, in all their biblical wisdom, decided that the lyric ventured into the realms of blasphemy. 'My Friend' was immediately withdrawn from the BBC playlists.

Now minus **Jeff Lynne**, the **Andicapps** were fortunate in obtaining the services of another fine guitarist, **Jeff 'Jake' Commander**.

"Jake was a whizzkid when it came to electrics and all that," said **Kex Gorin**. "The Andicapps did a tape at **Hollick and Taylor's** studio, and Jake managed to jam up the radio airwaves for a minute or so by broadcasting our tape before the authorities could track the signal! That would have been around 1965."

Freddie Garrity teaches John Singer a few steps

In the mid 1970's Jake Commander went on to produce the first album for the hard-hitting Brummie band, **Magnum**, with Kex Gorin on drums.

John Singer's fingers were itching for more action and his attention was drawn to the **Adelphi** ballroom in West Bromwich.

"The ballroom was owned by **John Gordon**, a director of West Bromwich Albion football club," said John, "And I managed to talk him into allowing me to rent it from him."

Using his shrewd business acumen, John Singer coaxed the Birmingham Planet newspaper into sponsoring a grand beat group contest at the Adelphi.

With the new line up of the

Andicapps raring to go, **Vic Sims**, their manager, confidently entered them into the contest. A double-decker bus was hired to ship the Andicapps fans from Shard End to West Bromwich. As far as the Andicapps could ascertain, the biggest obstacle to their winning was the **Saints Combo**, led by music shop salesman and guitar virtuoso, **Pete Oliver**. By coincidence, Pete Oliver was also head of the judging panel. Result? In first place, the Saints Combo! Disgruntled, but in no way disgraced, second place went to the Andicapps!

Showing at number forty-five on the charts in the first week of 1965 was a new version of the Big Joe Williams blues song, 'Baby Please Don't Go'.

"So I got a phone call from Phil Solomon, an agent in London," said **Mike Carroll**. "He wanted to sell me a Belfast group called **Them**. It was the old spiel, "Book 'em now and the price won't change when they're top five."

Mike Carroll had heard it all before, but booked Them for a fee of forty pounds.

"The night Them visited the **Mackadown** they were at number three," chuckled Mike. "The queue went all round the car park but the fee remained the same. I charged four and six on the door so you work it out."

As Mike Carroll struggled to organise the chaos, the licensee of the Mackadown, **Bert Bonfield**, informed him that the evening's main attraction, Them, had arrived and were in the bar.

Mike Carroll tells the tale, "Bert pointed out this long haired lad at the bar, so in total innocence I tapped him on the shoulder and asked 'Excuse me but are you one of Them?' Fortunately he said he was, and introduced himself — Van Morrison."

Dave Lacey was definitely not one of Them, but a **Corvette** and he intended to stay that way. **Ma Regan**, did as she had done with the **Cheetahs**, and switched Dave and the boys from Decca into the capable hands of **Johnny Franz** at Phillips.

"But it was the same old story with the material," said Dave Lacey. "Johnny Franz had me cut a country and western song, 'That's What They All Say', but I was no Tex Ritter. Then Phillips started talking about me splitting from the lads to go solo and I wouldn't hear of it."

Dave Lacey & the Corvettes at the Old Hill Plaza

$\mathbf{M}$eanwhile 'Soldier Boy', the Cheetahs' second release on Philips was marching towards the top thirty.

"Johnny Franz really got us working in the right direction," explained **Euan Rose**. "Johnny would demand original songs from us. He'd say, 'Come on lads, I've already got the Four Seasons. Give me the Cheetahs!' "

The Cheetahs provided him with a fair few original songs including 'Baby Goodbye', 'Whole Lotta Love' and 'The Party', a song credited with boxer **Johnny Prescott** as co-writer.

Capitol Systems at St Chad's Church Hall

$\mathbf{T}$here was a party going on at **St Chads Church Hall**, just off Tyburn Road in Erdington, on the evening of Saturday, 30th January. It was a case of local boys making good as four lads, just out of Great Barr Comprehensive and Marsh Hill Technical, had got themselves together as the **Capitol Systems**. With **Paul Sargeant** and **Dave Bailey** twanging away on their guitars, **Paul Whitehouse**'s bass riffs rode the groove that drummer **Rob Moore** was putting down.

"It was all down to the harmonies for us in those days," explained Rob Moore. "Plenty of Beach Boys stuff like 'Sloop John B', and 'Barbara Anne'. Anything with a goodtime feel."

Everything was capitol for the Systems when they became the talk of Erdington, landing the residency at the **Yenton Boys' Club** that met every Friday evening.

Finders Keepers

$\mathbf{O}$ver in Dudley, three of the **Strangers**, **'Dripper' Kent**, **Jake Elcock** and **Alan Clee** wanted to move their careers up a gear.

"We wanted to turn full-time professional," Alan Clee explained. "We felt we had something to offer but **Tony Dalloway** and **Mike Aston** weren't willing to make the switch to full-time."

Bringing in **Dave Williams** on drums and **Ralph Oakley** on rhythm guitar as enthusiastic replacements, the Strangers went for a change of name, and almost let their positive mood falter.

"The first idea was Losers Weepers," confessed Dripper, "But fortunately we settled on **Finders Keepers**.

Along with the professional status came a professional attitude and Finders Keepers began to make a big impression as confident entertainers.

Vincent Ladbrooke, a piano dealer with premises on Bristol Street, was a frustrated songwriter searching for success. What Mr Ladbroke needed was to get his songs down on tape for demonstration purposes. He'd heard from his neighbour on Bristol Street, Mr Griffin, of Griffin Hi-Fi, that two young men had started up in business as mobile recording engineers. **Johnny Haines**, who was still a student at St Peters College, Saltley, and **Jim Tetlow** had pooled what recording equipment they had, and were beginning to get results. Vincent Ladbrooke made contact with Mr Haines and Mr Tetlow, and arranged for a session to take place in his first floor organ showroom. With the primitive tape recorder and mixing desk in amongst the Farifisa and Lowry organs, the **Trevor Orton Trio** with **Roy Parry** on vocals made short work of the session. Impressed by the recording techniques, Vincent Ladbrooke, launched the **Ladbrooke Recording Studio** at the rear of his piano showrooms. Jim Tetlow and Johnny Haines were installed as in house sound engineers.

Ladbrooke Recording Studio

Mike Sheridan and his **Nightriders** were now confidently performing material written by their new guitarist, **Roy Wood**, and were pleasantly surprised when Norrie Paramor agreed to record and release one of Roy's songs, 'Make Them Understand'. "It was a good song for the time but I messed up pretty bad," admitted Mike Sheridan. "Tom Jones was massive by now with 'It's Not Unusual', but my attempt to do a 'Tom' with my approach to the vocal on the recording was a bit of a flop!"

Vintage Nightriders

Keith Powell
& the Valets

The Moody Blues

Αn appearance by **Keith Powell and the Valets** at Beat City in London's Oxford Street had made a big impression on Jean Lincoln. She ran an artiste management company which boasted entertainer Kenny Lynch among its clientele. After offering Keith a contract for exclusive representation and securing his signature, her next move was to introduce this new artiste to **John Schroeder** at Pye Records.

"John agreed with Jean Lincoln about my potential as a solo artiste and set about finding soul, and rhythm and blues material for me to record," said Keith. "It was a hard decision to make but with EMI not renewing my contract I had to move in other directions, and that meant quitting the Valets."

Keith Powell's first recording for Pye, which many believe to be one of his best, was 'People Get Ready'. This was quickly followed by a song that John Schroeder found on a visit to New York's Brill building. 'Goodbye Girl', composed by the 'writers in residence' team of Barry Mann and Cynthia Whiel, subsequently became a turntable hit.

Mal Ritter of the Valets picks up the tale, "With Keith Powell gone, life got tough but we had to keep going. **Stevie Horton** from the **Diplomats** was with us by now. **Colin Wood** hopped it down under to Australia so we pulled in **Dave Spence**, who had been in **Danny Storm's Strollers**, to play guitar."

Ιt was time for the **Applejacks** to pitch their fourth release at the record buying public. 'Chim Chim Cheree' from the film 'Mary Poppins' was scheduled to be the single for them, but in the name of street credibility, 'Bye Bye Girl' came out instead, only to quickly vanish from radar screens.

Phil Cash picks up the story, "We were now not earning much money. What little we did earn was being swallowed by us having two managers. **Joe Brannelly** took twenty per cent. **Arthur Smith** took ten per cent. We, the band, were six handed. Joe was taking the lion's share so we ditched him. It was the most stupid thing we ever did. In sacking Joe we said goodbye to any London connections we had, and the Applejacks were more or less back where they started."

Τhe **Moody Blues** had come a long way from where they started. Now residing in the most pleasant of surroundings, a communal abode in Rodene Crescent, Roehampton, the boys played host to the stars. An invitation to a Moody Blues party, where, it's said, the Beatles were more or less guaranteed to be in attendance, was like gold dust itself. The international stage was beckoning, America, the Promised Land of rock 'n' roll, should be theirs for the taking. All they had to do was smack them in the face with a worthy follow-up — they needed a 'Go Now II'.

"That was the problem," said **Clint Warwick**. "We soon found out the hard way that getting a second hit was easier said than done."

'I Don't Want To Go On Without You', a song written by American writers Bert Burns and Atlantic Records supremo, Gerry Wexler, was a strong heart-searching piece that again tested **Denny Laine**'s bluesy vocal delivery to the limit. And yet, even with the Moody Blues sounding moodier and indeed bluer than they had before, the record only managed number thirty-three on the charts.

"Already," said Clint, "In the space of three months, the public saw us as has-beens."

For their second shot at the hit parade, **Carl Wayne and the Vikings** delved into **Danny King**'s catalogue of compositions and found 'This Is Love'. As the Vikings were preparing for the recording session at Hollick and Taylor, Danny King arrived unannounced.

"It was a good job he did," Terry Wallace said. "**Ace Kefford**'s voice wasn't up to it that day, so Danny dubbed on the harmonies. Listen to that record now and you can hear Danny's style."

Danny King's unmistakable style was about to be re-assessed. When promoters **John Parsons** and **John Sabel**, of **Mayfair Entertainments**, took over the management of Danny and the **Jesters**, the first thing they proposed was a name change for the band. Upping the image of the band, and reflecting their company name, Mr Parsons and Mr Sabel re-launched them as Danny King and the **Mayfair Set**.

"The first time we appeared as the Mayfair Set," said **Trevor Burton**, "Was at the **Belfry** over in Wishaw. John Parsons got us dressed up as society toffs."

When Danny and the Mayfair Set were announced, they emerged from the back of the ballroom in top hats and capes and, brandishing walking canes, they danced their way through the crowd à la Fred Astaire. Once on the stage the Mayfair Set — Danny King, Trevor Burton, **Keith Smart**, **Roger Harris** and **Pete Allen**, removed their white gloves, took up their instruments and proved themselves to be first class musicians. Trevor Burton's harmonies enhanced Danny's voice superbly on songs like the Crickets' 'Please Don't Ever Change' and the Temptations' emotional 'My Girl'.

Danny King & the Mayfair Set

Pete Allen, the bass guitarist, was soon to be replaced in the Mayfair Set by **Dennis Ball**.

"Dennis's brother, Dave, played guitar and they lived in this grand baronial palace in Rectory Road, Sutton Coldfield," Keith Smart explained as best he could, "Jumping the story, Dennis and **Dave Ball** had a band, the **Scorcerers**, with **Cozy Powell** on drums. He was from Cirencester. I think I've got that right." Keith pondered slightly before driving his punchline home. "Yeah, that's it. Cozy Powell was brought to Birmingham by the Balls!"

Kingfishers at the Locarno

Lenny **Hall** recalls the progress that his band the **Kingfishers**, once called the **D'Fenders**, had made. They had run a close second to the **Concords** in the annual **Locarno** contest (a band called the **Freeways** took third place).

"That was in the early January and the bookings just rolled in, but by April things had changed. It was as if we'd become old fashioned overnight. We played the **Plaza**, Old Hill one night and felt bad vibes coming from the audience. Half way through the second song and the dance floor emptied faster than Rock Hudson's dressing room!"

The **Kestrals** were a vocal act that featured the voice of Londoner Tony Burrows, with two Bristolians, Roger Cook and Roger Greenaway, providing the harmonies. Roger Cook had enjoyed a taste of songwriting success with his 1963 composition, 'Parisian', which was included in the 'Maigret' television series. In the April of 1965, while the Kestrals were on tour with Herman's Hermits, Tony Burrows announced his decision to quit for a solo career. That's when the two Rogers decided to try their hand at song writing together.

Backstage in the Lincolnshire town of Cleethorpes, with Tony Burrows' departure from the Kestrals imminent, Roger Cook and Roger Greenaway rolled up their sleeves and very quickly composed their first song together. After recording a demo of the song, Messrs Cook and Greenaway handed the tape over to Cyril Gee, the song plugger at Mills Music, in the hope that he would place it with an international 'name' artiste. The song was entitled 'You've Got Your Troubles'.

William and the Conquerors had a few troubles themselves, having finished way down the field in the Locarno contest. To get back on track they began to feature blues and soul material heavily in their repertoire. **Brian Harbison**, the bass player was developing a singing voice that could handle the change in style. In fact he was becoming better suited to the new material than their lead vocalist.

"**Mick Fisher**, our singer up 'til then, couldn't really hack the soul stuff," explained Brian Harbison, "So we gave him a golden handshake of £45.00 and off he went perfectly happy, leaving us to become, for a while, just plain **William's Conquerors**."

As William's Conquerors, and with loads of Tamla songs in the set, they became firm favourites at such venues as the **Hopwood Caravan Club**, the **Meadway** pub and the **College Arms**, Kingstanding, where they would arrive in their converted 'Brooke Bond Tea' van to go Barefootin' every Wednesday evening.

The **Sovereigns**, back home from their debaucheries at Osmington Bay, and now highly experienced entertainers, were about to enter the world of cabaret with confidence. A corporate affair for the executive personnel of (coincidentally) Brooke Bond Tea was the occasion and the **Grand Hotel**, Colmore Row, was the place.

The Sovereigns at Pontins, Osmington Bay

"We were told we were sharing our dressing room with another cabaret act," **Dave Evans** of the Sovereigns explained. "The other act turned out to be the Brooke Bond TV chimps. It was frightening. The chimps were swinging on the coat rails and jumping from one side of the room to the other. If you moved a muscle, they'd be at you, nibbling at anything that twitched. It was murder trying to pull your trousers up!"

Denis Brown was acutely aware of the need to change. Having been the head cook and bottlewasher at the **Old Hill Plaza** for the past five years his nervous system could take no more.

"I'd arrive home from work at five o'clock and eat my dinner on the move," said Denis.

He would then drive to the Regan's home in Edgbaston to pick up the bar 'float' cash before arriving at Old Hill for seven-thirty to play the opening set with the house band. Overseeing the evening's events, Denis would balance the takings and, when everyone had gone, he'd lock and secure the building. Finally it was home to Sparkhill via Edgbaston, to deliver the takings to the Regans. Collapsed exhausted in bed, Denis would force himself to rise at seven o'clock when the whole process would start again. All this for four pounds a week!

Denis Brown

The **Barons**, from Smethwick, were no more. Stripped of his aristocratic title and finding himself at a loose end, guitarist **Ken Underhill** journeyed to the **Black Horse** at Northfield where the **Sombreros** were playing.

Sombreros

When Ken Underhill's availability became known to the band, the former Baron promptly became a Sombrero. And it wouldn't be long before the Sombreros needed someone on drums, to rattle the maracas.

Shaking it about was **Buzz Allen** with his **D'Fenders**, who were destined to play their farwell gig at **Gosta Green College**.

"We'd had two cracking years with barrels

of laughs," Alan 'Buzz' Burrows explains. "Then our drummer, **Albert Carr**, got poached by the Sombreros." Alan winces at the very thought. "With Albert gone, the rest of us were wondering whether to get another drummer in, or just pack up, but our minds were soon made up for us. Shortly after Albert's departure we were in our van driving over Frankley Beeches. As we passed a farmyard, we hit an animal that had strayed into the road and it caused so much damage that the van was a write-off."

Was it a cow?

"Not arf," sighed Alan, "We still owed three payments on it!"

The J4 van that the **Memphis Sounds** charged around in was bought and paid for, but totally unreliable. With a diary that contained such prestigious engagements as the **Rainbow Suite**, the **Cedar Club** and the **Queens Head** in Erdington, they were committing professional suicide by travelling about in such a rusty bucket. However, the only thing on their minds was the music. With **Dennis Ryland** installed as their new sax player, the Memphis Sounds were becoming grittier by the day.

"All that Wilson Pickett, Otis and Sam and Dave stuff was going a storm," recalled Dennis. "That is until we played the **Caves** pub in Dudley. It was like entering a time warp!"

The Memphis Sounds managed to arrive punctually but it was obvious that the clientele had not quite recovered from the mid 50s, either in musical taste or dress sense.

"We did 'Rock Around the Clock' and 'Alligator' quite a few times that night as a result of threats from the tattooed ladies at the bar," Dennis concluded.

Back in Birmingham, **Phil Myatt** was giving them one more chance to make the gigs on time without their van breaking down. He engaged the Memphis Sounds for an appearance at the **Carlton** ballroom.

The Memphis Sound

"Don't you dare loose me down!" warned Phil Myatt.

Vocalist **Brian Thompson** was taking no chances. He took loan of a J2 van from the garden centre in Withybed Lane, Alvechurch. When the Memphis Sounds loaded themselves and their equipment into the borrowed van they were careful not to disturb the potted plants and trays of seeds that took up most of the space. With the April showers lashing down from darkened skies, the Memphis Sounds set off in the garden centre's van. They made their way up Bristol Road towards the city centre, where they'd pick up the Lichfield Road and on to the Carlton where they would arrive with time to spare.

"As we sailed through the traffic lights at the Bristol picture house," said **Dave Challinor**, "A wheel came hurtling past us and we all collapsed laughing."

"Yeah," interrupted Dennis Ryland. "That's when the back end of the van dropped down with an almighty crash and the roller door flew up. There was sparks flying everywhere and flowerpots, drums and guitars went careering out into the Bristol Street rush hour."

Bristol Street route of the Memphis Sounds' wheel

It was their wheel. As one of the lads set about retrieving the wheel, which had come to rest on the steps of St Lukes' church, the panicking Memphis Sounds scurried around in the pouring rain in a desperate search for the missing wheel nuts. Dennis Ryland thought he spotted one in a puddle in the middle of Bristol Street. As he crawled on his hands and knees, the side of a number 62 bus brushed his ear.

Satellites with Ben E King

With the wheel back on the van and being held in place by two nuts, the Memphis Sounds continued their journey. Making good progress for at least a hundred yards until the throttle cable snapped. After frantic botching with string and plant ties they still managed to make it to the Carlton on time.

A full diary ensured that **Lee Stevens and the Satellites** had treacle on their pudding in more ways than one. The only thing bugging them was their name.

"Lee Stevens and the Satellites was beginning to sound a bit square," admitted **Norman 'Lee' Crandles**. "We needed a name to reflect the social awareness of mid-sixties rock musicians. We needed to get hip."

Satellites congratulate name completion winner

The Satellites themselves came up with a name that was in keeping with the good vibrations of Great Britain, or at least Saltley. Their suggestion, **Norman Crandles and the Roman Candles** however, met with total disapproval from Norman, who was determined to keep 'Lee Stevens' alive and kicking. An appeal was made on the band's behalf, via Midland Beat magazine. A crisp five-pound note was offered to the reader who suggested the best new name. After wading through sacks of postcards until the early hours, the Satellites were able to summon the gentlemen of the waiting press and announce that from that day forward, the boys would be known as, and here it comes, the **Lee Stevens Band**.

Four months after the opening of the **Ladbrooke Studio**, **Jim Tetlow** exited to set up his own studio on the Stratford Road in Sparkhill.

"I had my finals to finish so I went back to St Peters College for the exams," said **Johnny Haines**. "We hadn't done too badly. We'd had bands like **William's Conquerors** and **Frankie Spencer** and the **Cock-a-Hoops** in and that made for interesting times but, with Jim gone, it looked all over."

Frank Spencer & the Cock-a-Hoops

It certainly didn't look all over for promoter **Mike Carroll**. With the **Mackadown**, Kitts Green and the **Black Horse**, Northfield both bursting at the seams with punters, Mike added a third venue, the **Royal Oak** at Hockley Heath.

"In for a penny, in for a pound," said Mike. "I went for broke at the Royal Oak by opening Thursdays, Fridays, Saturdays and Sundays with 'live' bands. Discos still hadn't made their impact. I couldn't believe my luck. I'd have the likes of **Johnny Neal and the Starliners**, Johnny Carroll's group, the **Vogues** and a great blues band the **Boulevards**, all doing first class business for me. Also, for a year or so, I promoted the rowdier **Sydenham** and the **Gospel Oak** pubs from which I still carry the scars!"

Tony Clarkin of the Boulevards speaks highly of Mike Carroll, both as a promoter and a humanitarian: "Some promoters, who will remain nameless, would be so incredibly bullyboyish to young lads who were only trying to find their way. With Mike, that was never the case. He always was a perfect gent. Sometimes the Boulevards were not everybody's cup of tea. We'd do material that was a bit 'off the wall'. We never were a jukebox band. But Mike always respected our efforts."

DJ Doc Holliday at Arden Hall Disco

Mike Carroll, still wage earning at Scrivens' opticians in Hurst Street, reported for work one Monday morning to discover his promotional activities were in no way respected by his employers.

"I was summoned into the office by the hierarchy," chuckled Mike at the recollection. "They told me this rock 'n' roll business had to stop. I told them I earned more in a night than I did all week working for them. You can guess the outcome."

The outcome was that Mike Carroll's Brumbeat enterprises continued to thrive. Adding the **New Inns**, Handsworth and the **Breedon Cross** at Cotteridge to his list of promotions, at **Jimmy Powell**'s suggestion, he ventured into the management and agency side of the business. Firstly by acquiring sole representation of the **Sombreros**, who were beginning to specialise in close harmony songs, and then by managing a line up that had originally been known as **John E Law and the Trespassers**, but were now called the **Agency**. Also at Jimmy Powell's suggestion, he ventured north to the town of Bolton, where a town centre club, the Bone Yard, was, in Jimmy's words 'a goldmine, just there for the taking.'

The Agency

"So I went up and had a look at the Bone Yard," sighed Mike Carroll. "Jimmy was right — in as much as it was 'there for the taking' — it was dead on its feet! The brick walls were painted black and the tables were coffins. It was like Dracula's living room but I gave it a go."

Mike and Jimmy spent the week prior to the Sunday night launch pasting posters all over Bolton to advertise 'At the Bone Yard! Direct from Brum! The **Uglys**!' Unfortunately, as fast as Mike Carroll put up the posters, rival promoters ripped them down.

"It was that kind of town," said Mike.

Undeterred, Mike Carroll was determined to present Bolton with a taste of Brumbeat. "**Steve Gibbons** and the Uglys showed up and did their thing to about half a dozen punters. Ah well, put it all down to experience. We chucked it in and headed home. Bye-bye Bone Yard!" laughed Mike half-heartedly.

The Chucks

Never one for chucking it in, **Reg Jones**, the former powerhouse frontman of the **Chantelles**, with his brother **Chris**, put together the **Chucks**. With '**Mugsy**' **Morgan** strumming out the chords and **Keith Williams** laying down the bass lines, the line up was completed by drummer **Barry Smith**. Barry not only played drums, he also performed an incredible flame blowing routine!

"Folks would crowd around the stage to witness these spectacular antics," said Keith Williams, his eyes resembling bulldogs' proverbials.

At **Dudley Labour Club**, Barry Smith rose from his

stool and stepped from behind the drum kit. Bringing the spout of the bottle of petrol to his lips he tilted it, filling his mouth with the highly inflammable liquid. The crowd descended into a deep hush as he removed an England's Glory match from its box and struck a flame. As he did so, he developed an uncontrollable bout of hiccups, and in sheer panic he spat the petrol from his lips.

"Immediately, there was flames shooting everywhere!" exclaimed Keith, his eyes expanding to even greater proportions. In the ensuing pandemonium there were fortunately no serious casualties, but with the blaze of national publicity that it ignited, the Chucks were suddenly hot news.

When their manager **Brian Ennis,** who wrote for Midland Beat magazine, informed them that the agent **Billy Forrest** was in the market for bands to work in Germany, the Chucks were almost unanimously up for it. They auditioned at the **Moat House**, and a week later, as they were about to take stage at the Royal Oak, Hockley Heath, they received the news that they had prayed for. The Chucks were Germany bound.

"Keith Williams quit immediately," said Reg Jones. "He reckoned, with all the crazy stunts that was going on, being stuck in a foreign land with us lot would see him off!"

*Summer Hill Ice Rink —
a sedate gig*

Keith Williams headed for the sanity of the **Summer Hill Ice Rink** where he donned a monkey suit and a dicky bow to join up with two former **Astonaires,** guitarist **Dezi Pearce** and drummer **Alan Scott** to perform 'The Skaters Waltz' for folk that sought the more serene things in life.

For the German trip, **Melvyn Stanton** was recruited and the Chucks set off to perform eight hours per evening at the Star Palast Club, Karlstal.

"Sundays was murder," said Reg. "Two o'clock start, through until midnight."

The Chantelles

Singing guitarist Johnny Fincham set about resurrecting the Chantelles.

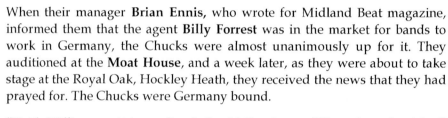

"In actual fact, Johnny was all that was left of the Chantelles!" said **Tim Bellamy,** once the drummer with **Johnny Dean's Dominators**. With Tim on drums, Johnny Fincham recruited **Pete Lewis** on bass and **Alan McCormack** on guitar. The new Chantelles were up and running and the Regan circuit welcomed them with open arms.

The **Rockin' Berries'** follow up to 'He's In Town' — 'What in the World's Come Over You' — had tickled the charts, but proved not to have been the wisest of choices. The Berries were rather hoping that their version of the **John Carter** and **Ken Lewis** song, 'Funny How Love Can Be' would be selected. However, John and Ken wanted it for their own **Ivy League** project, so the Berries version had to be tucked away on their album 'In Town with the Berries'.

"Our record producer **John Schroeder** was excited about a minor hit in the States by a band called the Reflections," said **Geoff Turton** of the Berries.

That song, 'Poor Man's Son', was dismantled and rebuilt on the studio floor when the Berries hit upon the idea of using three key changes. The song would kick off in D and move into E flat before concluding in E.

"Chuck's guitar sounded so full of body when we made it to E, but opening on a D strum sounded a bit plinky-plonky," explained Geoff Turton, getting technical.

Chuck Botfield came up with the answer. Tuning his guitar down a tone, his open E chord was pitched at D. When Geoff Turton delivered the opening line "I'm up each day with the risin' sun", 'Poor Man's Son' sounded like a full-blooded hit record should sound.

John Schroeder then put **Keith Powell**'s career under his microscope and came up with an idea. Jean Lincoln, Keith's manager, also managed a raunchy voiced young lady by the name of Elkie Brookes. Why not team them together?

Up the chute — the Moody Blues

"Which is what happened," Keith explained. "Elkie and I became a vocal duo and hit the road as a soul act. We'd planned to record a few things when we had it tight. On the road with us, we had a brother and sister backup vocal team, the Marionettes. They, later in the mid 70s, became Mac and Katie Kissoon and had their own hits."

For Keith Powell and Elkie Brookes though, things unfortunately didn't happen as Elkie began to develop a preference for jazz material.

The **Moody Blues** release for the summer of 1965, a **Denny Laine** composition 'From the Bottom of My Heart', sounded like a hit record, but in the rush to release it, the studio engineer failed to add the **Ray Thomas** flute part during the instrumental break to the final mix. "The result was a big musical hole," commented **Clint Warwick**, "But the strange thing is no one ever said anything about it. Not one single comment."

With or without the flute, 'From the Bottom of My Heart' faired a little better than their previous effort, making number twenty-two on the national charts.

"If nothing else it gave us a breathing space," added Clint.

Derrie Ryan & the Ravens with agent Nita Anderson

Norman Haines of the Brum Beats woke one morning to find their keyboard player, Terry Dews, or as he had re-named himself, Terry Guy, had gone AWOL. Norman's search finally found Terry with the Stringbeats, rehearsing at the Acorn, the pub that faces the gates of Winson Green Prison. The Stringbeats had been awarded the highly prestigious job of backing up the 'My Boy Lollipop' girl, Millie Small on a couple of local West Midlands dates, and needed someone with Terry's keyboard abilities.

"So someone had to play the Vox Continental in the Brum Beats," Norman Haines explained. "I asked Vic Wakelin, our manager, to let me have a go. I spent a week in solitary with the organ and reckoned I'd cracked it. We got a guitarist in, Graham Hill with Tony Quinn, who came from the Black Angels, on bass."

Terry Guy didn't hang around with the Stringbeats for too long though. Terry made the journey from Winson Green, through Cape Hill and beyond to the sleeping town of Oldbury where he discovered a band of Incas. "Could you blow a little harmonica for us?" asked their leader Derrie Ryan, producing an Echo Super Vamper from his trouser pocket.

Incas declare war

Derrie, from Tipton, had found public prominence with the Ravens, who operated under the guidance of Sedgley agent Nita Anderson. Fleeing the nest, Derrie travelled south to Oldbury to join with drummer Mac Poole and, from the Congressmen, guitarist Arthur Ray and bass player Doug Walker to make good as the Spectro Sonics. They soon decided, however, that the Spectro Sonics was far too much of a mouthful and settled for the snappier Incas.

Terry Guy couldn't come to terms with being an Inca and a surge of patriotism saw him enlist with Brian Yeates's John Bull Breed. At the Star Palace club at Kiel, in Germany, all was not well. The club's proprietor, Manfred Vykella, had gambled his boots on Screamin' Lord Sutch and the Savages pulling in the crowds. Kiel is the German seaport that was home to the U boats during the Second World War. With that history it followed that the audience would be made up of merchant seamen. Unfortunately, the seamen found these Savages rather too tame for their adventurous tastes. Ken Smith, the Cheshire agent who had formerly promoted the Say Mama in Sutton Coldfield was issued with orders from Herr Vykella to find a replacement. And quick!

The John Bull Breed came, saw and conquered the Star Palace. The seven-piece combo comprised of Brian Yeates on vocals, Terry Guy on keyboards, Mike Herd on guitar and Gene Rose on drums. Two sax players, Trevor Griffen and Graham Green gave the Breed a great honkin' sound that rode on the bass lines put down by ex-El Rioter John Lodge, who, for some reason took to calling himself **John Storm**. The Sam the Sham number "Wooly Bully" was the song that sold the John Bull Breed to the not so easily pleased German seamen and their fraulienes. Brian Yeates, in his best Mexican wetback accent would count the band in with "Uno! Dos! One, two, tres, quatro!" and the John Bull Breed were off and running. Being an ex-schoolboy gymnast, Brian would perform the splits on the song's accents, and with the audience going totally ape, he would dive onto the organ and demonstrate his ability in the handstand department.

"Manfred Vykella was always pleading poverty," Brian explained. "He drove a fabulous pink Cadillac but would always maintain, 'I have no money'. I asked him for an advance on our wages and again he repeated the fact that he had no money. I said that I'd take the Cadillac instead, and Manfred answered, 'You can have my wife but not the Cadillac!' "

John Bull Breed: 'What Cadillac?'

The **Rotundas** were using the McCabe family home in Crowhurst Road, Longbridge for rehearsals. In **Janice Nicholls'** weekly column in the Sunday Mercury, she reported that on her visit to the house she discovered the Rotundas deep in serious rehearsal. Janice went on to report that while the boys played, the McCabes' two poodles, Cindy and Suki, sat in judgement of the performance.

"If they dislike a number, angry barking fills the air," wrote Miss Nicholls, "However, if a song catches the poodles' fancy, their little ears prick up and delighted howls can be heard all around Longbridge."

Janice Nichols

Apparently, according to the article, when **Roger 'Twitty' Conway** and **Pete White** harmonized their way through the Everleys' 'Girl Sang the Blues', the ears of the little doggies did indeed prick up and both Cindy and Suki howled their approval. But oh dear, when **Roger Ottley** stepped up to growl out Bob Dylan's 'She Belongs To Me', their cute little ears dropped to collar level. The angry barking, which resounded down the full length of Crowhurst Road, brought the rehearsal to an abrupt ending. And it was all down to Master Ottley. The line about the hypnotist collector being a 'walking antique' had scared the daylights out of these poor little poodles.

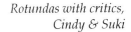

Rotundas with critics, Cindy & Suki

Thirty-six years on, Roger Ottley finally came clean on this totally absurd piece of creative journalism.

"You know, it never really happened like that," confided Roger, winking his eye and bringing his index finger to his lips to indicate confidentiality. "The dogs really loved the Dylan stuff!"

How those poodles would have reacted to the **Prospectors** is anyone's guess, but all was not well in Aston. **Hartley Cain** and **Len Ablethorpe** had been thrown out of the band for ungentlemenly conduct. 'H' and Len responded by recruiting bass player **Louis Clarke**, who immediately moved out of his palatial home in Bridgnorth and took a room above the dental surgery on Six Ways, Aston. The boys endeavoured to make music together, and the next twist to the tale came in the form of an advertisement which appeared in the music section of the 'Birmingham Mail'. It read quite simply, 'Singer requires band for nightclub.'

"Arh, that's right and it cost twelve-and-six," recalled the man who placed that advertisement, **Raymond Froggatt**. "My mate **Bunter Broadhurst**, who was a steel stockholder, had bought **'Titos'** nightclub on Soho Hill in Handsworth. He asked me to find some musicians that would be, shall we say, in residence." giggled Froggy in mock thespian tones. "Any road," said Raymond, reverting back to his native tongue, "This bunch of scruffs turned up at Bunter's house and that was it. **Froggy and the Tadpoles**, four hours a night, seven nights a week. Five quid each! We soon changed the name though, to the **Monopoly**."

The American country star, Roy Orbison was touring the United Kingdom in early '65 with the **Rockin' Berries** and Cliff Bennett and the Rebel Rousers as supporting acts. On bass guitar for the Rebel Rousers was **Bobby Thomson**, formerly of Liverpool's Rory Storm and the Hurricanes.

"It was the first time I'd ever seen anyone impersonate Norman Wisdom and I just fell about," said Bobby in praise of the Berries' **Clive Lea**, "Plus, **Chuck Botfield** was held in awe by everyone with his 'Scotty Moore' style of guitar playing."

Rory Storm & the Hurricanes with Ringo Starr on drums

In May of 1965, the Rockin' Berries made their debut on ATV's live variety show, 'Sunday Night at the London Palladium'. Bobby Thomson sat viewing the show in his apartment on Ealing Broadway and was greatly impressed by the Berries' performance, even though **Geoff Turton**'s voice dried with nerves for the first two lines. They were plugging their newly released single 'Poor Man's Son.'

"Next morning," said Bobby, "**Clive Lea** knocked on the door and asked me to join the band. **Roy Austin** had quit there and then."

Recommending Chas Hodges (now of 'Chas and Dave' fame) as his replacement in the Rebel Rousers, Bobby's first appearance as a Rockin' Berry came that very week, on 'Top of the Pops', miming to 'Poor Man's Son'.

"It seemed so weird," said Bobby, scratching his head. "I'd been on the previous week with Cliff Bennett!"

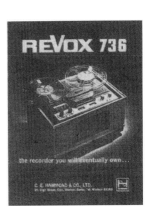

With his final examinations out of the way, recording engineer **Johnny Haines** was out into the big world, unemployed but rarin' to go. "I met up with **Vincent Ladbrooke** and he offered me the chance of renting the studio from him. I had the choice, studio engineer or schoolteacher. I didn't have any leather elbow patches for my tweed jacket then so I opted for the studio." Johnny explained.

Working on two Revox 736 tape machines (which are still in his posession!) he was able, with a little 'jiggery pokery' to ping-pong from one machine to the other and spread the word that **Ladbrooke Sound** had four-track facilities.

The business side of music was changing. "The word 'account' started to appear in the day to day vocabulary," said agent **Terry Matthews**. "One of my accounts was **Walsall Teachers' Training College**, they stipulated that every band I booked into there was paid at the end of the month by cheque."

Cheque — a word guaranteed to put the fear of God up any working musician. The bands raised merry hell but there was no way round the problem of having to wait weeks for their hard earned fees.

Terry Matthews recalls that one particular band got really uptight and the singer showed his displeasure in no uncertain fashion. "They were called the **Good Egg** and the young impatient lad was, oh yes, **Robert Plant**."

Roy Everett, who had been the featured screamer in the **Brand** now fronted a newly formed blues outfit appropriately called **Roy Everett's Blueshounds**, featuring bassist **Honri Edouarde**, drummer **Frank Devine**, sax player **Mike Burney**, organist **Gordon Bache** (who had a fetish for clocks!) and guitarist **Dave Pegg**, formerly of the **Crawdaddies**. Competing in the Melody Maker's national blues band contest, which was held at Wimbledon Palais, the lads came runner-up to a Cardiff band, the Ravens (who were led by Andy Fairweather Lowe, later to make it as leader of Amen Corner). Success in the contest generated interest in the Blueshounds from all over the country.

"Mike Burney always loved to play around the Crewe area," said Dave Pegg. "He was model railway enthusiast and would collect dust and soot from the Crewe sheds for his train set!"

"Never mind train sets!" interrupts Honri. "At Bamber Bridge, outside of Preston, we was parked up alongside a wall that surrounded the train sheds. Mike Burney produced a bag of tools and asked me to give him a hand in lifting a couple of souvenirs. Like a lamb to the slaughter, I agreed to help and we climbed over the wall."

As Mike Burney went to work on a nameplate, the distant sound of dogs barking could be faintly heard. Mike carried on regardless. As the barking drew nearer the two pilferers suddenly spotted two Alsatian dogs bounding across the tracks towards them.

"The railway cops was yellin' at us to stop but we kept runnin' for the wall." said Honri.

Honri Edouarde, feeling the teeth of one of the Alsatians scrape across his backside as he scrambled back over the wall, vowed that in future Mike Burney would pursue his hobbies solo!

The **Elbow Room**, situated next door to the Aston Hippodrome on Aston High Street, opened in June '65, courtesy of **Malcolm Hearn** and **Don Carloss**, formerly the proprietor of the **El Sombrero** coffee bar on Horsefair. Their policy was that only the grooviest of people would be allowed in. The **Blueshounds**, appointed as the house band, provided musical entertainment of the highest order.

El Sombrero Coffee Bar

The **Fortunes** were recording material of the highest order, revamping the Johnnie Ray top ten hit from February 1957, 'Look Homeward Angel', but still the charts eluded them. However, good fortune came their way whilst visiting the offices of Mills Music in search of the song that would justify Decca's faith in them.

"Cyril Gee told us to pick a song off the shelf and we helped ourselves to one entitled 'You've Got Your Troubles'. Easy as that." explained **Rod Allen**. "When Decca heard it they were hooked."

So was Les Reed, who was called in to arrange an orchestration for the song.

Rod continues, "Les agreed to come aboard if he could write the B side. Decca readily agreed."

*The Fortunes
at the London Palladium*

The master cut on 'You've Got Your Troubles' was an absolute gem of a commercial record. It was a highly melodic piece with an imaginative vocal arrangement that included catchy counter melodies. When Rod Allen's distinctive orchestral interpretation of Greenaway and Cook's lyric was added it was obvious that a massive hit was on the cards. Obvious to everyone except Roger Greenaway, who was incensed that Cyril Gee had pitched his song to an unknown act.

When 'You've Got Your Troubles' hit number two on the British charts in July of 1965, he felt a whole lot better.

"When it hit the American top ten," laughed Rod, "Roger readily ate his hat!"

John Singer, following **Ralph Horton's** departure from the Brum scene, had now joined the **Carlton** team of **Phil Myatt**, **Gary Surman** and **John 'Spud' Taylor**. Naming their new association as **Carlton Johns Entertainments**, they set up offices above a social club, formerly an officers billet during the First World War, at 110, Wake Green Road, Moseley.

"It made great sense for myself and the Carlton lads to merge." said John Singer. "We had a fair amount of sweet venues between us, the Carlton, the **Adelphi** and so we could bring in 'name' acts and 'double' them across the city. We had the likes of Lulu, Georgie Fame and Tom Jones doing the business for us. We even had Shirley Bassey at the Town Hall."

The premises of Carlton Johns Entertainment doing its bit in WW1

Dave Pegg recalls magical evenings at the Elbow Room when John Singer and Phil Myatt would call in with whoever they'd had appearing at the Carlton.

"John and Phil brought the Small Faces in. Steve Marriott and his keyboard player Nigel Pegram (who later went on to Steeleye Span) sat in with us and it was a crackin' night — as were most nights at the Elbow," said Dave, "Spencer Davis was always dropping our name to folks that mattered. He even sweet talked their London agent, George Webb, whose office was next door to the Palladium no less, to find us some gigs."

George Webb booked Roy Everett and the Blueshounds in to the Club a-Go-Go in Newcastle upon Tyne for a fee of fifteen pounds.

"That's the kind of pull George Webb had," chirped in Honri Eduoarde.

Mike Burney & Dave Pegg at the Elbow Room

For that fee, the Blueshounds would drive to Newcastle, a good six hour journey in those days, play an hour long set downstairs before moving their equipment upstairs for a late show.

Dave Pegg recalls his first encounter with theatrical digs, "Spencer and Stevie Winwood recommended a bed and breakfast place in Newcastle called 'George's'. The landlady didn't have strict rates. You paid what was in your pocket. If you had a pound, that was what you paid. My first night there I shared a room with a contortionist who was struggling to make ends meet. His act consisted of him hammering six-inch nails through his tongue, for which he charged a fee of seven pounds. 'If they want to see blood,' he said, 'the price goes up accordingly.' "

Hoping that their money would go up accordingly, thanks to a hit record, were the **Uglys**. Their manager, John Singer, had negotiated a recording contract with Pye Records, and **Steve Gibbons**, **Jim Holden** and **Bob Burlison** had composed the song that would be their recording debut, 'Wake Up My Mind'. Just prior to the session at the Pye studios, Steve had been browsing around the Bull Ring market stalls where he'd chanced upon a whacking great harmonica.

"I'd always been frustrated about the fact that I couldn't play anything," said Steve, "So I bought this really big harmonica. It had a sound like an accordion and we used it on the introduction for 'Wake Up My Mind'.

When 'Wake Up My Mind' was released it received only one radio plug, on Radio Luxembourg, before disappearing into oblivion. It was mid summer 1965 and the Uglys were touring Devon and Cornwall in the company of **Mike Sheridan and the Nightriders**, the **Hellions**, from Worcester, and Bobby Coral's Wolverhampton based **Zuider Zee**. Zuider Zee attempted to boost their booking fees by making out, in mock Dutch accents that they were 'Direct from Holland', even going as far as wearing traditional caps and clogs for stage wear.

The Uglys

"The summer tour was a great idea," said Steve Gibbons. "All village halls packed with locals and holidaymakers. During our act I'd pick up my huge harmonica and announce our latest recording."

It was whilst the Uglys were in North Devon that a telegram arrived from Carlton Johns, reading, 'Record in Australian top twenty!'

Thanks to Australia's number one disc jockey, Bob Rogers, 'Wake Up My Mind' had been played to awaken his listeners every morning on his breakfast show. After partying for the rest of the week, the Uglys received a further telegram. 'Congratulations, Record Number 1 in Australia.'

"We were so overwhelmed," Steve Gibbons explained. "With our first attempt, we'd hit a number one spot and we thought we were going to be loaded. Then we looked at the Pye contract. It was farthings here and farthings there."

Picking up pennies here and there but building a reputation as they did so were the **Stringbeats**. Sharing the bill with the American husband and wife team of Inez and Charlie Foxx had done wonders for them amongst the 'mod' fraternity but once the expenses had been deducted from the Stringbeats' gross income, it seemed there was very little left to spend on the luxuries of life.

"We were beginning to travel as far as Kidderminster, to **Frank Freeman's** ballroom," the Stringbeats' vocalist **Austin Griffith** (better known nowadays as **Mel Day**) explained. "It was there that we supported their local hero, **Jess Roden**, with his **Shakedown Sound**, who was just so great and was making waves on the London scene."

Inspired by Jess Roden's success in London, the Stringbeats punted around for a London engagement and came up with a date at Greenwich Town Hall.

"We weren't used to long distances and didn't have any money for overnight accommodation," said Austin.

So, armed with sleeping bags, soap, toothbrushes and shavers, the Stringbeats headed for the Smoke, for Greenwich, and whatever the future beheld. Delivering their high-energy show to the Town Hall revellers, while dodging the occasional falling piece of decorative plasterwork, the

Stringbeats excelled themselves. With the gig over and the gear packed, they drove back as far north as they could until overcome by the need for shuteye. This state descended on the Stringbeats even before they had passed Luton, and so they did the obvious thing and parked up... on the hard shoulder of the M1 motorway! Laying out their sleeping bags across amplifiers and speaker cabinets, five sleepy Stringbeats changed into their pyjamas, sipped stewed tea from a thermos flask and wished each other sweet dreams. Turning out the interior light, the Stringbeats drifted into golden slumbers.

"The motorway police went absolutely crazy!" said Austin, still bewildered by the authorities' reaction in the early-hours. "They were banging on the sides of the van, shouting 'Wake up inside there!' We climbed out in our dressing gowns and carpet slippers, wondering what the fuss was all about!"

The eighteen-year-old **Ace Kefford** and the sixteen-year-old **Trevor Burton** couldn't understand what the fuss was about.

"We just wanted to be mods," said Ace. "Everyone seemed older than us. We wanted to be part of what was really happening."

At the **Cedar Club**, Ace and Trevor witnessed a performance by the inspirational Jess Roden and the Shakedown Sound.

"The Shakedown Sound took our breath. Jess Roden, was doing this great song 'Leavin' Here', an Eddie Holland number that had the longest intro in the history of the pop record," Ace explained. "Plus Jess and his band had this tremendous mod image. Me and Trevor were trapped inside these Montague Burton outfits."

Itching with ambition, Trevor Burton and Ace Kefford nervously approached Jess Roden, inviting him to become part of a new and exciting project but their offer fell on deaf ears. Unperturbed, the two lads ventured once more to the Cedar to see a London mod band, managed by John Singer's former partner Ralph Horton, that had built a hot reputation for themselves — Davey Jones and the Upper Third.

"There was that song again!" exclaimed Ace. "Eddie Holland's 'Leavin' Here'."

Seeking an audience with Davey Jones in the quieter atmosphere of the Cedar restaurant, Trevor and Ace were advised by the spikey haired mod to follow their dream. (Davey Jones followed his own dream, which eventually turned to reality four years later when his 'Space Oddity', featuring a Rolf Harris Stylophone, caught the public's imagination. By then he was known as David Bowie.)

"We laid it on **Roy Wood**," Trevor Burton recalls. "He was more our age group and had the same drive and ambition that we had."

Ace takes up the **Move** story. "Charlie Wayne guessed there was something in the air. He was four years older than us but he wanted in and agreed to change his image."

Oddity — 'Can you tell what it is yet?'

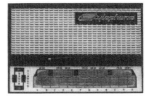

Carl Wayne had actually agreed to change his image some three or four months previously when the London agent, Roy Tempest, had shown great interest in promoting the careers of **Carl Wayne and the Vikings**. Making the point that the band's name was far too outdated for comfort, the whizzbanging agent had renamed them the **Sweet and Lovelies**.

"We may have been a lot of things but we were never sweet and lovely!" said Carl. "That idea didn't last too long."

Trevor Burton picks up, "With Carl Wayne aboard it seemed the natural thing to let **Bev Bevan** in on what was happening and we began to rehearse. From the start we knew we'd make it."

"That's exactly right," said Ace. "It was never "Whether we'd get there, it was always when we'd get there!"

Al **Jackson** had, in his opinion, given his blood in the name of Brumbeat. A version of the Kinks' 'I Go To Sleep' by the **Applejacks** had failed to awaken any excitement with the record buying public. Their next effort, 'I'm Through', meeting with the same negative reaction, was about to become Al's swansong. One of the last engagements Al Jackson had undertaken with the Applejacks was a concert in Copenhagen. Arriving at the port of Esberg, the Danish authorities refused to believe their claims that work permits had been obtained. The Applejacks spent a night in custody until the police had confirmation of the papers. Enough was enough as far as Al was concerned. Following in his father's footsteps, he headed for a career as a publican.

Heading for the nearest bar, which in this case was the **Elbow Room**, were the **Uglys**. Their second pitch at the charts, 'It's Alright', again an Uglys original, was given a spin by BBC disc jockey Alan 'Fluff' Freeman.

"After the record finished, Fluff declared, 'That's the Uglys! Looks like a big one!' Then the phone rang," chuckled Steve Gibbons, "It was **Jim Holden**. 'Did you 'ear what 'e just said?' he asked"

'It's Alright' was all right. On arrival at the Pye studios to record the song, the new keyboard player **Jimmy 'the Dish' O'Neill** (so called because 'Fab' magazine described him as 'dishy') had spotted a harpsichord standing idly in the corner. Intending to open 'It's Alright' on piano, Jimmy O'Neill discovered instead the joy of bringing a little 'Mozart' into the proceedings. **John Singer** called everyone involved to the Elbow Room for celebration drinks. 'It's Alright' had sold consistently enough over the week following the radio comments to more or less guarantee a chart position.

Steve continued, "Then the pressing factory went on strike and all the distribution collapsed. So we were back where we started."

Decca Records, in October of 1965, were busy pressing copies of the **Moody Blues** fifth single, 'Everyday'. It had been ten months since 'Go Now' had swept them to international stardom, but the all-important follow up top ten hit had eluded them. If the record buyers were losing faith with the Moody Blues, the hierarchy of the music business certainly wasn't. The Beatles had the utmost admiration for them, and their manager, Brian Epstein had enough belief in the Moody Blues to take them under his wing. 'Everyday' was released and given the necessary promotion to create interest. However the **Denny Laine** line in the song, 'Love comes and goes in a day', was strangely prophetic.

"That just about summed it all up," sighed **Clint Warwick**. "One minute you're headline news. Next minute you're yesterday's chip paper."

Through their business association with **Brian Epstein**, the Moody Blues found themselves out on tour with the Beatles around this time. To their surprise, Paul McCartney was as disappointed as they were about their failure to find the song that would put them back up where they belonged.

"Paul was so enthusiastic about a song he'd heard in a New York folk club." explained Clint. "It had been recorded by the Limelighters, but, according to Paul, the song had 'Moodies' written all over it."

The Moodies — still blue

When the Moody Blues gathered round a piano in a Scottish hotel to hear Paul McCartney give an impromptu performance of the song, before even hearing it, the Moodies believed it a mere formality before they would be back in favour with the nation.

"But after Paul finished another chorus of 'Those Were the Days', there was absolute silence before Denny refused point blank to give the song a second thought," said Clint. "Everyone thought Paul was off his rocker."

Three years later, the McCartney-produced recording of Mary Hopkin's 'Those Were the Days' was a worldwide smash hit.

In November '65 **Roy Everett** left the **Blueshounds** to take up the honourable profession of greengrocery. Replaced by **Pete Hodges**, Roy's farewell gig with the Blueshounds was the Zambezi Club in High Street, Hounslow, described by Dave Pegg as 'the worst gig on God's earth!'

Perhaps the Zambezi resembled a Chicken Shack. If it did, then that maybe it was the inspiration for Stourbridge's **Sounds of Blue** to change their name to, yes, **Chicken Shack**; although their flautist, **Chris Wood**, didn't hang around too long as he had a train to catch. He was about to board the **Locomotive**.

Sheet music specialists –
Crane & Sons,
& Kay Westorth's

Ayesha Brough

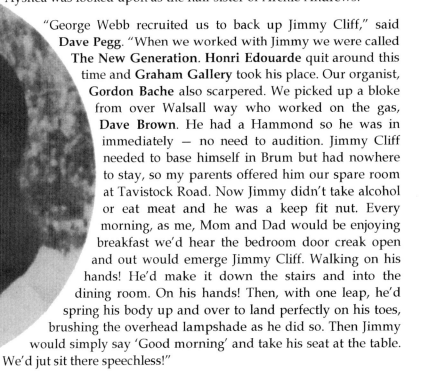

The **Monopoly** had been making the most of their residency at **Tito's** club on Soho Hill, building up a strong repertoire of material, enabling **Raymond Froggatt**'s confidence as a performer to grow stronger by the day.

"Monopoly had a motto, 'Don't just play it, listen to it!'" said Froggy, punching the air with his clenched fist.

Hartley Cain was always on the lookout for songs that would distinguish Monopoly from other outfits. 'H' would make regular trips to **Crane's** music shop or to **Kay Westworth's** in Cannon Street, where, under the supervision of **Bill Pickering**, sheet music was a speciality.

On one such excursion, Hartley Cain purchased, for the sum of two shillings and six pence, a copy of sheet music that would showcase their vocalist as, if audience reaction was anything to go by, the prospective candidate for the second coming of the Messiah. For half a crown, Hartley Cain provided Raymond Froggatt with a lyric that would firstly fire up Raymond's quite unique voice and charismatic stage presence and secondly plant a seed in his imagination that would eventually inspire him to weave his own dream. It would allow Raymond Froggatt to 'Hear laughter spinning madly across the sun that was far from the twisted reach of crazy sorrow'. The said purchase was Bob Dylan's four-verse poetic masterpiece 'Mr Tambourine Man'.

Meanwhile, back in London, **George Webb** had a new artiste under his wing. A Jamaican soul singing lad by the name of **Jimmy Cliff**, who had a female back up singer in permanent tow, **Ayshea Brough**. Her father, Peter, had carved himself a niche in life where skill was an optional extra. For years he'd made an excellent living as a ventriloquist performing on radio! For listeners of the BBC Light Programme's 'Educating Archie', Ayshea was looked upon as the half sister of Archie Andrews!

"George Webb recruited us to back up Jimmy Cliff," said **Dave Pegg**. "When we worked with Jimmy we were called **The New Generation**. **Honri Edouarde** quit around this time and **Graham Gallery** took his place. Our organist, **Gordon Bache** also scarpered. We picked up a bloke from over Walsall way who worked on the gas, **Dave Brown**. He had a Hammond so he was in immediately — no need to audition. Jimmy Cliff needed to base himself in Brum but had nowhere to stay, so my parents offered him our spare room at Tavistock Road. Now Jimmy didn't take alcohol or eat meat and he was a keep fit nut. Every morning, as me, Mom and Dad would be enjoying breakfast we'd hear the bedroom door creak open and out would emerge Jimmy Cliff. Walking on his hands! He'd make it down the stairs and into the dining room. On his hands! Then, with one leap, he'd spring his body up and over to land perfectly on his toes, brushing the overhead lampshade as he did so. Then Jimmy would simply say 'Good morning' and take his seat at the table. We'd jut sit there speechless!"

William's Conquerors were also speechless. After winning the Midland Beat contest back in June of 1965, and beating such talented opposition as the **UK Bonds**, the **Shooting Stars**, the **Martells**, **Size Six** and the **Telstars**, William's Conquerors were awarded a recording test with Alan Freeman of Pye Records. In October, four months later, as William's Conquerors played the Witch Doctor Club, on Hastings sea front of all places, they received the good news that Pye were offering a recording contract.

"That was one in the eye for all our doubters," said guitarist **Bob Adams**.

Having serious doubts about the future and what it held for him was **Pat Wayne**: "EMI had not renewed my contract and, as a result of the sax players scarpering, the **Beachcombers** were now down to a three piece with guitarist **Eric Ashcroft**, **Mel Edwards** on bass and **Brian Sharp** on the drums."

When Brian Sharp made known his intentions of retirement from the rapidly changing rock scene, Eric Ashcroft introduced the Beachcombers to young drummer who was looking for a break. At the **Three Men in a Boat** pub, Walsall, the young lad settled onto the drum stool to demonstrate his percussive prowess. Pat Wayne suggested trying what had been their most successful recording, 'Roll over Beethoven', and the lad at the kit counted the band in.

"Then whoosh!" exclaimed Pat. "Off he kicked. And how! That was our introduction to **John Bonham**."

John Bonham's first engagement with Pat Wayne and the Beachcombers was at the **Golden Diamond** club, Sutton in Ashfield, Nottinghamshire.

"John had the use of his father's delivery van," Pat explained, "A Ford Anglia van."

The Beachcombers called for John at the gents' outfitters in Redditch town centre, where he was working as an assistant, in order that he could follow the band to Sutton in Ashfield. With his drums crammed into the back of the small van, John pursued the Beachcombers as they whizzed around the back lanes of Earlswood and Solihull, en route to the East Midlands.

Pat tells the tale, "I kept John in my rear view so as not to lose him. In the middle of nowhere, two cars came thundering towards us, overtaking each other. I slammed on the brakes to let them through and shut my eyes, waiting for John to plough into the back of me…but he didn't."

Looking in his mirror, Pat could see John Bonham running frantically towards them in the middle of the country lane.

"Pat!" he cried, "I've turned the ol' man's van over. It's in the ditch back there!"

Piling John and his drums into their Bedford, the Beachcombers abandoned Mr Bonham's van and continued to the Golden Diamond club.

"We had 30watt amplifiers and, at the start, I had a voice," chuckled Pat. "John's drumming was magnificent, but it was a sheer powerhouse of volume. We couldn't make ourselves heard above it all. The manager of the Golden Diamond commented that the Beachcombers had become a 'drum-show'."

On the way home, and in the pouring rain, the Beachcombers, knee deep in mud and rainwater, managed to haul John Bonham's van out of the ditch. Fortunately the engine started first time, and the sorry looking convoy could limp home.

Shortly after this episode, the Beachcombers, arriving at an Irish pub in Kilburn, North London, were greeted by a poster in the hallway that proclaimed, 'Tonight — The Beachcombers, featuring the glamorous Pat Wayne.'

"I thought there and then, this is where I came in," mused Pat.

Bookers became extremely wary of John Bonham's drumming volume, and the Beachcombers, already in decline, were heading straight for the rocks. For what were to be their last few engagements, the Beachcombers chose to use the services of **Mike Kellie**, who was just feeling his way into the **Blueshounds**.

Six years later, with **Led Zeppelin** flying high around the world, Pat Wayne and John Bonham sat, one sunny afternoon, in the back garden of John's house at Hagley.

"We were having a few beers and laughing about the old days and I asked John if he remembered the Golden Diamond night and turning his dad's van over." said Pat. "John stood up, smiled, and said, 'Follow me.' We walked down the garden, and there, behind the rose bushes was the old Anglia van. 'It's there to remind me of the good times we shared.' he said."

Carlton Dance Orchestra at St Paul's Hall, Moseley "That's my memory of John Bonham. He was a very thoughtful and most gentle man. At his funeral, and please don't take what I'm about to say as flippant or disrespectful, his mother hugged me and sighed, 'Oh Pat, if only John had stayed with you.' God bless you John."

Kings Norton's **Sovereigns** had given their all to making music a professional career but, after riding the waves at a Pontins holiday camp, it was back to semi-professional status for them. Whilst at Pontins, the Sovereigns had been approached by two ambitious London based songwriters who had a few sovereigns of their own to blow away.

"These blokes booked us into Advision studios for the day," **Dave Evans** of the Sovereigns explained, "and we put down the backing track for one of their songs, 'If I Ever Lost Your Love'. We put the vocals on at Abbey Road, all paid for by these two blokes. But, in all honesty, the song was just too square."

With everything looking too square for the Sovereigns they disbanded. **Tony Lawrence**, their lead guitarist, joined the **Karlton Squares**, a combo that had the Kings Norton rock scene more or less sewn up. A scene that comprised of the **Saracen's Head** youth club, **St Nicholas Church Hall** and the odd bash at the **Breedon Cross** pub. The Karlton Squares; guitarist **Derek Crump**, drummer **Dave Templar** and bass player **Malc Edwards**, had vocalists **Ernie Barnhurst** and **Jill Gittins** doing their 'Pearl Carr and Teddy Johnson' bits out front. The band was actually a continuation of the **Carlton Dance Orchestra** that accordionist **Percy Edwards** (Malc's father) and had led in the late thirties. In those days the orchestra, which performed regularly at **St Paul's Hall**, Moseley Road, Balsall Heath, featured, the heart-throb crooner, **Dicky Marson**. Dick, a Small Heath man, had turned the ladies' heads with a little soul coaxing by way of 'Mexicali Rose' or maybe 'South of the Border', à la Al Bowley.

Spencer Davis Group

The first week of December 1965 saw the **Spencer Davis Group's** fourth single 'Keep On Runnin'' hit the number one slot on the charts in no uncertain terms. It was far removed from the demo recording that the composer, Jackie Edwards, had submitted to Fontana boss Jack Baverstock. The original 'feel' was laid back ska with a quaintly soft guide vocal. However, on the Spencer Davis cut, **Muff Winwood's** bass line rode raucously on the groove that drummer **Pete York** dictated. Influenced by Keith Richard's use of the fuzz-box on the Rolling Stone's Summer hit, 'Satisfaction', **Stevie Winwood** applied the newly discovered effect liberally when accentuating the featured chord change which held the piece together. With regard to his vocal delivery, Stevie's approach to the song and the result that he achieved was simply superb.

Let's party – the Bobcats at the Custard House

Burning with ambition to hammer the daylights out of the drums was thirteen-year-old **Les Fortnam**. In 1963 his father, Tony, had been licensee of the **Acorn** pub in Wheeler Street, Lozells, which housed the **Downbeat Club**. At every session Les would gaze in awe at the man behind the sacred kit, and yearn that one day he would be that man. One night at the Downbeat, his prayers were answered.

"What dad was sticking in the beer was anyone's guess," said Les, "But this drummer arrived, had a couple of pints and passed out!"

Whilst Tony Fortnam walked the poor lad up and down Wheeler Street in an effort to sober him up, his son Les took to the drum stool. Picking up the sticks he counted the band in, and let them have it. Two years on and his family were now in charge of the **Custard House**, Blake Lane, Small Heath. Three schoolboys, **Dave Cowley**, **Garry Hedges** and **Paul Willington,** all from Alderlea School at Shard End arrived with their guitars, to participate in the weekend free-and-easy at the pub. With the addition of drummer Les, the boys, with an average age of fourteen, became the **Bobcats**.

It wasn't so much age as size with Great Barr's **Little People**. Formerly known as the **Ramblers**, their singer, **Jeff Keane**, informed manager **Bruce Jordan** that with a marriage pending, his the rock 'n' roll days were over. **John Starkey** was the guitarist with the Little People and he immediately alerted his old Senator pal, **Ronny Smith**, that a situation was about to become vacant in the bird-pulling department. There was an added incentive. Bruce Jordan had convinced producer **Reg Watson,** of ATV, that the Little People were worthy of an appearance on 'For Teenagers Only'. Ronny Smith arrived confidently at the Co-op Rooms, just across from the Clifton cinema at Great Barr and completed his audition successfully, satisfying **Paul Simms**, the keyboard player, bass player **Mick Avery** and drummer **Dave Potter** of his worthiness to be a Little People person. Ronny now looked forward to his television debut as Ronny Smith, having shaken off the Tab Memphis tab. Then came the bad news. With the Little People already rehearsed for camera angles, ATV stated that Ronny Smith would not be required for the live transmission. Sick with burning envy, Ronny could only sit at home, his dinner balanced precariously on his knees, and wait for the Little People to come bouncing out of his nineteen-inch Bush television screen.

"There they were," said Ronny, "The Little People parading about, dressed up as tin toy soldiers. I've never been so happy to be left out of anything in my life!"

At Rediffusion House, the offices of ATV, in Edmund Street, the cast and crew of the popular Birmingham-based soap opera 'Crossroads' were holding their Christmas party, and had engaged the services of the **Blueshounds**.

"**Frankie Devine**, our drummer, was an angry young man," explained **Dave Pegg**, "We just soldiered through the gig but all the bull got too much for Frankie."

The angry young man expressed his frustrations by head-butting a window. Unfortunately Frank Devine's 'Glasgow kiss' shattered the glass. **Noele Gordon**, 'Crossroads' principle 'luvvie', placed a comforting arm around the

Danny King & the Mayfair Set

shoulders of the rebel without a cause.

"Never mind," she said sweetly, "He's through the pane now."

Pain of the emotional kind was about to present itself to **Terry Wallace** on the afternoon of Christmas Eve, 1965. His band, the **Vikings**, keen researchers of Indian cuisine and its effects on the digestive system, met for a late lunch at the **Bombay**, a restaurant on the corner of Essex Street, before carrying on up Bristol Road for an evening performance at the **Station** pub, Selly Oak. Also present at the festive curry bash along with Vikings Terry Wallace, **Carl Wayne** and **Ace Kefford**, were **Danny King** and **Trevor Burton** of the **Mayfair Set**.

"We all had the Christmas spirit," said Terry, "None of us were making it big but it didn't seem to matter, or so I believed. Then came the bombshell. Carl Wayne was facing me over the table and suddenly said, 'Terry, I want you to listen to what I have to say. I'm leaving the band.' My reaction was

Carl Wayne & the Vikings at Coleshill Youth Club

'Oh, here we go again.' Carl was always going to leave, but he never ever did. As I laughed, he interrupted quite sternly. 'Terry,' he said so forcibly that a hush fell over the rest of the company, 'This time it's for real. I'm leaving and I'm taking Bev and Ace with me. What you do is up to you but for us, it's over. Roy Wood and Trevor are joining us. We're making a move.' At the Station pub that night, the atmosphere was awful. **Johnny Mann** arrived and I broke the bad news. He, like me, took it personally. We both quit there and then. After seven years hard slog, building the band from nothing, the Vikings were all washed up."

Chapter Five

1966

IN THE JINGLE JANGLE MORNING

"Roy Wood was such an intrinsic part of our show," said **Mike Sheridan**. "It was such a blow. I know it sounds corny but for me, Roy was irreplaceable. He'd figure so strongly in the **Nightriders'** cabaret routine. **Roger Spencer** used to do his 'Jimmy Saville' bit with a huge cigar, "Ow's about that then guys and gals!' and introduce Roy who'd be wigged up as Dusty Springfield!"

An early Move gig at Coleshill Youth Club

Roger Spencer had had his own suspicions that things were changing. "Me and Mike Sheridan called into Roy's house the week before Christmas," said Roger, "And there sat the young dudes, Ace, Bev, and Trevor with **Carl Wayne**. It was obvious they'd been rehearsing."

"That's when we had to come clean," said **Ace Kefford**. "The truth was we hated ourselves for being so secretive to blokes who were mates, but we had to bust out of Birmingham before it was too late. But what's important is we were so inspirational to the Brum scene."

New Years eve 1965 saw **'Sprike' Hopkins** topping up his Christmas coffers as a temporary Viking, while at the **Belfry**, Wishaw, **William's Conquerors** were making their last appearance as semi-professional musicians. From now on they were to be regarded as full time pros. To let the New Year in good and proper, guitarist **Bob Adams**, arriving home from the Belfry, ploughed the group's van straight through the substantial double wooden doors of his garage. This drunken error of judgement had such a profound effect on drummer **Bryan Miles** that he decided that the rock 'n' roll lifestyle was no longer for him, and made way for **Derek 'Pecker' Woodward**. Derek had recently returned from an engagement in France with the Yardley Wood outfit, **Deuces Wild**. Whilst in France, they had existed solely on a diet of red wine and cheese.

"They'd been smashed and constipated for the whole trip!" commented the Deuces' **Brian Harbison**.

R oy Wood and **Trevor Burton** took advantage of the lull that always follows the storm of Hogmanay hootenannies to make their final preparations for the launch of the **Move**. Their live debut appearance was at the **Belfry**, and by January 28th they were making their first recording for radio. It was a rude awakening for the sound engineers at the BBC studios on Broad Street, who were more used to mellow melody makers like the **Ken Rattenbury Band**.

The programme, entitled 'One Night Stand', was presented by local broadcaster **Tom Coyne**, and transmitted on 2nd February. Alongside the Move on the show were **William's Conquerors**, who, like the Move, were newcomers to the airwaves. They performed 'Education', by Bob Adams and 'She', the Brian Harbison song that was scheduled to be their first release on the Pye label.

Ken Rattenbury Band with Stan Upcot on guitar, at the BBC's Broad Street studio

S cheduled to be pulling up at the Crown, Hill Street, just at the rear of New Street Station, was the **Locomotive**. The Locomotive were an exciting re-shape of the **Blueshounds** with **Pete Hodges** laying down his soulful 'Otis' touch. Alongside Pete was a powerhouse of brass that was **Jim Simpson, John Barry** and **Brian 'Monk' Finch**. Bass player **Pete Allen** and drummer **Mike Kellie** laid down the groove, while Hammond organ duties were in the hands of a young Geordie lad, **Rick Storey**. Rick, originally from Whickham, Tyne and Weir, was a teacher at Sundial Junior School, Great Barr. Recording engineer **Johnny Haines** had met Rick whilst they were studying together at Venerable Bede College, County Durham.

"Rick Storey was the keyboard player in a local band up there, the Rakes." said Johnny. "I sold Rick on the idea of moving to Birmingham. Once he was here I had him doing the sessions at my studio and that's how he met with the Jim Simpson fraternity."

S oon to be mixing with the elite fraternity of the nation's hit makers, the Liberators were a bunch of lads from Rugby, the town which happened to be the base location of pop music entrepreneur **Reg Calvert** and his pop star academy. The Liberators — singing guitarists **Tony Newman** and **Tom Long**, bassist **Barry Bernard**, drummer **Dave Holland**, and **Sam 'Pinkerton' Kempe**, who rippled the autoharp — had been doing the rounds of the Regan ballrooms and pretty well anywhere else that would accommodate

them. Feeling quietly confident, the Liberators took a stroll along to **Clifton Hall**, seeking the career guidance of Mr Calvert. Could he open doors for them as he had for others? His reaction was more than positive. He kitted them out with colourful jackets, and, making use of Sam Kempe's nickname, launched the boys as **Pinkerton's Assorted Colours**. Reg then secured them a deal with Decca Records, and by mid-January of 1966 they were in the top ten, with the Tony Newman composition 'Mirror Mirror'.

Pinkerton's Assorted Colours on Ready Steady Go

Keeping company with the Pinkertons in the January charts, Birmingham's **Second City Sound** were bringing a classical flavour to the hit parade, with their instrumental single, 'Tchaikovsky One'. Combining first class musicianship and professional stage presentation, the Second City Sound's driving force was pianist **Ken Freeman**. Not only was Ken an outstanding maestro on the piano, he was also an impressive exponent of electronic keyboards, and his expert use of the Clavioline demonstrated these skills perfectly. Ken Freeman had been, pre Second City Sound, a member of the **Unsquare Men**, as had guitarist **Alan Nicklin** and drummer **Dan Conboy**. **Billy Gilbert**, their bass player, and vocalist **Des Ryan**, had served their apprenticeships with the **Plainsmen** showband, which regularly entertained the 'excitable' audiences of the **Shamrock** and the **Pink Elephant** clubs. Fortunately for Des and Billy, albeit a slow process, the wounds were beginning to heal.

Second City Sound

If crowd pulling was anything to go by, the Second City Sound would have been right there at the toppermost of the poppermost! Their residencies at the **Viking** pub, Ulleries Road, Solihull and the **Raven** at Stechford caused queues to start forming a good hour before opening time. Once inside, the punters were treated not just to fine musicianship, but also to the delights of guest vocalist **Polly Brown**, whose smooth romantic tones caused many a strong man to buckle at the knees. Polly, or to be correct, Pauline, had briefly been a member of **Carl and the Cheetahs** back in 1963.

"Pauline called me up and asked if she could do a couple of songs with us," explained **Euan Rose**, drummer with the Cheetahs. "This was way before our EMI deal and she came along to the **Black Cat Club** at Colmores Farm School, Rubery. She was tremendous and oozed class. I was sure that one day she'd make it good."

Euan Rose was correct of course. Polly Brown emerged, in 1970, to lay her velvet tones on 'That Same Old Feeling' and '(It's Like a) Sad Old Kinda Movie', which were both big hits for the band Pickettywitch.

Second City Sound with Polly Brown

Getting that same old feeling of looking round for a guitarist were the Uglys. Auditions were held at the **Carlton**, Erdington, and **Roger Hill** and **Dave Pegg** were among the hopefuls.

"The job went to Roger," said Dave, "But I took it like a man."

Roger Hill & Dave Pegg

As Dave Pegg headed for the door, leader **Steve Gibbons** asked him if, by any chance he fancied filling another vacancy in the Uglys that was about to arise — on bass guitar!

"The decision to become a bass player, and incidentally I bought **Dave Husthwaite**'s Fender Precision bass off him there and then, completely changed my working life, and so much for the better." said Dave

Without any knowledge whatsoever of the instrument or comprehension of bass patterns, Dave Pegg set to work in order to master the necessary techniques.

Also addressing his technique on bass guitar was **Les Hemming**. His outfit, the **Casemakers** could now be considered a travelling band. They were playing engagements as far away as Walsall! Coming heavily under the influence of the jazzy styled Peddlers, Les chose to ape their bass guitarist and perch himself on a stool whilst picking out his very own two to the bar improvisations.

At the **Caves Club**, Walsall, one evening in the spring of 1966, Les announced into his Reslo microphone, "Okay, all you good people out there, we're gonna take five. So stay real cruel and we'll catch you later." Les removed his Burns Trisonic bass from around his neck, leant it against the wall and reached for his Nut Brown ale.

Les Hemming continues, "A local hard-knock, Sammy Holmes, walked through the door at that very moment and a chilling gasp shuddered around the room."

Sammy Holmes had, that morning, been released from HM Winson Green Prison. Seeking the whereabouts of his estranged wife, Sammy's search had led him to the Caves, where he found his lady in the arms of another man. Reaching for the nearest object, in this case Les's Trisonic bass, Sammy smashed it over the head of his wife's lover. To compensate for his son's loss, Mr Hemming senior bought, in ignorance, from a shy and reserved used car salesman, an extremely rare Fender Jaguar guitar for fifty pounds. At the Jones and Crossland music shop, young Les exchanged the Jaguar guitar for a brand new blonde Epiphone bass, as used by the Peddlers' bass guitarist. The Casemakers all fired up, arrived at **Zella** studios to record the Les Hemming composition 'I'm Gonna Make a Habit of Loving You'.

"As we were getting a sound balance there was a young kid jamming on the keyboard over in the corner," Les explained. "He asked me if it was okay for him to sit in on the session and I said only if he worked for nothing. No royalties, no nothing, and he agreed. I still have the tape of **Stevie Winwood** sitting in with us that day."

A master of the 'play it cool' technique, **Danny King** played it cool in his efforts to replace **Trevor Burton**, now a member of the **Move**.

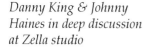

Danny King & Johnny Haines in deep discussion at Zella studio

"**Roger Harris**, our keyboard player, was talking on the phone to someone who'd called about Trevor's job," Danny explained. "Roger passed me the

phone and I asked the caller to tell me a little about himself. He said his name was **Dave Morgan** and he played guitar, sang and wrote songs. I told him he could start the following Monday!"

The Move 'backstage' at the Silver Blades Ice Rink

"I got the Move one of their earliest gigs and like all new bands, they needed the work," **Johnny Haines** recalls. "It was a Saturday dance at my old college, **St Peters**, Saltley. **Charlie Wayne** and his lot were going a storm. Then the principle of the college, Cannon Platton, asked me to tell the Move to pack up as it was turned midnight."

When John Haines refused to interfere, the good Cannon leapt on stage and, crawling round the back of the amplifiers, began tugging at mains leads in a desperate effort to silence the band.

"We're now into the seventh day, and on the seventh day God rested!" shouted the extremely reverend Cannon Platton to Carl Wayne.

Carl just snarled back, "Keep messing with them wires mate and you'll be having your Sunday dinner with him!"

The redundant **Viking**, **Johnny Mann** had by this time, swapped his grey suit for a tartan blazer to become a **Nightrider**. With the new boy in place **Mike Sheridan** and the boys were engaged to appear on the local events television show 'ATV Today'. With **Johnny Mann** fully installed there was no question as to who would be picking lead guitar on the small screen.

"**Fred Wood**, Roy's dad, did his nut," said **Roger Spencer**. "I told Fred not to worry. He'd soon be sick of seeing **Roy Wood** on the telly!"

For Mike Sheridan however, the fun days were over and he soon took early retirement (his first of many) from the music scene, to take up what he describes as 'a 'tater round', selling potatoes from the back of a truck!

Seeking a career for themselves were the four schoolboys, the **Bobcats**. **Fred Cowley**, who could play a fair tune on the mouth organ, and whose son Dave was guitarist with the band, was appointed their manager. With successful appearances at the **Custard House** pub free and easies, the Bobcats were plunged into the world of showbusiness. Their first engagement was at the **Tyseley Workingmen's Club** on Warwick Road, just below Yardley Grammar School. From there they progressed to both **Old** and **New Oscott** social clubs and word spread like wildfire across the domino and crib tables that these Bobcats were cool dudes, even though they arrived and departed from engagements in full school uniform!

The Uglys

Dave Pegg could well be described as a real cool dude. It was a glorious Cornish Sunday morning. He and his band, the **Uglys**, had appeared at

the Flamingo Ballroom, Portreath the night before. Waking to the sounds of the seagulls and the Wilfred Pickles' 'Have A Go' radio programme, Dave figured there was nothing more likely to fire the appetite for a seaside breakfast than a morning stroll. Strolling along the coastal path he slipped and plummeted two hundred feet down the side of the cliffs.

"They got me into Truro hospital but I was okay. The Uglys were ecstatic," said Dave. "The story made the Daily Sketch!"

Johnny Washington, formerly known as **George E Washington** of the **Congressmen**, was more of a 'Birmingham Mail' man. Whilst browsing through the early edition, his attention was drawn to an advertisement. A nationally known band with chart success needed a singer urgently for a cruising engagement aboard the Cunard liner the 'Queen Mary'. However, whilst being welcomed aboard the **Applejacks** 'trip around the bay', Johnny Washington was unwittingly joining a sinking ship.

Johnny Washington

"Next to parting company with **Joe Brannelly**, working the liners was the most stupid thing the Applejacks did," stated **Phil Cash**. "We should have stuck out for another couple of hits and traded on our name instead of clearing off around the world in such confined space."

Feeling the pressure of confined space whilst a member of **the Fortunes** was guitarist and vocalist **Glen Dale**.

"After 'Troubles', Les Reed and Barry Mason wrote 'Here it Comes Again' especially for us," said **Rod Allen**. "It even had the chat line in the middle."

Rod continues, "We couldn't have wished for a better song and it was a top five smash. For our next release we chose another Greenaway and Cook song, 'This Golden Ring' which made the top twenty, but not with the same zest as the other two had. Glen felt his future prospects would be better as a solo artist."

The Fortunes replaced Glen Dale temporarily with **Peter Lee Stirling**, formerly of Tommy Bruce's Bruisers, and now established as a jobbing songwriter. Perhaps that was part of the reason for Peter being asked into the line up.

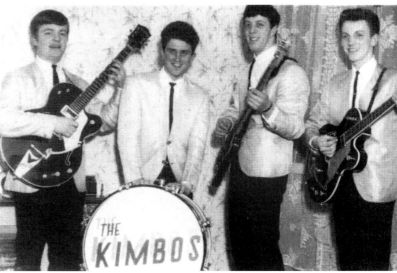

The Kimbos

"I'd known Reg Calvert for years as he used to book us when we were the original **Beachcombers**," said Peter. "Of course it followed that the Fortunes were mates from the early days back in Birmingham. I remember doing a few dates down on the south coast and then a couple of shows in Ireland and Scotland with them."

When the Fortunes made it to the Olympia ballroom, in East Kilbride, Scotland, they couldn't help but be impressed with the singing guitarist who was fronting the house band, the **Kimbos**. **Andy Semple**, or, as he was to become professionally known, **Shel Macrae**, was in possession of a voice that would marry quite perfectly into the Fortunes' format.

Dusting himself down was **Johnny Carroll**, who'd decided to hang up his dustman dungarees for good and, as with the others who made up the **Vogues**, **Ron Dickson**, **Brian Betteridge** and **Steve Price**, become a full time member of the music profession.

"Turning professional meant the North, and the clubs," said Johnny. "We did the Princess and Domino Club in Manchester for a week, with the comedian Ken Goodwin. He was an extremely funny man."

Such was the effect of Ken Goodwin's humour on the Vogues that, during the homeward journey, they relived every word of every gag amongst themselves, collapsing hysterically at the silly nonsensical punchlines. Back from their Manchester club experiences, the Vogues arrived, courtesy of booker **Roger Allen**, at **the Cleveland Arms** pub, Willenhall Road, Wolverhampton.

"And we froze with nerves," recalled Johnny Carroll. "It was a sit down affair. The audience was used to showgroups like the Montanas and Finders Keepers, but we were just really a basic pop group for dancing."

Steve Price, drummer with the Vogues solved the problem. Quickly making a list of all Ken Goodwin's jokes, he placed the list on his tom tom drum, so that when Steve felt the Vogues were in danger of losing the audience's attention, he would feed Johnny Carroll a couple of quick-fire jokes to break up the show.

The Vogues at the Atlas Ballroom, Stetchford

"At the end of a song, I'd hear a shout from behind the drums, "The housewife and the milkman!'" laughed Johnny. "So I'd do the gag about the housewife calling to the milkman, 'Have you got 'alf a Stork on today,' and the milkman shouting back, 'No, it's the way the wind's blowin' my apron!' All that seaside postcard stuff got us by at the sit down cabarets that were becoming more the kind of places to play."

Eventually, Johnny Carroll mustered up the confidence to perform a fifteen-minute stand up comedy spot without the assistance of a prompt.

"Here I was again," said Johnny. "I never asked to be a singer or lead guitar player and I certainly didn't ask to be a comic."

Nevertheless, that's what he was fast becoming, and to quote the man himself with what became his catchphrase, "I'm bloody good ain' I!"

The **White Hart** pub at Headless Cross, Redditch, offered a challenge to **Mike Carroll**. He had promoted, with some success, at the **Forest** pub in nearby Lickey End. Mike had, on numerous occasions, made use of the talents of Wolverhampton's **Montanas**. They were now Pye recording artistes enjoying their first release 'All That Is Mine Can Be Yours'. Guitarist **Bill Hayward**, drummer **Graham Crew** and all rounder **Terry Rowley** were first class musicians who, with their quite superb vocalist **Johnny Jones**, performed a highly entertaining comedy mime act. With the Montanas confirmed in his diary, Mike Carroll opened for business at the White Hart.

The Montanas

"Panic over," thought Mike as the 'House Full' notice was displayed long before Johnny Jones and the lads had even plugged in.

"But I felt an uneasy atmosphere around the room," said Mike. "Then someone slipped me the word that the **Brookes brothers**, **Knocker** and **Hooter**, infamous scrappers around the Redditch area, were in."

Mike Carroll immediately offered Knocker and Hooter positions as doormen.

"You will be my security men," Mike informed them, "For which you will be well fed and watered."

Proudly the brothers, Hooter and Knocker Brookes, took stance at the entrance to the function room. Mike Carroll was a contented man. The problem had been dealt with. With the Montanas playing a blinder, Johnny Jones did a little soul coaxing by whispering into the microphone "Baby baby, I'll get down on my knees for you. If you would only…"

As Johnny Jones went for broke (and his Equity card) his meaningful tone was so cruelly interrupted by the sound of bare knuckles smacking viciously against a jawbone.

"Hooter and Knocker were punching the daylights out of each other," explained Mike Carroll, wincing slightly. "Everyone ran for it. The Montanas, the crowd and the bar staff!"

Johnny Jones still trembles at the memory of the night of unmerciful violence that remains etched in the social history of Headless Cross.

"We thought the Montanas were fireproof," said Johnny. "After all, we'd only recently finished a nationwide tour with the Walker Brothers and thought we were entitled to some respect. We had to lock ourselves in a broom cupboard with a microphone stand rammed through the door handles to stop the fight getting to us!"

The furniture had been reduced to firewood but the Montanas were safe. The fight had spilled out onto the car park. Across from the White Hart, in amongst a row of quaint village shops, was an electrical store. By the time the panda cars arrived, Hooter had sent Knocker flying through the plate glass window of that store. As police grappled with Hooter, Knocker lay sprawled out amongst the toasters, reading lamps, hair dryers and vacuum cleaners. Mike Carroll opened and closed the White Hart that evening.

Did Mike regret this impulsive and negative action? The wise man of Kings Norton chose the wording of his reply most carefully. Raising the index finger of his right hand, Mike Carroll quoted the proverb that had been his guidance throughout as he had ridden the turbulence of promoting rock 'n' roll in the ale houses of Birmingham and its surrounding areas.

Billie Davis & Keith Powell

" 'Tis only the hairs on a gooseberry that prevent it from being a grape," was the profound reply.

John Schroeder, at Pye Records, still had a profound interest in **Keith Powell**'s career and, although the professional pairing of Keith with Elkie Brookes hadn't been successful, John still believed that the answer was to find a girl singer to work alongside Keith Powell. "John came up with **Billie Davis** and she proved an absolute knockout," recalled Keith.

Billie Davis had already experienced visits to the top twenty as a solo artiste with 'Will I What' in 1962, and 'Tell Him' in 1963. When teamed with Keith Powell, the pair went for the jugular with their first recording together, handing out the advice, 'When You Move You Lose.'

As well as picking up an immense amount of radio and television plugs, Keith and Billy also picked up respect from within the rock 'n' roll hierarchy. Rolling Stone Bill Wyman managed an excellent bunch of musicians, The End, and was only too happy to have them back Billie and Keith on live appearances. The highlight of their acclaimed stage act saw Keith Powell and Billie Davis performing a quite stunning rendition of the Sam and Dave song 'You Don't Know Like I Know'. Such was audience reaction throughout the country to this routine that John Schroeder had them commit the song to tape. The recording turned out easily as powerful as the original Sam and Dave cut.

Returning from Germany were the Jones brothers, Reg and Chris. **The Chucks** had chucked it in but the Jones brothers were looking for a new way of life.

"That's what we called the band," said Reg, "**The Way of Life**."

Calling upon the services of **Sprike Hopkins** as guitarist to work alongside **Chris Jones**, they had **Tony Clarkson** to play bass and upfront, alongside Reg, the legendary **Nicky James**.

"We'd started putting gigs into the diary," continued Reg, "but we hadn't found a drummer."

The first appearance was to be on a Sunday evening at the **Cedar club**. The Way of Life spent that Sunday afternoon at the Cedar putting would-be Ringos through their paces.

Nightriders & Vikings at the Cedar Club with Danny Burns & Eddie Fewtrell

"**John Bonham** showed up and demanded the job," recalled Reg Jones. "He told all the other hopefuls to go home!"

The Way of Life played the Cedar that evening and settled into a routine of being a regular feature at the club. **Eddie Fewtrell** was a happy man. His punters loved The Way of Life. The Way of Life loved the atmosphere of Eddie's club. Mixing in with the in-crowd was a warm and special experience. **Reg Jones**, at the end of yet another successful show at the Cedar, approached Eddie Fewtrell for the band's fee, only to be told that Nicky James had run up a considerable bar tab.

"Sort it out with Nicky," advised Eddie Fewtrell, "He's flattened the lot."

"Nicky James didn't hang around very long after that!" said Reg.

Johnny Fincham, the lad who had kept the **Chantelles** alive when the Jones boys had moved on, had now altered course with a new look Chantelles. Along with a new look came a rather sophisticated new musical direction with an element of jazz creeping in to their bluesy approach. With Johnny Fincham on bass and **Tim Bellamy** from the original line up on drums, saxophonist **Tony Allen** and guitarist **Richard Tandy** were welcomed into the fold. At the **59 Club** in John Bright Street, a dark and dank cellar beneath Birmingham Skin Hospital, out-of-town commercial travellers canoodled with painted ladies of the night. In the glow of flickering candles that were rammed into milk bottles, the Chantelles enhanced hot blooded feelings with highly emotional versions of 'A New Way of Makin' You Mine' and the aptly titled 'When the Lights Go Out'. Then, just when the commercial travellers were more or less crippled with frustration, from the Chantelles would come their jump jive number, 'Life's Gettin' Tougher than Tough.'

Life wasn't so tough for Tim Bellamy, who had begun to supplement his income by becoming a part time male model. Tim, for some strange reason, chose to keep this occupational venture a little 'hush hush'. However, this aspect of his career could be contained no more when Tim was featured as the 'Barretts of Feckenham' man, appearing on High Street advertising hoardings and regularly on ATV's commercial slot 'Midlands Parade'. Posing for the camera in a Barretts sheepskin coat, the handsome and debonair Tim Bellamy adopted what is known in certain circles as the 'teapot stance' — left hand on hip, while the other hand hangs limply from the wrist. Tim Bellamy, after receiving fan mail from a lonely sailor, retired gracefully from the Chantelles to be replaced by **John 'Pank' Panteny**. To celebrate this new wave of enthusiasm within the Chantelles, manager **John 'Upsy' Downing** decided to rename the band the **New Wave**.

On the road —
the Chantelles

Digbeth Civic Hall – home of the Jug O' Punch Folk Club

With the advent of a certain Robert Zimmerman, folk music was now playing a healthy part in the Birmingham scene. **The Crown** pub, across from the Law Courts, in Corporation Street, was home to the **Peanuts** club. At the renowned **Golden Eagle** pub on Hill Street, the **Eagle** folk club met. A perambulation along Colmore Row and into Livery Street would see the **Skillet Pot** club in progress in the small assembly room above the **Old Contemptibles**. Directly facing that famous alehouse, in converted livery stables, was **Le Metro Club**. As part of its various musical events, Le Metro, on Tuesdays, was the home of **McDonalds** folk club. At the rear of the Hall of Memory, at the **Shakespeare** pub, was the **Holy Ground**, but the place to be was **Digbeth Civic Hall**, a venue that played host to arguably the most important club in the country at that time, the **Jug O' Punch**. There, in residence, was the **Ian Campbell Folk Group**. Ian ran the club himself, utilising the talents of singer songwriter **Harvey Andrews**, a talent that **Johnny Haines** at **Zella** studios rated so highly.

"Harvey came in with this great song," recalled Johnny. " 'I'm on the M1 with me pop art sweater. Yeah, I'm a clever trendsetter!' What a song!"

Harvey Andrews takes great delight in recalling a young American folk singer and songwriter arriving to perform at the club a week early by mistake.

Tray chic – the mademoiselles of the Metro club

"Ian was pointing to the poster on the wall," recalls Harvey. "He stared down at the lad and growled in his Highland brogue 'See here! *Next* week! Paul Simon! Now go away and get yourself orrraganized!' "

Le Metro club was highly organised. Its directors, **Terry** and **John Mullett** and **Alec Cooper** had chosen a Parisian theme to present their evenings of folk, traditional jazz, and rhythm and blues evenings. French beer mats were laid upon French tablecloths and the snap of a finger would bring Parisian mademoiselles, laden with pints of Watneys Red Barrel, scurrying to the table. Photographs of Edith Piaf, Maurice Chevalier and Johnny Halliday adorned the walls. A spiral staircase, linking the upstairs and downstairs bars, dominated the ground floor. The club even employed a French compere, **Boris Gogny**, to put a little 'ooh lala' into the stage announcements. The poster in the Le Metro's foyer described Boris as 'madly gay'.

The Capitols

Madly gay were the **Capitols**, and so busy that they needed to advertise for a vocalist, which is how they found **Ken Fryer**, a Cotteridge lad who had previously sung with the **Stormriders**, a band formed to appear at the **St Agnes Church Youth Club**. In the parlour of guitarist **Keith Grant's** house, in Alton Road, Selly Oak, Ken successfully went through his paces to become a Capitol, alongside **Martin McLeogh** on drums and, on bass, electronics whizzkid, **Lyndon Laney.** On organ was the former Carpetbagger **Malc Bourne**. Shortly after Ken Fryer's arrival, Keith Grant quit and was replaced by big **Al Johnson**, another former Carpetbagger, and, following an appearance at **the Tyburn House** pub, the Capitols took on a manager in the shape of **Bob Thomas**, whose father was licensee of the **Queens Head** pub in Erdington.

With the record buying public crying out for a follow up to the **Spencer Davis Group** number one, 'Keep On Runnin'', Jack Baverstock, of Fontana Records lined up another potential screecher for **Stevie Winwood** to lacerate his vocal chords on. As the Spencer Davis Group prepared to lay down their backing track, Jack Baverstock nodded at the fuzz box on the studio floor. "Don't forget. Give it plenty of that on the guitar," he said to Stevie Winwood before pressing the 'record 'button.

Come the end of March 1966, the track with plenty of fuzz box, 'Somebody Help Me', was the country's best selling single.

ROCK AND TWIST FOR ALL OCCASIONS

The "Couriers" Rythm Group

Sole Representative
Mr R. DALEY

33. LABURNUM ROAD,
BOURNVILLE,
BIRMINGHAM, 30.

Shingles were rife and highly contagious around Weoley Castle. These Shingles were made up from the left overs from the **Couriers**. Guitarists **Derek Arnold** and **Tony Collinge** were joined by singer **Steve Wardle**, drummer **Paul Hancocks** and, from the **Exchequers**, came **Tony Russell**. When the Shingles broke out at the **Weoley Castle Community Centre**, the poster in the entrance foyer read 'Tonight! The Shingles! Spot Prizes Galore!'

The Exchequers were actually a continuation of the fifties outfit, the **Chequers**, which had, at various times seen the likes of **Mike Sheridan, Max 'the Nub' Griffiths** and **Mike Pinder** pass through its ranks, the common factor from day one being the band's manager, **Cyril Viles**. Now the Exchequers had drummer and vocalist **Kenny Wood** with guitarist **Ken Lunt**, formerly of Wolverhampton's Zuider Zee. They also had a 'chords only' guitarist and singer, **Laurie Hornsby**, who nigh on ruined his marriage prospects in a nightly attempt to hit the top 'A' note when singing the Easybeats' hit of the day, 'Friday On My Mind'.

Having achieved second place in the **Locarno** Beat contest, where they won a microphone stand, **Monopoly** were itching to break out of **Tito's** club and play an active part in the bubbling rock scene. That chance came when they were invited to appear at the **Birmingham Council House**, performing in the presence of the City's Lord Mayor and his good lady wife. **Sonny Rose** and his Orchestra would be making the short trip across from the **West End Ballroom** to play for strict tempo dancing whilst the Monopoly would provide the pop element for such daring abandons as the twist.

"I offered Sonny Rose full use of our microphone stand," said **Raymond Froggatt**. "Some bloke in a uniform showed us to our dressing room. I don't know why — we hadn't got anything to change into!"

Sonny Rose announced the first waltz of the evening, and the crowd stood and applauded as the Lord Mayor escorted his good lady wife to the dance floor. After a selection of quicksteps and slow foxtrots, a 'free for all' atmosphere abounded amidst the happy gathering as both the orchestra and the dancers went for broke with a blast of 'March of the Mods'. Bandleader Sonny Rose finally brought his troops to a resounding halt and, with the breathless dancers staggering back to their respective tables, Mr Rose announced that a session of shaking and twitching would follow, and the audience would be 'in the capable hands of the Monopoly!'

As the four hairy troubadours stepped onto the stage, the good lady wife of the Lord Mayor encountered her first sighting of the Monopoly and began to scream hysterically. Social climbers swiftly attended the scene.

"I s'pose to her, we looked like we'd just escaped from Rampton," sighed Froggy, "But we were there to play and that's what we intended to do."

An air of tranquillity was returning to the Lord Mayor's table. His good lady wife had been assured that these Monopoly boys were not hooligans but of good Aston stock. Demolishing a 'family sized' gin and tonic in one gulp, the good lady allowed herself to be escorted to a chair by her devoted husband. Unfortunately, the chair selected was the one placed directly in front of the public address speaker.

The Monopoly struck up the shuffling rhythm of 'Shotgun Wedding'. Gentlemen in evening suits, legs already slithering, began to encourage female partners to discard apprehension and 'join in the fun'. Even the good lady wife was seen to be attempting the hand jive. Obviously she winced a little as Raymond's gritty vocal crackled out of the speaker and straight down her ear but this was, after all, the swinging sixties. Go man, go!

The Roy C recording of 'Shotgun Wedding' was a hot one in the dance halls at that time. Not only did it have an infectious swing and a great hook line for dancers to pick up on, but also the sound effect of a gun firing and ricocheting loudly. This was an essential part of the production in Raymond Froggatt's view, and he had his own little trick to recreate an approximation of the effect.

"People are standin' all around," sang Froggy, one hand waving freely whilst the other remained fixed to the newly acquired microphone stand.

"There was smiles all round and I got well into it," laughed Froggy. "I got to the hook line, sang out 'Shotgun' and gave the PA amplifier a good kick." (The reverb effect in those days was created by a sensitive, amplified spring arrangement within the amp) "The reverb twang crashed out of the speakers and exploded round the room, and this poor woman by the speaker went six feet up in the air. Again I sang "Shotgun," and walloped the amplifier a few times more. She was screaming blue murder by now and the Lord Mayor was runnin' round in his Dick Turpin hat, beggin' us to stop!"

Sonny Rose and his Orchestra returned to the stage immediately and the Monopoly were requested to leave the building, which they did, taking their microphone stand with them.

"I was back at the Council House a few years after," sighed Raymond half heartedly. "They give me some 'Brummie of the year' award."

Froggy & the Monopoly

The **Bobcats** (still average age fourteen) were picking up awards. At the **Adelphi**, in West Bromwich, they entered and won the beat group contest. Not only did they win the contest, they won the confidence of promoter and agent **John Singer**, who immediately became their sole agent. He began putting engagements into their diaries that, only twelve months earlier, would simply have been schoolboy dreams. Engagements like the **Carlton** club at Erdington where the boys supported Geno Washington and the Ram Jam Band. When the headmaster at Alderlea School was alerted to his pupils' outside activities, an arrangement was made whereby the Bobcats would only perform at weekends.

Award-winning Bobcats, regulars at the Crown

"We'd do places like **Parkinson Cowan Social Club** at Stechford, where everyone knew us. We'd finish early and tell them we were going home. Then we'd be off to do a spot at the **Crown** in Hill Street," recalled **Les Fortnam**.

It was at the Carlton club that **John Carter** of the **Ivy League** called in to witness a performance by the **Boulevards**. No longer a purely blues outfit, the Boulevards were putting over soul in a deep and meaningful way.

Drawing from the creations of Wilson Pickett and Billy 'Fatboy' Stewart for their material, vocalist **Geoff Greaves** would beg his audience 'Don't Fight It', and then shuffle along to '634 5789', before introducing a little romance into the proceedings with the emotionally charged 'Sittin' in the Park'. The performance was everything John Carter had been led to expect and, shortly after their meeting, a demonstration tape of the John Carter and **Ken Lewis** song, 'Please Mr Heartache' arrived, for the attention of the Boulevards. The arrival of the tape coincided with a trip to Germany for the boys, who now were sporting a new bass guitarist, **Stuart 'Tiny Tim' Duncan**. Stuart was an excellent musician with leanings toward jazz. He could also see off four chicken and mushroom pies in one sitting at Alex's pie stand!

"In Germany," explained **Tony Clarkin**, lead guitarist with the Boulevards, "We set to work on 'Please Mr Heartache', the Carter Lewis song, changing the arrangement quite considerably to suit our style."

Back home, the Boulevards were summoned to London. At Regent Sound studios they recorded their new version of 'Please Mr Heartache'.

"Unfortunately for us, Tin Pan Alley didn't see things our way," said Tony Clarkin. "In fact they hated everything we'd done to the song and we came home with our tails between our legs."

The Boulevards

The **Ian Campbell group** had begun to make records for the Transatlantic label and had enjoyed a minor tickle at the top fifty during March 1965, with Bob Dylan's observation that 'The Times They Are A-Changin'.' Although strictly traditional in their approach to musical performances, they had a wide ability with Ian, **Brian Clarke** and **John Dunkerly** on guitars, **Dave Swarbrick** on fiddle, and Ian's sister, **Lorna**, adding her quite superb voice into the equation. The head of Transatlantic Records, **Nat Joseph** was keen to cash in on the thriving popularity of pop/folk artistes. Nat, himself a thoroughbred Brummie, arranged with the band's manager, **Ioan Allen**, for the group to record a couple of songs that had been submitted to Transatlantic. Nat Joseph then booked time at the famous Olympic Sound Studios in Baker Street, London.

"I was asked to the session," explains **Johnny Haines**, "Because I'd recorded the Campbells many times before. Ioan was desperate for a hit in order to move the Ian Campbell group into the big league."

Engineering the session was Keith Grant, a sound man who was developing a first class reputation that, over the next few years would see him become a much sought after producer. One of the songs the Ian Campbell group recorded that day was a South American folk song entitled 'Guantanamera'.

"The band, the song, Lorna's voice, everything sounded simply beautiful," said Johnny. "Olympic, in those days, was a brick cellar with stone pillars. It was just perfect for an acoustic sound."

At the end of the take, Keith Grant looked up from the mixing desk and announced to Nat Joseph that, in his opinion, Transatlantic had a smash hit on their hands. Nat Joseph was hoping for something a little more akin to the Seekers or Brian Epstein's recent signings, the Silkie, who had charted with John Lennon's 'You've Got To Hide Your Love Away'. In the belief that engineers should be seen and not heard, Nat Joseph ignored Keith Grant's comment. Seven months later, in September 1966, an American folk group, the Sandpipers, sold two million copies of 'Guantanamera'.

"I know for a fact that the thought of 'Guantanamera' slipping through their fingers made John Dunkerly quite ill with stress," recalled Johnny Haines.

Breaking free of the stress of working all day and performing all night were the **Sombreros**. Burning with ambition, they had quit their daytime occupations to make music their full time profession. **Peter Smith**, a joiner by nature, had served his apprenticeship admirably as a carpenter and **Grant Kearney** had carved out a career behind the bacon counter at Wrensons' grocery shop in Northfield.

"I sat on the slicer and got a little behind with the orders," said Grant,

Sombreros

struggling desperately to get a laugh.

Picking up the rashers from the slicer and packing them into the basket on the front of his Wrensons' bike was the new delivery boy at the Northfield branch. It was all part of a day's hard work as far as the new lad was concerned. When Grant Kearney heard that this lad was a locally rated exponent of the guitar and could sing a few songs into the bargain, the lad was talked into abandoning his delivery bike and putting in with the Sombreros.

"That's how we found **Rick Price**," Grant explained. "There was something for everyone at Wrensons!"

Germany beckoned and the boys, with **Joe Dignam** now drumming for them, found themselves in Dortmond, with accommodation that still bore the bomb damage that it had acquired twenty-two years previously.

"The exterior wall was pretty non-existent," said Pete Smith. "When it rained the water used to pour in."

At the end of the evening's work, maybe three, sometimes even four in the morning, the Sombreros would visit the all night public baths just to keep warm!

Alerted by the management of the **Whiskey a Go-Go** club, situated above **Chetwyn's**, the gents' outfitters, in Navigation Street, **Tony Secunda,** of Marquee Artistes, visited the venue to view a performance by the **Move**. What Tony Secunda witnessed that evening was a typical 'early days' Move performance of Tamla Motown material with **Bev Bevan** throwing in 'Zing Went the Strings of My Heart' for good measure. It was enough, however, to set the wheels in motion that would carry the Move to the Marquee club in Wardour Street, Soho, to take up a Wednesday night residency. The Marquee was the place to be seen. The eyes and ears of the pop music industry would be on them — the dream was on course.

The dream was still on course for the **Fortunes**. Their first hit 'You've got Your Troubles', having top tenned in America was making them hot news on the other side of the pond. It was the same for the **Moody Blues**, 'Go Now' had made such an impact with the American audiences. The

Moodys and the Fortunes found themselves sharing the bill with 'Mr Soulman' himself, Wilson Pickett, at the Brooklyn Fox Theatre, New York. The occasion was the 'Murray the K' television show and they played twice nightly for one week to a packed and frenzied house, their performances being filmed for coast to coast transmission.

"We did the first two nights without **Barry Pritchard**," Rod Allen explains. "**Denny Laine** took him out on the town as soon as we arrived and Barry ended up so smashed out of it. Murray the K was none too happy."

At the end of the week **Clint Warwick** was out of it. Out of the Moody Blues and out of the music business.

"I was the only one in the band with a family to look after," said Clint, "And we hadn't really followed 'Go Now' with anything near as good."

Earlier, in the spring of 1966, John Lennon and Paul McCartney had paid one of their many social visits to the Moody Blues' house in Roehampton.

Clint Warwick picks up, "I asked Paul if they had anything decent in the pipeline and he said he was working on a song about a bloke who fancied his chances as a paperback writer. Paul picked up Denny's guitar and sang a few words, 'Dear sir or madam will you read my book.' And I said 'Yeah, that'll do for us,' but Paul said they were keeping it for themselves."

Roy Wood puts his signature on the bottom of the Move's unusual record contract

"So back at the Brooklyn Fox, New York, everybody gave me a farewell hug and Wilson Pickett handed me his bottle of bourbon to take a few swigs. Alister Taylor, Brian Epstein's right hand man, was booked on the same flight back to London and gave me a lift to Kennedy airport. At Heathrow, Alister shook my hand and I said my goodbyes to the music business."

The Moody Blues quickly replaced Clint with **Rod Clarke**, a musician from Great Yarmouth, who had no problems understanding the Brummie accent, having served time strumming guitar for John Carter and Ken Lewis in the Southerners.

Clint, on arrival home in Birmingham, became a carpenter. "The only planes I saw after that was the ones I pulled out the toolbag," he sighed.

Reg Cavert

As the Fortunes returned home a drama was starting to unfold involving their mentor, **Reg Calvert**. An entrepreneur that was always itching to be part of whatever was going on, Reg had entered the rat race of pirate radio by purchasing Radio Sutch, a station that was broadcasting from a former defence fort on Shivering Sands, in the Thames estuary. Renaming the station Radio City, Reg Calvert steered his station so successfully that in mid

Radio City

June of 1966 a merger with Radio Caroline was rumoured to be on the cards. But, in the meantime, a stormy relationship had developed between Reg Calvert and a rival station — Radio London. On the afternoon of the 20th June, Major Oliver Smedley, representing Radio London, led a party that boarded the Radio City fort and removed its transmitter. Reg Calvert was raging at such an action and next evening, the 21st, he drove to Major Smedley's cottage in Saffron Walden, Essex for a showdown. On answering the front door, Major Smedley's housekeeper tried to refuse Reg Calvert entry and, as they struggled in the hallway, Smedley appeared on the staircase brandishing a shotgun.

Reg Calvert was shot dead. He was thirty-eight years of age. The police report revealed that an un-discharged gas gun had been found on Mr Calvert's person.

With their new record 'Don't Stop Lovin' Me Baby' in the shops, **Pinkerton's Colours** were out on the promotion road and appearing in Barnsley when they heard the sad news regarding their manager on the radio.

Tony Newman, the band's vocalist and guitarist explains, "I'd actually driven Reg down to Whitstable, on the banks of the Thames estuary, and put him on a boat with the new transmitter a few days previously. I had to call the police for confirmation of the news story."

Major Smedley's plea of not guilty on the grounds of self-defence was accepted by the court, and the Major was acquitted of all charges.

A few weeks prior to the events of Reg Calvert's death, coinciding with their new record release, Pinkerton's Assorted Colours had welcomed into their ranks a new bass guitarist, **Stuart Colman**. Their original man, **Barry Bernard** had left to form the outfit Jigsaw. In the mid 1970s Jigsaw went on to write and produce the top twenty hit, 'Who Do You Think You Are' for the band Candlewick Green and make the top ten themselves, performing their song 'Sky High'. Stuart Colman didn't fair too badly either. In the early to mid 1980s he was to produce a dozen or so top ten smashes for Shakin' Stevens.

Rockin' Berries at the Forty Thieves Club

Cruise ship pianist, **Terry Brennan**, originally from Stoke on Trent, had gone ashore in the Bahamas, liked what he saw and decided to remain there. After a period of wheeling and dealing, he made good and was now proprietor of the **Forty Thieves Club** in Hamilton, Bermuda. Whilst seeking inspiration for entertainment at the club, his thoughts went back to England. He was recalling a memorable performance by the **Rockin' Berries**, which he had seen at the Grosvenor House, Park Lane, Mayfair, in the January of 1966. Although aware of the limitations of their comedy routines with regard to American audiences, Terry Brennan had every confidence in the Berries as a rock attraction. Easter time, 1966, to coincide with the American 'college weeks' vacation, the Rockin' Berries played a hugely successful six-week season at the Forty Thieves. Delving into their past rhythm and blues repertoire, the Berries delivered the goods to the hip American students with such soulful songs as Jimmy Reed's 'Baby Take Out Insurance On Me', **Bobby Thomson** coaxing everything from his grizzly vocal cords. **Clive Lea** could not let his gift as an impressionist go to waste and would do a 'Bob Dylan' on 'Rainy Day Women', leading the packed audiences to join in the lyric 'Everybody must get stoned!' In all, the Rockin' Berries went on to perform nine six-week seasons at the Forty Thieves Club!

At the end of their first stint in the Bahamas, **Chuck Botfield** and **Terry Bond** broke their homeward journey to take time in New York and possibly seek out fresh material for future recording. 'Poor Man's Son' had happened for them a year ago, and in the record industry a year is a lifetime. Amongst the pile of records Chuck and Terry brought home was one by a New York outfit, the Left Banke, entitled 'Walk Away Renee'. Upping the key and the tempo, the Berries recorded a backing track that became, when layered with reverberation, positively 'Motown'. With Bobby Thomson's gritty and soulful vocals tracked on, the effect was, as they say in music circles, too much.

"Everyone involved with the Berries knew we'd cut a winner," Bobby Thomson recalls. "This was to be a whole new start for us. Then, for some reason, John Schroeder, the Artiste and Repertoire executive, lost his nerve and said 'Walk Away Renee' sounded too 'black' for the Rockin' Berries. We were back where we started."

Definitely not going back were Wolverhampton's **'N Betweens**. They'd started the year as a five-piece combo that featured **Johnny Howles** on vocals. However their rhythm guitarist, **Neville 'Noddy' Holder**, formerly of the **Memphis Cutouts**, was too much of a character to be suppressed. By the summer of 1966, Johnny Howles had departed leaving Noddy, **Dave Hill** and **Don Powell**, (previously of Wolverhampton's **Vendors**) and **Jim Lea**, (one time member of Codsall's **Nick and the Axemen**) to move forward to where they wanted to be.

The 'N Betweens

"Noddy and the lads were so much louder than all of us put together," explained **Johnny Jones** of the **Montanas**. "They were a real mix and match with their amplifiers all wired together. When they kicked off it was like an avalanche of screeching guitars hitting you!"

From the **George hotel** in Walsall, to the **Park Hall** in Wolverhampton; from **Aldridge Community Centre** to **Alcester Trades and Labour club**; when the curtains swung back, Noddy Holder's incredibly powerful voice, over the mountain of sound, would be telling the whole of the Midlands — 'I Saw Her Again Last Night'. So true were they to the Mamas and Papas original recording of the song, the 'N Betweens even had the John Phillips vocal mishap, where he makes a false start after the bridge, 'I saw her — I saw her again'.

Cheetahs Nigel & Rodney

The Star Club, Hamburg

Hopping around the world famous Hamburg Star Club, in their world famous sweatbox stage suits, were the **Cheetahs**. After their six-week stint of playing rock 'n' roll music for eight hours a night, laden heavily with cheetah skin, they were nominated collectively for the 'Slimmer of the Year' award. Back home, a few of mother's Sunday dinners soon put the meat back on their frail skeletons and they were off to spend springtime in Vienna at the San Remo club. George Kunov, the club's proprietor, (who had been head of the Austrian resistance during World War Two) proved the perfect host for the Cheetahs. With sensible playing times, good accommodation with meals slung in, who could ask for more? George Kunov's all time favourite was George Gershwin's 'Summertime'. Whenever the boys chose to play 'Summertime' a tray of beer would arrive at the stage, compliments of the house. Even in the middle of their newly choreographed comedy sketch, the Cheetahs would somehow manage to shoehorn 'Summertime' into the routine!

The Beach Boys were in town to play a concert at Vienna's Strata Halle. As the ten thousand strong audience took their seats for a magical evening spent in the company of the masters of the Californian surf sound, the Cheetahs admirably performed the support duties, rating the event as the highlight of their musical careers.

"When we finished," said **Euan Rose**, "Bruce Johnson commented that we sounded like Herman's Hermits ought to sound!"

Bass guitarist **Tony Clarkson** had become tired of the **Way of Life**. The void created by his departure was filled by Mr Brumbeat himself, **Danny King** of the now defunct **Mayfair Set**. With their reputation growing, the Way of Life had caught the eye of **Rick Gunnel**, the London based agent and club owner. When Rick Gunnel booked them into the **Bag O' Nails** club in Soho, the boys could hardly believe their luck. As the Way of Life got into their stride so the audience's interest began to grow. Such faces as Tom Jones, Manitas De Plata and Paul McCartney could be picked out in the enthusiastic crowd. As **Reg Jones** announced their next song to the star studded room, Danny King took a Park Drive cigarette pack and a box of England's Glory matches from his pocket and lit up. Suddenly a drumstick went spinning through the air and bounced off Danny's head.

"This is the Bag O' Nails you know!" screamed **John Bonham**.

"I loved Bonham," said Danny, gently rubbing the back of his head. "Beneath all the big front was a very warm and gentle man."

The **Applejacks** management of ADSEL, Arthur Douglas Smith Enterprises Ltd, was literally going up in the world. Moving from his office on Stratford Road, Sparkhill, **Arthur Smith** had taken a whole suite of offices on the 12th floor of Hagley House, standing proudly on the Hagley Road, Edgbaston. Nominated to oversee promotions was, **John Parsons** from the Belfry. Handling the 'one off gigs' was the leader of the **John Bull Breed**, **Brian Yeates**. In May of 1966, as a result of the business relationship that existed between ADSEL and Polydor Records, the **UK Bonds** and the John Bull Breed were able to release single records. The UK Bonds choice of release was entitled 'The Whole Wide World' with 'Can't Chance a Break Up', a cover of an Ike and Tina Turner recording, being the choice of the John Bull Breed. With the excitement of a record release comes the thrill and challenge of promotion. By arrangement with the Scottish agent 'Drunken' Duncan, a mini tour of the Highlands for the John Bull Breed was put in place.

John Parsons

"**Micky Heard** was always the last to be picked up," Brian Yeates explained. "We got to his house at Castle Bromwich at eleven-thirty in the morning and we couldn't wake him. We had to climb into the back garden and rattle the clothes line prop against his bedroom window!"

Their first Scottish engagement was at Buckie, on the Moray Firth. 'Drunken' Duncan had arranged overnight accommodation in Elgin with a Mrs McBean. At breakfast, the following morning, a bleary-eyed Micky Heard asked Mrs McBean, "How come you lot up here make such awful porridge?" According to 'Drunken' Duncan's worksheet, the John Bull Breed were to appear at a Dumfries ballroom the following evening. On arrival, they set up and were testing their microphones when the ballroom manager made his entrance.

Brian Yeates

"There must be some mistake," said the manager. "I don't have foreign bands on a Friday!"

UK Bonds

Back in Birmingham, the John Bull Breed took stock. Micky Heard was pleased to see proper porridge — 'Ready Brek' — gracing his breakfast table. A couple of trips across the Irish Sea to Dublin, as the John Bull Showband, soon put the colour back into their cheeks.

"Then came the gig that would make or break us," said Brian Yeates. "Polydor Records had arranged for us to appear at Tiles, a basement club in Oxford Street, London. Not only that, a critic from the New Musical Express would be there to review our performance."

The date of this prestigious showcase was Saturday, 30th July 1966. The John

The John Bull Breed

Bull Breed loaded their equipment into the back of their Ford Thames van in record time lest they should miss England kicking off against Germany in the World Cup final at Wembley Stadium. The football match went into extra time and the John Bull Breed stayed glued to the television set. Finally, with the immortal words of commentator Kenneth Wolstenholme, "They think it's all over -- it is now!" still ringing in their ears, the John Bull Breed tore themselves from the screen. They leapt into the van and headed for the Smoke and to Tiles club, arriving at eight o'clock on that evening.

"The management of Tiles weren't at all pleased at us being so late," Brian Yeates explained. "It became a slanging match and we told them to shove the gig."

If nothing else, the John Bull Breed had their pride. The following morning, back in Birmingham, they remembered about the New Musical Express critic that was due to show. Brian Yeates and company felt sick with nerves all week. Living in dread of the awful article that would appear in the NME about them and their non-appearance.

Brian Yeates continues, "The following Friday morning I scooted down to the newsagent's for the New Musical Express. There, in bold print was a review of our show at Tiles. It read 'The John Bull Breed put up a terrific show. These boys obviously know their trade and are surely bound for the top.' "

Bound for the top, or so they hoped, were four lads from Dudley. As members of the **Strangers**, they'd contributed to Decca's 1964 Brum Beat album. Now, fully professional, vocalist **Dripper Kent** and guitarists **Alan Clee**, **Jake Elcock** and **Dave Williams** climbed aboard the showbiz carousel as the highly entertaining **Finders Keepers**. With professional status came professional confidence and they soon found themselves appearing alongside top flight acts such as Morecambe and Wise and Tom Jones as they plied their talents on the tough Northern club circuit. These talents didn't go unnoticed and the boys were signed to London's Maurice King agency who were looking after the interests of the Rockin' Berries and the Walker Brothers. It was this association that led to Finders Keepers becoming Scott Walker's guinea pigs as Scott began to find his feet as a record producer. Their first collaboration was the country song, 'Mention My Name In Sheboygan'. This went unreleased and Dripper Kent found himself being summoned to the Decca Studios in the company of such session men as Tony Meehan, Big Jim Sullivan and the Ladybirds. There Scott Walker produced the recording that became their first release— 'Light'.

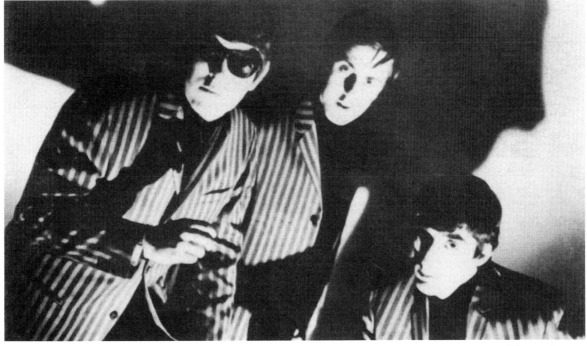

The Ivy League

The **Crescendos**, now enjoying the benefits of **Norman Haines** on keyboards and **Pete Allen** on six string bass, had been recommended to Polydor by Arthur Smith of the ADSEL agency. The evening prior to the recording test, the Crescendos rehearsed a Norman Haines composition 'When the Sun Goes Down', until the early hours. They arrived promptly for their eleven o'clock appointment at the Advision studios in New Bond Street, only to wait three hours while producer Terry Kennedy finished an Ivy League recording session.

"We set up, plugged in and slammed down the Norman Haines song we'd spent the previous night rehearsing," **Trevor Greaves** recalled. "Result? Absolutely lousy!"

Bev Bevan & John Sabel

The **Belfry** Hotel at Wishaw, near Sutton Coldfield, was the place for the discerning patron every Monday and Saturday.

"Actually," recalls **John Ford**, "The class punters favoured Mondays. Saturdays tended to be pick and mix. It was a posers paradise."

Promoting the happenings at the Belfry was the front line team of **John Parsons, John Sabel** and **John Morgan**.

"Myself and **Tony Sofiano** were the dogsbodies," said John Ford, who performed disc jockey duties in the guise of **Doc Holliday**.

Always in the market for untapped talent, John Parsons presented the **Monopoly** to his Monday night clientele.

Raymond Froggatt remembers his Belfry debut well. "I'd always found playing dances hard going and quite honestly I dreaded them. We started with 'You're So Good To Me' and no one danced. The crowd stood and applauded everything we did. When it was time to wind up I could feel these great vibes. **H Cain** rippled out the introduction to 'Tambourine Man' and the roof came in."

John Parsons, being well impressed, found a European outlet for Raymond Froggatt and Monopoly. In his capacity as an agent, he booked them for an eight week engagement at the Whiskey club, Nice, on the French Riviera. Borrowing fifty pounds for expenses from Hartley Cain's mother, the Monopoly drove their clapped out Ford Thames van to Dover and the Calais ferry. As they rolled off the ferry onto French soil, the accelerator cable snapped. With impatient tourists blasting their car horns, Hartley Cain calmly fixed the problem with a guitar string. En route to Nice, the band stopped over in Paris to appear at the Locomotive Club. The Parisian audience, in the main students, were overwhelmed by the stage presence of Raymond Froggatt, and the Monopoly played a set of three hours duration. On to Nice and half way across the Alps, a spring snapped and the exhaust pipe fell off their van but, with God on their side, Monopoly arrived outside the Whiskey club, 'on the prom', at Nice. Here Raymond Froggatt, Hartley Cain, **Len Ablethorpe** and **Louis Clark** performed six hours a night, every night except Sundays, when they would play for ten hours!

When it was time to return home to Birmingham the problem of the snapped spring had to be addressed. Once again H Cain had the answer. He temporarily repaired the damaged spring by clamping the broken strips of metal together with six guitar capodastras. The exhaust problem had to be ignored and with monetary funds extremely low, H recommended that they existed solely on biscuits until reaching Calais. He then took it upon himself to spend what funds the band had on a plentiful supply of biscuits from a nearby grocery store. As the Monopoly made their return journey back across the Alps, they experienced problems in biting through the biscuits. Louis Clark examined the goods. Being the educated one, Louis was able to translate the print on the wrappers. Hartley Cain, mechanic supreme, had spent all their money on dog biscuits!

Stardom, it seemed, was just around the corner for the **Uglys**. In mid-May, after a gig in Somerset, the lads climbed into their lipstick caked Commer van and headed, via Denmark, for Finland where they were to be featured in a television show.

It was a trip similar to the one that the **Applejacks** had made seven months previously. If only the Applejacks could have forewarned the Uglys. Oh, if only…

At Harwich the Uglys boarded the Esberg ferry. After a restless night spent sprawled out over the lounge seats, they disembarked, driving into the Danish sunshine. **Dave Pegg** was on foreign soil for the first time in his life. Port officials in their decorative uniforms were smiling with gay abandon, waving excited tourists through the customs zone.

"As we neared the front of the line an official signalled for us to pull over and park up. We all jumped out enthusiastically, expecting to sign autographs for his daughter or something," explained Dave.

Five Uglys were about to conquer the world, or at least Scandinavia. Police arrived and started shouting at them in Danish. It might as well have been Chinese. The van was impounded whilst **Steve Gibbons** and his fellow Uglys were frog marched down to police headquarters, stripped, searched and thrown into individual cells where previous occupants had scratched off the passing days and weeks on the cold bricked walls. Pleas from the lads for a call to the British Consul went ignored. Twenty-six hours later they were released without charge. All their money was confiscated before the Uglys were bundled back onto the Harwich bound ferry. Stamped on their passports was the word 'Deported'.

" I'd only had mine five minutes!" said Dave Pegg.

The Uglys,
bound for Finland

Complaints to the authorities at Harwich resulted in Her Majesty's Customs officials ripping the backs off their amplifiers in a desperate search for contraband. It took the Uglys five hours to piece their equipment back together. A telephone call to the Carlton Johns Agency resulted in money being wired to them.

Dave Pegg continues, "We managed to get up to Grimsby and book a ride on a cargo boat direct to Finland. Pure magic! Three days of drinking and singing all the old songs with the crew got that nightmare out of our heads."

The **Nightriders** were beginning to think that they might have slipped up with their choice of replacement for **Roy Wood**.

Roger Spencer picks up the tale, "**Johnny Mann**, God rest his soul, was a lovely gentle man and this was reflected in his guitar playing. To please the crowd the Nightriders needed a guitarist who had the necessary aggression in his playing, so it was reluctantly agreed that we would advertise for someone to replace him."

When an enthusiastic youth telephoned in answer to the advertisement in the Birmingham Mail, Roger suggested that he should 'stroll round' for a chat after work. Replacing the receiver Roger re-read the notes he had scribbled down during the call, 'sounds keen — day job — car spares shop — **Jeff Lynne**.'

Party time at the Silver Blades Rink

Roger Spencer paused for a few seconds. "Just think about that. Roy Wood walks out the door and then Jeff Lynne walks in! Immediately we were all born again. We got a feel good factor going and it was obvious from the start that Jeff was incredibly creative. **Dave Pritchard** thought up the new name. He, as I recall, came up with the Idyll Race, which we all loved. Somewhere along the line it got changed to the **Idle Race**, but either way, life suddenly changed for the better."

Gerry **Day**, formerly of the **Dukes**, was pulled back into the rock business by **Ray Snelson**, the guitarist that he had worked with in the **Del Saints**. Along with bassist **Gerry Marsden**, (no, not that one) Ray had put together a soul band in keeping with the public trend for black music, called the **Marshall Sounds**. To give them an authentic feel, organist **Alan Clifford** was along to provide the 'Booker T' sound.

Robert Plant

"We did all the places like the **Silver Blades Ice Rink**, the **Hobmoor** at Hay Mills, the **Rainbow Suite** in High Street and what was the biggest pub in Europe at the time, the **Swan**, at Yardley," Gerry Day recalls.

"I couldn't really handle the material," he continued with a painful expression, "All the Otis and Wilson Pickett stuff. 'Can't Turn You Loose' and 'Midnight Hour'. Next morning I was soundin' like Louis Armstrong when I spoke."

Working hard to acquire the knack of sounding like Louis Armstrong, or even Big Bill Broonzy was the young vocalist in a band with the most unusual name, **Listen**. **Robert Plant** was the singer in question and with **John Crutchley** on guitar, **Roger Beamer** on bass and **Geoff Thompson** on drums, Listen were the band for the mods that frequented the **Rainbow Suite**. Not only were Listen dedicated followers of fashion, they also had a great song going for them, 'The Pakistani Rent Collector', that set them far apart from all other competition. That song was guaranteed to get the pork pie hats bobbing!

All over the place during the summer of 1966 were a Handsworth based surfing group known as **Andy's Clappers**. Going like the clappers around the Rhine Valley and the Italian Riviera in a converted London Transport double-decker bus (no smoking downstairs and spitting strictly prohibited) were guitarists **Andy Preston**, **Bob Neale** and **Dave Kaye**, with **Roy Saywood** doing a pretty good job of 'Wipeout' on the tom toms. At the keyboard, and putting in a few Chopin fills beneath the falsetto harmonies, sat the classically trained and ever so attractive **Jan Jefferies**. Prior to their European 'Summer Holiday' style tour the Andy's Clappers had appeared at the **Black Horse**, Northfield, parking the big red London bus for all to view on the pub car park. As the rest of the band changed into their beach wear, Roy Saywood popped across to the telephone box on the other side of the Bristol Road. There, he plugged his Remington shaver into the light bulb socket, and received a stern reprimand from a passing constable for doing so.

With stories flying around of the **Rockin' Berries** lording it up in the Bahamas; of the **Monopoly** getting film star treatment on the French Riviera; of the **Cheetahs** taking tea with the Beach Boys in Viennese delicatessens and of the **Andicapps** and the **Uglys** enjoying royal status in the Scandinavian lands of free love, people in Birmingham were quite understandably feeling a little left out of things. Especially the **Little People**. **Ronny Smith**'s old schoolpal from Moseley Grammar, **Jasper Carrott**, had somehow found himself quite literally in the driving seat as far as the Little People were concerned. He was appointed road manager with a free hand to pursue new opportunities for the band.

Bumper problems for John Starkey & Jasper Carrott

"It was agreed that Jasper would use all his hustling skills to find us a gig that would put the Little People in with the beautiful people," explained Ronny.

Following a day of hard sell on the telephone to various international impresarios, Jasper was able to announce proudly, "Lads, we're off to . . . er . . . Barmouth!"

The Little People go west

New Moody – John Lodge

Okay Barmouth, that quaint Welsh seaside town that lies just the other side of nowhere, was not exactly San Francisco, but it was definitely West Coast! The engagement was for the boys to play nightly for one week at the church hall, just off the promenade. A caravan was available for accommodation. So after a performance at **Walsall Arboretum**, the five Little People, with Jasper at the wheel and his pal **Dave 'Yogi' College** navigating, set a course for Barmouth.

Arriving at five-thirty the following morning on the esplanade, seven weary travellers scrambled gasping from their aging Thames van in a bid to escape the combination of engine fumes and flatulence. Once washed and brushed, they presented themselves at the church hall only to be informed that the caravan was no longer available to musicians, due to the sinful and obnoxious antics of its previous occupants — the **Nightriders**.

Being of middle class stock and having the ability to turn on a genuine full thoroughbred Solihull accent, **John Starkey** was the person chosen to plead their case to the vicar. Christian charity prevailed. **The Little People** would be allowed to rearrange the church pews to form a communal bed. The Little People would also be allowed to take down the stage curtains at the end of every performance to use as blankets.

Den Caney, the entrepreneurial manager of the **Vogues**, had no difficulty in providing his boys with a full date sheet, week in, week out.

"The only problem was money," explained the Vogues' frontman, **Johnny Carroll**. "It was a fiver here, a fiver there. What we needed was a record. And a hit one at that."

Manager Den Caney was on the case immediately and within a short while had 'sold' the idea of the Vogues to EMI Records A&R man David Paramor, son of Norrie.

American West Coast folk rock music was now the order of the day and so David Paramor tapped into the songbook of the Lovin' Spoonful to come up with John Sebastion's 'Younger Girl'.

"She's one of those girls that come in the spring. One look in her eyes and you forget everything!" sang Johnny Carroll as he reminisced about the time the Vogues spent at Abbey Road recording studios.

"Just as we were entering the building, Ringo Starr and George Harrison walked past and said 'Good morning' to me." said Johnny. "That was it. I was totally lost for the day and couldn't concentrate on recording. Isn't it daft now when you look back?"

When the Vogues returned the next day to hear the engineer's mix on 'Younger Girl', Johnny, hearing some weird sounds drifting around the corridor, noticed a studio door was ajar and couldn't resist a peep.

"There they were," said Johnny Carroll. "The Beatles sat listening to 'Strawberry Fields Forever' being played back to them."

The John Lennon lyric 'Livin' is easy with eyes closed' would probably have described **John Lodge**'s feelings as he sat at his office desk. He was now a qualified draughtsman, having completed his apprenticeship at the Parkinson Cowan works at Stechford. Life was good. Sure he'd had his fair share of the ups and downs of the rock 'n' roll business in his time spent with **El Riot and the Rebels** and, more recently, the **John Bull Breed**, but that was all in the past. Oh Satan, get thee behind me! Pop music? What a mug's game!

If John was ever to be in need of a new gas cooker, all he had to do was fill in a form to receive the most favourable of staff discount. What a piece of cake. There was also the works' Christmas party to look forward to. He wasn't contributing two bob a week for nothing. And let's not forget the two weeks holiday, the Brummagem fortnight, with pay, if you don't mind. Yes indeed, this was the life. Rattling a 2H pencil against his teeth, John leaned back and watched through the office window as the number 11 bus wended its way past the folks queuing outside the Atlas bingo hall for the morning 'housey-housey' session. As the bus rocked gently over Stechford railway bridge, John dipped a 'Jammy Dodger' biscuit into his eleven o'clock cuppa. As his mind wandered, he reminisced about those freezing cold nights spent in the back of a broken down band wagon, with a speaker cabinet for a pillow, and of waking, arid of mouth and chilled to the bone. 'Beat groups? Who needs 'em?' he thought, and with that picked up the telephone to inform the **Moody Blues** that he was ready, willing and able to rock 'n' roll all night. And so John Lodge was welcomed with open arms into the Moody Blues. They had a short trip to Belgium in the diary and John's first duty would be to sell off some of his bass equipment to finance the band's travelling expenses.

Also selling off whatever he could in order to meet day-to-day expenditure was a twenty-year-old lad, **Justin Hayward**. Beginning his professional career in his hometown of Swindon, Justin had been a member of the group **All Things Bright**, before an advertisement in the Melody Maker led him to 1950s heart throb Marty Wilde. During the early 60s Marty Wilde had enjoyed two top twenty hits, 'Rubber Ball' and 'Jezebel' before the arrival of the Beatles had condemned him to the northern circuit of cabaret clubs. Justin Hayward's engagement as guitarist and vocalist with the **Wilde Three**, (Marty's wife Joyce making up the three), lasted until September 1965, when, after signing a publishing contract with Lonnie Donegan's Tyler Music, he began a solo career. However, after the release of two flop singles, Justin Hayward got word that Eric Burdon was in the process of reshaping the Animals and was in the market for a guitarist. Justin's application for the position arrived too late, but Eric Burdon did not discard his letter.

Justin Hayward with Joyce & Marty Wilde

At night, the Hill Street area jumped to the sound of the **Locomotive** thundering away in the function room above the **Crown** pub. Immediately after the gig, the band members would cruise their way through Newtown to partake in the groovin' that abounded at the **Elbow Room**.

"We were the Elbow crowd," explained drummer **Mike Kellie**. "We'd all jam together. Pals like **Jim Capaldi**, **Stevie Winwood** and flute player **Chris Wood**, who was, by now, with me in the Locomotive."

On arrival home at Marston Green, Mike Kellie would grab a couple of hours shut-eye before reporting for work at Cartwright's Lumberyard in Olton.

"Then Stevie Winwood recommended me to Chris Blackwell at Island Records," said Mike Kellie. "Chris had just picked up a band that had been roughing it round London, playing clubs like the Cromwellian and the Scotch of St James in order to try and crack it."

That band, originally from Carlisle, were the **VIPs**. When Mike Kellie received the offer to become a VIP, he was on the next train to London.

"I never had time to tell them at Cartwright's!" said Mike.

The VIPs had a single in the shops at that time, 'I Wanna Be Free', and Mike's first gig as a VIP was the Unicef televised benefit concert from Paris. Other acts on the bill were Danny Kaye, the **Spencer Davis Group** and Marlon Brando. With promotion like that, it followed that 'I Wanna Be Free' was a big hit in France.

In early October of 1966 the folks of Birmingham were introduced to the cabaret club experience when entrepreneur **John Reeve** converted a three storey warehouse in Bradford Street into a supper club, the likes of which have never been seen since. Carpeted throughout with a sand effect that bore footprints as a pattern, there were palm trees and tropical plants in abundance. The sound effect of a rippling seashore and the odd squawking parrot filtering through a camouflaged hi-fi system. Roped bridges dangled perilously overhead. Table waitresses wore grass skirts and had garlands of fresh flowers around their necks. With its resident band, the **Waikiki Islanders**, featuring a cute little hula-hula girl out front, the whole place was everyone's dream of what it was like to be cast away on some remote desert island. In fact, that's what it was. It was the **Castaways**.

Entertainment at the Castaways was of the highest order. In the top floor cabaret room the audience washed down their dinners with pints of mother nature's remedy for constipation, Watney's Red Barrel. For those who preferred not to hang loose, a couple of shots of the house Caribbean firewater would guarantee double vision as the talents of the likes of Tom Jones, Dusty Springfield, Adam Faith or the pony tailed PJ Proby were paraded.

Two hundred yards down the road apiece on Digbeth, was, but only for a short while, the jumping joint **Midnight City**. Midnight City set out to be just that, its reception area was a market of clothes and record stalls. The main entertainment room was down the stairs and into the cellar where the finest rock acts on that current British music scene performed. Indeed the opening night at Midnight City saw the Who as its main attraction. With five top ten smashes already under their belts, the Who proved a massive draw. As the crowds piled into Midnight City, the sound of Robert Parker's 'Let's Go Where the Action Is' came pumping out of the house speakers, courtesy of resident disc jockey, **Erskine T**.

Spikey haired Mods, in their bespoke tailored mohair suits and celluloid collars, from Hawkins of Corporation Street, cooljerked from one side of the dance area to the other, while the more refined waited, in anticipation, for the explosive Who to make their appearance. When the Who's road crew arrived, they found a concrete stage floor awaiting them, making the 'spiking' of Keith Moon's bass drum nigh impossible. In front of a full house, the road crew hammered and chiselled two holes out of the concrete floor and tried, with a degree of success, to stabilise the drum kit.

The following weekend, the newly formed Cream – Eric Clapton, Jack Bruce and Ginger Baker – were foraging on their knees around the dimly lit stage, looking for the holes in the concrete to give purchase to Ginger Baker's bass drum spurs.

With the Birmingham Watch Committee refusing the stallholders permission to trade at such unearthly hours, Midnight City closed pretty quickly, but not before the Graham Bond Organisation, Alexis Korner, the Victor Brox Blues Band and Skip Bifferty had paid a visit, complete with hammers and chisels.

Carl Wayne at the Marquee

Carl **Wayne** preferred an axe. During the Move's act, effigies of political world leaders were placed around the front of the stage and television sets would be stacked high at the sides. As the **Move**, bathed in a psychedelic lighting effect, created ear splitting feedback through their amplifiers, Carl, wielding his axe like a man possessed, would lay into the effigies and televisions, creating absolute havoc on stage and amongst the audience.

"Whatever Tony Secunda asked us do, we did it," said Carl "We never questioned him and he always came up trumps."

Shoppers in Manchester town centre stared in amazement as the Move wagged a replica of an H-bomb around the streets. That evening they appeared on a Granada television show that was broadcast live throughout the Northwest of England. Also on the show were the 'Hooray Henrys' of psychedelic pop, Pink Floyd. At the rehearsal, the show's producer sternly instructed the Move to forget any ideas of performing their smashing up routine on air. On overhearing the producer's lecture, the 'Hooray Henrys' began to rib the Move for being egotistical common hooligans.

"They were probably right," commented **Ace Kefford**. "But ribbing us was the worst thing they could have done."

Tony Secunda sensed a headline and smuggled the axe into the studio, hiding it behind the amplifiers, winking at Carl Wayne as he did so. Live on air, the Move could well be described as loose cannons. The song they had chosen to perform, Bobby Parker's 'Watch Your Step', was appropriately named. With **Roy Wood** breaking into a guitar solo, Carl produced the axe and began to lay into the stack of television sets that had been piled there purely for visual effect. After fifteen seconds of total mayhem, with Ace Kefford and **Trevor Burton** hopping around, trying to watch their step, the producer pulled the plug and the whole Granada network audience found itself staring at a blank screen. The voice of announcer Trevor Lucas apologised profusely and informed the viewers that normal service would be resumed as soon as possible.

"In the meantime, some light music for your pleasure," he said.

"And Pink Floyd never got on the screen!" laughed Ace.

Smoke bombs were also a prominent feature of the Move's stage show. As the act climaxed, the smoke bombs would be triggered. At the Marquee, one late summer's evening in 1966, Tony Secunda ordered road manager **'Upsy' Downing** to 'double the dose' of smoke bombs. With Carl Wayne swinging his axe into the political dolls and the television screens, the smoke bombs were fired into action. Almost immediately, the Central London Fire Brigade received an emergency call to attend the Marquee club in Wardour Street. Next morning the national newspapers carried photographs of firemen in gas masks, armed with water hoses, weaving around the individual members of the Move as they played on through the thick choking clouds of smoke.

At it again — the Move

By the time Deram Records, a subsidiary of Decca, had secured the rights to the Move's recordings, the nation was already well aware of them. An investigation made later revealed that the call for Fire Brigade assistance came from a Wardour Street public telephone kiosk. The caller, a Mr Secunda, had been taking evening perambulation when he became aware of choking smoke in the vicinity of the Marquee club. He was only doing what any decent minded member of the public would do. After all, England expects every man to do his duty.

Expected to do their duty in the land of free love and sauna baths were Shard End's **Andicapps**. With **Micky Heard** now initiated as an Andicapp the boys made the treck across the North Sea to Finland where they found, holed up in Helsinki, another Birmingham bunch, the **Renegades**.

"They'd gone over eighteen months previously. Did well. Sold a right few records of their song 'Cadillac', fell in love with the place and stayed," **Kex Gorin** explained.

Did the Andicapps do their duty in the land of free love?

"No comment!" was the stern reply.

Doing his duty to the best of his ability was **Geoff Turton** of the **Rockin' Berries**. But a worksheet that was bulging at the seams with concerts, television and radio appearances, with recording sessions slotted in according to availability, proved too much for him.

"We never ever had a day off. To be honest, I was cracking up. A voice inside me was saying that enough was enough and so I went down to the factory in Hockley where I'd worked before and asked for my old job back."

With the story of Geoff's retirement from a job that paid £250 per week making the national press, applications from would-be 'poor man's sons' arrived by the sack-full. Auditions were hastily arranged at the Rainbow Suite, Dale End.

"We were lucky in that **Rod Clarke**, who'd filled **Clint Warwick**'s shoes with the Moody Blues so well, was still lingering around Birmingham and he fitted in perfectly with the Berries formula," **Bobby Thomson** explained.

Geoff Turton picks up the tale, "I'd been gone a couple of months. It was hard graft in the factory but I was happy enough. Then **Maurice King**, the Berries manager, sent me a telegram. Would I rejoin?"

"Rod Clarke had been an ideal replacement," Bobby Thomson continued, "but the public had this image of how the Berries should be and sound and that bothered Maurice King."

Geoff Turton was assured that if he returned, the workload would ease considerably. So Geoff asked the foreman for his National Insurance cards and returned to the Berries, but did the workload lighten?

"Of course it didn't," said Geoff. "In fact, as the Berries pushed further into the growing cabaret market, the worksheet became even more intense."

What wouldn't the Vogues have given for the Berries worksheet. But it ain't that easy. Their single 'Younger Girl', although receiving plays on Radio Luxembourg, hadn't exactly happened.

However, a chance to perform the song on national television came their way in late 1966, when they were invited to participate in the Hughie Green talent show, 'Opportunity Knocks', which they had auditioned for earlier in the year.

"We turned up at the Thames TV studios, bubbling with the chance to do 'Younger Girl', but the producer told us that we'd have to do a song that was more in keeping with the format of a family variety show," **Johnny Carroll** explained.

Hughie Green gave his pat announcement, "For the Vogues — opportunity knocks!" and the boys gave their all, wiggling around Edmundo Ross style, to the standard samba song 'Brazil'.

"The show did us no favours at all," said Johnny Carroll, "But I told Hughie Green that I was thinking of having a go as a comedian. He told me he was sure I'd do well. That was good enough for me."

Hoping he was good enough to impress Freddie 'Mr Superbad' Mac was the vocalist with the **Stringbeats, Austin Griffith**. The Freddie Mac Soul Band were in town, at the **Top Rank**, Dale End, and a friend of Austin's knew Freddie personally and asked him to give the boy a shot at singing with the band. With the soul explosion still erupting, the Freddie Mac show had managed to pack the Top Rank ballroom.

"Freddie wasn't that keen on giving me a chance but he relented and I went on cold," explained Austin Griffith. "The brass section just willed me to sing and I recall doing 'Knock On Wood', 'Midnight Hour' and 'Mr Pitiful'. Freddie was well pleased."

Freddie Mac was so well pleased and impressed that he immediately contacted Claire Frances at Polydor Records and advised her immediate attention should be drawn to the **Stringbeats**. Within weeks the Stringbeats were in London, recording 'I Can't Get Enough Of You' for the Polydor label. However, when the mention of promotion came up, which would mean becoming professional musicians, two of the Stringbeats refused to surrender the security of their twenty-pounds-a-week factory jobs and the record fizzled away into oblivion.

The Ebonites and . . .
. . . the Ebonies

"The Stringbeats would have been Birmingham's first black recording band," pointed out Austin Griffith.

Austin was quite correct, as both the **Ebonies** and the **Ebonites** were quite happy as they were and, even on a national basis, the Stringbeats would have been two years ahead of Eddie Grant's Equals. If they were not to be Britain's first successful black recording band, then they would have to be content with being the first local black outfit to be regularly featured at Eddie Fewtrell's **Cedar Club.**

Denny Laine of the **Moody Blues** still had that burning will inside to hang on in there. With frustration at an all time high as a result of efforts to recapture the glory days of eighteen months ago, Denny decided to quit the Moody Blues and pursue a highly ambitious project, the **Incredible String Band**. During the period of this project, Denny composed a song with lyrics and chords so beautifully crafted that it sounded satisfyingly simple. Denny's little masterpiece, 'Say You Don't Mind' went on to provide Colin

Blunstone, formerly of the Zombies with a top twenty single in February 1972.

Messrs Thomas, Edge, Pinder and Lodge could mind all they wished, but with Denny Laine gone, they had to do something, and fast. Being a typical Brummie, **Ray Thomas** headed for the nearest pub to take consolation in a few pints of ale. Alongside Ray at the bar stood Eric Burdon of the Animals. When Eric heard the news of Denny Laine's departure, he reached into his pocket and produced the letter he'd received from a desperately hungry guitarist who could sing and could also write songs to a professional standard. The world was just one year away from 'Nights in White Satin'.

The Capitols

At the **Capitols** camp, **Lyndon Laney** and manager **Bob Thomas**, being enterprising gentlemen, became knights in white cowgowns as they went into the business of making amplifiers. Calling their company 'Laney' they set up shop in a workspace at the old Birds Custard Factory in Digbeth.

"They talked me into buying the first PA amplifier they made," said **Ken Fryer** of the Capitols. "It looked great and the covering smelled fantastic. But it was just like singing down a rolled up Argus! Credit to Lyndon though, he got it bang on after that."

Mike **Sheridan**'s head was going bang with the pressures of being in the potato business. Fed up to the gills with lighthearted jibes about his 'taters', Mike had to regain his street credibility. The result was **Sheridan's Lot**, and this Lot were **Pete Oliver**, **Terry Wallace** and **Colin Timmins** on guitars with **Joe Dignam** at the drums. The chance of a four-week engagement at the recently opened **Rum Runner** club presented itself to Sheridan's Lot. The Rum Runner, on Broad Street, lay between Gas Street and Bridge Street, and facing King Edward's Place. Either way for Sheridan's Lot, the Rum Runner was a high profile engagement. The only drawback was performing until the early hours when daytime occupations now figured in many of the once-professional musicians' lives.

The Rum Runner, Broad Street

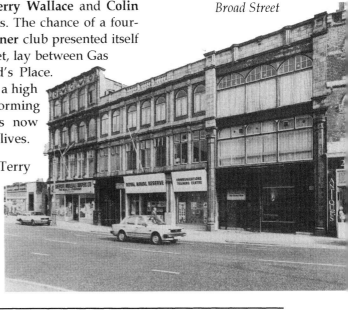

"I was working at Leyland in Drew's Lane," said Terry Wallace "But the old rock 'n' roll feeling was still there. Then on the Friday night, half way through the four week run, Sheridan casually mentioned that he'd booked a week's holiday in Weston-super-Mare. I asked him when he was going and he said, "Tomorrow morning, first thing." That was the end of Sheridan's Lot!"

So, down the alleyway off Broad Street that led to the Rum Rummer club, came the **Bobby Ash Sound**. 'Bobby' (**Graham Ashford**) had, in pre-Beatles days, led Rednal's **Ekos** before they became the **Cheetahs** and more recently had figured in the **Brumbeats**. Once again firing on all cylinders, Bobby had recruited guitarists **Bob Watkins** and **'Fats' Surplice** along with bassist **Roy 'Tank' Davis** and **John 'Jigger' Evans** at the kit. When 'Fats' Surplice became surplus to requirement, they had gone for broke as a three piece until, at the Rum Runner bar one evening, **Dennis Ryland**, the saxophonist, was spotted partaking in cocktails and pocket billiards.

"I'd had a few," said Dennis, "and I was worried about my sax being left in my car outside. Graham Ashford suggested that I did something useful and sit in with them and that's how I joined the Bobby Ash Sound."

"The band changed for the better with Dennis aboard," commented Bob Watkins. "He's a great flautist, so we started to put all the Manfred Mann stuff into the set."

With material like Dylan's 'If You Gotta Go, Go Now', 'Just Like a Woman' and 'Mighty Quinn' all figuring prominently in the programme of the Bobby Ash Sound, the combo had a gig list to be envied.

The Bobby Ash Sound outside the Black Horse, Northfield

"Our diary was always crammed full," said **Bobby Ash**. "I was then working for **Pete Gittins** as the booker. He'd give me his agency date sheet to fill in. So I did, giving most dates to the **Bobby Ash Sound**!"

In early 1968 Bobby Ash sold his PA system to Robert Plant for £100 and set

off for America, eventually settling in Los Angeles, where he became general service manager of Rolls Royce Motors in Beverley Hills. However music was not discarded totally as, at the Star Recording Studios, Bobby provided backing vocals on many an occasion for the likes of David Gates and Steve Miller. Venturing further into the arts, Bobby discovered an incredible outlet for his paintings. His own art gallery!

Now in early retirement, Graham lives in Hawaii. Under near permanent blue skies and to the sound of the crystal clear Pacific waters rippling onto a white sandy beach, he still performs as 'Bobby Ash' to an audience of garland laden hula-hula girls. A far cry indeed from Underhill Road, Alum Rock!

Brian Nicholls of the **Shanes** was feeling like a bit of a castaway, or 'cast off' himself. **Max 'the Nub' Griffiths** had headhunted the front man of the Shanes, **Mick Lawson**, and claimed him for the **D'Fenders**. At the same time drummer **Ken Horden** got word from the horse's mouth that **Tony Finister** was vacating the drum stool with the **Modernaires**. With the drum stool still warm, Ken became one of the Mods.

Brian was able to keep his hand in by re-uniting with his old mate **Vic Jarvis**, now serving in the **Little People**. Standing at five feet six inches, Brian just qualified for the job.

The Modernaires

What had qualified **Freddie Mac** as a heavyweight boxer was his enormous frame. "If Freddie said it was Wednesday, it was Wednesday!" recalled promoter **Mike Carroll**.

Freddie Mac had seen out his career in the ring by acting as sparring partner to the world champion himself, Cassius Clay. However it was as a soul man that he'd make his presence in Britain known.

Mike Carroll explains, "I got a call from a London agent asking if I'd take the Freddie 'Mr Superbad' Mac Soul Show for a three night run, the Thursday, Friday and Saturday. Soul was what my punters were demanding. I'd heard that Freddie had this great band blowing for him and normally I wouldn't have been able to afford them, but as they were passing through the Midlands en route to the North, I picked them for more or less travel expenses."

The D'fenders

Again the Gods smiled on Mike Carroll. Having recently come to an arrangement with Bromsgrove Council, he had started promoting dances at **Bromsgrove Baths**, the **Dolphin Suite** to be precise, on Saturday evenings throughout the winter of 1966.

"The Freddie Mac Soul Show had to be seen to be believed," said Mike Carroll. "The crowds loved every second. I had them at the **Black Horse**, Northfield on the Thursday and the **Royal Oak** at Hockley Heath on the Friday. The word was hot and I had to organise coaches to ferry people in from the surrounding areas of Longbridge and Redditch to Bromsgrove Baths. Unbelievable!"

The audience at Bromsgrove Baths that night found the support band, the **Exchequers**, quite unbelievable. After being totally zapped by the sheer energy of Freddie Mac and his powerful brass section, the audience stood in anticipation as the Exchequers shuffled on stage. Guitarist and vocalist **Laurie Hornsby** tried desperately to maintain the soulful vibes of the room with a meaningful interpretation of the John Sebastian song 'You Didn't Have To Be So Nice'. Receiving minimum applause, Laurie's attention was drawn to the wings where promoter Mike Carroll beckoned the lad who, by now, was drowning in his own sweat, to 'Come off son. It ain't worth it!'

Perhaps if Freddie Mac had stayed a little longer in the Bromsgrove area he would have attended one of the 'Fight Nights', presented in the canteen at the Austin Motor works at Longbridge. Representing the team from **Kyle Hall**, Aston was **Albert Chapman**, the feared doorman of the

Plaza, Handsworth. Albert's opponent that particular evening was, from Leamington Spa, **Dave 'Banger' Walsh**, who later became the world heavyweight wrestling champion.

Albert Chapman tells the tale, "He was called 'Banger' because he came out like a man possessed, wanting to bang somebody, and quick. I was scared and nervous and when the bell went 'Banger' came charging out and swung one at me. I dodged, saw he was wide open and lamped him one on the 'ooter."

In twenty seconds Albert Chapman had knocked out 'Banger' Walsh. Also knocked out with Albert's performance was **Ray Berrow**, owner of the **Rum Runner** club. He immediately offered Albert a position at the club, working with its manager, the former Redcap himself, **Mick Walker**. For his conquest over 'Banger' Walsh, Albert was presented with the evening's star prize, a blanket!

"That meant I could finally take the overcoat off the bed!" said Albert, wiping a tear from his eye.

Unbelievably cold in the cellar beneath the All Saints Mission Hall, Station Road, Witton, across from the Aston Villa football ground, four lads who called themselves the **Approach** were rehearsing.

"We couldn't find a drummer and we only had one amplifier," **Jeff Hibbard** explained. "It was me and a bloke I worked with at Bush Motors on Chester Road with our guitars, and a bass player. We spent hours down that cellar practising Eddie Floyd's 'Knock on Wood'. With no heating whatsoever, our fingers used to be frozen to the bone!"

Fortunately for the singer in the Approach, **John Osborne** (who everyone called 'Ozzy') there were four inputs on the amplifier, which meant that there was room for Ozzie's microphone. Staring menacingly at the cold, dank walls of the church cellar Ozzy would broadcast to the vicinity of Witton Lodge Road that 'I don't wanna lose this good thing!' Informing the neighbourhood that 'It's like thunder! Lightning! The way you love me is frightening!' John Osborne's breath would freeze as it left his lips!

The Bobcats at Pye Studios

Knocking on wood were the **Bobcats**. Agent **John Singer** announced that he had secured twenty-thousand pounds worth of work on the their behalf, but things got tricky when the authorities came down on them for working under-age. The ensuing national press headlines didn't go amiss though, and on the strength of their obvious appeal, John Singer also negotiated a contract with Pye Records for a single release.

Written by **Uglys Steve Gibbons**

and **Dave Pegg**, 'Can't See for Lookin'' was recorded at Pye's Marble Arch studios under the supervision of producer Alan Freeman.

"We were fifteen and appearing on the David Frost Show!" recalled drummer **Les Fortnam**,

Although still schoolboys, the Bobcats were so hip in the fashion stakes that when **Grey's** store, in Bull Street, launched an in house boutique, the Birdcage, who did their marketing people invite to cut the ribbon and proclaim the Birdcage open? Why, the Bobcats of course! But the sweetest trip of all for the boys was when they were invited to play 'Can't See for Lookin'' live, on the Blue Peter children's television show. With the show recorded in the morning, the Bobcats were back in Birmingham in time for the evening transmission. It was a proud moment indeed when Dave, Paul, Gary and Les received their Blue Peter badges from Valerie Singleton and John Noakes.

After the disappointment of the Polydor recording test with the Crescendos, **Norman Haines** discovered that the man could be removed from Brumbeat, but Brumbeat could not be removed from the man, as he returned to the **Brum Beats**. However the Brum Beats were taken out of the Brumbeat when, for a short while, they operated as the **Ladies Gentlemen**, a bunch of highly formal looking soul men. With a repertoire that was very black in influence, the Ladies Gentlemen wore black suits and black bowler hats.

"They matched our fingernails," Norman commented.

Formal dressing counted for nothing when the Ladies Gentlemen were awakened one morning with the bad news that their van, with all their equipment aboard, had been stolen.

"The coppers found the van and some empty drum cases but the rest had gone," said Norman. " I sulked around for a few days then psyched myself

The Ladies Gentlemen

up again. I had to. By now I was a married man and we had the flat over Sutcliffe's other record shop on Smethwick High Street. As you can imagine, living in that area, I was getting very influenced by the ska and the blue beat music that went with the territory."

So influenced was Norman that he managed to find the down payment on a Vox organ and a PA system. A few 'cold calls' to various establishments in the Handsworth and Smethwick areas of the city resulted in a residency at the **Continental** club, on Soho Road. An advertisement in the 'Birmingham Mail' brought drummer **Jimmy Skidmore** and bassist **Alan Taylor** to Norman, who came up with a suitable sunny Caribbean name for them, the **Delmore Lee Sound**.

The **Continental** club faced **Tito's**, where **David Broadhurst**, now that **Monopoly** were striking blows for musical freedom, began to regularly present a new band, **The Rest**. With **Tony Iommi** on lead and **Vic Radford** on rhythm, the Rest also had **Mike Pountney** on bass and **Bill Ward** crashing away on drums. They were a pretty exciting bunch that supplied an up-tempo set that was well stocked with the groovy stuff and kept the punters happy. Tony Iommi had been pals at Birchfield Road School with **Albert Chapman**, who was by now working at the Rum Runner.

"I lived in Franchise Street, just round from the school," said Albert. "Tony had his gear set up in our front room so he could start practising immediately after the school bell sounded. My old man would be in the other room trying to eat his tea in peace. 'Turn that bleedin' noise down!' he'd shout."

Mr Chapman senior and Tony Iommi had been working together at a factory in Aston in 1963 when Tony met with a horrific accident that threatened any ambition he had as a guitarist. Whilst working a guillotine he sliced the tips off his right hand fingers. Being left-handed meant that these were the fingertips used to press the strings against the fretboard.

"Tony refused to be beaten," said Albert. "He used to collect 'Squeezy' washing up liquid bottles and cut them into little pieces. Then he'd weld the pieces together to make thimbles!"

Highly strung – H Cain

The **Monopoly** were now making rapid progress and gaining recognition as a fine folk/rock outfit. Hartley Cain has always acknowledged the Byrds' guitarist, Roger McGuinn as his guiding light.

"At the time I had a Gibson 335 guitar which I'd spent out on. Roger McGuinn was using a twelve string Rickenbecker for that 'jingle jangle' sound, but I could never afford one in a million years," said 'H'.

After giving the problem some thought, with typical Hartley Cain logic, he came up with a solution. He drilled three holes in the bridge of the Gibson and wired three banjo strings on to make it a nine-string guitar. Still dissatisfied with being three strings short, Hartley Cain drew up a master plan to give the Monopoly a guitar sound that they could confidently refer to as 'all their very own'. **Raymond Froggatt** marked out a piece of wood what was to become the body of a totally unique guitar. Mr Cain senior made the necessary metal parts and young 'H' then fitted the neck of a Fender Precision bass to the body. A motorcar's clutch cable, stretched at the rear of the neck, ensured that the tension was maintained.

Hartley Cain then proceeded to fit the strings onto this newly created instrument, the eighteen-string guitar!

Through their association with John Parsons, the Monopoly became known to ADSEL managing director, Arthur Smith. He was quick to recommend them to Polydor Records' talent scouts.

"We did a test at the **Hollick and Taylor** studio," recalled Froggy. "Johnny Hawkins and Richard Hill came up from London on behalf of Polydor. At the end of the test Richard told us that normally the tape would be analysed and all that claptrap, but in our case he told us the result there and then. Yes!"

The Monopoly would be contracted as Polydor artistes. The scruff bags had made good!

The **Hellions**, from Worcester, weren't scruff bags by any means but they had decided to move with the times and go for a name change. When, in October of 1966, they played at the opening night of entrepreneur **Tony Green**'s new **Penthouse** club (above the **Surfside Stop** late night café on Constitution Hill) they were introduced as **Deep Feeling**. Whether performing or simply socialising, **Jim Capaldi** and guitarist **Dave Mason** were now regular faces on the Brumbeat scene, especially at the **Elbow Room**. They would be the guest musicians for the evening, or perhaps, if coaxed from the bar, participants in a little jamming with their close friend **Stevie Winwood**.

Upstairs – the Penthouse Club Downstairs – the Surfside Stop

At the **Surfside Stop**, two of the **Boll Weevils** — **John Rowlands** and **Geoff Nichols** — sat at a table drumming their fingers to the deep muffled sound of Deep Feeling that was leaking from the club upstairs. The two lads were there to meet with a young man who had answered their newspaper advertisement for a drummer who could sing harmonies.

The Incas

"**Mac Poole** had been with the **Incas**, **Derry Ryan's** band, from Oldbury," explained John Rowlands. "When Mac arrived we bought him a cup of coffee. Me and Geoff then started singing the song, 'Barbara Anne', and asked Mac to put a harmony on the top so we could check his voice out."

In 'barber shop' harmony, the two Boll Weevils plus an out of work Inca provided the Surfside Stop waitresses with an impromptu performance

The Seed

of what the Brum rock scene could expect over the next few months or so. Mac Poole tapped his spoon on the sugar bowl to keep everyone in tempo as they 'Saw Mary Lou, Tried Peggy Sue', before collapsing in fits of hysteria. Just as the Beach Boys had done on the master recording. Mac joined up immediately but a mutual decision was made to rename the band. Having entered the Surfside as the Boll Weevils, they departed as the **Seed**.

John Rowlands continues the story, "As we drove home, Geoff Nicholls suddenly looked at me and said, 'What happens if he can't play the drums?' "

Stevie Winwood was approached to do the soundtrack for the film 'Here We Go Round the Mulberry Bush'. It was taken for granted by the powers that be that Stevie would work with the rest of the Spencer Davis Group on the project. Instead he chose to be assisted by **Jim Capaldi**, **Dave Mason** (who was supplementing his Deep Feeling wages by acting as a roadie for the Spencer Davis Group) and the flautist from Locomotive, **Chris Wood**.

Stevie Winwood was definitely working with the Spencer Davis crew in the autumn of '66. Brother Muff began by creating a lick on his bass guitar. The lick was worked around the octave, with emphasis on the lower registered note. So infectious was the lick that Spencer Davis could not help but play accompanying chords that, for him, seemed immediately tailor made. As his fingers fumbled from an E chord to the G, Stevie Winwood, stabbing the keys of the Hammond organ, sang the line "So glad we made it." The Spencer Davis Group *had* made it. As the song reached the all important hook, came the movement from the first to the fourth chord. A movement that, when graced with Stevie Winwood's lyric would have the groovers on every dancefloor in Britain pleading 'Gimme Some Lovin''.

Hoping like crazy to grab the ears of the record buying public were **William's Conquerors**, who had spent the summer in and out of **Ladbroke Sound Studios** and **Jim Tetlow**'s studio on Stratford Road, Sparkbrook.

Not only had they come up with new material, they also had a new name that was more in keeping with the mod image that they had adopted, enhanced by a shopping excursion to Carnaby Street. In September, **William's Conquerors** became the **Frame**. By October, RCA Victor, Elvis's label no less, had them under contract and by November, the Frame had released the **Brian Harbison** song 'She'. Despite live appearances on Radio

Luxembourg, from Tiles club, London; and the lunchtime BBC Light Programme show, 'Pop Inn', sales were pretty disappointing.

Whilst supporting the Who at **Birmingham University**, bass player Brian Harbison, in showing off his skills as the world's next John Entwhistle, blew his bass speaker to smithereens. Next morning, **Bob Adams** set out, in their Thames van to **Ringway Music**, on Moor Street with a view to having the speaker repaired.

"The speaker cabinet toppled from the back seat and I reached over to steady it," said Bob innocently.

Meanwhile, unfortunately, with no one at the helm, the van wrapped itself round a tree. Bob was okay though — that is until the rest of the band got a hold of him!

The Frame

Desperate to make good was **Norman Haines** with his **Delmore Lee Sound**. Always willing to travel, Norman made the mile-long trek from the **Continental Club** on Soho Road to Rookery Road in Handsworth, to appear at the **Plaza** ballroom. There had been a slight disruption at the Plaza the previous night when the **Memphis Sounds** had appeared. On setting up their equipment, they discovered that they had forgotten to pack their mains plugboards.

"Someone had the bright idea of bodging the bare wires into the power points and wedging them with matchsticks," **Dave Challinor** recalled.

Jim Simpson on trumpet at the Swing Shift

Such demand was too much for an antiquated electrical wiring system that had been in place since the building had opened as the Rookery Cinema in the 1930s.

"There was a flash and an almighty bang. We'd fused the whole lot," said Dave. "We never played on the Regan circuit again!"

With power restored, the **Locomotive** were the bill toppers the following evening. Their trumpet player and manager, **Jim Simpson**, was well impressed with Norman Haines. Jim had made his presence felt within the Brumbeat scene as the number one photographer of the action in and around the city. His photographs were part of the fixtures and fittings of the magazine, Midland Beat.

Norman Haines

Norman Haines picks up the tale, "Locomotive, at that time featured Jim, **Monk Finch** and **Chris Wood** with **Pete Allen** on bass. **Rick Storey** played keyboards and **Pete Hodges** handled the vocals. A couple of weeks later, Jim Simpson called and we arranged to meet for a liquid lunch at the Jester pub on the corner of Smallbrook Ringway. He asked if I fancied joining Locomotive as the keyboard player. I told him I'd join if I could do the vocals as well. Jim replied that I'd have to sort that one out for myself!"

Norman needn't have worried. Pete Hodges, after a couple of weeks of trying to strum a guitar whilst Norman scatted his way through some fine songs, decided to leave of his own volition. Jim Simpson paid the deposit on a Hammond organ and Norman Haines was aboard the Locomotive with his career right on track.

Blaises

Right where he wanted to be was a former motor racing driver and enthusiast turned carpet salesman in the family business based at Hall Green. **Martin Hone**, a self confessed 'jazz nut', had no experience whatsoever of running a bar, club or restaurant, and yet had a wish and a will to do something for the people of Birmingham that would be good for himself and his family. Converting canalside stables in Gas Street, Martin Hone launched his club, the **Opposite Lock,** on 21st December, 1966.

"With an hour to go and a queue along the towpath, there I was in a dress suit, nailing drape curtains behind the reception desk," chuckled Martin. "The principle of the Opposite Lock was to provide great music in a wholesome atmosphere with a good supper."

As canal barges chugged by to moor up in Gas Street Basin, the discerning clientele sat at candle-lit tables and bathed in the romantic atmosphere created by pianist **Al Bevins** and his trio. Then, at midnight, the Lock came alive to the jive, compliments of the disco, featuring the hip-to-the-tip sounds of Roger 'Our Man' Harris. **Roger Harris**'s previous showbiz career had been as keyboard player with the **Concords**. With the band now defunct, Roger had sought pastures new as a DJ.

Bass guitarist **Bob Doyle**, along with drummer **Keith Smart**, keyboard player **Terry Guy**, vocalist **Bill James** and guitarist **Dave Morgan**, were figuring in the plans of **Mayfair Entertainments** man, **John Parsons**. With his ADSEL involvement, John Parsons envisaged a new outfit that would trigger some interest within Polydor Records. Shrewdly naming his new project after the Soho club where the hierarchy of the music business did their socialising, John Parsons thought that selling the idea of **Blaises** as a band would be a cinch.

"But the Polydor thing never worked out," explained Keith Smart. "And we needed to work."

Blaises weren't on their own. The **Move** needed to work. They were now a force to be reckoned with on the London scene, thanks to their successful Marquee residency. When the Who played the opening night of the Roundhouse, at Chalk Farm, North London, the Move took the prestigious support spot.

"Give 'em loads of old rock 'n' roll," **Tony Secunda** advised his protégés, and the Move obediently carried out his instructions. Taking to the stage

Axeman Carl Wayne in action at the Roundhouse

they began to deliver a set that was in no way for the faint hearted. With **Trevor Burton** tearing his throat apart on Eddie Cochran's 'Somethin' Else', two female strippers appeared on stage. As Trevor screamed the lines "She's sure fine lookin' man! Wow! She's somethin' else!" the scantily clad ladies more or less revealed their all to a Roundhouse audience that was simmering towards hysteria. Trevor Burton was now pointing to something that was being shunted down from the back of the room.

"That car's fine lookin' man! Wow! That's somethin' else!"

And it was. A silver coloured Cadillac car was driven to the stage and Carl Wayne, clutching his famous axe, leapt onto the car's bonnet, and plunged the axe straight through the roof!

"The stage got invaded," recalled **Ace Kefford**, shaking his head. "It was an hour before the Who could get on. Christ only knows what happened to the strippers!"

The Move at Windsor Festival 1966

Ace 'the Face' Kefford

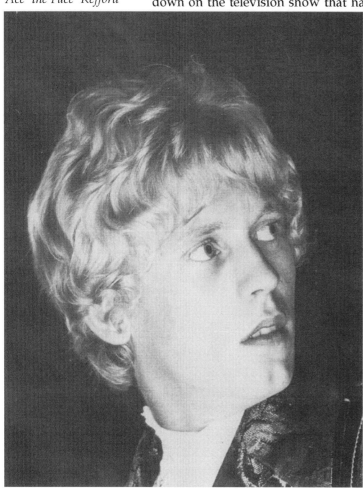

With such razzmatazz publicity aiding their course, the Move's first single, 'Night of Fear', began to show in the top twenty. Riding on the riff of Tchaikovsky's '1812 Overture', minus the cannons, **Roy Wood**'s lyric told of eyesight being affected by green and purple lights and images on bedroom walls.

A slot in what was to be the very last transmission of the Friday night pop television show, 'Ready Steady Go' was secured to add further weight to the promotion of 'Night Of Fear'. Tony Secunda had already decided that the band should adopt a 'Roaring Twenties' gangster type image to carry the song. When the show's running order was devised it was revealed that the Move were to bring the curtain down on the television show that had done so much for mid-sixties British youth culture. Presenter Cathy McGowan giggled out sentimental 'Thank you' messages from all over the universe before introducing the grand finale, "The Move with their absolutely spiffing new record, 'Night of Fear!'"

Menacing as ever, and staring directly into the camera, **Carl Wayne** spelled out to the nation that what they were hearing was 'too much for your mind'. Viewers, taking their Friday night tea of steamed fish, reeled in shock as 'Ace the Face' made the most of his camera close up, telling everyone, in no uncertain terms, that he was "Just about to flip your mind. Just about to trip your mind."

Proceedings were then bought to an end with an almighty crescendo of feedback and crashing drums. With the studio audience showing their appreciation a midget, dressed in 'Bugsy Malone' attire, burst from inside of **Bev Bevan's** bass drum, leapt down from the stage and began to 'machine gun' them!

"As far as Secunda's promotional pranks went," said Ace, "That one *Poised for chart success –* bordered on genius." *the Move*

Credits rolled and Cathy McGowan could be seen congratulating the Move on another explosive performance. Also caught quite clearly on camera was the sight of the three-foot tall midget desperately fighting a losing battle to clamber back up onto the four-foot high stage!

Chapter Six

1967 Rainbows in the Evening

In January '67 **Dave Pegg**, **Roger Hill** and **Bugsy Eastwood**, a Kingstanding lad who was not only an amazing drummer, but also by now a terrific songwriter, pooled their exceptional talents to make up the **Exception**. Rehearsals were held at the **Prince Rupert** pub in Nechells. When everything looked and sounded shipshape, Dave Pegg's close friend **Robert Plant** introduced them to Eddie Kassner. Eddie had formed Kassner Music back in the 40s when, for a few bucks, he purchased the rights to a throwaway song that no one else in the music business was remotely interested in. The song was Max Friedman's 'Rock Around the Clock'.

*The Exception —
left out of the charts*

Kassner Music had a record label, President, which gave the Exception their first release entitled 'The Eagle Flies on Friday'

"**Bobby Hill**, Roger's brother, had a brainwave to buy the record into the charts," said Dave Pegg, "So he toured the shops buying our single by the box full."

Unfortunately, on that very week, the Melody Maker and New Musical Express had been made aware of various stings taking place intended to influence the sales charts. So that week the retail figures were ignored and so called experts, who'd never heard of the Exception or 'The Eagle Flies on Friday', were called upon to estimate chart positions. Bobby Hill was left disastrously out of pocket.

Leaving Birmingham on the first Friday of the New Year, **Blaises**, the band put together by **John Parsons**, were off to Turkey.

"And we went by train!" drummer **Keith Smart** exclaimed. "All the way from London Victoria to Istanbul, humping the gear with us!"

Blaises' destination was the American Air Force base at Adana, in southern Turkey, famous for being the base from which spy pilot Gary Powers took off. In line with all engagements of this nature, a female vocalist was an absolute necessity and Blaises were able to call upon the services of 'Little Miss Dynamite' herself, **Brenda Bosworth**, formerly of the **Grasshoppers** and the **Creators** (who were briefly known as the **Block**).

"Struggling with the gear on and off trains was sheer murder," said Brenda, pulling a pained face. "On at Victoria, off at Folkestone and onto the boat; off the boat and onto the Paris train; off again, then on for one last time to Istanbul. Great! Off to the sun! Or so we thought."

Explosive –
Brenda Bosworth

Somewhere in the bowels of Yugoslavia, the Istanbul train made a short stop. The four little Brummie lads and one little Brummie girl were hanging out of the train windows, taking in the Yugoslavian sights as the train pulled out the station. That's when Blaises noticed their equipment – stacked on the platform. A porter had unloaded it by mistake!

Keith Smart described the scene at Istanbul railway station as Blaises stepped down from the carriage, stressed out with worry about their equipment.

"It was like that film, 'Midnight Express'. There was coppers pointing guns at people, busting open suitcases and emptying the contents all over the platform. Nobody spoke a word of English."

No one except a Turkish taxi driver who happened by; luckily he spoke the most perfect Queen's English.

"What the Blaises is going on?" he asked.

With his help their equipment was dispatched to them via the next train from Yugoslavia. Blaises, in the middle of a freezing Turkish January night set off across the mountains for Adana. Travelling on a rickety old bus, with their gear hurled haphazardly up and onto the rusty roof rack, Miss Bosworth and Messrs Morgan, Doyle, Guy and Smart, sat terrified, clinging to their seats as the old bucket bounced around the road, which was no more than a dirt track, with sheer drops of hundreds of feet on either side.

Blaises –
hot band in cold Turkey

"The driver kept turning his head round and talking to us," said Brenda. "I was thinking, 'This is it. It ain't been a bad life but it's all over now.' "

The American servicemen warmed to Blaises immediately. With a set that was soul orientated, the songs they performed fitted in perfectly with the way that the entertainment room functioned.

"There were whites on one side, who switched on to **Dave Morgan's** songs and blacks on the other side, who were into my raunchy stuff, you know, 'I can't turn you loose!' " sang Brenda, doing a quick Otis impression.

IT'S BROOM AND ZOOM AT BRUM AIRPORT !

IT'S a real flying take-off every Monday evening at the Caravelle Club, the latest entertainment spot to crash-dive the Midlands.

It's certainly a club with a difference, 'cos it's held in the Observation Lounge, which overlooks the runways of Birmingham Airport.

Top marks to the famous Scotch Clubs of London for introducing a club zoom full of atmosphere, where you can watch the planes taxi-ing along the runways while dancing to the discs from the top fifty presented by D.J. Andy Ferris.

Or sample the live entertainment from groups like the Action and the Way of Life, and top-liners like Zoot Money and Chris Farlowe, as aircraft arrive and take off for London and the Continent.

It's " chocks away " on the dance floor, where you might find yourself raving it up alongside Chris Farlowe, Normie Rowe or Steve Winwood.

Some ravers even fly in from Manchester and London especially to dig this great scene.

The gear here is really more varied than at most clubs. From silk mod suits for the sophisticated guys to cord hipsters and fringed suede jackets for guys who dig the Westerner look.

While skirts—whether they're kilts or just plain—are short, short, short ! Dresses, too, are definitely mini, in wild fabrics, and fab cat suits worn by long-legged lasses are catching everybody's eye.

Great for travelling and raving is this natty navy and white striped shirt dress from British Home Stores, which costs only 55s.

And flying high with the boys was a gal in this purple smock dress with decorative pearl buttons by Shelana at 99s 6d.

Address : Observation Lounge, Birmingham Airport.
Open Mondays 8.30 - 12.
Membership 2s 6d per year plus entrance fee, which varies with artiste.
Average age : 18.
Fully licensed.

Doc Holliday and fans (taken just a split-second before the impact?)

Although their record, 'The Eagle Flies on Friday', was not deemed a classic, the **Exception** still played on regardless at places like the **Mews** on Moseley Road, just down from the Prince of Wales pub; **St Peters College**, Saltley; **Mossley Youth Club**, Bloxwich; the **Belfry** at Wishaw; the **Mackadown**, Kitts Green; and the **Cofton Country Club**, which was the former roller skating rink on the fairground site in Warren Lane at the Lickey Hills. There was also the **Caravelle Club**, Elmdon airport, where disc jockey **Doc Holliday** would announce, far too often, that a thief had been 'apprehended by the hangers.' The **Carnaby Club**, which was the back room of the **Hobmoor** pub at Yardley. The **Penthouse**, over the top of the Surfside Stop café on Constitution Hill, just down from the **Cedar Club**, and the **Crown and Cushion** at Perry Barr.

Venues of this nature meant little to the **Applejacks**. Enjoying every moment of life on the ocean waves, they were now firm favourites as entertainers aboard the Cunard liner, 'The Queen Elizabeth'. **Gerry Freeman** could well be described as the sailor with the navy blue eyes.

"We were on the Southampton to New York crossing for months at a time," he recalls. "That meant I could utilise my time ashore in the Big Apple by taking drum lessons from some of the finest percussion tutors in the world. I'm not putting the Applejacks down, but working with top-class reading musicians was what I intended to do, once we'd finished as a band."

Pitching again at the charts, the Applejacks released what was to be their final record. 'You've Been Cheatin'', featuring **Johnny Washington** on vocals, made little or no impact. It was hardly surprising as the Applejacks were far too busy cruising the Caribbean and the South Pacific to worry about such an irrelevant thing as promoting a pop record.

Taking their promotional work very seriously was the **Spencer Davis Group**. Their previous single, 'Gimme Some Lovin'' was still 'hot and selling' but, with the song, 'I'm a Man', already done and dusted, Spencer and the boys, in late January of 1967, were again amongst the nation's top ten best

Working for Cunard —
the Applejacks
Stevie Winwood

selling singles. However all was not well as rumours abounded regarding the future of **Stevie Winwood** and his position within the Spencer Davis Group. All was revealed when, in April of 1967, an amicable split was announced. Stevie, along with drummer **Jim Capaldi** and guitarist **Dave Mason**, was forming a new band that would be called **Traffic**. **Chris Wood**, the flautist, would also be included in the line-up, and future releases would be on the Island label, the independent label owned by Stevie's manager, **Chris Blackwell**. A further dent was made in the Spencer Davis group when **Muff Winwood** announced his retirement from playing as a musician to take up a position in the Artiste and Repertoire department of Island Records. Spencer Davis wasted no time at all in replacing Muff and Steve Winwood with two London musicians, guitarist **Phil Sawyer** and organist **Eddie Hardin**, whose previous band, A Wild Uncertainty, had recently covered an Everley Brothers' song, 'A Man With Money'. As the spring bank holiday day trippers headed for the coast, the sound of Traffic could be heard crackling out of their transistor radios.

"So you think you're having good times," sang Stevie Winwood. You better believe it! Everyone was having good times to Traffic's 'Paper Sun'.

With a spring in their step, **Jeff Hibbard** and **Ozzy Osbourne** headed for the Birmingham City centre and the **George Clay** music store in their old and battered van. The name **The Approach** was daubed on its sides.

The boys had decided that a move from their rehearsal room, the church cellar in Witton, to the **Underwood School Hall** on the Lyndhurst estate at Erdington would be musically beneficial.

"The school hall was bigger than what we were used to," said Jeff Hibbard. "Ozzy went in for a Vox PA system and a microphone. I got myself a Vox Conqueror amplifier. Of course it was all on the drip."

The salesman at George Clay's, **Cedric Viles**, tried in vain to talk Ozzy Osbourne into going the distance and buying a microphone stand.

"No thanks. I don't use 'em," replied Ozzy bluntly.

With new equipment and a new drummer, the Approach entered into a weekly thrash at Underwood School Hall. Folks would gather in the playground to hear Ozzy Osbourne's voice jumping from his recently purchased microphone system, warbling out the Jimi Hendrix song, 'Purple Haze', which had newly been added to the band's repertoire.

George Clay Music Centre's Cedrick Viles

"People would ask us to play at weddings and birthdays and them kind of do's," Jeff Hibbard explained. "We always gave the same answer. "When we're ready, we'll start taking bookings." Just as we were nearly ready, the Approach called it a day!"

Decca Records were seriously thinking about calling it a day with the **Moody Blues**. Two and a half years on from 'Go Now', the Moodys could now be found endeavouring to be creatively inspired while parading their unquestionable talents amongst the bingo ping-pong ball machines, and weekly tote result boards that cluttered up the stages of the soul destroying northern cabaret clubs. Stuck in a 'Catch 22' situation, the Moody Blues were trying to strike the happy balance of earning a half-decent living wage as credible musicians whilst struggling to ignore the demands from the audience to 'play something we know for Christ's sake!' And then, as if by miracle, came a lifeline. **Tony Clarke**, an in-house producer at Decca, was given the task of rescuing the recording career of the Moody Blues. More by luck than judgement, Decca could not have appointed a better man for the job. Tony Clarke was a Coventry lad and therefore had no problems with the Brummie accent. Also, in the early 60s, Tony had played bass with a Coventry outfit, **Danny Storme and the Strollers**, performing on the same dance hall circuits as **El Riot and the Rebels** and the **Avengers**. When spirits are down, having the same backyard in common can prove to be the vital uniting factor. In 1963 Tony Clarke had decided to learn the record business from scratch and under the guidance of **Tony Hall**, had taken employment in the promotions department at Decca Records. Rising through the ranks, Tony Clarke was granted the producer's chair when Decca signed **Pinkerton's Assorted Colours** and the combination had produced the hit 'Mirror Mirror'.

The Tony Clarke/Moody Blues partnership did not meet with instant chart approval. Their first effort, the **Justin Hayward** song, 'Fly Me High' did not fly too high, and likewise their second attempt, **Mike Pinder**'s 'Love and Beauty' passed unnoticed during the beautiful summer of love. But the Moodies were finding their feet, and a heavyweight keyboard salvaged from the cobwebbed wings of the **Dunlop Sports and Social Club** in Erdington was playing its part. The instrument that Mike Pinder had been workshop testing three years earlier, the Mellotron, was providing a distinctive atmosphere for their creations. The band was fired up and resurrected. **John Parsons**' agency, **Mayfair Entertainments**, was providing them with their bread and butter, presenting them at venues such as the **Belfry**, Wishaw and the **Punchbowl** at Lapworth. The experiences of flat-capped, ale-swilling masters-of-ceremony were hopefully behind them forever.

Ready and raring to re-launch were Wolverhampton's new look **Montanas**. Earlier in the year they had beefed up their sound and presentation by welcoming in **Jake Elcock** from **Finders Keepers**, on bass guitar. This allowed **Terry Rowley** to demonstrate his skills at the keyboards. Impressed by the new line up, Tony Hatch at Pye Records committed himself to the cause of finding a suitable song for the Montanas. Delving into the catalogue of American writer Scott English, Tony Hatch came up with 'Ciao Baby'. The song was a perfect vehicle for Johnny Jones' voice. If Tony Hatch had delved a little deeper he may have found another Scott English song, 'Brandy'. Whilst plotting to launch a solo career two years later, Barry Manilow explored the same Scott English catalogue. Unhappy at the way 'Brandy' rolled off the tongue he requested permission to change the subject's name to 'Mandy'.

Although 'Ciao Baby' didn't chart, it certainly helped strengthen the popularity of the Montanas through the amount of radio play the record

*Montanas –
down the hatch*

received. Most Sunday lunchtimes would see the Montanas appearing at the **Cleveland Arms** in Wolverhampton. **Trevor Westwood**, a keen follower of the Black Country music scene, recalls arriving at the Cleveland by eleven-thirty at the latest, to be sure of a seat for a Montanas performance.

"You had to queue even though the doors never opened for another hour," said Trevor. "Me and the brother-in-law

Wires investor, Bev Pegg

Cliff Ward

would go home to Chase Terrace after the session, sleep off the beer, and be back at the Cleveland for six o'clock with our wives to queue for the Montanas' evening show!

In the grand old town of Stourport-upon-Severn, just up from the fairground, stands the **Crown** pub. **Cliff Ward** and his band, the **Cruisers**, **Graham Dew**, **Ken Wright**, and **Terry Clarke** had been experiencing similar crowd success for a couple of years, because they were, without doubt, fine exponents of Tamla Motown material. However, Cliff Ward realised that the way forward was to create his own style. A few miles up the A449, on the other side of Kidderminster, in the village of Kinver, Cliff's old pal **Bev Pegg** had made a useful investment. Bev was now the proud owner of a tape recorder and a couple of studio accessories. Bev, always the entrepreneur, immediately saw possibilities and set up a recording studio at Bowcliffe House, aided and abetted by guitarist and writer, **Dave Cartwright**. (Dave would find national acclaim in the early 70s as a folk singer/songwriter with numerous appearances on BBC's lunchtime television show, 'Pebble Mill at One') With the combination of Cliff Ward's early writing efforts and Bev Pegg's twiddling of the knobs on the primitive mixing desk, the CBS Record Company were suitably impressed enough to put out a single, 'Infatuation'. With the name 'The Cruisers' sounding a little dated the artistes were credited as **Martyn Raynor and the Secrets**. For some strange reason, another recording by Cliff Ward, 'Who's a Naughty Boy' was credited to **Simon's Secrets.**

Northfield's very own mischievous little boy, **Jimmy Powell**, had heard on the grapevine that the BBC television soap opera 'The Newcomers' was to feature a pop group performing in its fictional pub, the Bulls Head. In reality the exterior of the **Bulls Head** pub on Kings Norton Green was used for outdoor location shots. Never a lad to let the grass grow under his feet, Jimmy telephoned the show's producer, **St John Howell**, offering the services of **Jimmy Powell and the Dimensions**. On hearing that the BBC had already engaged the services of another local band, **New Street Station**, Jimmy Powell wished St John Howell every success with his production and reminded him that, should anything go haywire, he could be assured that Jimmy Powell's professional services would be readily available. Strangely enough, things did go a little haywire. The band, New Street Station, who had been previously known as the **Outer Limits**, suddenly received an offer that would take them to the outer limits. It was an offer of a four-week engagement in Switzerland. The boys had been highly recommended to the club's owner and, with New Street Station being professional musicians, such offers could not be passed over. Especially when the offer carried the phrase 'plus accommodation'. Regrettably New Street Station had to withdraw from 'The Newcomers' schedule. St John Howell, being a gentleman of the old school, fully understood their dilemma and made contact with Jimmy Powell. Jimmy was sympathetic to the cause and only too happy to be of service. He would, of course, be performing his new single that had been released on Strike Records, a label in which Jimmy had a major interest. Based on Bristol Road South, Northfield, Strike Records had the prestigious postal address of 'Rear of Smoky Joe's Transport Café.' Immediately Jimmy Powell contacted Selmar amplification. Selmar readily agreed to supply their current range of products to be featured on the television camera shots that would be beamed nationwide.

"We will get all this equipment back?" queried the marketing director as Jimmy stacked his transit van full of brand spanking new Selmar goodies. Jimmy Powell and the Dimensions made their television appearance and enjoyed the benefits of being billed as television personalities. Jimmy adjusted their future booking fees accordingly and the Selmar marketing director held his breath.

Meanwhile, over in Switzerland, things weren't all roses for New Street Station. The playing times were horrendous and the accommodation provided could best be described as sparse. After two weeks the boys approached the club owner and asked who had actually recommended them for what was, after all, just a mundane engagement.

"It was a chap from Birmingham, Jimmy Powell," answered the club owner.

Jimmy Powell's new record, incidentally, was prophetically entitled 'I Can Go Down'.

Going down in a big way at the **Plaza,** Old Hill, was drummer **Kenny Wood**. Kenny, along with **Laurie Hornsby**, had moved on from the **Exchequers** to put in with three ex-members of the **Rotundas**, **Roger Ottley**, **Phil Pearce** and vocalist **Roger 'Twitty' Conway**, to perform as **Today's Post**. As the lads finished their set and staggered off the Plaza's revolving stage, it was to be love at first sight for Kenny Wood and one of the regular Plaza girls. Unable to command privacy in the dressing room, Kenny escorted the young lady out through the Plaza emergency fire door and onto the roof of the neighbouring George pub. Giving the courting couple all of two minutes to canoodle in the darkness, Roger Ottley and Laurie Hornsby burst open the fire door and selfishly began to mock the loving couple.

"Come on love," said Kenny Wood to the star stuck young lady, "We'll have a stroll round the corner." Roger looked strangely at Laurie. Laurie thought he'd misheard. The young lady gasped in disbelief. Like the two nosey lads, she knew every inch of the roof. She'd been up there many times, with Roger and with Laurie. There was no 'round the corner'. In total innocence, Kenny Wood, by now near crippled with frustration, stepped further into the darkness and crashed down fourteen feet into the back yard of the George pub, landing amongst the empty beer barrels and smashing his ankle in the process. Credit to Kenny though, despite his injuries, he clambered back up a drainpipe like a real professional, to make sure, in true showbiz style, that the young lady went home thoroughly entertained!

Today's Post at the Ringway Club

G oing down to the Midlands Arts Centre in Cannon Hill Park to join in with the jamming was bass player **Les Hemming**.

Les picks up the story: "The **MAC**, as we called it, was a wonderful place to be if you were young and into expressing yourself creatively in any form of the arts. I well remember **Bob Carolgees** as the assistant manager. Bob did very nicely for himself a few years later with his 'Spit the dog' comedy routine."

Scott Morris Blues Combo Les Hemming continues, "Musically, it was all so far out, as we used to say, meeting other players, the **Dolan Brothers**, **Mike** and **Steve**, and piano players **Frankie Spencer** and **Bob Brady**. That's how we evolved the **Scott Morris Blues Combo**."

Eager to break in the big world of the Birmingham music scene, the Scott Morris Blues Combo put their name down for the Warwickshire Group Contest to be held at the **Locarno** ballroom, Hurst Street in the July of 1967.

Smelling of roses – the Frame

E ntering the Finnish port of Helsinki on a slow boat from Grimsby were the **Frame**. They were on a mission to generate a few sales of their recent single 'Doctor Doctor'.

"We were amazed at our reception," recalled **Brian Harbison**. "There were loads of groupie girls. We called them 'roses', and they knew all about us and our records. The roses used to supply us with illegal booze. They'd follow us everywhere. Even into the sauna. It was a tough trip but someone had to do it!"

After a gig on the Russian border, at the town of Kotka, the Frame were homeward bound. There were plenty of roses crammed in the group's van for their farewell rides. Two hours out of Koska, as the Frame bathed in the fragrance of the roses, it suddenly dawned on them that guitarist **Mick Webley** had been left behind!

Traction

Planning to leave England behind was bass guitarist **Danny Gallagher**. With **Johnny Shane and the Solitaires** long gone, Danny had his emigration papers signed and sealed. He was off to Canada and nothing would change his mind.

"Then **Malc Palmer**, a saxophone player, knocked my door and offered me a job with his soul band, **Traction**," Danny explained. "I went down for a session with them and we got on like a house on fire. But it was the female singer who sold me on the idea of forgetting Canada. The tag 'Little Miss Dynamite' was in no way wasted on **Brenda Bosworth**."

In Sparkhill, the distant hurdy gurdy chimes of a Mr Whippy ice cream van could be heard ringing out ye olde English tune 'Greensleeves', causing the kiddies of that suburb to tear around its back streets, in search of the sacred vehicle. Dispensing the cornets and wearing a pageboy box hat was the former Beachcomber himself, **Pat Wayne**. With the **Beachcombers** no more, and Pat a self-confessed workaholic, he took great delight in serving the community as the Mr Whippy man. Operating strictly on a 'one for them, one for me' basis with regard to cash transactions, Pat achieved the blissful contentment of job satisfaction.

John Rooney's Plainsmen

"Then a punter recognised me and said that a bloke in Ivor Road, **John Rooney**, had a showband, the **Plainsmen**, and they needed a singer," said Pat. With a few more blasts of 'Greensleeves' and a couple of stops in Ivor Road, one of which included a meeting with **John Rooney**, Pat Wayne returned the van to the depot. Once there he told the depot's manager exactly what to do with the remaining cornets.

Heading down the M1 motorway in their Commer van, the **Way Of Life** were bound for Dover and the Channel ferry. London agent Rick Gunnell had booked them to open a brand new club in Leige, Belgium. Not only was the engagement 'a nice little earner', but two of the Pan's People dance troupe, Flick Colby and Babs Lord would be acting as their on stage go-go dancers. Nearing London, the Commer van began to cough and splutter until it finally ground to a halt on the North Circular Road.

"Rick Gunnell sent us out another van, and we pushed the Commer off the road and carried on to Belgium." explained **Reg Jones**.

On arrival in Leige the following morning, The Way of Life were treated by the promoter to a hearty English breakfast. Reg Jones continues, "**Sprike Hopkins** was panicking. He'd never had free food before."

By the time The Way of Life arrived back from their travels, they found their Commer van on the North Circular Road reduced to a shell, having been stripped of all removable parts!

Stripped of all the ambition he ever had in the pop music circus was **Johnny Carroll** of the **Vogues**. One-time dustman, turned full time pop musician, Johnny was now back in Council dungarees and reporting for duty at Lifford Lane refuse disposal site; although he was still spending his evenings as the singer-come-cheekie-chappie of the Vogues.

"I'd more or less left the band," said Johnny "So I did a solo spot at the **Variety Artistes Club** in Aston for nothing. A bloke in a crombie overcoat and smoking a fat cigar offered me a job at **Perry Common British Legion**. "Do me twenty minutes and it's worth a fiver to you," he said. "I don't want nothing out of it."

From there Johnny moved on to **Balsall Heath Labour club** where he turned the place upside down. When the secretary asked Johnny how much his fee was, Johnny Carroll, popping his banjo back in its plastic carrier bag, put his shoulders back. "Six," he said, pausing to reflect on the excellent entertainment he had just provided. The secretary ferreted amongst the notes in the bar till. "Guineas!" added Johnny.

The following weekend Johnny Carroll earned twenty pounds as a comedian by more or less performing Ken Goodwin's act.

Johnny Carroll

"I even did a couple on the banjo, just like Ken," admitted Johnny. "I was earning eighteen pounds gross on the dust, so I handed the Council their dungarees back!"

A Birmingham band under a Black Country banner was **Varsity Rag**. Formed in June '67, their mission was to play pop and soul music. "Actually," admits singer **Mick Lawson**, "It was all old Drifters stuff!"

The boys, Mick, **Ken Horden** and bassist **John Fox** had recruited **Brian Nicholls** from the **Capitols** and were represented by the **Roger Allen** Agency of Wolverhampton.

"I knew with Roger behind us there'd be plenty of work," admitted Brian

Nicholls, rubbing the tips of his fingers to indicate financial gain.

Roger Allen was a leading light in a network of agents. **Pete Gittins** of Great Barr worked in league with Roger. One Saturday afternoon the recently formed Varsity Rag committed the unforgivable sin. They dared to knock on Pete Gittins' front door, in Tideswell Road, Great Barr, at precisely four-thirty.

"Pete answered in a rage and a Noel Coward dressing gown," explained Brian Nicholls. " 'You boys have been told that you must never knock my door when the wrestling's on!' Pete screamed, shaking with temper. 'It's Ironman Logan for God's sake!' slamming the door in our faces. I haven't seen Pete for years," sighed Brian, "But he still writes."

When, in early 1968, Brian Nicholls quit Varsity Rag and professional status, **Max 'the Nub' Griffiths** was recruited into the line up. Shortly after this Mick Lawson decided to leave commercial music far behind him, in order to study and perform the works of Bob Dylan. How much his quest would be aided by promptly becoming a Redcoat at Butlin's Ocean Hotel, at Saltdean, Brighton, only time would tell. Before he left, Mick Lawson spent a whole day teaching his replacement, **Laurie Hornsby** (whose head was already crammed full with the works of Bob Dylan) the lyrics and arrangements to the songs of the Varsity Rag set — Drifters songs, interspersed with blue-beat and ska with obscure titles like 'Bang Bang Lulu' and 'It Miek'. It was also drilled into Laurie's brain that these songs must always be delivered in his best Caribbean accent.

*Under the boardwalk —
Varsity Rag*

Mick Lawson would eventually adopt the professional name of **Emmit Till**, from the title of a Bob Dylan song that told the story of the last black man to hang in America. As Emmit Till, in the mid-seventies, Mick was chosen as the supporting act for the up and coming Bruce Springsteen during his European tour.

Writing his notice of resignation from the Cadbury factory in Bournville was **Laurie Mansfield**. The staff discount on Christmas selection boxes was a handy perk to have but Laurie Mansfield, a self confessed Buddy Holly fruit and nut, yearned to make a career for himself in show business. This young and ambitious gentleman bade farewell to a world of chocolate buttons to become a rep with the record wholesaler E A Woods.

"I'd pick up my stock from New Street Station. Plonk the boxes of records on the back seat of my car and off I'd go, whizzing around Derby, Nottingham and Stoke, which was my designated patch," recalled Laurie. "It doesn't sound much but it introduced me to the greatest business on earth."

Trevor Burton – court with a bird on each arm

The **Move** had the feeling that they were in the greatest business on earth. Spring was in the air. The daffodils were out and their second single 'I Can Hear the Grass Grow' was at number five on the charts, confirming their pop star status. Homeward bound from Yorkshire in the early hours, the Move happened upon the 'Robin Hood' all-night café on the outskirts of Nottingham.

Trevor Burton tells the tale, "It was three in the morning and there was no one in the place. I'd bought a mug of tea and our roadie, '**Dumpy**' nicked it. I called him a couple of nice names and a copper arrested me for causing an affray."

A telephone call to manager **Tony Secunda** set the publicity wheels in motion.

"Secunda was amazing," Trevor Burton stated. "You can see where Malcolm McLaren got his ideas for the Sex Pistols from."

When Tony Secunda looked into the details of the pending court case he found a charter made way back in medieval times, which decreed that, for such public order offences, the fine could be paid with a sack of grain, a pig or a couple of ducks. Trevor Burton pleaded guilty to his charge at Nottingham Magistrates Court, and a substantial fine was handed down as punishment. When asked how he intended to pay, Trevor reached under his kaftan and produced a couple of ducks!

The Move were now an established hit act. Eighteen months on from their launch, their success was surprising many. **Johnny Haines**, of Ladbroke studios was not, however, one of the many.

"I'd recorded their first efforts, and although they were still miles away from 'Night of Fear', I felt from day one that they were very together as a band. Denny Cordell at Deram really got 'em buzzin'."

Impresario Larry Parnes intended to get the Move buzzin', playing second billing to Billy Fury at the Royal Aquarium Theatre, Great Yarmouth, for a series of Sunday concerts. **Billy Fury**, the golden boy of the Larry Parnes stable, hadn't experienced serious chart action since his hit of July '65, 'In Thoughts of You', but in Mr Parnes' shillings-and-pence estimation he was still far better box office than the Move. Billy Fury's backing band were to be none other than the **Plainsmen**.

Billy Fury with Tommy Bruce and Georgie Fame at Terry Wallace's house

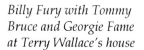

Top London agent George Cooper had heard glowing reports of the Plainsmen and offered them the prestigious job. **Tony Finister**, the Plainsmen's drummer, immediately asked George Cooper how much take home pay he could expect. George Cooper, a stammerer, asked why Tony was so concerned about such a minor issue as money. Tony Finister informed Mr Cooper of a recent addition to his family. He explained in some detail how this new addition would add f-f-further burden to the f-f-financial outgoings of the f-f-Finister household.

George Cooper's eyes peered over the rim of his wire-rimmed spectacles as he interrupted heartlessly, "How'd you f-f-flippin' like to hear my f-f-f-flippin' problems?"

With **Brian Ford** taking over the drum stool, the Plainsmen, now augmented by **Mike Burney** on sax, blew a course for Great Yarmouth. The Move, whether Larry Parnes liked it or not, were a current hot act with two top ten singles under their belt. Larry Parnes did not like it and, after the Move's first appearance for him, demanded that when they next perform, the following Sunday evening, they should reduce their volume considerably.

"It was the worst thing Larry Parnes could have said," said **John Rooney** of the Plainsmen. "The Move played twice as loud. You could have heard them in Lowestoft."

The next morning Larry Parnes cancelled the Move from all future shows and replaced them with Whistling Jack Smith!

*Mean & moody –
the Move*

W histling with sheer delight were the **Uglys** after receiving the news that they were to spend the month of August 1967, at the Top Ten Club, Torremolinos, on the Costa Del Sol. The personnel of the Uglys at this time was **Steve Gibbons**, **Jim Holden** and **Jimmy O'Neill** with **Dave Morgan** on bass and **Willie Hammond** on guitar. Unfortunately for Willie Hammond, he never sorted out his passport in time and was left behind.

The Uglys

August is the busiest and hottest time of the year on the Costa Del Sol. The Top Ten Club heaved every evening to the folk and rock sounds of the Uglys' diverse repertoire: Bob Dylan and Stevie Wonder songs, and tracks from the Beatles' newly released 'Sgt Pepper' album, as well as their own homegrown songs. With the crowds packed in like sardines, for the Uglys it was like performing in a sauna bath. For Steve Gibbons' voice it was unmerciful, and not even half way through the stay, his voice was reduced to no more than a whisper.

"I never spoke a word during the day," said Steve. "When I sang at night, the pain in my throat was excruciating, but somehow I kept going."

Moody Blues

The **Ladbroke Sound Studio** was by now trading as **Zella Records**. 'Zella' coming from the name of a family friend, 'Hazel', who had taught children in Thailand.

"When the kids tried to say 'Hazel' it came out 'Zella'," explained Johnny Haines.

A hundred yards from Zella, down Essex Street, on the corner of Bromsgrove Street, was the **Ringway Club**, formerly the **Garden of Eden**. The advertising hoardings around Birmingham city centre, in that midsummer of 1967, were informing everyone that the **Moody Blues** were back in business and back in town to show off the two new additions to their line-up, **John Lodge** and **Justin Hayward**. The Moody Blues, hit recorders of 'Go Now' were to play the Ringway Club. On the morning of the gig, as Johnny Haines sat at his transistorised mixing desk, **Ray Thomas** and **Graeme Edge** popped their heads around the door.

"Can you ask old man Ladbroke if we can hire a piano at the right money for tonight?" they politely asked. "There's no piano at the Ringway for **Micky Pinder** to play."

"Mr Ladbroke was only too pleased to help out," said Johnny Haines. "The Moodys chose a piano and Mr Ladbroke and I loaded it onto a trolley and wheeled it down Essex Street, over Bromsgrove Street, into the Ringway Club. Up the narrow stairs we humped it, and onto the stage, leaving the collapsible trolley in the corner."

The next morning **Vincent Ladbroke** and Johnny Haines returned for the piano.

"Poor Mr Ladbroke," chuckled Johnny Haines. "The Moodys had 'opped it with his trolley."

Methodically loading their instruments onto the open back of a five-ton truck that was parked outside the **Locarno** in Hurst Street, were the **Method**. The boys were clutching the trophy they had just been awarded as outright winners of the 'Band of the Year' contest. Once they were precariously seated on the speaker cabinets, the truck roared off down Smallbrook Ringway for its home base at Wheeler's timber yard in Erdington.

"**Bob Johnson**, our bass player, had a van but he went on holiday the same time as the final," drummer **Jimmy Bromley** explained. "My old man took us down on the truck from his wood yard. When Bob got home, complete with his all-over suntan, he asked us how we got on in the final. I told him that we, with the emphasis on the 'we', had done okay."

The Method had actually won convincingly over joint runners up, the

Elegant Set and the **Pinch**. Behind these came the **Scott Morris Blues Combo** from the Midland Arts Centre, performing admirable renditions of the Pierre Richard Tubbs song, 'I Can Go Down' and Oscar Brown's 'Brother Where Are You'. The Blues Combo - pianist **Baz Jones**, guitarist **Ken Cole**, bass player **Al Ray**, drummer **Bob Franklin** and **Les Hemming** handling the vocal duties - did well to finish ahead of the almost-all-black **Heartbeats** and the psychedelic **Breakthru**; two bands handled by the **Richardson** brothers, **Peter** and **John**, who operated their agency from premises in High Street, Harborne.

The Heartbeat's whiter shade of organ player, Mike Lavender

On the dance floors of Birmingham, folks, used to **Dave Pritchard's** vocal interpretation of 'Paper Sun', **Roger Spencer's** 'Cool Jerk' or **Jeff Lynne's** 'Darlin'' or even 'Runaway', were delighted by the announcement from the **Idle Race** that "the next song is our new single!"

Without grand press headlines, the Idle Race had signed to United Artistes Records and all releases would appear on the Liberty label.

"We got so worked up," admitted Roger Spencer. "We knew we had a good band going and now we had an excellent commercial recording."

'Here We Go Round the Lemon Tree' had, in fact, been written by **Roy Wood** and was perfect for them. It was also time for the **Move** to release their third single so, to all intent and purpose, it was party time all round. Liberty Records dreamed up a terrific gimmick to plug 'Lemon Tree'. All promotional material was lemon scented. As the first batch of Idle Race 'bumf' was circulated and wafted around the media, news filtered through from the Move camp that they had switched labels from Deram to Regal Zonophone. Until then, the best known act on the Regal Zonophone label

Idle Race

was the Salvation Army's very own Joystrings. Also came the news that the Move's version of 'Here We Go Round the Lemon Tree' was to be the B side of their new single 'Flowers in the Rain'. Liberty Records refused to compete with what was destined to be a massive seller for the Move, especially when 'Flowers in the Rain' was granted the honour of being the very first record played on Radio One when it took to the airwaves.

With promotion like that behind them," said Roger Spencer, "We'd have been left for dead. Liberty just pulled the plug on 'Lemon Tree'."

Tony Secunda decided that a little more headline grabbing wouldn't go amiss. He commissioned a cartoonist friend to draw a caricature of the Prime Minister, Harold Wilson, in a compromising position with his personal secretary, Marcia Williams, graphically depicting a totally unfounded rumour that was 'doing the rounds'. This artwork was reproduced in postcard

form. At number 10 Downing Street, the Prime Minister was taking breakfast. As he dipped his toasted soldiers into the yolk of his boiled egg, the morning post arrived. On top of the pile of envelopes was the libellous postcard. With 'Flowers in the Rain' making its way up the charts and the Move being so controversial an act, the lads gave little thought to the massive press presence as they arrived at a ballroom in the Home Counties to play a 'bread and butter' engagement.

"Secunda was waiting for us when we arrived," recalled **Ace Kefford**. "He spelled out what he'd done. He looked scared out of his wits."

"We finished the gig, walked out of the stage door and into the flashguns of the world's press," explained **Trevor Burton**. "That's when we started getting scared out of our wits too."

Ace Kefford accompanied Tony Secunda back to his London apartment, and at four-thirty the following morning they made the trip to Piccadilly Circus to pick up the first editions of the national morning papers. Tony Secunda was ecstatic at what he saw on the news seller's boards. The Move had made the headlines on every front page.

"Secunda was dancing around on the pavement," said Ace. "He opened the car door and threw the newspapers all over me!"

Tony Secunda & the Move en-route to the Old Bailey

Ace made his way back to the Move's hotel, the Madison, Sussex Gardens, Paddington. The Madison provided bed and breakfast for travelling musicians seeking overnight accommodation in London, and extra business for the local pharmacy, which did a roaring trade in Blue Unction Escabiol Lotion.

Ace continued, "Back at the hotel I packed my bags. That was the start of me getting out of it all."

The 'Flowers in the Rain' postcard trial was heard at the Old Bailey on 22nd September 1967. Arriving half an hour late, the Move found all business done and dusted.

"The barristers were waiting for us. We were informed of an arrangement whereby all proceeds from 'Flowers in the Rain' would go to a charity of the Prime Minister's choice," said **Carl Wayne**. "What we should have done was to plead our innocence. It was nothing to do with us. But then the postcard would have had to have been produced," added Carl, tapping his temples. "The Move always did whatever Secunda told us to do."

In accordance with the High Court ruling, the Move bade farewell to any royalties for their part as artistes; and **Roy Wood**, as composer, was forced to forsake any entitlements from mechanical and performing rights of the said recorded work.

Protesting at this outcome, Roy Wood composed a tongue-in-cheek song, 'Vote For Me' and enlisted the services of **Derry Ryan** for the master recording. Unfortunately the work proved far too hot to handle and the recording went unreleased. So, putting all the Old Bailey nastiness behind them, the Move hit the road, sharing top billing with the American guitarist Jimi Hendrix and his band, the Experience — bass player Noel Redding and drummer Mitch Mitchell (who, six years previously, had gained dubious celebrity status as one the 'Ovaltinies' in the bedtime drink commercial!)

Raymond Froggatt and the **Monopoly** could have done with a mug or two of Ovaltine to help them through a few restless nights that lay before them. Polydor Records were revelling in the success of 'New York Mining Disaster 1941', a hit written and performed by their recent discovery, the Bee Gees. When asked to provide a song for the Monopoly, the brothers Gibb obliged with 'House of Lords'.

"It's gotta be the worst song they ever wrote," said Froggy, shaking his head. "Fortunately the record vanished without trace. It just wasn't us."

When Froggy turned down a song written by two of the Hollies, his producer Terry Kennedy challenged him to produce original material. Raymond Froggatt picked up the gauntlet and was back in London a week later. Taking a seat in Polydor's offices, he strummed his acoustic guitar and sang out his self-penned lines,

"In and out of the red balloon. Marry the farmer's daughter. Sleepy heads in the afternoon. Callow la, callow la vita"

Through his work with the likes of Donovan and the Ivy League, Terry Kennedy knew a hit song when he heard one.

Froggy & the Monopoly

"That song," he announced, pointing at Froggy's acoustic Gibson guitar, will sell millions. By the way, what's it called?"

"Callow La Vita." answered Froggy

"What's that supposed to mean?" asked Terry Kennedy.

"How warm is life," was the reply.

Terry Wallace's life was about to become a little warmer. "There was this advert in the 'Birmingham Mail' saying that **The Ray Mond Set** required a couple of guitarists," Terry recalls. "When I rolled up at the audition, **Pete Oliver** was also there and the Ray Mond Set was just this bloke dressed as a cowboy. His big song was 'Ghost Riders in the Sky' complete with the 'Yippee-yi-ay!' yodels. I had my wife **Cheryl** with me. Pete suggested she join in. We stuck a tambourine in her hand and in no time we were up and running around the Black Country and its working men's clubs."

Dave Pegg parted company with the **Exception** in Sept '67 to join **The Way of Life**, replacing **Danny King** as bass guitarist. Replacing Dave in the Exception was **John Rowlands** of the **Seed**. Auditions were held at the scout hut on Oscott Hill. Fortunately for John Rowlands, he knew the Exception programme pretty well. When asked to perform their recorded works, 'The Eagle Flies on Friday', and 'The Gabardine Saturday Night Street Walker', both **Bugsy Eastwood** compositions, John was only too happy to oblige.

"The Way of Life initially rehearsed with Dave Pegg at the Warstock pub and it sounded good," said **Reg Jones**. "Our first gig was at the **Crown and Cushion** pub, Perry Barr. We opened with 'You Keep Me Hangin' On', the Supremes song but with the Vanilla Fudge treatment. I know it sounds big headed, but the roof came in." commented a modest Reg.

However, as The Way of Life's confidence soared, so did the volume of **John Bonham**'s drumming.

The Way of Life with shed-builder supreme — John Bonham

"In some instances promoters sent us home after the first spot," said Dave Pegg. "We never, ever got rebooked."

John Bonham saw the problem a different way. The drums weren't too loud – the band was too quiet! He came up with his own solution — the Way of Life needed bigger speaker cabinets. John, being a carpenter, built speaker cabinets that were the business. Covered with orange Rexine with lime green speaker cloth, the cabinets looked sensational — but unfortunately the Way of Life were now just louder than ever!

Out on the road with Billy Fury, the **Plainsmen** didn't have orange speaker cabinets, but a little glittering of gold did filter into their lives. A 'remote shack somewhere in the Rhonnda Valley' was how sax player **Mike Burney** described a particular venue where the band, and

Billy Fury, had arrived late for their performance.

"We were franticly trying to get changed in this cramped dressing room," Mike Burney explained, "And the compere was shouting that we only had five minutes before we were on."

Pat Wayne, immaculately clad as always, glanced lovingly at his own reflection in the mirror.

"Oooh, she'll want you tonight," he sighed to himself, stroking his black wavy hair with his hands. Noticing an aerosol can on the window ledge, Pat reached out for it. Shaking it well, he gave his immaculate locks a few sharp blasts of what he presumed to be hair lacquer.

"I knew immediately there was something wrong," said Pat. "The room went silent and then exploded with hysterical noise. I looked at the can and then looked in the mirror. It was gold car paint!"

With his hair still prematurely gold, Pat Wayne and the Plainsmen arrived at their next scheduled date, Aberystwyth, where they were again to provide accompaniment for Billy Fury. To save on overnight accommodation expenses, the Plainsmen had invested in a camping tent from Barrett's of Feckenham.

"John Rooney reckoned we'd each be a pound a night better off. All that meant was we drank more!" said a bemused Mike Burney.

The Aberystwyth show was a great success and, as the Plainsmen began to pack away their gear, two gentlemen leant a helping hand, loading the equipment into the waiting van.

"Oi, Goldilocks! Anything else to go?" one of the helpful gents asked Pat Wayne, who was busy writing down his phone number on the back of a discarded raffle ticket for a starry eyed coal miner's daughter.

"Just the suitcases." answered Pat, nodding at the luggage, happy to feel the warm glow of human kindness.

Pat's expression then took a turn for the worse. "We never saw the suitcases again," he said. "Them blokes just kept walkin'!"

Walking tall with ambition were the **'N Betweens**. As the Wolverhampton scene still called out for pop groups that could intersperse highly polished comedy routines, Messrs Holder, Hill, Lea and Powell were still in search of a dream. The local pub scene held nothing for them now. The odd appearance at **Wolverhampton Civic Hall**, supporting the likes of Eric Clapton's Cream was as good as it got. London seemed to hold the answers. A one-off gig at Tiles, a basement club in Oxford Street accommodated their wall of sound without any moans or groans. When it came to their 'big' song of that period, the Young Rascals 'You Better Run', Oxford Street was theirs for the taking. In the audience was the legendary American music hustler Kim Fowley. Before the boys knew it 'You Better Run' was out as a single on EMI and the 'N Betweens returned as heroes to their hometown.

MEANWHILE ELSEWHERE . . .

*1967 - Donald Campbell dies in Bluebell speedboat- Torrey Canyon bombed by RAF to disperse oil - Muhammad Ali jailed for refusing Vietnam draft - Concorde flies - De Gaulle vetoes British entry to Common Market - gay laws reformed - Barnard performs first ever heart transplant - pirate radio stations closed - BBC creates Radios 1-4 - Otis Redding dies in plane crash - Sgt Pepper released - **TV** - The Prisoner - The Forsyte Saga - **Cinema** - The Graduate - Bonnie & Clyde . . .*

Inspired by Terry Kennedy's reaction to his song 'Red Balloon', Raymond Froggatt began to pull other songs out of the hat.

"It was ridiculous," **Hartley Cain** recalled. "It was a song a day, and every one a gem. Songs like 'Roly', 'Seaside' and 'The Old Accordion' came pouring out of Froggy." 'H' paused, then made the point: "Up to then we'd played rock like Dylan and the Byrds. Now our own stuff was very English. Very 'folky'.

Dave Pegg's taste in music was becoming very 'folky'. He'd palled up with folk singer **Harvey Andrews** when they both had girlfriends working at the Inland Revenue offices in the town centre.

"We all became friends," said Harvey "and Dave and **Christine Pegg** began coming to the Jug O' Punch club. That was Dave's introduction to the folk scene."

Ioan Allen, who managed the **Ian Campbell Folk Group**, had arranged a recording session for the band at the **Ladbroke Studio** in Essex Street. An electric bass player was required for the session because their regular bassist **Mansell Davis** only played upright string bass. **Johnny Haines**, the sound engineer at the studio, booked Dave Pegg for the session.

"That," said Dave, "was the start of my career in folk music."

Once Dave Pegg had discovered his ear for folk songs, he was intrigued with a song that **Steve Gibbons** had recently written.

Ian Campbell Folk Group

Steve recalls, "In my frustration at not being able to play an instrument, I literally stumbled across a hunting horn in a junk shop. I'd played bugle in the Boys' Brigade so I was halfway there."

The hunting horn, which Steve purchased, proved to be the inspiration behind his song 'Squire Blues Horn', which protested against fox hunting. When Dave Pegg heard the song, Steve was immediately summoned to the Jug O' Punch club to lay his lyric onto the appreciative audience.

'The foxes quake inside their holes,
The wires vibrate on telegraph poles,
But the lovers who are lying in the corn,
Don't hear the dogs a barking, so they carry on a larking,
And the Squire blows his hunting horn.'

The producer, Mike Smith, in his wisdom, put these 'horsey horsey' backing vocals on," Steve said. "When I recorded my part, I had to blow the horn six feet away from the mic to prevent the VU meters from going permanently into the red!"

The late autumn of 1967 saw the **Rockin' Berries** rubbing shoulders with the privileged when they were selected to appear in front of Her Majesty, Queen Elizabeth and Prince Philip, Duke of Edinburgh, as part of the annual Royal Command Performance.

The Uglys with DJ Barmy Barry

Geoff Turton, of the Berries, recalls very little of their performance. "I was in bits with nerves. We all were. I was okay until we were informed that the television audience would be twenty-one million!"

The after-show presentation of the artistes to the Royal couple was always an extremely disciplined affair. One should only speak when spoken to. The Queen would be initially addressed as 'Your Majesty' and then, if another response was called for, 'Ma'am'.

"I was near Tommy Cooper in the line up," said Geoff. "The Queen thanked Tommy for his services and turned away. As she did so, Tommy called out "Excuse me Ma'am. Do you follow the football?"

"Not really," replied the Queen, a little startled by the sudden impertinence of a commoner.

"In that case," asked Tommy Cooper, sniffing, "Can I have your Cup Final tickets?"

Although it wasn't exactly a sword on the shoulder job for the Berries, it did wonders for their diary and their fees went up accordingly. The **Ringway Club** in Bromsgrove Street was one of the first venues to take advantage of the Berries new wave of popularity following their Royal Command appearance.

"Our audience was a gang of navvies propping up the bar," recalls **Bobby Thomson**.

The Rockin' Berries were, if nothing else, model professionals, and took to the stage to perform their hit records, peppered with bouts of novelty humour which met with little or no reaction. With fifteen minutes left on the clock, **Clive Lea** pushed the panic button and plunged headfirst into his Norman Wisdom impersonation. Geoff Turton sang 'Don't laugh at me 'cause I'm a fool' and Clive, with peaked cap at forty-five degrees, and in fine 'Mr Grimsdale' voice begged, "'Ere I wanna sing! Let me sing!"

Chuck Botfield viciously grabbed Clive by his jacket lapels and delivered, quite clearly, the rehearsed dialogue of the routine. "Clear off! Grow up stupid!"

"I did grow up stupid!" was the Christmas cracker response from Clive before the sound of a pint glass being slammed down on the bar resounded out around the room.

"Suddenly this bloke jumped on stage," giggled Bobby Thomson. "He stuck his fist under Chuck's chin and threatened, "Let de little fella thing, or elth!"

Needless to say the little fellow sang. The Berries picked up the cheque and scooted.

Having seen the success of the **Move**'s dynamic stage act, **Raymond Froggatt** devised a routine that would leave his audience spell bound. His stage act would climax with him being hanged at the gallows until dead. **Hartley Cain** was commissioned to purchase the necessary wood for the construction of the gallows. Following a month of hammering, banging and cursing, the black thumbed Raymond Froggatt began performing his illusion in confident manner.

At the **Mackadown** pub, Froggy was winding his act up with his recently penned stomping closer, 'Always Goodbye'. Singing the line, "Passing my hat around. Got both feet on the ground," Froggy skipped across the front of the stage, holding out his tambourine in playful gesture for any loose coins.

"I wish you all goodbye!" he sang in true old time music hall fashion, skipping backward, shaking the tambourine behind his head as if it were a straw boater. A roll on **Lenny Ablethorpe**'s drums signalled that the gallows were in position and ready for mounting. Raymond climbed the steps and, head bowed, stood still as the noose was placed around his neck. Silence fell around Kitts Green as folk prepared for the execution of their hero. The hangman kicked the steps from under Froggy's legs, the audience gasped. Then Froggy gasped.

"It all went wrong and I was choking to death!" recalled Raymond. "The last thing I remember was kicking my legs out in panic!"

Froggy's kicks caused the gallows to topple into the audience, taking him along for the ride over half a dozen or so tables. Pints of brown and mild, bottles of Ansells 'Special' light ale, 'Cherry Bs' and Babychams, some enhanced with cocktail cherries, were sent flying around the ballroom. The Monopoly were forced to use their wages to replace the tables of drinks that had been demolished. The rest of the money went towards impending dry cleaning bills. Needless to say, Raymond Froggatt never performed his hanging routine again, and, for six months, the rope burns around his neck served to remind him of his folly.

A Bedford van with Smokestacks on the roof

John Bonham wasn't hanging around either. Tired of persistent complaints of the sheer brute force of his drumming, he'd been hearing on the grapevine, glowing reports of a joyous soul and blues band called, strangely enough, the **Band of Joy**, and their vocalist, **Robert Plant**. This Band of Joy had endeavoured to gain crowd reaction by painting their faces like Red Indians on the warpath. Unfortunately they had only succeeded in scaring the living daylights out of folk as Robert Plant, painted up for the kill, hurled himself off the stage of the **Rainbow Suite** and chased terrified Mods around the hallowed corridors of the Birmingham Co-operative building. But it was the feel of the band that had attracted John Bonham's attention, and with the Band of Joy now clean of warpaint following liberal scrubdowns in turpentine, he joined their ranks.

"We turned up at his mother's place in Astwood Bank and John wasn't there," **Reg Jones** of the **Way of Life** explained. "So I phoned the venue, the **Majestic ballroom** in Wellington, and told them John Bonham wasn't available and so the Way of Life couldn't appear."

The management of the Majestic, to Reg's surprise, informed him that John Bonham had arrived at the Majestic, was set up and ready to rock with Robert Plant and the Band of Joy!

"That was the start of the partnership that put John and Robert on the road to the top," said Reg, proud of his input to what was to become a worldwide musical phenomenon.

Hoping to become a musical phenomenon were Erdington's **Capitol Systems**. Once a four piece, the boys, **Rob Moore**, **Dave Bailey**, **Paul Whitehouse** and **Paul Sargeant** decided that, if they were to compete in the big league, they needed a person of substance out front to lead them. An advertisement brought them **Bob Catley**, who had been crooning his tunes with the **Smokestacks**.

"The Smokestacks were a youth club and community hall band," said Bob Catley. "We were from Bordsley Green and one of our early gigs was a pub down by the St Andrews football ground. The gaffer paid us with a bar of chocolate each!"

Managed by **Vic Sims**, who had once handled the affairs of Shard End's **Andicapps**, the Capitol Systems began to rub shoulders with the elite. Moving out of Yenton Boys' Club they began to discover the delights of the **Ringway Club**, the **Chalet** at the Lickey Hills, the salubrious **Penthouse Club** on Constitution Hill and the **Santa Rosa** club, formerly **Titos**, on Soho Road. The Capitol Systems spent hours rehearsing at the **Atlas Bingo Hall** in Stechford where Vic Sims was now the manager.

Capitol Systems

Bob Catley recalls the audiences at the Atlas bingo sessions, "Vic smartened us up and bought us 'butcher's boy' trousers, blue and white pin stripes. We'd kill the audience, all two dozen of them! They'd sit there with their bingo boards, felt tips, cheese cobs and tea, and I'd do an Elvis drawl on 'Let the Heartaches Begin'."

The perseverance paid off when the boys became full-time professionals, and began to venture to London where they would play the Empire Rooms on Tottenham Court Road.

The Southerners

Bob Hatch

Not venturing too far but trying to figure out a method for success were indeed the **Method**. Now that the billboards proclaimed the Method as 'Winners of the All Midland Beat Contest', their leader, organist **John Goble** decided to bring two new faces into his already powerful line up that had **John Bond** on bass and **Phil Savage** providing the vocals. Out of the **Rest**, and into the Method went drummer **Bill Ward** and guitarist **Tony Iommi**.

All stoked up, the **Locomotive** regularly steamed down to London. **Jim Simpson** knew all the right places to be seen, and made sure that the band played all the 'in' venues. Locomotive, which now had **Mick Hinks** from Tipton on bass, and **Bob Lamb** from Sheldon on drums, were the 'fave raves' at establishments frequented by the beautiful people — clubs like the Bag O' Nails and Eel Pie Island would feature them regularly.

"I thought the **Continental** on Soho Road was hip," sighed **Norman Haines**. "But when we were doing the Bag O' Nails, I knew we were flying high up there."

In the audience and also flying were Tom Jones and the Rockin' Berries, who were, at the time, sharing the honours at the London Palladium.

"Me and Tom were staggering out of the Bag O' Nails and I could hear a woman shrieking with pain," said **Bobby Thomson**. "My cuff link had somehow got tangled in her wig as I passed. It must have been well pinned on, 'cause I'd dragged the poor girl out of her seat and across a couple of tables!"

Wooden songs (an American term for acoustic folk music) were gaining in popularity, and **Terry Wallace** was becoming more appreciative of the gentle approach. Working at his bench at the Leyland factory in Drews Lane, Washwood Heath, he was introduced to a fellow worker, **Robbie Harper**.

"Robbie had been in the **Brumbeats** a couple of years earlier and had heard that me and the wife, **Cheryl**, were performers," said Terry. "Anyway, it emerged that we all shared a common love for these folk songs that were coming from the likes of Simon and Garfunkel, Peter, Paul and Mary and the Seekers. So me, Cheryl and Robbie became the **Southerners**, and I have to say that it was the most enjoyable time I ever had in the music business. We were doing folk clubs where the crowd hung on your every word. We'd do top class variety shows with wonderfully talented artistes like that great Brummie comedian **Bob Hatch**. What a contrast to the days back in Germany with the **Vikings**, playing the hard hitting stuff non-stop for seven hours a night!"

About to enter that hard hitting German life of seven hours a night were **Fading Colour**, an outfit made up of vocalist **Dave Brecknall**, guitarists **Roy Davis** and **Steve Brown** with **Kex Gorin** on drums.

"We went with good hearts, earned a few bob and collected a few memories," chuckled Kex Gorin. "That's about as good as it got."

In October 1967, the **Idle Race** finally enjoyed the release of a **Jeff Lynne** song, 'Imposters of Life's Magazine' and, two weeks later, debuted on Radio One's 'Top Gear'. Sessions took place at the BBC's Maida Vale studios and were produced by Bernie Andrews and Jeff Griffin. With inquisitive eyes and ears, Jeff Lynne was absorbing quite a few tricks of the recording trade. Even to the point of copying the appropriate style of dress — arriving back in Birmingham after the sessions, the first thing Jeff did was to buy a pair of corduroy trousers!

Fading Colour

Idle Race

Not wearing corduroys but a pin stripe suit was **Ken Wright**, formerly of **Cliff Ward and the Cruisers**. Ken was now working for the BBC in London as an accountant so he was the ideal courier to deliver tapes of songs directly to the inner sanctums of Radio 1.

Bev Pegg picks up the tale: "We, that's **Cliff Ward**, **Dave Cartwright** and myself, had a few of Cliff's songs down on tape. With Ken Wright at the BBC every day, we asked him to give someone, anyone really, the demonstration tape."

Arriving at the BBC offices the following Monday morning, Ken Wright, had the tape in his briefcase. As he stepped from the lift, the first face he encountered was John Peel.

"John Peel came back to us within

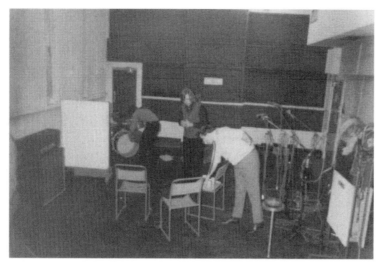

Cliff Ward & Johnny Haines at Zella Studio

days," recalled Bev Pegg. "Our timing was perfect. John was about to launch his own label, Dandelion."

With John Peel's backing, the boys from Kidderminster booked **Zella** studio to record the Clifford T Ward album, 'Singer Songwriter'.

Stereo was finally coming of age by 1967, and Decca's Deram record label were determined to stand out from the crowd with a system they called 'Deramic Stereo'. They hatched a plan to release a promotional LP that would demonstrate the virtues of this 'wall to wall' sound, for both classical and rock music. It made economic sense to use in-house resources, so the idea was to bring together their own roster of session players, the London Festival Orchestra, and the chart-shy **Moody Blues**. With **Tony Clarke** producing, and conductor **Peter Knight** providing the orchestral arrangements, the brief was to record a version of Dvorak's 'New World Symphony', which would contrast their musical styles and reveal this new technology in all its glory. Peter Knight and the Moodys were, however, less interested in championing the cause of 'Deramic Stereo' and more interested in exploiting this golden opportunity to further their own artistic careers! In a masterpiece of judicious manoeuvring, they somehow dumped Dvorak, to turn the LP into a showcase for their respective talents, entitled 'Days of Future Passed'.

Ian Campbell Folk Group

What record company in its right mind would have bankrolled a band, without a hit to its name in three years, to record a symphonic rock concept album? Engineered into one continuous piece of music, the tracks on 'Days of Future Passed' were effectively 'movements' of an elaborate work exploring times of day, from dawn until dark. It was **Justin Hayward**'s interpretation of the dark hours that provided the long awaited Moody hit single. At last, in early December of 1967, the Moody Blues were back in the nation's top ten chart, with the haunting 'Nights in White Satin', and two months on, 'Days of Future Passed' provided them with their first hit album.

Swapping his '62 Fender Stratocaster for a double bass, a transaction that he still kicks himself for, **Dave Pegg** became a permanent member of the **Ian Campbell Folk Group**. With Ian and **Lorna Campbell**, Dave found himself working alongside **John Dunkerly** on banjo and accordion, and **Brian Clark** on guitar.

"It was working in this environment that got me started on the mandolin," said Dave.

Getting ahead and hacking it in theatre — the Rockin' Berries

Beginning to work in a different environment were the **Rockin' Berries**. The Globe Theatre in Stockton on Tees had offered them a season in the Christmas pantomime 'Jack and the Beanstalk', which they gladly accepted. It was two months guaranteed wages and the chance to share the stage with the actor Bill Maynard, who was playing Dame.

"There were two weeks of daytime rehearsals prior to the opening," recalled **Bobby Thomson**. "Which meant that the nights were free to do as you pleased."

This spelled danger as it gave Bobby the chance to enjoy 'a few scoops' with his old pal from the early Liverpool days, Billy J Kramer, who, with guitarist Mick Green, from the late Johnny Kidd's Pirates, was playing the Stockton Fiesta Club for the week. After a particular heavy night, Bobby Thomson arrived at the Globe for rehearsals, nursing a thunderous hangover and suffering from complete loss of memory. As he joined the rest of the cast on stage for the director's morning briefing, footsteps were heard approaching. Stepping from the wings, a uniformed policeman sternly announced that he was "henquiring into the where-habouts of a Robert Thomson."

It had been alleged that Robert Thomson of the Rocking Berries had assaulted a taxi driver outside the Fiesta Club in the early hours.

"I felt my whole system drain and I admitted I'd been so drunk I couldn't remember a thing," said Bobby.

The policeman then suggested confidentially to Bobby, that should a sincere apology and a couple of complimentary tickets be forthcoming, the injured taxi driver might be prepared to drop the assault charge. Readily agreeing to this, Bobby Thomson marched out of the Globe Theatre and across the road to the taxi office, where the alleged assault had taken place.

"All the cast and even the director followed me," said Bobby. " 'I'm the bloke who beat up your driver last night and I'm just so sorry and ashamed for what I did,' I said to the chap at the desk. My legs were like jelly. He looked puzzled and asked, 'What are you talkin' about mate?' I looked round and everyone was in bits. The whole thing was a set up. They'd used a uniform from the theatre wardrobe and got an actor to play the copper!"

The Berries opened to a box office sell-out. Christmas was around the corner and all they had to worry about was buying back Bill Maynard's cow, which they'd sold for a bag of magic beans. In the dinginess of their cramped dressing room, the Rockin' Berries pulled on their bright red theatrical tights. It was a sight that was guaranteed to put anyone off glasshouse tomatoes for life!

Interested to see which records would be riding the charts through the lucrative festive season into 1968, the Rockin' Berries gathered around the latest copy of Melody Maker. There, taking the number three slot was the Four Tops recording of 'Walk Away Renee'.

"Everything was a total lift from our arrangement," sighed Bobby Thomson. "Our version had been used as a demo. That record would have resurrected our careers as recording artistes, if only John Schroeder hadn't rejected it for sounding too 'black'. That was the very sound that made it a hit — but not for us."

B LUEBIRD FLYING HIGH

Chapter Seven

1968

Cool sounds – Erskin T

Robert Plant at the Belfry

When **Phil Myatt** decided to re-christen the **Carlton Club**, he chose the name of the fictional fifties speakeasy bar visited by Ronald Reagan in an American B movie — **Mothers**. Any connection with the past, however, began and ended there. It was certainly the first place that any Brummie had ever seen the magic box that could, in seconds, turn a harmless cold pasty into a scalding, molten, lethal snack! But it was not hot food, but cool sounds on which the club's reputation would be built. DJ **Erskine T** would set the mood each night, intoxicating Birmingham's Woodstock generation with the warm vibes of peace and love.

John Singer looks back fondly at that truly magical era of **Mothers**. "It was the norm for our members to enjoy the likes of Derek and the Dominoes, Joe Cocker, The Who, Van Morrison and Fleetwood Mac at Mothers. "We'd also use local acts like the **Moody Blues**, **Raymond Froggatt**, **Trapeze**, **Black Sabbath** and who can forget **Robert Plant** and **John Bonham** with their **Band of Joy**, and later with **Led Zeppelin**.

"Talking as a booker, I can say that in those days, nothing was impossible. I booked Jethro Tull when they were huge. Their fee was four hundred quid. At today's rates, multiply that by twenty. What would you get for eight grand now? Chicken-and-chips-style cabaret perhaps, but nothing of the stature that Jethro Tull had at that time. I used to peep out of the top window and estimate how many people were queuing up Erdington High Street. Then I'd decide on the door charge!"

With their single 'The Skeleton and the Roundabout' released and regular appearances on the Radio One's 'Top Gear', the **Idle Race** never seemed to be off the airwaves.

"I remember once when we were playing Mothers, **Reg Jones** of the **Way of Life**

Idle Race

Traction

commented that the Idle Race sounded like a London band," recalled **Roger Spencer**. "We walked on air after hearing that remark."

Walking on air was the soul outfit **Traction**. Although the soul explosion had peaked by this time, Traction were busier than ever, now managed by **Peter Martin** of **Intercity Artistes**, where **John Tanner** was the booking agent. **Luddy Sammes**, a great black soul singer in the mould of Marvin Gaye, now fronted Traction's powerful stage show. Added to this was the fact that Traction were also in demand for their ability to provide professional musical accompaniment for three visiting black American acts. Week in, week out, all over Great Britain, Traction would lay down the groove for the Temptations to sing 'My Girl', the Miracles to perform 'You've Really Got a Hold on Me' or the Drifters to bring the house down with 'Save the Last Dance for Me'. That was until a Sunday newspaper exposed the fact that all of these 'original' American vocal groups seemed to share the same personnel. The four black gentlemen that made up the Drifters were the same four that made up the Temptations, and indeed the Miracles as well

"Honestly, we were in the dark," said **Danny Gallagher**, tongue firmly in cheek, "These guys were working the same stroke going out as the Crystals and the Chiffons as well!"

When regular frontman Luddy Sammes departed, Traction got themselves back on track by bringing in the former Redcap, **Dave Walker**, to provide the earthy vocals required; and when Dave moved on to the Savoy Brown Blues Band, Traction were fortunate to find vocalist **Phil Savage** available.

Danny Gallagher explains: "Phil's voice was more jazzy than Dave Walker's, so, with the advent of outfits like David Clayton's Blood, Sweat and Tears, that was the road we went down musically."

Taking the road down Halesowen High Street to what had been the **Star and Garter** pub was a bunch of budding professional musicians who called themselves the **Magic Roundabout**.

"The Star and Garter closed and re-opened as the **Star** coffee bar," explained **Keith Evans**, who doubled on sax and trumpet with the Magic Roundabout. "The Star became our residency, if you like. We'd rehearse down in what had been the pub cellar and do our performances upstairs in the old function room. **Robert Plant** was a regular visitor, he'd get up and do the odd song or two."

Magic Roundabout at the Star Coffee Bar

Other personnel lined up along with Keith Evans were fellow sax player **Chris Norton**, vocalist **Mick Woods**, guitarists **Alan Batty** and **Dave Neil**, drummer **Dave Donovan**, bass man **Roy Williams** and former **Heartbeats** organist, **Mike Lavender**. Together as Magic Roundabout they scooped first prize at the **Adelphi** ballroom and were awarded the title 'Midland Band of the Year'. They were also offered their choice of brand new Laney amplification at fifty per cent discount, and promptly upgraded their sound system.

"We also got an offer to go to Switzerland and then on to Germany," said Keith. "Mike Lavender wasn't old enough to get a work permit, so he got left at home. By the time we made Germany, **Bob Brady** had joined us on piano."

"**D**umped!" said Mike Lavender faking a wistful sigh, "But there were no hard feelings. I took up with a new soul band that was forming, named after the Ventures' instrumental track, **Ram Bunk Shush**."

In order to do justice to the Sam and Dave material that featured heavily in the act, the band was fronted by two excellent black singers. In fact their names were usually added to the billing, to produce a compere's nightmare — **Rip 'n' Lan and the Ram Bunk Shush**. Along with **Paul Barratt** on guitar and **Colin 'Slash' Nash** on drums, were saxman **Phil Cross**, trumpeter **Roy 'Coil' Blake**, and looking after bass and transport, **Roger Philpotts**. For quite some time Roger was the only one in the band with both a vehicle and a driving licence. "Poor bloke," said Mike Lavender, "It was a hundred mile trip to pick all of the band up, and the same again to drop them off after the gig, so on a good week he'd driven a thousand miles before he'd even started!"

Rip 'n' Lan & the Ram Bunk Shush

The **Exception** were now holding down a regular Wednesday night residency at the Marquee club in Wardour Street. With a European tour alongside Eddy Grant's Equals about to commence, things were looking good for the Exception, but a record release would make life even sweeter. Eddie Kassner of President Records engaged the services of producer Roger Bolton, and brought the Exception into the studio to record two **Bugsy Eastwood** songs. The A side, 'Rub It Down', had a ska feel while the B side, 'Snowing in the Desert' was more of a novelty number.

Lemon Tree

Johnny Neal & the Starliners

The band once known as the **Agency** were making a fresh start. Taking a new name from the **Roy Wood** song, the **Lemon Tree** entered into a management deal with **Ron King**, of Galaxy Entertainments in London, and soon it began to bear fruit. The Lemon Tree were vocalist **Micky Taylor**, guitarist **Terry Meredith**, organist **Gary Wortley**, with **Derek Arnold** on bass. Drummer **Carl Palmer**, who also played with the **King Bees** (later known as **Craig**) was replaced by **Keith Smart**. Keith's long-time friends **Trevor Burton** and **Ace Kefford** came up with a song for the Lemon Tree entitled 'William Chalker's Time Machine'. Manager Ron King immediately saw the potential of recording a song written by the nation's current pin-up pop stars, and wasted no time in selling the idea of a single release to Parlophone Records. To promote the record, Parlophone commissioned producer Mike Mansfield to film the Lemon Tree performing 'William Chalker's Time Machine' at the Esso oil refinery at Fawley, Southampton, making full use of the pipes, pumps and control panels to simulate a 'time machine' environment.

Johnny Neal and the **Starliners** line up was now featuring **Malc Priddey** on drums, **Johnny Andrews** on Hammond organ and **Barry Gray** on bass.

"We were doing loads of nights at **Gary Finn's Executive Club**, which was on the third floor of Malcolm House on Moseley Road, just across from the bus depot. Every time we played the place, we had to hump the Hammond up three flights of stairs, through a pokey little door and down the length of the room, then lift it onto the stage," moaned Johnny Neal, reliving the agony. "It nigh on killed us and when we were due on, our arms still felt like they were about to drop off!

"This went on for months on end. One night Johnny Andrews said to me, 'Nothing personal but me and Priddey are off on the QE2 with **Mick Walker** from the **Rum Runner**. Please don't be angry.'

"Me? Angry?" quizzed Johnny Neal. "It was like winning the pools!"

Into the Starliners came **Roger Craythorne** on drums, and on keyboards, **Geoff 'Cuckoo' Nichols**. So called because of his ritual of putting his hair in rollers before retiring to bed. It was at this time, and with this line up of Starliners, that Johnny Neal took the chance of auditioning for Hughie Green's 'Opportunity Knocks' at the Midland Hotel, New Street.

Johnny Neal

The **Rum Runner**'s highly popular resident band were the **Katz Whiskers** and they never failed to impress **Laurie Mansfield** whenever he visited the club. Now working for Monty Babson's company, Morgan Records, based in Willesden, North London, it was Laurie's job to oversee distribution of the company's output. Being the ambitious type, Laurie Mansfield had shrewdly arranged with Monty Babson that he too should be allowed to do some production if a suitable act caught his ear. Katz Whiskers seemed a good starting point.

"I changed their name to **Cinnamon Quill** and set to work with them. Although nothing we did set the woods on fire, I was learning all the time," explained Laurie.

Also on for a name change were the **Sombreros**. "I thought Sombreros was a bit old hat," said manager **Mike Carroll**, "Then one Sunday I was reading the Mercury and an advert for a typing course just caught my eye. In bold letters, jumping off the page, there it was, **Sight 'n' Sound**.

Publicising Ebeneza –
Sight 'n' Sound
('n' Smell?)

Guitarist, **Rick Price**, had by now formed a songwriting partnership with **Mike Sheridan**. One of their songs, 'Ebeneza' told of a dilatory tramp who had the ability to peel an orange in his pocket. Rumour had it that the story was based on **Danny King's** ability to suddenly produce a lighted Park Drive cigarette from its packet. Either way, 'Ebeneezer' provided Sight 'n' Sound with plenty of national airplay.

'Rub It Down' by the **Exception** did not, for some reason, enjoy anywhere near the airplay and sales it deserved. The boys, **Bugsy Eastwood**, **Roger Hill** and **John Rowlands** had been touring Holland, Belgium and Germany; performing the song on German television; doing interviews on American Forces Radio, as well as playing numerous concerts with the Equals, but all to no avail. On returning home, they were looking forward to at least picking up their earnings from the Equals tour. Instead they

Trevor Burton

walked into a contractual dispute with Kassner Music, who had recouped the recording costs and so-called promotional expenses of 'Rub It Down' against the band's bread and butter earnings.

"I'd started in 1963 with the **Boll Weevils** and had four great years as part of the Brum scene." said John Rowlands. "It seemed the moment we went for the big one with the Exception, we experienced the nastier side of the rock 'n' roll business."

Back to their grand and glorious rock 'n' roll roots went the **Move**. Their fourth single 'Fire Brigade', complete with fire engine bells, was a great throwback to the late 50s, with the **Roy Wood** vocal arriving on a typical Duane-Eddy-type guitar twang on the bass string. The Move's stage act was now as rock 'n' roll as it had been in the early days of the **Vikings**, the **Nightriders** and the **Everglades**. Raw and raunchy versions of Eddy Cochran's 'Somethin' Else' and 'Weekend' or the Jerry Lee Lewis barnstormer 'It'll Be Me' came pumping out of their hundred-watt speakers. This was the kind of stuff that had driven **Ace Kefford** down the rock 'n' roll highway, from humble beginnings at the Warstock pub, to being the instigator of one of Britain's most influential pop groups

"But I just couldn't handle it any more and I cracked up," said Ace. "My granddad had laid into me something awful about the Harold Wilson affair. He'd always been a proud supporter of the Labour Party and its cause, and I'd let him down. We even had MI5 following us for a while because of all that. It was like a scene out of the 'Harry Lime' film. There'd be blokes in raincoats and trilby hats outside the house every time you peeped through the curtains."

In April of 1968, during a Move rehearsal, Ace Kefford, in a fit of frustration, hurled his beloved bass guitar at the wall and went home to bed.

"**Charlie Wayne** came to see me as I lay there," recalled Ace, "I said I'd had enough and I was through. Charlie nodded, gave me a bunch of grapes and agreed that it was for the best."

For the lad who had initially dreamed up the concept of the Move, the dream was over.

The recording 'You Better Run' by the **'N Betweens** certainly hadn't given them cause to run to the off-licence but the elusive dream was still there to be had. Their manager, **Roger Allen**, somehow persuaded Jack Baverstock of Fontana Records to audition them. On hearing the band, Jack immediately bought off Roger Allen for three hundred pounds, and buried the name the 'N Betweens, believing the name conjured images of bisexuality. In pre-Freddie-Mercury Britain, that would not be a shrewd commercial tactic. The office girl at Fontana thought up a new name. It was to be **Ambrose Slade**. The boys didn't dare complain -- there was a recording contract at stake!

Finders Keepers, from Dudley, incurred no such name problems when their single 'Sadie, the Cleaning Lady', written by producer **Des Champ**, was released. By now their former roadie, **Ian 'Sludge' Lees**, was fronting Finders Keepers.

"What happened," explained former leader **Dripper Kent**, "Was that Finders Keepers, was me, **Alan Clee** on lead, **Dave Williams** on drums and **Phil Overfield** on bass, and we went off to Cologne, Germany, with Sludge as our roadie. The boss came in and started ranting in German about how he was paying for a five-piece and there were only four of us. I spoke good German and told him that our roadie was also a featured vocalist with us. I'd remembered that Ian had once sung with the Cannock outfit, the **Telstars** back in '64. That's how Sludge Lees began his professional career."

Back home Finders Keepers found themselves heavily in demand on the northern cabaret club circuit, where their highly comical Black Country personalities really hit home at places like La Strada and Wetheralls in Sunderland and La Dolce Vita in Newcastle.

A couple of months later Dripper Kent took a well earned rest from the road. Sludge, having completed his crash course in professional entertainment, became their sole frontman. Finders Keepers then found (and kept) guitarist, **Mel Galley**, to play alongside **Alan Clee**. **Dave Holland**, a powerhouse of a drummer from **Pinkerton's Colours** was also recruited, and the icing on the cake came when Alan Clee spotted a youngster playing bass with the **In Pack**, one of their support bands. He was a Cannock lad, **Glen Hughes**.

Alan Clee recalls their 1968 German trip: "It was our last night there. I checked the ferry timetable and our sailing was six o'clock. I presumed it meant six am so we drove through the night to make the sailing. Of course I got it wrong. The sailing was six pm. We had to sit for twelve hours in the freezing cold waiting for the boat!"

Locomotive

For **Big Bear Music**, the agency that had been created by photographer and trumpeter **Jim Simpson**, the ship was about to come in. By 1968, he was running a very busy office. Jim had to relinquish his role as a working member of **Locomotive**.

"Jim would be hustling away all day, setting up concerts all over the place, then rush to a Locomotive gig and nine times out of ten, he'd be late," explained **Norman Haines**, "Besides, he was enthusing over these Aston lads he'd found and endeavouring to launch them on an unsuspecting public. They were called **Earth** at that time. I'd been writing a fair few songs and Jim got us a release on Immediate Records with my song 'Broken Hearts'. The good thing about 'Broken Hearts' was that it was the last record ever to be played on 'Juke Box Jury'. The bad thing was — they voted it a miss. Katy Boyle said that this was one Locomotive that should never have left the station!"

L eaving the station and bound for the Advision studios in London were the **Monopoly**, now billing themselves simply as '**Raymond Froggatt**.' The boys were there to record Raymond's 'Callow La Vita'. With an orchestration by **Phil Dennis**, who had worked wonders with the novelty song 'Cinderella Rockefella', **Terry Kennedy** had decided to re-title their song 'The Red Balloon'. In every sense the master cut is a classic example of late-sixties pop. It was released in June 1968 and every radio show plugged it solidly for two months, but it made no impression on the charts.

"We just didn't have any organisation behind us," said Froggy. "Polydor were only a small outfit then and didn't have good distribution facilities. Our little gem just died a slow death."

Out of the dark comes the light. Dave Clark, leader of the famous Five, the outfit that gave the world the 'Tottenham Sound', needed a good song badly. It had been twelve months since Les Reed provided them with the 'weepy' 'Everybody Knows'. Prior to that chart showing, the Dave Clark Five hadn't figured in the public's mind for two years. Radio Two's 'Early Show' was always referred to as 'The Milk Show', as the music industry took the view that only milkmen could possibly listen to it. Dave Clark was listening in on his car radio as he drove home early one July morning in 1968 and heard 'The Red Balloon' being broadcast. As his fingers tapped on the steering wheel he found himself joining in on the hook, 'Callow la vita! Callow la vita!' The next evening, Stuart Reid of E H Morris Music Corporation entertained Raymond Froggatt, **Hartley Cain**, **Len Ablethorpe** and **Louis Clark**. Over an expensive dinner at Ishooh's, an exclusive West End restaurant favoured by the show business hierarchy, Stuart Reid informed them that the Dave Clark Five's next release would be 'The Red Balloon'.

By September 1968, the Dave Clark Five were back in the Britain's top ten. Not to be outdone, Marie Laforet, one of Europe's premier artistes, held the number one position on the French charts with 'The Red Balloon'.

"We were still skint but now we had the class!" laughed Froggy.

Showbiz luminaries Ma Regan & Ray Bridger at Ishoo's Restaurant

E arth were skint and without any trace of social class whatsoever. They were guitarists **Tony Iommi**, bassist **Terry 'Geezer' Butler**, and drummer **Bill Ward**. On sax was **Acker Clark** and adding the slide guitar was **Jimmy Phillips**. **Polka Tulk** had been a Pakistani clothing store in Newtown, Aston, and the boys, in search of an inspiration had worked under that name for a while. Again renamed, to suit the prevailing mood of the late sixties, they became Earth. And the Earth moved from a mainstream musical policy to a shuffle beat that rode on a solid, pumping bass part providing a foundation to a sliding, distorted guitar. The equation was completed with the addition of a vocalist in the form of the somewhat extrovert **John 'Ozzy' Osbourne**. John's claims to fame prior to his elevation to the heavy metal world of Earth, were stints with the **Approach** and the **Rare Breed**, having a tattoo of a face on each kneecap, and possessing the ability to open a bottle of Newcastle Brown Ale with his teeth! To introduce themselves to the Brum scene, Earth took a gig at **Henry's Blueshouse**, a club that met in the function room above the **Crown** pub in Hill Street, organised by **Jim Simpson**. The agreed reward for their debut performance at Henry's was a tee shirt apiece!

J immy Page, former guitarist with **John Carter** and **Ken Lewis's Southerners**, had gained an excellent reputation as a top session musician Looking for some live action in 1966, he had moved onto bass to replace Paul Samwell-Smith in the legendary **Yardbirds**, but soon swapped roles with Chris Dreja to become the Yardbirds' joint lead guitarist, alongside Jeff Beck. After Jeff (who had replaced Eric Clapton in the band, early in '65) moved on to form his own band, a rift between Jimmy Page's heavy blues approach, and the more acoustic taste of the other Yardbirds gradually began to develop.

John Paul Jones, a musician very much on Jimmy Page's wavelength, had provided the string arrangements for what was to be the Yardbird's final album in 1967. As the band drifted apart Jimmy started accepting session work, and the spring of 1968 found him working alongside John Paul Jones once again, on Donovan's 'Hurdy Gurdy Man' recording session. Jones made it clear to Page that he would jump at the chance to work with him if the opportunity ever arose. When the Yardbirds finally parted company in July 1968, after a gig at Luton Technical College, it fell to Jimmy to put together an outfit that could fulfil the outstanding autumn engagements.

With bass player Chris Dreja prepared to stay on board for a while, Jimmy Page's top priority was to fill the drum and vocal vacancies. His first call was to Terry Reid, the former singer with Great Yarmouth's Peter Jay and the Jaywalkers. Terry chose to turn down the offer, but spoke highly of a lad who could sing the blues with so much power and feel. Terry had experienced the vocal capabilities of this young man who was fronting the **Band of Joy** when the Jaywalkers had made a stopover in Birmingham. He reckoned he had witnessed the 'best rendition of 'Stormy Monday' this side of the Atlantic.'

Enquiries were made as to this man's whereabouts. The Band of Joy was no more, but their singer, **Robert Plant**, was alive and kicking, doing the all too infrequent gig with a band called **Hobbstweedle**. In the audience, when Hobbstweedle played at **Walsall Teacher's Training College**, were Jimmy Page and John Paul Jones. Page had, by now, lined up Jones to take over on bass in the new lineup, and together they experienced the sheer power and presence of Robert Plant. Following a brief word with him after the show, they said they'd be in touch, and left with the distinct impression that they would be able to prize this man away from Hobbstweedle. Robert Plant would not take much persuading; to supplement his musical income he was working by day with a tarmac gang in the West Bromwich area.

Austin Griffith of the **Stringbeats** recalls the backbreaking days, "Robert and the Stringbeats went back to the days of **Listen**. When he wasn't singing with Listen, he'd be with us. I'd meet him for lunch when he was working with the Irishmen, digging up West Bromwich High Street. We'd drink from the same cup and eat from the same plate at the **Zachachico** café on the High Street. I remember the day we were together at the **Three Men in a Boat** pub in Walsall, Robert showed me a letter. He was open mouthed. 'The Yardbirds want me,' was all he could manage to say."

When **Martin Hone** opened his **Opposite Lock** club, **Eddie Fewtrell** said that he'd give it three months at the most. "He said I was barmy!" said Martin, "Because my policy was to specialise in presenting jazz, with no gambling or girlie stuff!"

It was now eighteen months on, and with the Opposite Lock continuing to do exceptional trade, Martin could well have rested on his laurels, "But I was having to turn away the young rock fans. Remember that **Mothers** was out in the suburbs at Erdington, and Eddie Fewtrell's rock club, **Barbarellas**, didn't happen until 1971. There was no rock venue as such in Birmingham city centre."

Martin Hone's mind was made up to bring rock to town. He acquired the four-storey building next-door to the Opposite Lock at the bottom of Gas Street. When he took possession of the former warehouse, he found parts of the building crammed full of Christmas crackers! Undaunted he rolled up his sleeves, and with the help of his brothers, **Ian** and **Garth**, work on the conversion pushed ahead. The Birmingham rock music scene was about to have a brand new venue, the **Factory**, with a quite superb psychedelic atmosphere created by lighting expert **Paul Molineux**. To open with a bang on the 29th June 1968, Martin Hone engaged an outfit whose superb musicianship he'd long admired. A band that had a dozen or so top twenty hits to their credit — **Manfred Mann**.

"Oh we opened with a bang all right," chuckled Martin. "It took all afternoon for the Manfreds' road crew to load in and sound check. The Factory was heaving for its opening night. Disc jockey **Pete York** kept everyone in the groove before introducing the Manfred Mann band onto the stage. Manfred and the boys then played for all of twenty seconds before the main fuse blew!"

The Ace Kefford Stand

Eager to start blowing fuses again was **Ace Kefford**. A phone call from **Dennis Ball**, formerly of the **Mayfair Set** gave Ace the chance to once again make a stand, literally, the **Ace Kefford Stand**.

"Dennis called me and asked if I'd team up with him and his guitar playing brother Dave. They'd been playing as the **Scorcerers** with drummer **Cozy Powell**, who'd moved up from Cirencester to work with them. Did you know Cozy was brought to

Birmingham by the Balls?" asked Ace. "Oh, **Keith Smart** has already done that one has he?"

With Ace the Face upfront and without his bass guitar as it was still awaiting repair as a result of being hurled at the wall, the Ace Kefford Stand made an appearance at the **Belfry** at Wishaw. Impressed by the content and presentation of the Stand, promoter **John Parsons** made an approach, on the band's behalf, to Phil Carson, head of Artistes and Repertoire at Atlantic Records. Although still hazy in the head from his **Move** experiences, Ace Kefford, with his Stand, covered, on Atlantic Records, the Graham Gouldman song, 'For Your Love', which the Yardbirds had taken into the top ten in the spring of 1965. Sales didn't exactly go through the roof, but the Ace Kefford Stand created enough interest to tour Germany as a 'name' outfit.

"When we got back home, Phil Carson found us a song by one of Atlantic's contracted house writers," Ace explained. "We recorded the song 'This World's an Apple' and then we waited and waited. Eventually Dave Ball quit and went to Procol Harum and Cozy put in with Jeff Beck. For me it was all too soon after throwing my bass up the wall."

Although the Yardbirds material hadn't done the business for Ace, it was about to for **John Bonham**. The new look Yardbirds, **Jimmy Page**, **John Paul Jones** and **Robert Plant** needed someone as solid as a rock to provide the necessary energy to enhance the musicianship of Page and Jones, and give Plant a base from which to holler the blues.

Martin Hone takes up the theme: "I had the American singer songwriter Tim Rose, of 'Morning Dew' fame playing at the **Factory**. With him were **Steve Dolan** on bass, and John Bonham on drums. I'd noticed a couple of hairy blokes at the bar, watching the drummer intently. A member of my staff told me that one of them was a local artiste, Robert Plant and the other was none other than guitarist Jimmy Page. Something was cooking."

Hard Meat

When the Tim Rose engagements ceased, Steve Dolan became re-united with his guitarist brother Mike. Together, after recruiting drummer **Nick Carlaton**, a Devonshire lad, they cooked up the band **Hard Meat**.

"You could say we were moderately successful," said **Mike Dolan**, "Warner Brothers signed us for two albums that sold okay. The first was entitled 'Hard Meat', and the second 'Through a Window'.

Magic Roundabout at the Adelphi

Peeping through the window at the **Queen Mary** ballroom, in the middle of Dudley Zoo was **Dripper Kent**. He was now working as a booker for Wolverhampton's Astra agency and was always on the lookout for up and coming talent.

"I'd actually booked this band **Purple Onion** for the evening without knowing anything about them other than they'd been known as the **Magic Roundabout** prior to setting off for Germany," Dripper explained. "When I saw them that evening they blew me away, only I wasn't too keen on the name Purple Onion."

"Neither was our new guitarist, **Jimmy Phillips**," said saxist **Keith Evans**, "But I convinced him that the world was Purple Onion's oyster. Jimmy was in **Earth** at the time with Messrs **Iommi**, **Osbourne**, **Butler** and **Ward**. What chance had they got?"

Dripper Kent came up with the new name. "I told Purple Onion they'd go an absolute storm on the new university scene that was just taking off. And that's just what they did. As **Rock Rebellion**."

With Joe Cocker and Chris Farlowe preparing to enter into a Dutch auction for **John Bonham**'s services, John followed his heart and put in with **Robert Plant** and the **New Yardbirds**.

Led Zeppelin

"I drove John and Robert to their first engagement as **Led Zeppelin** in my Jaguar," recalls **Reg Jones**. "It was at Surrey University. There was a huge banner hanging outside that read, in big letters, 'Tonight! The Ex-Yardbirds'. Underneath, in smaller lettering, it said 'Led Zeppelin'. After the gig I couldn't start the Jaguar and we all came home on the train."

However, it wouldn't be too long before transport problems would be behind Led Zeppelin. Manager Peter Grant had negotiated a recording contract with Phil Carson at Atlantic Records and their debut album, 'Led Zeppelin', was recorded (in under thirty hours studio time) and parcelled up ready for release in the January of 1969. Phil Carson could hardly contain his excitement on hearing Led Zeppelin's ground-breaking tracks punching their way out of his office hi-fi system. He immediately telephoned Peter Grant to ask his opinion on which track should be chosen as a single release to whet the record buying public's appetite. Peter Grant, being an ex-wrestler and an ex-debt collector, in other words, a right hard knock, was not in the habit of pulling punches when it came to making his business plans known.

"We don't do singles. Only albums." was his brusque reply.

September of 1968 saw the eagerly awaited release of the **Moody Blues** next album, 'In Search of the Lost Chord'. The record buying public had been baited by the quality of the product when a single from the album, 'Voices in the Sky' had been released during mid-summer. With ambitious string arrangements courtesy of **Mike Pinder** and his Mellotron, and lyrics that demanded serious attention, it was obvious that the Moody Blues meant business this time around. Dedicated followers were treated to a live preview of the new material when the Moodys appeared at the **Belfry**, Wishaw to coincide with the album's release.

"Me and Mike Pinder spent all that afternoon humping the Mellotron into the Belfry and onto the stage," recalled **John Ford**, alias disc jockey **Doc Holliday**. "That's when I did my back in. Even today, thirty three years on, my back still gives me gyp!"

So a ride on a see-saw would have been out of the question for the good Doc, but the nation went along for a spin when the **John Lodge** song 'Ride My See-Saw' charted in October 1968

Unperturbed by the absolute failure of their record 'Broken Hearts', the **Locomotive** and their manager **Jim Simpson** were determined to pitch another effort once more into the London based music machine. Jim Simpson found sympathetic ears with Tony Hall, the former head of promotions at Decca, now heading his own talent spotting and publishing house from an office in Noel Street, in London's Soho area.

Tony Hall, a soul man through and through, liked what he heard on tape, comparing **Norman Haines**'s voice to that of Gary Brooker, whose song, the haunting 'Whiter Shade of Pale' had been adopted by the world as its signature tune throughout the summer of love.

"All they need is the right song," Tony Hall stated, "It's as easy as that."

Such a remark from anyone else would be taken as frivolous. From the man who for many years, from the mid-fifties to the mid-sixties, had been head of promotions for one of the biggest record companies in the world in its day, Decca

Locomotive

Locomotive

Records, this was praise indeed. In the late summer of 1968 Tony Hall journeyed from London to Birmingham to take in a typical Locomotive club performance at the **Cedar Club** on Constitution Hill. What Tony witnessed on that night was probably typical of how certain breeds of band had engulfed themselves in self-indulgence. 'Dying the death' is the expression chosen by Norman Haines to describe the evening that was to be quite a milestone in his career.

"All our songs met with total indifference. We were trying to be too clever. Then we found we were out of songs and still had five minutes to go before the disc jockey came on to steal the limelight. To kill time I announced a song that we'd roughly rehearsed to use in such emergencies."

Whilst living in the accommodation over Sutcliffe's record shop, on Smethwick High Street, Norman Haines had fallen under the influence of the rhythm of that suburb.

"It was 'Rudi this, Rudi that, Rudi's dead, Rudi, a message to you' thing," Norman explained. "I'd loved the groove of that music and the use of the soft sounding major seventh chords on the records. So I wrote a song, 'Rudi's in Love', using those ingredients. When we struck into the song at the Cedar that night, the dance floor filled immediately. On the chorus, the whole club was chanting 'Rudi, Rudi's in love'. When we came off Jim Simpson was beaming. 'Tony Hall is going to record 'Rudi's in Love,' said Jim, hardly containing himself. 'Tony says it's a certain hit!' "

Tony Hall was correct in his prediction. 'Rudi's in Love' was recorded at EMI's Abbey Road Studios, and entrusted with the producer's seat was the young Gus Dudgeon. The recording made number 20 on the charts in October of 1968, setting the airwaves alight with its infectious rhythm and is acknowledged as the very first ska song to register on the nation's record charts. Gus Dudgeon, as a result of his production success with 'Rudi', went on to produce records for Elton John.

"The success of the **Factory** left me breathless," said its proprietor, **Martin Hone**. "We'd only been open a matter of weeks but folks just seemed to come from everywhere to see what I was putting on for them. The Moody Blues with their Mellotron, Locomotive, and Joe Cocker with his Greaseband all played within a short time of my opening. I paid Joe £65 the first time. The second time he had 'A Little Help From My Friends' up there for him and he cost me a quite a few bob more. But he was worth it!"

Chateau Impney, Droitwich

"I'd say so," commented **Les Hemming**, who, as a member of **Jasper Stubbs Gloryland Band**, had supported Joe and the Greaseband one sunny Sunday afternoon in the grounds of the **Chateau Impney** at Droitwich. "It was a year on from the summer of love but you could still feel the vibes," said Les, slipping quite easily into hippie-speak. "When you think about such an event as that Sunday afternoon. There was Joe Cocker, Geno Washington and the Ram Jam band, who were something else by the way. Robert Plant and his Band of Joy, and us, Jasper Stubbs. And all for a couple of shillings at the main gates."

Jasper Stubbs and the Gloryland Band, previously known as **Calgary Stampede**, were, for the record, **Les Hemming** at the microphone with **Stephan 'Nosher' Bouthanovski** playing the saxophone, **Barry McCourt** sticking down the bass riffs, **Johnny Soul** thrashing the drums and **Roger Shropshall** stabbing the Hammond organ.

"We seemed to steal a lot of Jefferson Airplane material," confessed Les. "All that West Coast, up-in-the-air stuff like 'Spanish Castle Magic' and 'One Pill Makes You Larger'. When we'd play 'Granny Takes a Trip', the whole band would dance the Charleston!"

The Gloryland Band must have done something right as they performed, on a regular basis at London's **Marquee**, and also the **Playboy Club** of all places.

"If you could take the travelling and the late nights, it was a great way to make a living," said Les, faking a yawn.

In late October of 1968, **Martin Hone** took a phone call from Jimmy Parsons, the manager of Ronnie Scott's club in Frith Street, London. Could Martin accommodate, at the **Factory**, a new band that he and Ronnie had an investment in? The band, Gun, featuring the creative talents of guitarist Adrian Gurvitz, was endeavouring to promote their record, 'Race With The Devil'. Unfortunately the record wasn't racing and the band needed exposure pretty quickly. When Gun appeared at the Factory, in late November of 1968, they had performed 'Race with the Devil' on Top of the Pops the previous evening, and the record was showing at number eight on the charts.

"The queues for Gun that evening were incredible," said Martin, "Folks queued the length of Gas Street and round into Broad Street, almost down as far as the Rum Runner!"

A casual knock on the door one evening, by **Roger Spencer** at the Lynne family home in Shard End Crescent, interrupted a makeshift recording session to demo a new **Roy Wood** song, 'Blackberry Way'.

"Jeff was in the corner, messing around on his Mellotron," Roger explained.

"To separate Roy Wood's vocals, I held cushions either side of his face as he sang his wonderful lyric into a microphone that was wired into Jeff's Bang and Oluffson sound-on-sound tape recorder. 'Boats on the lake, unattended now the laughter drowned, I'm incredibly down.' What a song!"

Following a thumbs-up all round to **Jeff Lynne**'s demo, the **Move** went on to record the master of 'Blackberry Way'.

"The problem we incurred in the studio," said **Trevor Burton**, "was the tempo. It was too slow for drummer **Bev Bevan** to get into the groove."

The solution was to up the tempo while the drums were being recorded, then slow the recording down when the time came to layer on their vocals. "It's a good job we did," chuckled Trevor Burton, "At the recorded speed, the opening guitar riff is revealed as the intro to the James Bond Theme!"

The Rockin' Berries

Slowing down in more ways than one were the **Rockin' Berries**. Late September of 1968 saw the conclusion of their highly successful summer season at Great Yarmouth in the company of comedian Jimmy Tarbuck, the delightful Anita Harris, and the ever-kilted Kenneth McKellar. The switch to variety, although successful, was proving frustrating for the five young Berries who were, after all was said and done, rock 'n' roll musicians.

"We still felt that we had a few more years recording left in us," said **Geoff Turton**. "It had been over three years since 'Poor Man's Son'. Life was a lot of fun, but I wasn't singing anything anymore."

Geoff Turton quit the Rockin' Berries with a vague notion of perhaps a solo career. Record producer John Schroeder was interested enough to promise that he'd look around for a good song for Geoff.

In the late autumn of 1968 **Derry Ryan** and his outfit, **Stacks**, received the telephone call that every band dreads. Their equipment had been stolen from their van. In desperation, Derry made a call to **Carl Wayne**.

"Come on round. I'll put the kettle on," was Carl's solution to the crisis.

"Carl had a garage full of amplifiers and speakers that had been given to the **Move** by suppliers eager to promote their products," said Derry.

In late November, as Stacks were playing the **Rum Runner** with equipment courtesy of the Move, in popped the Move for a late drink.

"One thing led to another," continued Derry, "And the Move took to the stage and performed 'Blackberry Way' for the first time to a **Rum Runner** audience of no more than thirty people. And it sounded magic!"

Idle Racer Roger Spencer has his own recollection about the song, "When 'Blackberry Way' came out we were in the offices of Liberty Records in London. One of the executives commented that the Move were beginning to sound more like the Idle Race than we did!"

As the haunting 'Blackberry Way' climbed on its way to the top of the charts in the closing week of 1968, **Trevor Burton** made a New Year's resolution to quit the Move, citing musical differences as the reason.

"I was simply looking to play some music I could get my teeth into," recalled Trevor. "All those tales of me hating the Move's records are total nonsense. The truth is quite the opposite and I'm proud of my input. 'Fire

Brigade' is, for me, still an absolute gem of a rock 'n' roll record. But there again, they all are. It was just a case of me hanging out with the likes of Noel Redding from Jimi Hendrix's band. We actually shared a house together. Noel and Chris Wood of Traffic got me into more 'bluesy' music. I just didn't want to be in a pop band any longer."

When offered a position with Britain's number one pop act, **Jeff Lynne** politely refused and immersed himself in the production of the **Idle Race**'s next album entitled 'Idle Race'.

Stacks

"Jeff always worked better in his corduroy slacks," said **Roger Spencer**, "He fondly referred to those cords his 'producers trousers'!"

Not wearing corduroys but a thinking cap was **Raymond Froggatt**. He'd been asked by his publisher, Stuart Reid, to compose something for the wee Heelan' lassy herself, Lulu. The Eurovision Song Contest was looming and Lulu was to be Britain's representative. Raymond's effort for Lulu, 'Big Ship' was eventually rejected. The selection panel much preferred the subtly titled 'Boom Bang-a-Bang'. However, Lulu's producer, Mickey Most, thought 'Big Ship' too good a song to be passed over. Herman's Hermits were summoned to the studio to record a version, but the session didn't gel and was eventually abandoned. 'Big Ship' was in dry-dock for the foreseeable future, but it would soon be cruising — and how!

Chapter Eight

LIKE A TRUE NATURE'S CHILD

At the **Cedar Club**, during the first week's trading of 1969, the Christmas tree was stripped of its decorative lights, plastic bells and trimmings before being carted off to the refuse tip. The tree was occupying valuable stage space that was required for the first 'big name' of the year, the American soul singer Junior Walker who, with his All Stars, would be guaranteed to be 'Road Running' up and down Constitution Hill. Warming up the crowds during that bitterly cold January were Cedar favourites, **Sight 'n' Sound**. As the boys demonstrated their vocal harmony skills by performing the Raymond Lefevre number, 'Soul Coaxing', it became apparent that a new voice was enhancing the boys' instantly recognisable sound. The voice belonged to **Geoff Turton**, formerly of the **Rockin' Berries**.

Sight 'n' Sound

"What Geoff brought to Sight 'n' Sound was the feel of the American harmony group, the Fifth Dimension," said their manager **Mike Carroll**. "This was a tremendous help as I was trying to break them into the lucrative cabaret market."

To be a high earning band on the cabaret circuit entailed dressing accordingly. Black evening suit with a frilly shirt, and a velvet wasp throttling the neck was an absolute must. **John Dawson** was a guitar-playing member of Sight 'n' Sound during the period of 1969 and met the code of dress with enthusiasm and immense pride.

"I had the boys cruising on the Mediterranean for two weeks aboard the liner, the Chusan," Mike Carroll explained. "The shipping company, P&O Cruises, very kindly sent me a colour photograph of Sight 'n' Sound with the ship's captain at his cocktail party. There stood John Dawson, resplendent in his black evening suit — and brown boots!"

Pete Smith, frontman of Sight 'n' Sound, unfortunately had his 'boys made good' outfit stolen from the back seat of his car when it was parked on Broad Street, outside the **Rum Runner**, in the early hours of one morning. However, it was not all doom and gloom as the thief very kindly left his clothes in exchange for Pete's stage wear. Pete Smith, returning to his vehicle, found an old donkey jacket, grimy jeans and a muddy pair of builders' boots waiting for him.

Also embarking down that road of sit-down cabaret, but not bothering with monkey suits were the remnants of the **Vogues**. With their former leader, **Johnny Carroll**, now King of the Clubs in his newfound role as a stand-up comedian, the only survivor of the original Vogues was bass player **Ron Dickson**. Revamping the line up, Ron brought in guitarist **Keith Locke**, organist **Richard Brown**, drummer **Tony Harrison**, and frontman, the cheeky little chappie himself, **Roy 'Dripper' Kent**. Out of the darkness comes the light and from the Vogues came **Light Fantastic**.

Light Fantastic in the park . . .

"The song 'The Monster Mash' was going over big," explained Dripper. "Ron Dickson decided to expand the song and from that came our notorious horror act."

At the Stella Ballroom, Dublin, Light Fantastic were booked onto the TV show 'Live Now', sharing the bill with local heroes, Thin Lizzy.

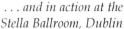

. . . and in action at the Stella Ballroom, Dublin

Dripper continues, "When the cameras rolled we went into 'Monster Mash' and Ron went to town with his horror antics. We sensed we were on a winner."

Back home, Light Fantastic were booked into the **Hen and Chickens** on the Wolverhampton Road, and knew full well that they had to make an impression. To make that impression they hired the services of four girls for a fee of five pounds each. The girls' instructions were to faint as Ron Dickson, all ghosted up, emerged from a flaming coffin, his mouth seeping with imitation blood.

"Contagious hysteria followed," chuckled Dripper. "The girls fainted alright. Along with about half the room!"

The word was out. Light Fantastic were hot news and bookers engaged them with confidence. At **Pelsall Community Centre**, Light Fantastic arrived early, way before the audience, in order to rehearse even more scary routines for their fiery stage act.

"We were experimenting with the pyrotechnics in the dressing room and suddenly the whole lot went up like a volcano," said Dripper Kent. "The Fire Brigade was there for days!"

The former 'Fire Brigade' twanger himself, **Trevor Burton** had by now quit the **Move**, confessing to **Keith Smart** that one of the reasons for his departure was a need to play 'some decent gritty guitar licks'. Keith was now an **Ugly** who, along with guitarist **Willie Hammond**, bassist **Dave Morgan** and keyboard player **Richard Tandy**, was giving out the gritty licks and feel being demanded by the bluesy tones of **Steve Gibbons**' voice.

"Then someone suggested to Willie that he'd be better off elsewhere, and, with Trevor Burton conveniently waiting in the wings, Trevor became an Ugly," explained Keith Smart wryly.

Waiting in the wings at the **Factory**, Gas Street, for the **Freddie Mac Soul Band** to take the stage was proprietor **Martin Hone**.

The Uglies

"I loved the Freddie Mac show," recalled Martin. "Everything about it — the brass section, the rhythm section, the back up singers and dancers — was just too much. I had them down at my place quite a few times."

On this particular evening, Martin was pleasantly surprised to detect a hint of a Brummie accent in the lead vocal.

"Yeah, it was me," owned up **Austin Griffith**, late of the **Stringbeats**. "Freddie Mac made contact and asked me to move to London and be with the show."

This he did, and, on Freddie Mac's insistence, Austin Griffith adopted the professional name of **Mel Day**. When the Freddie Mac Soul Band performed the Percy Sledge song, 'When A Man Loves A Woman', on that early spring evening in 1969, Birmingham became switched on to the soulful voice of Mel Day.

Thanks to Martin Hone, Birmingham also switched on to what proved to be a memorable evening in its history of presenting outstanding musical events. Martin Hone brought to Birmingham, to the Factory in Gas Street, the chance for folks to be entertained and enthralled by the sensational **Count Basie and his Orchestra**.

"I got the opportunity to present the Count and his Orchestra, in my own front room as it were, to my best friends — the folks of Birmingham," said Martin. "I'd have needed to take three times the door money to get near to breaking even, but so what? As the Count played the grand piano, people were milling round him. In between numbers he was shaking hands and joining in conversations. It was a truly magical evening that will remain with me, and I imagine everyone else that was present, forever."

The following morning, saxophonist Eddy 'Lockjaw' Davis gave his considered opinion to the Birmingham Mail: "It was a gas down Gas Street!"

Martin Hone at the Factory with Count Basie

Geoff Turton had been busy in the studio since his departure from the **Rockin' Berries**, making numerous demos with John Schroeder of Pye Records, in the hope of stumbling across the right song to launch his solo career. In January of 1969, a package containing a rough recording arrived from John Schroeder for Geoff's attention. The song 'Colour of My Love' had been written and performed by Paul Ryan, who, with his twin brother Barry, had enjoyed top twenty status in November of 1965 with 'Don't Bring Me Your Heartaches'.

"Personally, I didn't rate it. The song was disjointed and the hook wasn't very strong," said Geoff, "But I wasn't prepared to argue with John's judgement."

When Geoff Turton arrived at Pye Studios to cut the master of 'Colour of My Love' however, he found that arranger Lou Warburton had worked miracles. What had initially appeared to be just a very ordinary song had come to life, with Geoff's distinctive voice married perfectly to a wonderful orchestral score. For the release of the single Geoff adopted the name **Jefferson**.

"But it was still a case of 'let's wait and see', so I came back to Birmingham and continued with **Sight 'n' Sound**, putting the record to the back of my mind." said Geoff.

Serious and Southbound on the M1, **Terry Rowley** and **Johnny Jones** of the **Montanas** were on a mission.

"We'd seen the **Idle Race** with these WEM speakers, and myself and Terry were driving to meet with Charlie Watkins, who made the speakers, to order some for ourselves," Johnny explained. "It was own up time and Terry and I both agreed that, although the Montanas still did the business, it was

Grounded — Montanas

Flying — Trapeze

becoming a tired performance. We needed a change. To do more ambitious things."

During the drive back from the WEM workshop to Wolverhampton, Terry Rowley and Johnny Jones decided just who would be approached to make up the personnel for this ambitious project of theirs. Bass guitarist **Glen Hughes**, guitarist **Mel Galley** and drummer **Dave Holland** would be, in the gentlest of ways, pillaged from **Finders Keepers**. When it came to naming this super duper outfit, Johnny Jones drew on the geometrical knowledge that he had acquired during his education at Dudley Grammar School.

"The band Pentangle were cracking it big," explained Johnny, "So I thought of another weird shape and came up with Trapezium. That quickly got shortened to **Trapeze**. All this happened on the drive back from London."

Alan Clee, of Finders Keepers, was entrusted with the role of sound engineer. It was to be his responsibility to create a studio sound for Trapeze on their live performances.

"Terry Rowley was quite inventive," said Alan. "He was recording backing tracks to augment the Trapeze stage sound years before anyone else thought of that approach."

Traction had lost its grip and ground to a halt, but three members were determined to put together a new band. Progressive rock had surfaced from underground minority status, and vocalist **Phil Savage** was working with guitarist **Gerry Earsdon** on ideas for an all-original set. With bass player **Danny Gallagher** still on board, a well-heeled drummer from Hertfordshire was recruited. He had the use of an isolated cottage on a Welsh mountain near Machynlleth, the ideal place to write and rehearse. **John Tully** from **Peter Martin**'s **Intercity Artists** promised to fill their diary with work, and roadie **Johnny McCourt** was all ready to rev up his J4 van. It was all coming together. With the fine arsenal of sound equipment that they had amassed, this was going to be a solid powerful band. The first gig in the book was for the 14th of February — only weeks away — and the race was on to find a keyboard player to complete the line-up. That was a tall order. He must have a creative mind and nimble fingers. He must be available immediately, and hungry for professional work. Most importantly, the keyboard must be a Hammond organ and the amplification must be big. Big enough to do Marshall combat with their own formidable 'stacks'.

Ever the lateral-thinking man of action, Phil Savage went straight to **Yardleys** and grilled the staff like a detective. He was investigating recent sales of powerful amplification to Hammond organists. Whatever Yardleys' strengths in those days, data protection was not one of them. Phil left the shop armed with a name and address from their files, and hopped aboard a Quinton-bound number nine to seek out **Mike Lavender**.

With the line-up complete, Johnny McCourt braved the late January snow to deliver the band and all their gear to the Welsh retreat. The cottage was a truly inspirational place, two miles from the nearest habitation with panoramic views across the valleys. The band, to be called **Frosty Moses**, set to work, but it soon became clear that an error had been made on the choice of drummer. Fortunately he departed on good terms. *Un*fortunately he had been the only one in the cottage with any money in his pockets! Gerry knew a drummer of the calibre required — his brother **Maurice Earsdon** — but was convinced that he would not be persuaded from his comfortable set-up back home in Hexham, Northumberland. Gerry hadn't reckoned on the determination of Phil and Danny. Without even the small change for a phone box, they set out over the snow-covered fields!

Walking and hitching, hitching and walking, they finally made it from the frozen wilderness of Wales to the relative comfort of Johnny McCourt's feeble gas fire in Sparkhill. Now it would just be a matter of persuading Johnny to take them to Northumberland; convincing drummer Maurice to up sticks and join a starving rock band; and asking brick-built Johnny nicely if he would mind dropping them all off in Wales on his way back to Birmingham!

"Mission accomplished!" shouted Danny, as he marched Maurice through the back doorway and into the cottage.

The creative process now began in earnest. Maurice slotted into the band perfectly — positive, confident and accomplished. Telegrams of encour-agement saying that bookings were rolling in came from John Tully, bringing cheer to all, except the long-suffering postman on his pushbike.

The new show got its first airing at **Thimblemill Baths** to a polite and appreciative audience. Frosty Moses then piled into the van to play the late spot at the **Elbow Room**. This was much more their scene. From a packed house, the band received the response to the new material that they were hoping for. Frosty Moses were on their way. Looking for the first time at the string of dates that John Tully had lined up however, their positive mood faltered. The gaps outnumbered the gigs ten to one! The struggle was only just beginning.

Frosty Moses

Raymond Froggatt & Co

L ater that February, producer Micky Most gave an interview to the Melody Maker. Airing his views on the Eurovision Song Contest, he mentioned that a **Raymond Froggatt** song, 'Big Ship', had sailed close to being selected as Lulu's entry and was, in his view, an extremely well crafted pop song. Peter Gormley was a man who read every word the music press printed. He also happened to be the manager of Cliff Richard. Peter's mission in life was to keep the production line of hit singles in motion.

"Remember," said Raymond Froggatt. "Cliff had scored so heavily with Britain's entry of the previous year, 'Congratulations'.

Peter Gormley made contact with publisher Stuart Reid regarding the Raymond Froggatt catalogue.

"The next thing I know is that Cliff's version of 'Big Ship' is in the top ten and I'm a very hot and sought after songwriter!" chuckled Froggy.

H ot and sought after was a bunch of Brummies who had headed south as the **World of Oz**. Guitarists **Chris Evans** and **Geoff Nichols**, with **Tony Clarkson** on bass, had originally left Birmingham for London with drummer **Dave Reay**.

Rob Moore of the **Capitol Systems** picks up the story: "Deram Records had signed the World of Oz but Dave, who'd drummed briefly in Danny King's Jesters, fancied getting from behind the kit and going into management. So when they sent for me. I was there like a shot!"

Produced by Wayne Bickerton, who went on to produce hits for the Rubettes in the 70s, the album 'The World Of Oz' was packed full of cleverly constructed songs. The BBC, in their wisdom, gave the World of Oz the chance to exhibit their talents to the nation by featuring them in their contemporary music show 'Colour Me Pop' on the evening of Saturday, the 8th March 1969. One song in particular, 'The Muffin Man', written by Chris Evans, was chosen as a single release and became a top five seller in Holland and Germany. When, in the early 1970s, the World of Oz had finally run its course, Rob Moore reunited himself with pianist **Dave Bailey** to form **Kansas Hook**, along with bassist **Charlie Harrison** and the American guitarist **Richard Cole**. Kansas Hook provided backing for the legendary Gene Vincent on his final British tour. They also recorded with him for the Johnny Walker Show at the BBC's Maida Vale studios. The tracks committed to tape were 'Say Mama', 'Be Bop a Lula', 'Roll Over Beethoven' and a totally off-the-cuff version of the Jim Reeves country hit, 'Distant Drums'. The recordings were eventually made commercially available and are, today, extremely sought after.

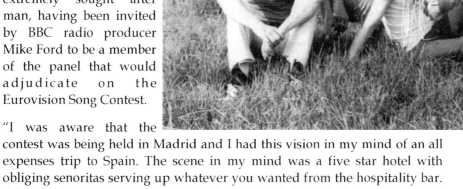

Kansas Hook

Mike Carroll, in early 1969, was an extremely sought after man, having been invited by BBC radio producer Mike Ford to be a member of the panel that would adjudicate on the Eurovision Song Contest.

"I was aware that the contest was being held in Madrid and I had this vision in my mind of an all expenses trip to Spain. The scene in my mind was a five star hotel with obliging senoritas serving up whatever you wanted from the hospitality bar. I'd be laid out on a sun-lounger with a copy of the Melody Maker open at the jazz page," sighed Mike.

"Then the paperwork arrived. I was to report to Wood Green studios in London where the British adjudication would take place under the supervision of Michael Aspel."

Did Mike Carroll enjoy his Eurovision experience? The wise man of Kings Norton sipped at the foamy crust on his freshly pulled pint of ale, "Does the eagle fly on one wing?" he asked, raising an eyebrow inscrutably.

What Mike Carroll needed was a little excitement injected into his mundane existence. His flagship act, **Sight 'n' Sound** were, as they say in the trade, 'ripping up trees' with their vocal harmony and comedy cabaret act. On a Sunday evening in late January of 1969, at the **Chesterfield Club**, Castle Bromwich, guitarist **Rick Price** had literally paralysed the audience with his send up, complete with hairy wig, of Roy Wood. On leaving the Chesterfield, Rick encountered the hairy man himself waiting on the car park. "How do you fancy a job with the Move?" asked Roy.

Rick Price sat up all night debating his future. At seven-thirty next morning, he rattled the door of the Carroll household. A bleary and red-eyed Mike Carroll finally answered. He had spent the previous evening at the **Rio Grande Lounge**, rear of the Yew Tree pub, where he promoted his hard rock disco. This had been followed with a session of the old 'George Rafters' until the early hours. The dear boy had only been in bed an hour. Mike Carroll was a little peeved, to say the least, about the loss of his guitarist, but consoled himself that he still had the voice of **Geoff Turton** as a major selling point.

Jeff Lynne & Greg Masters

Roger Spencer

The **Idle Race** still had **Jeff Lynne**, who had rejected Roy Wood's offer to join the Move. The band was stronger and more focused than ever.

"What a lot of folks didn't realise," explains drummer **Roger Spencer**, "Is that there were two Idle Races. The one Idle Race featured us performing Jeff's whimsical and melodic songs, whilst the other Idle Race rocked like crazy. **Dave Pritchard** had a great Leadbelly style of country rock. **Greg Masters** was so solid with his bass playing, and I just stuck it down without all the frills. Jeff Lynne always was a great blues guitarist. That was our secret. No one did anybody else's job."

With **Trevor Burton** now doing **Willie Hammond**'s job of playing gritty guitar licks with the **Uglys**, it was decided that the Uglys as a name was a little too far out the other way for comfort.

"We all met up at **Steve Gibbons'** house," said **Keith Smart**. "After loads of suggestions for a new name, we went with the one that accurately described the style and feel of Trevor's guitar playing."

In the late spring of 1969, the Uglys became **Balls**. Keith Smart continues the story: "**Tony Secunda**, the former Move manager, worshipped the ground Trevor walked on, and firmly believed that the switch from the Move to new ground with the reborn Uglys was a terrific business plan for us all."

Warner Brothers Music were alerted by Tony Secunda to the existence of Balls, and the fact that Balls would be the next big thing to hit the British progressive music scene. All Balls needed was a healthy advance of money to 'get it together'. When the first payment arrived, Balls rolled south, from Birmingham to Fordingbridge, a quaint little place on the edge of the New Forest in Hampshire, where they took rent of a cottage to enhance their creative flow.

"The first thing that we did to help the flow was open an account at the village off-licence," recalled Keith Smart.

When **Denny Laine** heard that good times were rollin' down in Fordingbridge, he suddenly discovered his own creativity was flowing again and turned up on the cottage doorstep. Tony Secunda, on hearing of Denny Laine's presence, informed Warner Brothers Music that not only did Balls have the vital spark of the Move, they also had the voice of 'Go Now' and the creative talent that was behind the Incredible String Band. Warner Brothers responded by advancing more money. The proprietor of the village off-licence pinched himself and stocked up his cellar accordingly. After three months of 'getting it together', Balls managed to perform just one show. This was at Fordingbridge Village Hall. When asked by Keith Smart to display a poster in his window to advertise the forthcoming Village Hall event, the gentleman at the off-licence was only too happy to oblige.

Rolling south on the A435 out of Moseley, bound for the village of Studley, where their intention was to hang out and stay loose, were a strange looking bunch of hippies by the name of **Tea and Symphony**.

"**James Langston**'s father had a farm there," drummer **Pete Chatfield** explained, "So it was an obvious place for us to get it together."

Prior to Pete's arrival in the band, Tea and Symphony's vocalist James Langston, with multi instrumentalists **Nigel Phillips** and **Geoff Daw**, put out their progressively constructed folk songs to an accompaniment of flutes, recorders, accordions, acoustic guitars and whatever else they could lay their hands on. Their unique, thought-provoking, yet endearing style quickly caught Brum's imagination. It also led them to the management services of **Jim Simpson** who, in turn, led them to the offices of music publisher **Tony Hall**. Always on the lookout for the fresh approach, hence the name of his publishing house, 'Fresh Air Music', Tony introduced Tea and Symphony to producer **Gus Dudgeon** and the hippie EMI label, Harvest Records.

These introductions resulted in Tea and Symphony's highly acclaimed debut album, 'An Asylum for the Musically Insane'. This album contained such obscure, but priceless gems of songs as the poetic 'Feel How So Cool the Wind' and 'Armchair Theatre', a clever slant on the television series that was showing at the time.

The **Bull's Head** pub, on St Mary's Row in Moseley village, was attracting the 'Monty Python' brigade like moths around a flame during the summer of 1969. The reason for this was that on the bar, next to the mild and bitter pulls, was a plastic model of a lump of ice advertising the availability of a revolutionary tipple. For the price of two shillings and four pence, a pint of keg lager, served up at forty-eight degrees Fahrenheit (six degrees colder than your average drop of wallop) was there for the taking. Word travelled fast around the educated circles about the wonders of this chilled continental

Tea & Symphony in Cannon Hill Park

sherbet and weekend evenings would see St Mary's Row crammed full of Triumph Spitfires. **Pete Chatfield** needed some intellectual company, having become artistically suffocated within the confines of his Sheldon surroundings. Hearing that the Bulls Head was the place for love, peace and a few pints of the gassy stuff, Pete stepped inside and encountered Tea and Symphony propping up the bar.

"They wanted to expand and become a little more 'Tyrannosaurus Rex' in style. You know, sitting cross legged with African drums all over the place," said Pete. "So, into Tea and Symphony I went, along with guitarists **Bob Wilson** and **Dave Carroll**."

Adopting a policy of 'the freakier the better', T&S played venues such as

Henry's Blueshouse, the **Elbow Room**, the **Arts Lab** on Summer Row and **St Peter's College**, Saltley. With their audiences under the spell of bewildering lyrics, crazy rhythms and olde English instrumentation that abounded on the tracks of their second Harvest album, 'Jo Sago', Tea and Symphony would play their ace card. In an act of sheer psychedelic surrealism vocalist James Langston would step into the rays of the hypnotic strobe lighting, clad in a pink PVC lobster suit!

Open-air festivals were now the order of the day in that pleasant summer of 1969, and the hippie vibrations that Tea and Symphony radiated were much in demand. At the Great Western Festival, Boston Lincolnshire, they gave terrific support to the newly put together line up of the Faces, which included Rod Stewart and Ronny Wood and down in sunny Cornwall, at Truro, the Crazy World of Arthur Brown didn't exactly have it all their own way. Neither did a four-piece outfit that were actually billed beneath Tea and Symphony on that afternoon — Queen!

*Manic moments —
Frosty Moses in the park*

Birmingham's open-air celebration of rock was hosted by the **Midland Arts Centre** in Canon Hill Park, which had its own scaled-down Roman amphitheatre. Tea and Symphony were there to cast their unique spell on the proceedings, but topping the bill was the manic yet melodic **Frosty Moses**. They had grafted and hustled their way through the spring to become a force to be reckoned with; from **Gary Finn**'s curiously named **Executive Club**, with its free goat curry and lovely Rita, the embarrassingly topless barmaid; to **Mothers**, where **Phil Myatt** was hatching plans to get Frosty Moses into the big-time. In London too, they were making in-roads with the in-crowd, at **Blaises**, the **Marquee**, and the **Speakeasy**, where **Tony Hall** was making sure that the band was getting noticed by all the right people. Their prestige booking at Chalk Farm's **Roundhouse** was jeopardised by the breakdown of the Minivan that was carrying vital extra equipment that would not fit in the J4. No problem. They towed the Minivan, and its load, down the M1 to the engagement — and back again afterwards!

Frosty Moses were also chipping their way into the record business, recording demos for **Island** at **Morgan Studios**, and with **Nirvana**'s **Patrick Campbell-Lyons** at **Pye**. That was where **Phil Savage** risked his entire personal record collection on a wager.

The Pye studio was in the basement of the Marble Arch building, down three steep wide flights of stairs. After a long session, roadie **Johnny McCourt**, single-handed, was getting the band's equipment back up to ground level. When he came to **Mike Lavender**'s Hammond organ (similar in size and weight to an upright piano) Phil casually quipped, "So let's see you trot up the stairs on your own with *that* thing!"

Now, Johnny took a pride in his trade. A long, stoned debate ensued. Phil had, good-as, called him a weakling. If Phil was so convinced that Johnny wasn't up to the job, he should put his money (or whatever other tangible asset he could claim to own) where his mouth was. Phil was in a corner, but then again, how could he lose? The task was beyond any mortal man! Hands were shaken — the bet was made. Johnny, having been careful not to claim that he could actually lift the organ, commandeered the other four band members to tilt the instrument backwards, as Phil looked on with increasing unease. Johnny then instructed them to lift it as high as they could (which was all of four feet), until he could take up a suitable position beneath, and have it gently lowered onto his back, shoulders and outstretched arms. Like the man in the song, big John let out a mighty groan, steadied his balance, and proceeded with ungainly but unstoppable dignity, to climb the three flights to ground level. At the top, Phil Savage, eyes now closed, didn't even watch as the rest of the band carefully relieved Johnny McCourt of his burden; he was too busy mourning the loss of his record collection.

Idle Race

That same summer saw the **Idle Race**, at a festival at Nottingham racecourse, playing support to Status Quo (a band who had previously been known as the Spectres, before changing briefly to Traffic and then Traffic Jam). The Idle Race's set included powerful classics like the Grateful Dead's 'Hey Grandma' and Steppenwolf's 'Born to be Wild' interspersed with such **Jeff Lynne** gems as 'Come With Me' and 'Days of Broken Arrows'. Status Quo could only gaze in awe at the Idle Race, dreading the prospect of following such progressive and creative talent. Quo's set leant heavily on performances of their two top twenty successes, 'Pictures of Matchstick Men' and 'Ice in the Sun'.

"Francis Rossi told me some time later that the Idle Race had changed the Quo's whole outlook on their musical style," said **Roger Spencer**.

A change of style and presentation were on the agenda for the **Move**. "People tend to think that I took the Move into cabaret," commented **Carl Wayne**, "That is not so."

The success of 'Blackberry Way' at the close of 1968, had coincided with the Move seeking a change in professional representation. **Peter Walsh** of **Starlite Artistes** approached the Move with a management offer. It was a strange proposition considering the Move's public reputation as hooligans compared to the squeaky clean image of Starlite's other managed acts, Marmalade, the Tremeloes and Vanity Fair, but by early February of 1969, the Move were in the hands of Peter Walsh. Now, with a diary full of cabaret clubs, their presentation tactics were forced to change from shock to schmaltz.

"Once we'd signed, Peter Walsh then declared that there was a big circuit of cabaret clubs out there waiting for us," Carl Wayne explained. "It was the first we'd ever heard of the Bailey Organisation. The Baileys wanted the Move, and Peter Walsh did the deal. It was nothing to do with me."

The single that **Geoff 'Jefferson' Turton** had recorded four months ago, 'Colour of My Love', was picking up radio plays.

"Geoff was always down-to-earth," said **Mike Carroll**. "He genuinely thought the record was dead and buried. Then apparently a radio jockey over in Ireland gave it a couple of spins. Radio One picked it up and the record just shot away, and as a result, soon after, so did Geoff Turton!"

'Colour of My Love', made number twenty-two on the charts in April of 1969, resulting in Geoff Turton breaking away from **Sight 'n' Sound** to embark on a solo career.

Overcoming personnel problems was now seen as an ongoing occupational hazard for Sight 'n' Sound. They soon found themselves back in the spotlight when they performed at the grand opening evening of **Eddie Fewtrell**'s latest contribution to Birmingham's nightlife, **Rebecca's**, which was situated on the corner of Lower Severn Street. Mike Carroll was also able to engage, for that opening night, the services of one of the most popular disc jockeys on Britain's airwaves. Radio One's Stuart Henry found himself being carried onto the stage, shoulder-high, to the triumphal din of half a dozen kilted bagpipers!

Geoff 'Jefferson' Turton

Once Mike Carroll was satisfied that everything was again ship shape and Bristol fashion at his Kings Norton office, he decided to ease his somewhat troubled mind, and head south where **Jimmy Powell and the Dimensions** were playing a short season at the Royal Hotel in St Helier, Jersey.

"I have to say that promoting Jimmy Powell had been an absolute magic carpet ride for me through the sixties decade. He was the most exciting act I ever booked." commented Mike. "He was also a great pal and when he invited me to Jersey for the weekend, to get away from it all, I was there like a shot."

The accommodation for Jimmy and his band was in the loft of a farmhouse at St Saviours Bay.

"Dawn was breaking and Jimmy and I were still wide awake. Nights were pretty wild in those far-out days of the late sixties," said Mike, reminiscing. "As the birds twittered so the sound of cows mooing could be heard and I confessed to Jimmy that I'd always wanted to milk a cow."

Wearing only a shirt, shoes and a pair of Y-fronts, and armed with a pint pot, Mike Carroll found himself being spirited across the farmyard by Jimmy Powell to a field where a few cows were standing.

"Mind the wire Mike, it's electrified," warned Jimmy.

Taking great care, Mike and Jimmy stepped over the electrified wire to arrive at the side of a real live Jersey cow.

Jimmy Powell

"My feet were soaked with the morning dew." Mike explained. "But here I was, about to fulfil an ambition of a lifetime."

Jimmy Powell took hold of the cow's head. He knew the procedure.

"I'll blow up her nose," said Jimmy in passable Yorkshire tones, "While you go to work on her udders. Daisy loves her udders feeled."

Mike continues the tale: "So I'm down there, stroking away and the cow's looking at me like it wants to get engaged. Jimmy's blowing up the cow's nose and suddenly it happened. The milk started squirting out and I filled the pint pot. Don't ask me why I expected it to be ice cold for some reason, but I'd done it!"

With his pot full to the brim, Mike turned and made his way back to the farmhouse. Swinging his leg across the electrified wire, he held his pint of milk up high in the air for the entire world to share in his achievement. Unfortunately, Mike didn't swing his leg high enough and his wedding tackle brushed against the wire.

"When I eventually returned to Earth, the pot was empty," a wincing Mike Carroll recalled, adding, "But I s'pose it's not worth crying over."

Also returning to **Earth** was guitarist, **Tony Iommi**, who had actually departed from his long time pals and, indeed, Birmingham, to make a curious career move to **Ian Anderson**'s ground-breaking outfit, **Jethro Tull**.

After two weeks, Tony was back in Hill Street, at **Henry's Blueshouse**, describing his brief flirtation with stardom as a nine-to-five job with no camaraderie. It was then that the clientele of Henry's began to feel the earth move under their feet as Messrs Osborne, Butler, Iommi and Ward embarked on a course of writing their own material. Influenced by the writer Dennis Wheatley, their songs took on a most definite feel of the occult in their character. One such song, so dark and so menacing, was entitled 'Black Sabbath'.

When Earth performed 'Black Sabbath', the audience did not chat amongst themselves. They didn't have the choice, the band played so ear-splittingly loud! From then on, the way was clear. Earth would be renamed **Black Sabbath**.

The way was clear for the **Move** to return to Birmingham. In July of 1969, they were back to perform the cabaret act they had spent the past few weeks honing in the northern supper clubs of the Bailey Organisation.

They were booked to play two shows a night for a solid week. An early show at the **Cavendish Club**, which was situated over the Swan Shopping Centre at Yardley, followed by a late show at **La Dolce Vita**. This upmarket venue, opened in October of 1967, occupied the former premises of a health and fitness club on the corner of Hurst Street and Smallbrook Ringway.

"To be brutally honest," said **Carl Wayne**, "for me, losing **Ace Kefford** and then **Trevor Burton**, the Move was already finished."

On that balmy Sunday evening, a packed Cavendish Club waited in anticipation as roadie **John 'Upsy' Downing** positioned the Move's amplifiers on stage; to a piano, bass and drums accompaniment of 'The Girl From Ipanema', courtesy of the **Brian Ford Trio**. With the three front line microphones in place, a monkey-suited compere stepped into the spotlight to announce that should anyone wish to make use of the club's gaming facilities, then they'd be pleased to hear that the brakes on the roulette wheel had been re-lined. Riding on a wave of minimal titters, the cheeky chappie went on to say that should anyone fancy playing blackjack, then black Jack would be in the building by midnight. Spotting a John the Baptist look-alike in the audience, the master of ceremonies asked if the gentleman's moustache was, in reality, his eyebrows that had popped down for a drink. Receiving a threat that was peppered with Anglo Saxon slang, the genial host coughed nervously before proudly announcing, "Here they are! The Move! And don't forget Bob Monkhouse next week!"

Carl Wayne, the ultimate professional, looked every inch the star in his white tuxedo, tailored black trousers and black patent sensible shoes that would cover practically every inch of the cabaret floor in his efforts to entertain the chicken-in-the-basket diners. For the Bailey Organisation to

The Move

obtain the services of an act that was currently high on the charts was unprecedented, but it happened that week. 'Curly', their seventh single, and rumoured to be about Sight 'n' Sound's roadie, Curly Williams, was in at number twelve.

The act that the Move presented to their loyal Birmingham following contained no smashing of televisions, or smoke bombs being fired off. In fact the only sign of controversy was when Carl Wayne compared Roy Wood's hairstyle to an explosion in a mattress factory. It was a rehearsed line that slotted in well with the format. An ambitious and quite beautiful interpretation of 'Ave Maria' was climaxed with a highly emotionally charged version of Marvin Gaye's 'Abraham, Martin and John'. As soon as Carl Wayne had delivered the lyric 'They freed a lot of people but it seems the good die young. I just turned around and they were gone', so too were the Move.

The compere pleaded, "One more! Thank you!" but it wasn't to be. The Move, as Birmingham knew them, as everyone knew them, had moved on.

Everyone seemed to be moving on. **Derry Ryan**, from the defunct **Stacks**, now found himself fronting **Copperfield**, who were, along with Derry, **'Sprike' Hopkins** and **Bob Duffurn** on guitars, **Derek Arnold** on bass and **Malcolm Cope** on drums. Their manager was **Wilf Pine**, formerly of the powerful **Don Arden Organisation**. Having a manager with such experience and contacts, Copperfield found themselves with a Parlophone recording contract. Their first release was 'Any Old Time', and Wilf Pine, being the smooth operator that he was, was able to obtain thirty minutes of prime time television for Copperfield by negotiating an appearance on BBC 2's 'Colour Me Pop'.

"We started rehearsing at nine in the morning. Broke for an hour for lunch then recorded the show until one the following morning." recalled Derry Ryan. "I was sick of the song by then."

Although 'Any Old Time' didn't make the national charts, the record made number eighteen on the Birmingham Mail top twenty in July of 1969. The composer of that song, **Tony McCauley**, was now writing hits like a housewife shells peas. Hits for the likes of the Foundations and Long John Baldry had made Tony McCauley an extremely sought after composer.

Copperfield

When the master requested the presence of **Pinkerton's Assorted Colours** at Pye recording studios, the lads from Rugby were there like a shot. Tony McCauley's song for them, 'Baby Make It Soon', seemed the ideal vehicle to project Pinkerton's Colours back into the charts after a three-year absence. When the Scottish outfit Marmalade picked up on the song after hearing the constant radio plays, they wasted no time in putting out a version of their own. Fresh from their chart success with 'Ob-La-Di Ob-La-Da', Marmalade

soon scooped the market with their version of 'Baby Make It Soon'.

By now, Tony McCauley's contribution of songs to the hit parade was phenomenal. 'Build Me Up Buttercup' and 'Sorry Suzanne' were just a couple of the titles that he had going for him at the time. By late summer, Tony McCauley came up with a song for Pinkerton's Assorted Colours that, when released would go down in history as possibly the most remembered 'one that got away'. 'Smile a Little Smile' was an absolute gem of a three-minute pop song that was simply tailored for the pathos of Tony Newman's

Pinkerton's Assorted Colours

vocal delivery. But even the addition of an oboe (an idea borrowed from the Honeybus's 'I Can't Let Maggie Go') and despite intense radio play, 'Smile a Little Smile', failed to chart.

Gerry Levene, at this time, was approached by Tony McCauley to record two of his songs, 'That's All Any Man Can Say' and 'Hold Back the Daybreak'. Gerry Levene, sensing chart success, was on the all-time high.

"After the session, the end result of which I thought was wonderful, me, Tony McCauley and his associates retired to the pub where I ordered the drinks," recalls Gerry Levene with slight embarrassment.

Gerry ordered port and brandies all round without realising that, at London prices, he didn't have anywhere near enough money to pay for them. Tony McCauley, after being landed with the bill, informed Gerry Levene that he not only sounded like a Jewish tailor, he also acted like one! A change of name was called for.

"David Essex was beginning to create waves within the business at the time, so there and then Tony came up with the name of **David Lincoln** for me," explained Gerry.

Downing the port and brandy in one massive gulp that made his eyes water, Gerry Levene was frog marched to a boutique on Tottenham Court Road. Sweeping aside the cutely effeminate salesman, clothes of the latest fashion were removed from their hangers by these new acquaintances and handed to Gerry, with the order to 'stick these on, quick'.

With Gerry looking 'a real Bobby Dazzler', he was ushered outside onto the street where a waiting photographer quickly fired off a few shots for publicity purposes. Once the photographs had been taken, the bewildered shop assistant was handed back the fashionable garments and told "Thanks, but no thanks. Not his size."

Now re-dressed in his grubby hooded duffle coat and Aston Villa supporter's scarf, Gerry Levene was hurried along Oxford Street to the powerhouse offices of the highflying theatrical agent, Sidney Rose. Sidney, on acquiring the signature of 'David Lincoln' on a management contract, told Gerry to return to Birmingham and await further instructions. Instructions that would lead to the career of David Lincoln blossoming beyond his wildest of dreams.

Gerry Levene tells it exactly how it was: " I never heard a thing from Sidney Rose or any of 'em ever again!"

David Lincon alias
Gerry Levene

Trapeze were in the big city of dreams to play **Rasputin's** club, in Oxford Street. No strangers to the club, which was owned by brothers Rick and John Gunnel, Trapeze believed that if they kept at it, sooner or later the man with the big cigar would appear. Sure enough, as they took to the stage, Chas Chandler, once of the Animals, and now manager of the guitarist Jimi Hendrix, came into the club. Could this be the big one?

Johnny Jones, vocalist with Trapeze tells the story: "We went down really well that night at Rasputin's club and we got word about Chas Chandler hanging around on a scouting mission."

Hopes were high when the dressing door knocked, but it was not Chandler, it was the **Moody Blues**, and they made it perfectly clear that they wished to be associated with Trapeze.

The Moody Blues were now right back where they belonged; their recent album 'On the Threshold of a Dream' had received both critical and public acclaim. When they took to the road that autumn of 1969, Trapeze were there to play support. Trapeze were also there to promote their new single 'Send Me No More Letters', a **Terry Rowley** composition that was released on the Moody Blues' own Threshold label.

"The tour culminated at the Albert Hall," Johnny Jones recalled. "I drove down on the afternoon with our management team but we got stuck in fog on the M1 motorway."

When Johnny finally made it to the stage door of the Albert Hall, the audience was already seated.

"My first look at the Albert Hall was when we walked out to perform," said Johnny. "That view from the stage just took my breath. The music business can steal your soul but not your memories."

Alan Clee, Trapeze's sound engineer, has his own memories of the Albert Hall concert: "The format was that as soon as Trapeze finished their last song, I was to remove their equipment from the stage to make way for the Moody Blues. The arrangement had worked fine throughout the tour. What happened at the Albert Hall? As I quickly cleared the stage, the audience broke into claps and cheers, demanding an encore from the band. In front of a full Albert Hall, and it took me five long minutes, I had to re-set the stage for Trapeze!"

Back at Rasputin's club, Chas Chandler once again stepped out of the shadows to be totally zapped by the energy that was being generated by the Wolverhampton outfit, **Ambrose Slade**. The song that they closed with that evening was a raving crowd rouser entitled 'Get Down and Get With It'. Their encounter with Chas that night set the wheels in motion for the band's success, but it wasn't until two years later, in June 1971, that 'Get Down and Get With It' became their first entry onto the charts, with Chas Chandler promoting them as **Slade**. They would go on to make sixteen visits to the top ten charts, six of them hitting the number one slot with a bullet.

Gloucester's answer to Elvis Presley, **Dave Scarlet** was hoping to visit the number one slot. Arriving at **Zella** studios were three members of **Locomotive** — organist **Norman Haines**, drummer **Bob Lamb** and bassist **Mick Hinks**.

"I'd had a call from Dave Scarlet," said sound engineer **Johnny Haines**. "He wanted to cut a demo of one of his rockabilly songs. Could I provide the session musicians?"

With instruments and tape deck at the ready, Messrs, Haines, Lamb and Hinks awaited the arrival of the Gloucestershire hillbilly cat.

"I was on the corner of Essex Street, watching for him," Johnny Haines explained. "A chauffeur driven black Humber came cruising along the Horsefair, and into Essex Street. The chauffeur opened the back passenger door and out stepped Dave Scarlet in his Elvis cape and shades. Under his arm was an electric guitar that was worth all of ten quid!"

Johnny Haines wrote on the top of the track sheet, 'Dave Scarlet' and asked, "What's the song called?"

Applying a deep Southern drawl to his West Country farmyard tones, Dave Scarlet slipped the guitar round his neck, and turning to the waiting musicians he half whispered," 'Scalled 'Ma Hatty Batty' an' I guess this is how it goes one tarm."

Curling his lip and shaking a leg, Dave Scarlet proceeded to knock the living daylights out of his 'tupenny-ha'penny' guitar. Breaking into a Chuck Berry duckwalk, he did two laps of the studio floor before laying his song onto the astonished onlookers. "A she's my Hatty Bahatty! Oh yeah! Ma Hatty Bahatty!"

"It really was your mother or a priest," confessed Johnny Haines, holding his ribs.

Johnny Haines' next session would see him holding his ears when the sheer force of **Black Sabbath** was let loose in his Essex Street studio.

"**Jim Simpson** brought them down to see if the live feel, which they were creating at **Henry's Blueshouse**, would transfer onto tape," Johnny explained.

Jim Simpson, in fact, had already spoken with **Tony Hall** and **David Platz**, partners in Tony Hall Enterprises, about the band of heavy metallers who were, if they weren't careful, going to be worldbeaters. Tony Hall, a veteran of the music business, had heard it all before, but had the utmost respect for Jim Simpson's judgement. He not only agreed to look in on the Black Sabbath Zella session, he also provided the services of hitmaker **Gus Dudgeon** to engineer the proceedings. On the morning of the session Tony Hall stepped out of his Green Street apartment in London's Mayfair, climbed behind the wheel of his white Rolls Royce and headed north on the M1 motorway to Birmingham. Making the area of Deritend, he turned right, under the Digbeth 'temporary' flyover to behold the Rotunda building. As luck would have it, he also beheld a beat bobby standing outside the Haddon and Stokes factory. Pulling into the kerb, Tony Hall leaned across and was about to ask directions for Essex Street.

"You're lookin' for Johnny 'Aines's studio ain' ya," said the helmeted constable, opening the passenger door of the prestigious vehicle.

"Why yes, as a matter of fact I am," said Tony, a little taken aback with the welcome.

"Aarhh, Johnny said there was some bloke comin' up from London. Carry on up to the Rotunda, down the Ringway and hang a left." Leaning into the car, the constable began to gently stroke the stained oak dashboard and tanned leather upholstery of the Rolls Royce interior sighing, "And they say there's no money about."

Pretty soon there would be sackfulls of the green stuff winging its way into the accounts of the **Led Zeppelin** personnel. When **Peter Grant** had made the revolutionary decision not to release any singles, it immediately set Led Zeppelin apart, and fired them into a market place that was to be theirs and theirs alone. Six months after its release, their first LP, having peaked at number six, was still in the album charts and would remain so for a further year. Their second album, 'Led Zeppelin 2' was now in the shops, and about to become a major milestone in the history of rock. In November '69 it provided the band with their first number one hit, and it would be almost three years before it finally dropped out of the album chart!

Pat **Wayne**'s records, 'Go Back to Daddy' and 'Roll Over Beethoven' had faired remarkably well with the Scandinavian market. Even his lighter material, 'My Friend' and 'Come Dance With Me' had shown with some distinction on the Swedish charts. In his Stockholm hotel room, as Pat prepared to take in the fine Scandinavian air during afternoon perambulation, the telephone interrupted the lacing up of his tennis pumps.

"It was **John Bonham**," said Pat. "Zeppelin were playing the City Hall and John invited me down for a drink."

Musically it was an experience Pat Wayne will remember for the rest of his days.

"I could feel the sheer force of Led Zeppelin hitting my chest. It really was that powerful," he chuckled.

Backstage, as John Bonham and Pat Wayne wet their whistles and brought

Pat Wayne

each other up to date with stories that still remain, to this day, unprintable, an ultra-hip female journalist from one of the trendy Scandinavian 'glossies' endeavoured to prise a couple of quotes from John Bonham.

"She poked her little tape recorder under John's nose and asked if there were any hidden mystical messages within their songs," explained Pat.

"Oh yeah," replied John, "Deferably."

Pat continued, "So she then asked John where exactly these mystical messages came from."

"From Mrs Smith and her five little boys," John Bonham replied, biting his lip.

When Pat Wayne returned to his Swedish cabaret engagement he found the South African booker Val de Angelis waiting for him. Informing Pat that an untapped, yet highly lucrative market awaited him in Zambia, 'My Friend' having scored heavily in their charts. Pat Wayne, on hearing such news,

Cabaret time —
Pat Wayne in South Africa

kitted himself out with a Daktari outfit and was off like a shot. Word spread fast and furious through the South African network of the handsome and debonair British entertainer that was 'on safari' around the Zambian hotel circuit. These words reached the ears of Solly Kershner, proprietor of a highly prestigious chain of hotels in Johannesburg and Capetown.

"Solly immediately moved me down south to front his hotel floorshows," explained Pat Wayne, "Which I did for the next two years before (and I still can't think why I did it) I returned home. I must have been raving mad!"

By the mid 1970s, Solly Kershner had opened up his very own town, Sun City, the South African equivalent to Las Vegas.

Although not quite in the Las Vegas stakes, **Laurie Mansfield** was steadily learning the ropes of highflying showbusiness. A **Mike Sheridan** and **Rick Price** collaboration, both as artistes and writers, 'Top Ten Record', which Laurie produced, unfortunately didn't live up to its name, but some novelty recordings, made with the comedian Charlie Drake, had triggered a spark within Laurie.

Mike Sheridan

Taking control of Charlie Drake's representation, Laurie Mansfield became a booker with the well-established firm International Artistes, of Regent Street, London. International Artistes had been in business since the forties, when Phyllis Rounce and Hugh Alexander signed the comedy actor Terry Thomas to a management contract. By the late 1960s International Artistes was truly a stable of established star names. When Laurie Mansfield joined the staff he had one ambition — to be present, on set, during a recording of 'Top of the Pops'. Moving swiftly through the ranks, Laurie's ambition would soon be realised.

"For some reason," said **Dave Pegg**, "work was quiet with the **Ian Campbell Group**, so I began making plans for another group in case things should fold."

With guitarist **Clem Clemson**, who had played with the Bakerloo Blues Band and drummer **Cozy Powell**, Dave Pegg came up with the idea of a band called the **Beast**.

"We put the feelers out for some gigs but then Clem left to join John Hiseman's Colosseum. Then Cozy got a call from Jeff Beck and he was off too."

Fairports Curthy, Swarbrick & Pegg, with Doc Holliday & Bev Bevan

Just when Dave Pegg was feeling alone and unloved, an offer for his services came from the folk group **Fairport Convention** who had spent that summer of 1969 on the charts with their version of a Bob Dylan song. After its lyrics were translated into French, the title came out as 'Si Tu Dois Partir', which we English recognised as 'If You Gotta Go', the Manfred Mann hit from four years earlier.

Geoff 'Jefferson' Turton would have loved to have spent the summer on the charts. To follow the success of 'Colour of My Love', Geoff was given a Tony McCauley song, 'Baby Take Me in Your Arms'. The song, an excellent choice, received plenty of airplay and was termed a turntable hit. However, all promotional work ceased when Jefferson, returning from a short tour of Scottish clubs, was involved in a horrendous car accident on

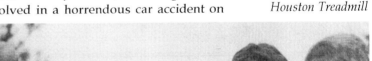

Houston Treadmill

the M6 motorway in Stafford. The good news for Geoff was that, whilst hospitalised, 'Baby Take Me in Your Arms', made number 11 on the American Billboard charts. Back on his feet and itching for the road again, Geoff Turton found himself an ideal backing band. **Houston Treadmill**, from the Warstock area were being led by Mr 'Little People' himself, **Ronny** (formerly of **Ronny and the Senators** fame) **Smith**.

The Burp Band

Ronny's colleagues in Houston Treadmill were, from Sight 'n' Sound, guitarist **Grant Kearney**, with former **Top Priority** members -- **Phil Copestake** on bass, **Steve Wheat** on drums and, on lead guitar, Ronny's neighbour, **Gerald 'Sid' Hood**, a lad with one green eye and one blue eye!

"I was still managing Zissman's Menswear at Sparkbrook, so when the others took to the road with Jefferson, I chose to stay with the shop." said Ronny Smith.

With the shop closed every Wednesday, Ronny filled his day off by lending a helping hand to a pal from his Moseley Grammar school days, **Bob Davis**, or, as everyone referred to him, Jasper, or even by now, **Jasper Carrot**.

Shades & wigs — it must be Burp at the Boggery

"We used to do Dudley Market every Wednesday," recalled Ronny. "Jasper called the stall 'Karrot's Kut Price Korner' and we'd sell soap, shampoo, scouring pads, bleach, clothes pegs and disinfectant in multiples of three. We'd be caked in all gooey stuff. Our stall was next to the gents' toilets. We used to put a peg over our nose to wash our hands clean every half hour!"

The boys also made sure that their hands were clean and scrubbed every Monday evening.

"Jasper had opened his own folk club, at the **Boggery**, in Solihull and we, as the **Burp Band** were the resident act, doormen and cloakroom attendants," said Ronny Smith, who, for the life of him, could not break the habit of dressing in womens' clothing.

"The Burp Band," Ronny continued, "Was me, with Jasper on his guitar, **Dave College** played washboard, **Hazel**, Jasper's missus, was on keyboard and **Malc Chapman** played trumpet in the style, he claimed, of Maynard Ferguson. For that reason we christened him **Massey Ferguson.**"

Frosty Moses

Down in London, **Chris Blackwell** had obviously taken a shine to **Frosty Moses**. He had solved their dire transport problems at a stroke, by providing them with a brand new six-wheel Ford Transit bus. He also arranged hotel accommodation for the band and ordered Island Records' legal department to draft out a record contract. Meanwhile a start was made on recording a debut album at Trident Studio, with **Gus Dudgeon** producing. When, two days into the project, Gus announced that he wanted to bring in a replacement drummer, the band were dumbstruck. They regarded **Maurice Earsdon** as one of the finest drummers in the country, and when Chris Blackwell backed Gus Dudgeon's decision, Frosty Moses could see only one choice. They handed back the shiny Ford key fob and the Transit's ignition keys, and set about getting themselves and their gear back to Brum.

Picking up where they had left off, Frosty Moses returned to writing and rehearsing into the early hours at the **Midland Arts Centre**, and striving for gigs at venues that were serious about rock. It was at just such a venue — **Mothers** in Erdington — that proprietor **Phil Myatt** spelled out a deal that he had cooked up for the band. He was not only offering to manage their live bookings, he had lined up Moody Blues producer **Alex Murray** to handle their recording career, and financier **John French** to fund the proceedings. Frosty Moses were impressed. This was a dream team. Phil would have all the connections on the progressive rock circuit; Alex had a great track record, not least with his production of the memorable first-ever pop video for the Moodies' 'Go Now'; and money-man John, an eloquent city slicker who exuded wealth, and would underwrite the entire enterprise.

John French

A five-year contract was promptly drawn up, guaranteeing the 'artistes' a minimum income of four thousand pounds a year each! Frosty Moses promptly signed it! John French asked the band to compile a 'wish list' of the instruments and equipment that they would choose if money were no object — and then went straight out and bought it all! Still pinching themselves, Frosty Moses were temporarily installed in John French's luxury West End apartment, while more permanent London accommodation was being sought. It seemed nothing could go wrong any more. Even their miss-billing as 'Frosty Noses' for a gig at the Lyceum produced valuable mentions the following week in Melody Maker and the New Musical Express.

At the Lyceum they had marvelled at the efficient road crew that John French must have organised. Making way for the headliners, **Led Zeppelin**, these goliaths cleared the stage of Frosty Moses' fine new equipment in record time. The band were yet to find out that the 'crew' were actually repo' men and that, but for some smooth-talk and a rubber cheque from John French, Frosty Moses would never have seen that gear again! The dream was about to turn into a nightmare.

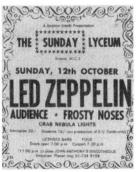

Everything (except cheques) was bouncing in the offices of International Artistes, where **Laurie Mansfield** was now entrusted with the affairs of Rolf Harris, Cleo Laine and Johnny Dankworth, and the outfit led by songwriter Roger Cook -- Blue Mink. It was the second week of December 1969 when Laurie's ambition to be present on the 'Top of the Pops' set came true. At number three that week were Blue Mink with their 'Melting Pot'. Laurie Mansfield, standing in the wings, smiled contentedly. Presenter Tony Blackburn announced the immortal words, "It's number one! It's this week's top of the pops! It's Rolf Harris with his tale of those 'Two Little Boys'!" The sentimental Victorian music hall song that told of heroism in the Crimea brought tears to the eyes of everyone present (be it for one reason or another). Everyone, that is, except the man wearing the big ecstatic grin — showbiz-hustler-turned-pop-tycoon, Laurie Mansfield.

Balls could have done with a lift upon the back of Rolf Harris' horse as they were slowly rolling back to Birmingham. The good times were over. **Dave Morgan** and **Richard Tandy** headed home to Birmingham, to be quickly followed by **Keith Smart**. The summer of 1969, for them, had been one long party but all that had been achieved was just the one appearance at the **Fordingbridge Village Hall**. The landlord asked for the keys to the cottage to be returned forthwith, and the gentleman at the village off-licence booked himself and his wife on a world cruise. **Steve Gibbons**, **Trevor Burton** and **Denny Laine** set out for the farm, to continue as Balls, with drummer **Mike Kellie**.

"In the Uglys, I'd been the major spokesman," said Steve Gibbons. "Soon as Balls got involved with **Tony Secunda**, I got locked into a five year contract with him and my views counted for nothing. Secunda sent my pals packing and I couldn't do a thing about it. I had to keep soldiering on. I was a family man by then. I'd given ten years of my life to rock 'n' roll and I was determined to get something back for my efforts."

New Balls

Keith Smart comments, "Balls was a crying shame because it was so good it was frightening, but it wasn't to be. I was fortunate. As soon as I got home, the band **Young Blood** came knocking on the door."

Young Blood were guitarists **Chris Moore** and **Terry Meredith**, on bass was **Roy Black** with vocalist **Ken Price**, who had, earlier in the decade had sung with the **Cadillacs**. With Keith Smart aboard the drum kit, Young Blood headed for the happy

Young Blood

hunting grounds of Germany. On their return Ken Price joined forces with **Brian Yeates** to launch the entertainment agency Yeates and Price.

In London, **Tony Hall** and **David Platz** were listening intently to the demonstration tape that **Black Sabbath** had recorded at **Zella Studios**. The more they listened, the more they liked it. The same could be said of the audience at Hamburg's **Star Club**, where Black Sabbath were smashing every box office record ever set. When Black Sabbath first arrived on the hallowed boards of the Star Club, **Ozzy Osbourne** had decided to use shock tactics to win the German audience by painting himself purple. Meeting with no reaction whatsoever, Ozzy was forced to spend five hours at a washtub filled with turpentine. Once cleansed, he and the rest of them, **Tony Iommi**, **Bill Ward** and **Geezer Butler** took the only route they knew in order to make the crowds shut up rattling and pay attention to what Black Sabbath were sticking down. They turned their amplifiers up to earsplitting level and let them have it!

"It was the same with our very last effort of the 1960s," said **Rod Allen** of the **Fortunes**. " 'Seasons in the Sun' was massive across Europe for us but it didn't do a blind thing in Britain."

So the final festive spirit of the decade began to creep into the pubs, clubs and discos of Birmingham, Rod Allen's distinct interpretation of the highly emotional Rod McEwan song touched everyone's hearts as he wished the 1960s farewell with the moving lyric, 'Goodbye to you my trusted friend.'

Returning home to Birmingham in that cold and bleak December, **Black Sabbath** were greeted as trusted friends by their manager, **Jim Simpson**. Arrangements had been made for them to record their debut album. **Tony Hall** and **David Platz** were putting up the necessary cash.

Tony Iommi & Albert Chapman

Studio time had been booked at **Regent Sound** studio on Tottenham Court Road. Production of the album would be in the hands of the highly rated **Roger Bain**.

Roger Bain's first thought was to have Black Sabbath thoroughly rehearsed before arrival at Regent Sound to avoid unnecessary time wasting. A rehearsal studio in East Purley was booked and the boys took full advantage of its facilities. The following morning Roger Bain received a telephone call from the caretaker of the rehearsal rooms.

"Mr Bain," said the caretaker, "I've got a viola player in the next cubicle to your boys. He's trying to get to grips with Ravell's 'Bolero'. The gentleman is an old and valued client. You do understand, don't you?"

Black Sabbath understood. Four days later, on the mixing desk of Regent Sound studio, lay the completed master tape of their first album — 'Black Sabbath'.

Chapter Nine

DAYS I'LL REMEMBER ALL MY LIFE

As dawn broke on that first morning of 1970, and those of us who were so heavily hung over lay pleading for bedroom curtains to remain drawn, teams of dedicated cleaning ladies waded through the slush coated pavements of Birmingham city centre to arrive at their relative places of employment.

At the **Cedar** club, **Rebeccas**, the **Opposite Lock**, the **Rum Runner**, the **Penthouse**, the **Top Rank** and other such places, these ladies began to sweep up the rubbish created by New Year's Eve revellers who had 'Ob-La De'd and Ob-La Da'd' their way out of the decade.

Could it be true? Were the 1960s really over?

The last smooch of the evening at the **Tower** ballroom had confirmed the rumour. From a primitive turntable, the house disc jockey signed off from 1969 with the **Fortunes'** recording of 'Seasons in the Sun'. It would at least give the lonely hearted one final chance of a shot at a consolation prize.

Blowing their chances along with their kazoos, well meaning party-hatted drunks clumsily stumbled over the feet of prospective female catches,

Black Sabath with Albert Chapman

endeavouring to waltz to a four beats to the bar time signature. Spilling from beer-drenched lips came those parting words of surrender, 'Oh we've had joy, we've had fun but the hills that we climbed are now seasons out of time.' Goodbye indeed my trusted friend.

Around the suburbs in pubs like the **Swan** at Yardley, the **Tyburn House** and the **Mackadown**, the morning saw blurry eyed bar staff, some still dizzy from the endless 'Lily the Pink' song and dance routine, collapsed over the beer pumps in a desperate effort to re-open for lunchtime 'business as usual' sessions.

Celebrating with bucketfuls of the old medicinal compound was **Black Sabbath**. Their hard-hitting approach was about to be unleashed on an unsuspecting world via the album 'Black Sabbath'.

By spring the world would be reeling from the stabs and blows of blistering guitar licks, a screaming vocal that proclaimed a dabbling into the occult, and a rhythm track that surely was powerful enough to awaken the dead. And if that wasn't enough for folks to get paranoid about, then, in the late summer, along came that very track, 'Paranoid' to demonstrate to the world exactly how a hard rock band was going to sound from then on.

With the record charting, Black Sabbath's menacing presence was beamed into the nation's sitting rooms by appearances on BBC TV's 'Top of the Pops'. There the 'airy Astonites were pitched against such switched-on opposition as the England World Cup Squad with their patriotic terrace rouser, 'Back Home'. Coincidentally, by the time of the programme's transmission, that was the exact location of the England soccer team!

Experiencing the flush of success – Robert Plant

Led **Zeppelin** kicked off the year with a gig at Birmingham Town Hall on January 7th. The band went on to spend the next nine months touring Europe and America, riding high on the worldwide success of their second album. Along with a vocal delivery from **Robert Plant** that would tear anyone else's larynx to shreds, one particular track on 'Led Zeppelin 2' had a heavy metal guitar riff to die for. 'Whole Lotta Love' took on a life of its own. The Zepps may have been happy to turn their backs on the world of pop singles, but this song was having none of it. Alexis Korner's band, CCS, recorded an instrumental version, and took it to number 13 in the singles chart. Then in 1972 the CCS cover was adopted by the BBC as the theme music for 'Top of the Pops', and the infectious energy of that riff went on to power the presentation of the show for the next ten years. Strange that a number written by the band that refused to release singles, would be played on around 500 editions of Britain's most influential pop-single TV show!

At the end of their 1970 tour, Led Zeppelin took time out to record their third album, and before the year was out, it provided them with their second number one – the second of eight consecutive number one albums! Led Zeppelin knew how to make records – in more ways than one.

Carl Wayne

The **Move** were also demonstrating ambitious intentions, even though Carl **Wayne** had now departed to pursue a successful solo career that would include the stamping of his distinctive voice on numerous advertising jingles and the recording of the song, 'You're A Star', used as the top and tail track for the ATV talent show of the 1970s, 'New Faces'.

Gaining invaluable experience in the performing arts from his role as 'Colin the milkman' in the ATV soap opera, 'Crossroads', Carl Wayne eventually made it to the West End Stage, spending six years as the narrator of Willie Russell's 'Blood Brothers'. In 1999, Carl would replace the retiring Alan Clarke as lead singer with a band whose catalogue contains no less than twenty instantly recognisable top-ten hits, the **Hollies**.

Finally, into the Move from the **Idle Race**, came **Jeff Lynne**, although Jeff is always keen to make the point that he joined the Move as a guitarist and therefore did not replace Carl Wayne.

"**Roy Wood** had courted Jeff's talent for a couple of years," said **Roger Spencer** of the Idle Race. "Jeff eventually agreed to work with Roy on the understanding that the Move would steer themselves even more towards the use of violins and cellos."

Jeff Lynne's position in the Idle Race was filled vocally by the former Redcap, **Dave Walker**, whilst **'Sprike' Hopkins** took over the lead guitar duties.

Jeff Lynne in a cool Move

"But there seemed an awful lot of rehearsing and, with Jeff gone, not too many performances," explains Roger Spencer. "We did a tour of blues clubs with the Canadian harmonica player, King Biscuit Boy, after which, for me, it was a career in cabaret, initially with **Sight 'n' Sound**."

The **Rockin' Berries** and the **Fortunes**, by the close of the 1960s, were firmly established as cabaret attractions.

"We had four great years after 1965 as a result of 'He's in Town' and 'Poor Man's Son', comments **Chuck Botfield** of the Rockin' Berries. "No complaints from us."

The Fortunes had no complaints as, after a five year absence from the charts, they returned, again courtesy of the Greenaway and Cook team, with the bouncy 'Freedom Come Freedom Go'. And just when everyone believed the Fortunes had gone, it was simply to be, a year later, a 'Storm in a Teacup', served up for them by the songwriter Lynsey De Paul.

Idle Race phase two

Showing on **Peter Green**'s worksheet, in the early days of 1970, was a recording session to demonstrate a handful of songs that had been composed by tunesmith **Geoff Stevens**.

"One of the songs, 'Daddy Don't You Walk So Fast', was intended for Elvis," explained Peter Green, "But the American country singer Wayne Newton heard it, moved quickly, and his recording hit the American top ten."

When Larry Page, of Penny Farthing Records, was made aware of this, he immediately released the original Peter Green demo of the song, crediting him as **Daniel Boone**. That record made the British top twenty in April 1971.

Delving further into the Peter Green catalogue, the tapes of which were stacked on his office shelf, Larry Page came across an instantly catchy song with a lyric that told of waking on a Sunday morning before taking a stroll in the park. The chorus would then lift the song so strongly as the vocal part, a chanting "Hi! Hi! Hi!" clicked in.

Released, in the spring of 1972, 'Beautiful Sunday' immediately charted worldwide, especially in Japan, where the song has become one of Japan's biggest selling single records.

"When the first royalty cheque arrived, I rang Larry Page and told him he'd scribbled a few too many zeros on the end," said a more than honest Peter Green.

It was then explained to Peter that, in the land of the rising Sony, 'Hi' translates as 'Yes', therefore providing the perfect morale booster to its far out and far east audience.

Despite the success they were enjoying on the progressive rock circuit, **Frosty Moses'** days were numbered. By the dawn of the 70s their management squad had split up, and the band were shacked up at various locations around London. **John French**'s last act of genius was to team the band up with **Jeff Beck**. After a promising start, rehearsing in the foyer lounge of the London Palladium (whilst a new set was being installed in the main theatre) it soon became clear that Beck and the band were not heading in the same musical direction. The proposed marriage was to be no more than a one-night stand.

Returning to Birmingham, Frosty Moses' bass player **Danny Gallagher** wound up running the **Crack PA Company**. Vocalist **Phil Savage** stayed on in London, working with a jazz/rock project codenamed **Superdrums**, but was eventually drawn back to Brum, where he set up **Outlaw Sound** studio. Organist **Mike Lavender** joined **Aardvark**, a promising London based hard rock group with a Deram album just released. But the circuit, which had built up through the 60s, of good live venues for middle-weight original bands was quickly disappearing.

"Life was getting a bit crazy in London," says Mike Lavender. "It dawned on me just how crazy one morning as I arrived back from a gig to my tiny room just off the Portobello Road. The sun was coming up and I'd just travelled for six hours to play at — the **Old Hill Plaza**!"

Turning his life the right way up, Mike returned to rock on in Birmingham. In 1977 however, he was lured down the M1 once more by **Noosha Fox**, whose single, 'Georgina Bailey', which he had played on, was tickling the charts. The trip was for the gig that no one turns down — 'Top of the Pops'

Taking a positive approach to the decade that lay ahead was **John Singer** of **Mothers** club.

"Come 1970 and the universities killed us off," said John. "In total innocence, we at Mothers had helped to create a market place that the club could no longer compete in. Universities had substantial funding and eventually the bands that did the business were enticed away, and who could blame them. But we certainly put Erdington High Street on the map didn't we!"

Mothers lasted only twelve months into the 1970s, closing its doors in early January of 1971.

Foreseeing the great business potential of speakeasy discos, John Singer channelled his efforts into the opening of his new venture, **Sloopys**, on Corporation Street.

Sloopys, Corporation Street

Meanwhile, at the other end of Corporation Street, where it meets New Street, outside the Midland Hotel, traffic chaos abounded. A 'Harold Steptoe' look-alike in a horse and cart, was being presented with a parking ticket.

A closer examination of the offending rag-and-bone man revealed the true identity of the reprobate. It was Small Heath's very own scrap man, **Johnny Neal**, who, with his **Starliners**, was promoting his new single, the gospel song that praised the healing abilities of the man from Galilee, 'Put Your Hand in the Hand'.

Johnny Neal & the Starliners

"Just when I thought it was all over for me, Hughie Green got in touch. Would I do his 'Opportunity Knocks' TV show?" explained Johnny.

Johnny Neal and the Starliners went on to win the ratings-topping television show six times. Johnny Neal enjoyed the glory such success brings until the bubble finally burst, then he headed for South Africa and its lucrative hotel cabaret circuit.

The combination of the powerful creative forces of **Jeff Lynne** and **Roy Wood** was a shot in the arm for the club-weary **Move**. Over the next two years they had four more hits, finally bowing out on a high with the memorable rocker, 'California Man'. But in the meantime Messrs Wood and Lynne, together with **Bev Bevan**, had created a worthy successor, the **Electric Light Orchestra**, and had a debut album already recorded. The album, and a single release, '10538 Overture' (which took its curious name from the serial number of the studio console that it was mixed on) were both climbing the charts as 'California Man' was descending. Their first Birmingham appearance was at **Eddie Fewtrell**'s **Barbarella's** club in Cumberland Street, but it was to be some time before their live performances would do justice to the ambitious orchestrated rock arrangements that worked so magnificently in the studio.

On the same team –
Roy Wood & Jeff Lynne

Wizzard

The downside of any collaboration is that it must inevitably involve an element of compromise and so it was that, having given the world their finest hour together, two of pop's finest creative masterminds parted company to take full control of their respective handiwork. Roy Wood took aboard **Rick Price** on bass, **Bill Hunt** on keyboards, saxists **Mike Burney** and **Nick Pentelow** and drummers **Keith Smart** and **Charlie Grima**, to create **Wizzard**. He wrote the songs and produced the recordings that gave the band half a dozen top ten smashes, including a couple of number ones, 'See My Baby Jive' and 'Angel Fingers'. He even found time to hit the top twenty with four solo singles, but his cynical sideswipe at Yuletide excesses in 1973 is the track that guarantees that Woody and Wizzard are remembered at least once every year. 'I Wish It Could Be Christmas Everyday' made it to number four on the charts, but any hopes of a Christmas number one were scuppered by Wolverhampton wailer **Noddy Holder** with **Slade**'s 'Merry Xmas Everybody'

After Roy Wood's departure ELO wasted no time in getting back into the studio. **Ronny Smith**, the former frontman of **Ronny and the Senators**, recalls, "I was in partnership with **Bev Bevan** in the 'Heavy Heads' record shop on Stratford Road, Sparkhill. Bev was with the band down at George Martin's Air Studios on Oxford Street when I got a call from him asking if we had a copy of 'Roll Over Beethoven' in stock."

The Chuck Berry masterpiece was to get the ELO treatment that day, the only snag was that no one in the band, in the whole building for that matter, could remember all the lyrics. Ronny Smith had no need to dig out a copy of the record. He just closed his eyes and in his mind he was back performing at the **Las Vegas** coffee bar. With Bev scribbling franticly at the other end of the telephone line, Ronny, having taken up a Gene Vincent stance, just belted it out — 'Gonna write a little letter, gonna mail it to my local DJ . . .'

Over the coming years, Jeff Lynne's songwriting skills soared to incredible heights as his expertly crafted lyrics were perfectly woven into haunting melody lines. 'Evil Woman', 'Strange Magic', 'Mr Blue Sky', 'Sweet Talkin' Woman' and 'Telephone Line' are just a handful of songs that demonstrate the creative genius of Jeff Lynne.

Jeff Lynn with John Landon & Trevor Francis

When, in 1975, **Jasper Carrott** was given a thousand pounds by DJM Records to fund the recording of a Chris Rohmann song, he knew his rock 'n' roll moment had come. He booked **Hollick and Taylor Studios**, and set about recruiting ELO as his backing band! In the event, Messrs Bevan, Lynne and **Richard Tandy** were joined by **Phil Tree** on bass, to create the all-too unforgettable biker anthem, 'Funky Moped'. Jasper wound up not only with enough money left over from the budget to buy the Martin guitar that he had been lusting over, but a bigger hit single than ELO themselves had yet achieved!

In the summer of 1971 a tour of the United States was entered into the diary of **Fairport Convention**, who were now such a worldwide pioneering force as an electric folk band.

Temporary pop star — Jasper Carrott

"The only snag was," explained **Dave Pegg**, "We were down to a duo. All that remained was me and fiddler **Dave Swarbrick**."

Richard Thompsom, Fairport's singing and songwriting guitarist had departed but Mr Pegg and Mr Swarbrick were determined not to let their fans down on the other side of the pond.

Fairport Convention

Drummer **Tom Farnell** and guitarist **Roger Hill** were slotted into the Convention. With the addition of a road crew that was made up of thoroughbreds **Andy Wheeler** and **George Tolley,** the result was a Fairport Convention that was, for the duration of the American tour, one hundred per cent Brummie.

"Maybe the music wasn't as traditional as the Americans were expecting," said a smiling Dave Pegg, "But I have to tell you, we had a ball on that tour!"

Albert Chapman – taking care of business for Black Sabbath

Tony **Iommi**, in early 1973, had a question for **Albert Chapman**, manager of the **Rum Runner** club.

Albert picks up the story, "It was a Thursday afternoon and Tony called me saying **Black Sabbath** were off to Australia on the Saturday for a month of concerts. Did I fancy going along?"

Eventually gaining Mrs Chapman's permission, Albert sought the blessing from his employers, the Berrows, a bookmaking family who owned the Rum Runner.

"**Ray Berrow** okayed it and off I went with Sabbath," said Albert.

The Australian trip for Black Sabbath was to be part of 'The British Rock and Roll Month', sharing the bill with Uriah Heap and Status Quo.

"Once there, I just started organising and sorting things out for the lads." Albert explained, adopting a sparring stance.

"That led me to being appointed tour manager until eventually I became business manager of Black Sabbath."

The **Moody Blues**, having survived the lean years, trying to stay afloat on the perilous northern club circuit, became a world-class force. The dramatic and quite stunning **Justin Hayward** song, 'Question', showcased their unquestionable brilliance, and gave them their biggest single since 'Go Now'. Classic hit albums like 'To Our Children's Children's Children' and 'A Question of Balance' demonstrated the enduring quality of their musical creations.

In 1974 they took a break and went their separate ways to pursue solo projects. **Mike Pinder** took off for America, which is where, four years later, the band hooked up together again to record the 'Octave' album. With a gruelling tour scheduled to follow its release, Pinder bowed out of the band, to be replaced by ex-Yes keyboardist, **Patrick Moraz**.

The Moody Blues continue to delight their fans, and keep box-office staff around the world busy; and the board of the M&B brewery can only dream at what might have been!

The Moody Blues

The one thing **Steve Gibbons** needed to get his career back on course was a business manager. With his colleagues, guitarists **Bob Wilson** and **Dave Carroll**, bass player **Bob Griffin** and drummer **Bob Lamb**, they were now, to all intent and purpose, operating as the **Idle Race**. **Greg Masters** and **Dave Pritchard** having long since departed.

By 1975, and taking up with the more obvious name of the **Steve Gibbons Band**, the lads had created quite a local following at their residency, the **Railway** pub, Curzon Street, Birmingham.

The Steve Gibbons Band

"But we also played a fair bit in London as well, trying to get noticed," said Steve Gibbons.

One such London gig was the Hope and Anchor pub in Islington, where, amongst the denim-clad audience, Steve Gibbons had noticed a sports jacket of some quality.

"A few nights later, at the Railway, and again in the middle of the denim was that same sports jacket," explained Steve.

"I'm hopeless with faces, but I never forget a jacket."

That jacket belonged to Peter Meadon, formerly of Tony Hall Enterprises and who also had once managed the Who.

"Peter Meadon promised to put Pete Townsend into the equation and I thought, 'Yeah, believe it when you see it.'"

Back in London a few days later, at Dingwalls club, Pete Townsend and his manager, Bill Curbishley, showed up to witness the magical charisma of Steve Gibbons. Steve, dressed as a Mississippi riverboat gambler, played his cards just right by holding the supercool London audience in the palms of his hands, leaving them spellbound.

With **Trevor Burton** now taking care of the bass guitar duties, Bill Curbishley took over the management affairs of the Steve Gibbons Band, booking them to support the Who during their 1977 British and American tour. And on that tour, the audiences were treated to a blistering version of a Chuck Berry classic rock 'n' roll poem that told of a police raid on a novelty shop, where, underneath the counter, 'the cream of the crop' was always readily available.

'Tulane', by the Steve Gibbons Band, in August of 1977, made number 12 on the national single charts.

Raymond Froggatt

Amongst the cream of the crop in the Nashville country music circles, in August of 1977, was Birmingham's **Raymond Froggatt**.

The standard of the songs on Raymond's albums, 'Voice and Writings' and 'Bleach' had not gone unnoticed.

At the Jack Clement studio, under the supervision of the legendary Larry Butler, and accompanied by Elvis Presley's vocal team, the Jordanaires, Raymond Froggatt recorded his critically acclaimed album 'Southern Fried Frog'.

Swiftly scaling the slippery rungs of the country music ladder, Raymond Froggatt, by the mid 1980s had received all the music media awards going, for being, by far, the number one British and European country music singer and songwriter.

And being the gentleman that he is, Froggy refrained from reminding Hughie Green about the time, back in 1964 at an 'Opportunity Knocks' audition, when he snapped at the young Raymond, in no uncertain terms, "Son, you're no country singer!"

Staying put and making his mark was **Laurie Mansfield**, the one time worker at the Cadbury factory in Bournville who'd made it to the dizzy heights of the mezzanine floor at 235 Regent Street, London. This is the prestigious address of International Artistes.

"I did a Victor Kiam," said Laurie, referring to the Remington shavers man. "I liked International Artistes so much, I bought the company!"

In 1999, Laurie Mansfield was granted the privilege (and the headache) of overseeing the Royal Command Variety Show, held that year in the presence of Her Royal Highness Queen Elizabeth and Prince Philip, Duke of Edinburgh, at the **Birmingham Hippodrome**. For a true son of the City of Birmingham, it was indeed an honour to perform such a duty.

All-star line up – Mansfield, Queen & Prince

A royal encounter of a far more surreal nature took place when the Queen of England met the Prince of Darkness! In 2002, having dined with president Bush at the White House, and starred in an Emmy-winning TV series, **Ozzy Osbourne** was invited to Buckingham Palace, to join in the Golden Jubilee celebrations. After the show, the Queen exchanged a few words with each of the celebrity performers. "I freaked out," said Ozzy. "The queen spoke to me, but I haven't a clue what she said. I was in shock!"

Long after the sound of 'Paranoid' had stopped reverberating around the palace, and the spectacular firework displays had subsided, the moonlight and comparative silence that descended on the stately grounds following that event would serve as a more poignant reminder of the passing of an era. The

At the Palace – Rod, Ozzy, Cliff & Paul

concert was a showcase of the highlights from 50 years of popular music; and yet half of the star performers were stalwart 60s troopers; and many of the remainder were passing new fads – singing 60s songs! Had so little of lasting substance happened in the intervening years? The Queen had moved on, and finally embraced a musical culture of revolution and innovation. Had rock 'n' roll merely marked time, and waited for the royal seal of approval? Had the pioneering spirit of rebellion and creativity, so prolific in those early years, simply stalled in the 70s?

In truth it had not, and there were a few notable icons from the superseding years to bear testament to that, but the scent seems to get colder as the decades have passed. High technology has proved to be no substitute for the intuitive zeal for discovery of the generation that got man to the Moon. The blueprints for almost every new aspect of trail-blazing pop music were drawn up in the 50s and 60s, be it moody and moving, rockin' and raunchy, electric, orchestral, or black and satanic!

Rock 'n' roll's reign began, as did that of Queen Elizabeth, in the 1950s, and amongst nearly 1000 singles that have made it to number one since that time, Birmingham has had more than its fair share. Meanwhile, in the album charts, and more importantly, in the 'real world' of live performance, Brum has flourished. Its musicians continue to respect their heritage whilst forging the future, living up to the motto on their city's official coat of arms — Forward.

For many people, there has only been one truly golden age of rock, and they are not just the nostalgic survivors of those heady hippie days. Do Birmingham's fledgling twenty-first-century guitarists look to manufactured 'boy bands' for inspiration, or do they instinctively begin by picking the emotive arpeggios of Led Zeppelin's 'Stairway to Heaven'? Do the young new keyboard players care about committee-built pop idol groups, or do they start trying to emulate Stevie Winwood's scalp-tingling Hammond sound on 'Gimme Some Lovin''? They know in their very bones that in the 60s, in the Midlands, Brum rocked on! And they recognise with pride that, in this brave new century their role is to pursue their destiny, and make sure that it always will.

PEOPLE

CASTLE Dave 33
CATLEY Bob 227
CELLARMEN 91
CHADS 96 119
CHALLINOR Dave 109 133 199
CHAMP Des 239
CHANTELLES 15 26 53 165
CHAPMAN Albert 82 193 196 277 284
CHAPMAN Malc 272
CHATFIELD Pete 259
CHEETAHS 11 46 68 86 87 103 176 183 192
CHEQUERS 168
CHICANES 94
CHICKEN SHACK 147
CHUCK BERRY 101
CHUCKS 135
CIMARRONS 30 69 81
CINNAMON QUILL 237
CITIZENS 113
CLARE Wilf 68
CLARK Acker 240
CLARK Brian 231
CLARK Louis 180 240
CLARK Mee 26
CLARKE Alan 92
CLARKE Brian 171
CLARKE Doug 113
CLARKE Louis 115 140
CLARKE Malc 42
CLARKE Rod 173 189
CLARKE Terry 208 210 230
CLARKIN Tony 98 134 170
CLARKSON Tony 114 164 256
CLAY George 208
CLEE Alan 72 126 179 239 254 267
CLEMSON Clem 271
CLIFF Jimmy 148
CLIFF WARD & THE CRUISERS 31 91 229
CLIFFORD Alan 182
CLIFFORD Mike 31
CLIFTONES 26 27
CLIMBERS 58 90
CLIVE LEA & THE PHANTOMS 80
COCK A HOOPS 117 134
COLE Ken 219
COLE Richard 256
COLIN DENNIS DUO 89
COLLEGE Dave 'Yogi' 184 272
COLLINGE Tony 167
COLLINS John 91
COLLYER Ken 109
COLMAN Stuart 174
COMMANDER Jeff 'Jake' 124
CONBOY Dan 156
CONCORDS 103 130 200
CONGRESSMEN 71 103 120 160
CONRAD Jess 39
CONWAY Roger 'Twitty' 62 139 211
COOPER Alec 166
COOPER Colin 29 89
COPE Brian 58
COPE Malcolm 265
COPESTAKE Phil 272
COPPERFIELD 265
CORAL Bobby 17 39
CORVETTES 64 74 125
COUNT BASIE & HIS ORCHESTRA 252
COUNTS 15
COURIERS 33 167
COWLEY Dave 152
COWLEY Fred 160

COYNE Tom 155
CRACK PA COMPANY 280
CRANDLES Norman 'Lee' 31 133
CRAWDADDIES 110 141
CRAWLING KINGSNAKES 71
CRAYTHORNE Roger 237
CREATORS 205
CRESCENDOS 29 89 93 116 195
CRESSIN Neil 63
CRESTAS 11 21 78
CREW Graham 162
CREWDSON Dave 61
CREWE Geoff 72
CROSS Phil 235
CRUISERS 31 91 210
CRUMP Derek 151
CRUTCHLEY John 182
CULLEN Paul 117
CUTAWAYS 42
DAKOTAS 58 78
DALE Glen 26 160
DALLOWAY Tony 72 73 126
DANNY BURNS & THE BURNETTES 118 120
DANNY BURNS & THE PHANTOMS 11 63
DANNY KING & THE JESTERS 53 66 77 123
DANNY KING & THE ROYALS 11 45 51
DANNY RAY & THE RAYVONS 31 37
DANNY STORME & THE STROLLERS 128 208
DANTE Troy 39 80
DANVERS WALKER Bob 102
DAVE & THE EMERALDS 63
DAVE LACEY & THE CORVETTES 64 73 125
DAVID Lloyd 52
DAVIS Billie 163
DAVIS Bob 272
DAVIS Gordon 94
DAVIS Mansell 224
DAVIS Megan 21 81
DAVIS Mick 86
DAVIS Roy 'Tank' 192 229
DAVIS Spencer 22 84 87 106 110 123
DAW Geoff 259
DAWES Barry 100
DAWSON John 250
DAWSON Phil 91
DAY Gerry 11 15 33 96 182
DAY Mel 52 144 252
DAY Tanya 87
DEAN Johnny 16
DEEP FEELING 197
DEL SAINTS 15 58 182
DELMORE LEE SOUND 195 199
DELTAS 18
DENNING Cal 63 69 81
DENNIS Colin 89
DENNIS Phil 240
DENNY LAINE & THE DIPLOMATS 11 19 49
DETHRIDGE Dennis 53 54
DETOURS 36
DEUCES WILD 155
DEVINE Frank 141 153
DEW Graham 210
DEWS Terry 39 115 138
D'FENDERS 94 100 130 131 193
DICKSON Ron 78 161 251
DIGNAM Joe 94 172
DIMENSIONS 109
DIPLOMATS 11 40 49 77 94 95 112 114 128
DIXON Billy 54
DM TRIO 42

DOC HOLLIDAY 134 245
DOLAN Mike 44 117 212
DOLAN Steve 44 117 212 243
DOMINETTES 11 19
DON ARDEN ORGANISATION 265
DONOVAN Dave 235
DOWNING John 'Upsy' 165 188 264
DOYLE Bob 201
DUDGEON Gus 269 273
DUFFURN Bob 265
DUKES 14 33 182
DUMPY 216
DUNCAN Johnny 57
DUNCAN Stuart 'Tiny Tim' 170
DUNKERLY John 171 231
EARL Bobby 15 26
EARSDON Gerry 254
EARSDON Maurice 255 273
EARTH 239 244 263
EASTWOOD Alan 'Bugsy' 76 204 222 236 237
EBONIES 190
EBONITES 190
ECCLES Albert 14
EDGE Graeme 35 77 95 218
EDOUARDE Honri 58 90 141 149
EDWARDS Malc 151
EDWARDS Mel 149
EDWARDS Percy 151
EKO 76 192
EL RIOT & THE REBELS 11 13 43 46 58 77 88 185 208
ELCOCK Jake 72 126 179 209
ELECTRIC LIGHT ORCHESTRA 282
ELEGANT SET 219
EMMIT TILL 215
ENNIS Brian 33 136
EPSTEIN Brian 92 147
ERSKINE T 187 233
EVANS Chris 256
EVANS Dave 'Effram' 28 99 131 151
EVANS John 'Jigger' 192
EVANS Keith 235 244 BC
EVERETT Roy 58 90 141 147
EVERGLADES 51 52 100 122 238
EXCELSIOR JAZZ BAND 22
EXCEPTION 204 205 222 236 237
EXCHEQUERS 167 193 211
FADING COLOUR 229
FAIRPORT CONVENTION 271 283
FALCONS 86
FARNELL Tom 283
FARREN Steve 26
FEWTRELL Eddie 164 262 282
FINCH Brian 'Monk' 155 200
FINCH Graham 74
FINCHAM Johnny 165
FINDERS KEEPERS 126 179 209 239 254
FINISTER Tony 68 193 216
FINN Gary 236 260
FIREBIRDS 68
FISHER Mick 37 130
FLANNAGAN Matt 98
FLEETWOODS 60 61 105
FLETCHER John 69
FORD Brian 217
FORD John 57 180 245
FORD Mal 83
FORREST Billy 136
FORTNAM Les 152 170 195
FORTUNES 12 58 96 142 160 172 275 277 279
FOX Noosha 281

FRAME 198 212
FRANCIS Roger 29
FRANCIS Trevor 283
FRANKLIN Bob 219
FRANKLIN Graham 118
FRANZ Johnny 103 125
FRED BRINKLOW BAND 10
FREDDIE MAC SOUL BAND 252
FREEMAN Alan 73
FREEMAN Frank 144
FREEMAN Gerry 21 40 81 206
FREEMAN Ken 156
FREEWAYS 130
FRENCH John 273 280
FRIARS AGENCY 96
FROGGATT Raymond 117 140 148 168 180 196
   221 226 233 240 249 256 286
FROGGY & THE TADPOLES 140
FROSTY MOSES 255 260 273 280
FRYER Ken 167 191
FRYER Kevin 91
FURY Billy 75
GAFFNEY Martin 97
GALLAGHER Danny 74 213 234 254 280
GALLERY Graham 76 148
GALLEY Mel 239 254
GARGAN Stuart 42
GARRITY Freddie 124
GARRY Tony 113
GAUNTLETT Roger 31
GERALD 'Sid' Hood 272
GERRY & THE PACEMAKERS 92
GERRY DAY & THE DUKES 11 33 77
GERRY LEVENE & THE AVENGERS 11 50 76
GIBBINS John 10 54 71
GIBBONS Steve 19 47 79 107 119 135 143 157
   194 217 224 252 258 274 285
GIBSON Denis 30
GILBERT Billy 98 156
GITTINS Jill 151
GITTINS Pete 192 215
GOBLE John 228
GOFFIN & KING 109
GOGNY Boris 166
GOOCH David 69
GOOD EGG 141
GORDON John 33 124
GORDON Noele 153
GORIN Kex 27 115 124 189 229
GOULD Don 21 80
GRAHAM Ricky 74
GRANT Keith 167
GRANT Peter 269
GRASSHOPPERS 14 105 205
GRAY Barry 236
GRAY Teddy 69
GRAYSON Larry 80
GREAVES Dennis 113
GREAVES Geoff 98 170
GREAVES Trevor 29 89 93 179
GREEN Bob 100
GREEN Dave 86
GREEN Graham 138
GREEN Hughie 116
GREEN Peter 11 16 39 45 65 279
GREEN Ray 61
GREEN Tony 197
GRIFFEN Chris 106
GRIFFIN Bob 67 285
GRIFFITH Austin 52 190 241 252
GRIFFITHS Max 'The Nub' 100 168 193 215

GRIMA Charlie 115 282
GROVES Maurice 'Moss' 68
GUNNEL Rick 176
GUY Terry 138 201
HAINES Johnny 127 134 141 155 159 171 216
   218 224 268
HAINES Norman 39 70 76 115 138 166 179 195
   199 228 239 245 268
HALEY Bill 108
HALL Brian 37
HALL Fred 30 38
HALL Kyle 193
HALL Lenny 94 130
HALL Terry 68
HALL Tony 80 208 245 259 260 268 275 276
HAMILTON Andy 85
HAMMOND Willie 71 252 258
HANCOCKS Paul 167
HANCOX John 40
HANCOX Ronnie 84
HARBISON Brian 37 130 198 212
HARBOR Barry 25 65
HARD MEAT 243
HARDIN Eddie 207
HARPER Robbie 228
HARRIS Roger 129 158 200
HARRISON Charlie 256
HARRISON Tony 251
HARVEY Grant 44
HATCH Bob 228
HAWKINS Al 29
HAYWARD Bill 162
HAYWARD Justin 185 209 218 230 285
HAYWARD Maurice 29
HEALEY Steve 106
HEARD Micky 177 189
HEARN Malcolm 142
HEARTBEATS 219 235
HEATH Fred 29
HEDGES Garry 152
HELLIONS 87 144 197
HEMMING Les 104 157 212 219 246 247
HENDERSON John 37
HEPCATS 16
HEPWORTH Kenny 98
HERD Micky 110 138
HI CARDS 35
HIBBARD Jeff 194 208
HICKS Alan 30
HIGHWAYMEN 42
HILL Benny 109
HILL Bobby 204
HILL Christine 33
HILL Dave 175
HILL Graham 138
HILL Jimmy 94
HILL Roger 67 76 157 204 237 283
HILL Tony 87
HINES Brian 16 19 40 56
HOBBIS Phil 91
HOBBSTWEEDLE 241
HODGES Pete 147 155 200
HOLDEN Jim 19 47 79 143 146 217
HOLDER Neville 'Noddy' 175 282
HOLLAND Dave 155 239 254
HOLLIDAY Doc 180 205
HOLLIES 79 92
HOLLIS Dave 25 98 122
HOLMES Christine 74
HOLMES Les 40
HOMER Stan 36

HONE Garth 242
HONE Ian 242
HONE Martin 200 241 243 246 247 252
HOOD Robbie 27 58 59 96
HOOK Kansas 256
HOOKER John Lee 106
HOPKINS 'Sprike' 35 94 154 164 214 265 279
HOPKINSON Roy 44
HORDEN Ken 105 214
HORNSBY Laurie 168 193 211 215
HORSLEY Dennis 29 89
HORTON Ralph 77 78 85 143
HORTON Stevie 94 128
HOUNSLOW Johnny 103
HOUSTON TREADMILL 271
HUGHES Brian 29
HUGHES Glen 239 254
HUMPHRIES Bert 74
HUNT Bill 282
HUNT Dennis 86
HUNTER Billy 51 118
HURRICANES 140
HYDE Ray 30
IAN CAMPBELL GROUP 166 171 224 231 271
IDLE RACE 182 219 229 233 248 249 253 258
   261 278 279 285
IN PACK 239
INCAS 138 197
INCREDIBLE STRING BAND 190
INTERCITY ARTISTES 234 254
IOMMI Tony 63 228 240 263 275 284
IRESON Trevor 51
IVY LEAGUE 97 137 170 179
JACEY Jeff 60
JACK Roger 44
JACKSON Gordon 87
JACKSON Harry 'Al' 37 40 81 146
JAGUARS 21 37 87
JAMES Bill 201
JAMES Nicky 49 63 88 113 164
JARVIS Vic 60 193
JASPER STUBBS GLORYLAND BANK 246
JAUNCY John 73
JAY Lenny 104
JAY Peter 46
JAYWALKERS 46
JEFFERIES Jan 183
JESTERS 77 119 129
JETHRO TULL 263
JIMMY POWELL & THE DIMENSIONS 210
   262
JINKS Dave 104
JINKS Johnny 104
JOHN BULL BREED 138 139 177 185
JOHN E LAW & THE TRESPASSERS 135
JOHNNY & THE ALPINES 37 91
JOHNNY DEAN & THE DOMINATORS 16 56
   136
JOHNNY DUNCAN & THE BLUEGRASS
   BOYS 57
JOHNNY SHANE & THE SOLITAIRES 74 213
JOHNSON Big Al 61 88 167
JOHNSON Bob 42 218
JOHNSON Dick 42
JOHNSON Graham 30
JONES Baz 219
JONES Chris 15 26 53 135 164
JONES Den 41
JONES John Paul 243
JONES Johnny 162 175 253 254
JONES Mo 68

OVERFIELD Phil 239
OWEN Tommy 94
PAGE Jimmy 241 243
PALER Malc 213
PALMER CARL 236
PANTENY John 'Pank' 165
PARAMOR Norrie 45 46 75 123
PARKER Dave 35
PARRY Roy 127
PARSONS John 129 177 180 204 209 243
PEACE Dave 110
PEARCE Dezi 136
PEARCE Phil 61 99 211
PEARSON Roger 69
PEGG Bev 210 229
PEGG Christine 224
PEGG Dave 40 63 110 141 143 148 153 157 160
   181 195 204 222 224 230 271 283
PEGG Pat 63
PENTELOW Nick 282
PERERA Vernon 52
PERFECT Christine 71
PERRY Doug 103
PETE TIERNEY & THE NIGHTHAWKS 95
PETER JAY & THE JAYWALKERS 46
PETERS Phil 50
PHANTOMS 11 50 67 103 118
PHIL KING & THE COURIERS 33 71
PHILLIPS Alan 114
PHILLIPS Jimmy 114 115 240 244
PHILLIPS Nigel 259
PHILPOTTS Roger 235
PICKERING Bill 148
PICKET Kenny 98
PINCH 219
PINDER Mike 59 68 77 112 168 209 218 245 284
PINE Wilf 265
PINKERTON'S ASSORTED COLOURS 156 174
   208 239 265
PINSON Roy 73
PIOVESANA Antonino 98
PLAINSMEN 156 213 216 222
PLANT Robert 71 141 182 204 226 235 241 243
   244 278
PLATZ David 268 275 276
PLAZENTS 76
PONTIN Fred 99
POOLE Mac 138 197
POTTER Dave 152
POUNTNEY Mike 196
POWELL Cozy 129 242 271
POWELL Don 175
POWELL Jimmy 23 36 47 55 66 109 117 135 210
   262
POWELL Keith 11 66 74 82 128 137 163
POWELL Ted 100
PREECE Maurice 30 82
PRESCOTT Johnny 126
PRESTON Andy 183
PRICE Ken 274
PRICE Rick 30 172 237 257 270 282
PRICE Steve 78 161
PRIDDEY Malcolm 31
PRITCHARD Barry 26 173
PRITCHARD Dave 182 219 258
PROSPECTORS 140
PRYKE FAMILY 77
PRYKE Rob 46
PURPLE ONION 244
PURSUERS 63
QUEDGLEY Dave 63

QUEDGLEY Keith 63
QUILLIAM Roy 33
QUINN Tony 138
RAINBOW BOYS 14
RALPH JOHNS AGENCY 85
RAM BUNK SHUSH 235
RAMBLERS 152
RARE BREED 240
RAVENS 138
RAY Al 219
RAY Arthur 103 120 138
RAY Danny 31 37
RAY MOND SET 222
RAYVONS 31 37
READ Graham 91
REAY Dave 256
REBELS 13 77
REDCAPS 50 101
REED Les 72 80 103
REEVE John 186
REGAN Joe 27 28 34 50 82
REGAN Mary 'Ma' 35 38 50 71 76 101 103 240
REID Stuart 65 69 84
RENEGADES 30 189
REST 196 228
RHYTHM & BLUES QUARTET 22 38
RICHARDS Keith 44
RICHARDS Ron 45
RICHARDSON John 219
RICHARDSON Peter 219
RIP 'N' LAN 235
RITTER Mal 128
ROBBIE HOOD & THE MERRIMEN 58
ROBERTS Geoff 98
ROBINSON John 42
ROCKETS 62
ROCK REBELLION 244
ROCKIN' BERRIES 11 12 23 36 47 64 71 74 79
   92 109 123 136 140 141 174 183 189 225 228
   231 248 250 253 279
ROCKIN' CHEVROLETS 62
ROCKIN' JAYMEN 11 18 46
ROCKIN' MODERNAIRES 14
ROCKIN' ROCKETS 61
RODEN Jess 144
RODGERS Lee 80
ROMAIN Robert 111
ROMAN CANDLES 133
RONNY & THE RENEGADES 18
RONNY & THE SENATORS 3 49 65 85 282
ROONEY BROTHERS 98
ROONEY John 213 217
ROSE Euan 64 86 126 157 176
ROSE Gene 138
ROSE Sonny 168
ROTUNDAS 62 99 139 211
ROWLANDS John 197 222 237
ROWLEY Terry 162 209 253 267
ROY EVERETT & THE CLIMBERS 90
ROY VEARS & THE STRANGERS 79
ROYALS 15 45
RUSSELL Tommy 68 101
RUSSELL Tony 167
RYAN Dermot 98
RYAN Derry 138 197 221 248 265
RYAN Des 98 156
RYAN John 35
RYLAND Dennis 47 132 192
SABEL John 129 180
SABRE 33 113
SAINT John 'Whispering Giant' 26

SAINTS & SINNERS 13
SAINTS COMBO 125
SAMBROOKS Dave 37
SAMMES Luddy 234
SARGENT Paul 126 227
SATELLITES 11 31 67 70 133
SAVAGE Phil 228 234 254 260 280
SAVILLE Jimmy 81
SAWYER Phil 207
SAYWOOD Roy 183
SCARLET Dave 268
SCHROEDER John 128 137 163
SCORCERERS 129 242
SCOTT Alan 136
SCOTT MORRIS BLUES COMBO 212 219
SEARCHERS 109
SECOND CITY SOUND 156
SECUNDA Tony 106 201 216 219 258 274
SEED 198 222
SEMPLE Andy 161
SENATORS 18 49 85 88
SHAKEDOWN SOUND 144
SHANE Johnny 74
SHANES 193
SHARP Brian 93 149
SHELDON Ray 35
SHEPHERD John 30
SHEPHERD Pauline 96
SHERIDAN Mike 11 20 46 79 88 127 144 154
   159 168 191 237 270
SHERIDAN's LOT 191
SHEWARD Rob 77 88
SHINGLES 167
SHIP John 17
SHIPTON Al 63
SHOOTING STARS 149
SHROPSHALL Roger 247
SIGHT 'N' SOUND 237 253 257 262 279
SIMMS Paul 152
SIMON'S SECRETS 210
SIMPSON Dave 91
SIMPSON Jim 155 199 228 239 241 245 259 268
SIMS Vic 115 227
SINGER John 57 84 85 114 119 124 143 146 170
   194 233 281
SIZE SIX 149
SKIDMORE Jimmy 195
SLADE 268 282
SLY John 68
SMALL Millie 138
SMART Keith 51 122 129 201 204 236 243 252
   258 274 282
SMITH Arthur 41 80 128 177
SMITH Barry 53 135
SMITH Ken 33 138
SMITH Mike 67 102
SMITH Peter 36 171 251
SMITH Roger 78
SMITH Ronny 18 34 49 63 88 122 152 183 271
   282
SMOKESTACKS 227
SNAPE Pete 113
SNELSON RAY 182
SOFIANO Tony 180
SOLITAIRES 74 75
SOLOMONS Phil 105
SOMBREROS 36 131 135 171 237
SOUL Johhny 247
SOUL PREACHERS 77
SOUNDS OF BLUE 71 147
SOUTHALL Cliff 68

SOUTHERNERS (Carter/Lewis) 241
SOUTHERNERS (Harper/Wallace) 228
SOVEREIGNS 80 99 131 150
SPECTRO SONICS 138
SPENCE Dave 128
SPENCER DAVIS GROUP 12 38 87 151 167 186
  207
SPENCER Frankie 117 134 212
SPENCER Geri 79
SPENCER Robert 28
SPENCER Roger 48 64 154 159 182 219 234 247
  248 249 258 261 279
SPIDERS 91
SPILLSBURY Dave 30
STACKS 248 249 265
STANTON Melvyn 136
STARKEY John 34 152 184
STARLINERS 11 81 134 236 281
STARLITE ARTISTES 262
STEELE Tony 94
STEVE GIBBONS BAND 285
STEVENS Geoff 80 280
STEVENS Lee 11 31 70 133
STEWART Rod 109
STEWART Roderick 55
STIRLING Peter Lee 45 51 65 69 70 84 161
STOREY Rick 155 200
STORM John 139
STORM Rory 140
STORME Danny 26
STORMRIDERS 167
STRANGERS 28 48 72 73 79 80 126 179
STRIDE Eddie 91
STRINGBEATS 52 53 138 144 190 241 252
STROLLERS 26 208
STUART Mark 11 78
SUBURBAN STOMPERS 22
SUNDOWNERS 20 44 46 59 96
SUPERDRUMS 280
SURMAN Gary 143
SURPLICE 'Fats' 192
SWARBRICK Dave 171 283
SWEET & LOVELIES 146
SWING SHIFT 10
SWINGIN' CHIMES 99
SYLVESTER Steve 52
TAB MEMPHIS 49
TANDY Richard 165 252 274 283
TANNER John 234
TANSELL Pete 91
TARMY Shel 58 96
TAYLOR Alan 195
TAYLOR John 'Spud' 60 103 143
TAYLOR Micky 236
TAYLOR Ray 99
TAYLOR Roy 58
TEA & SYMPHONY 259
TEENBEATS 72
TEENSCENES 29
TELSTARS 149 239
TEMPEST 44 45 100
TEMPLAR Dave 151
TERRY BLOOD AGENCY 92
TERRY MATTHEWS AGENCY 57 92
TERRY Ricky 100
TETLOW Jim 126 134 198
TEXTONES 60
THEM 125
THOMAS Bob 167 191

THOMAS Ray 13 58 68 77 120 137 191 218
THOMPSON Brian 109 132
THOMPSON Clive 109
THOMPSON Dougie 52 109 122 123
THOMPSON Geoff 182
THOMPSON Richard 283
THOMSON Bobby 7 140 175 189 225 228 231
THORNTON Jack 72
THREE Gs 29
TIERNEY Pete 95
TIMMINS Colin 191
TIPPER Tony 103
TODAY'S POST 211
TOLLEY George 283
TOMLINSON Mick 26
TOP PRIORITY 272
TORNADOS 116
TRACTION 213 234
TRAFFIC 207
TRAPEZE 233 254 267
TREE Phil 283
TREMORS 101
TRESPASSERS 40
TREVOR ORTON TRIO 127
TULLY John 254
TURNER Don 110
TURTON Geoff 'Jefferson' 47 109 137 140 189
  248 250 253 257 262 271
UDEY Barry 120
UGLYS 19 47 79 119 135 143 144 146 157 160
  181 183 194 217 252 258 274
UK BONDS 149 177
UNDERHILL Ken 29 39
UNSQUARE MEN 90 156
VALETS 66 82 128
VALLENDER Doug 113
VAN DELS 25 39 70
VAQUEROS 36
VARSITY RAG 214
VEARS Roy 28 79
VENDORS 175
VIKINGS 13 47 65 98 129 146 153 159 228 238
VILES Cedric 208
VILES Cyril 168
VINCENT Gene 88
VIP's 186
VOGUES 108 134 161 184 214 251
VYSE Dezi 17
WAIKIKI ISLANDERS 186
WAKELIN Vic 71 138
WALKER Dave 101 234 279
WALKER Doug 103 138
WALKER Mick 101 194 237
WALLACE Cheryl 222 228
WALLACE Terry 25 47 63 66 122 153 191 222
  228
WALPOLE Ray 42
WALSH Dave 'Banger' 194
WALSH Peter 262
WARD Bill 196 228 240 244 275
WARD Cliff 31 91 210 229
WARDLE Steve 167
WARWICK Clint 14 77 96 112 129 137 147 173
  189
WASHINGTON Denny 44
WASHINGTON George E 103 120 160
WASHINGTON Johnny 160 207
WATKINS Bob 33 113 192
WATSON Alan 35

WATSON Dave 27
WATSON Johnnie 115
WATSON Ronny 152
WATSON Willie 115
WAY OF LIFE 164 176 214 222 227 233
WAYNE Carl 'Charlie' 11 13 25 47 63 98 129
  146 153 154 159 187 202 220 238 248 262 264
  278
WAYNE Pat 11 18 46 51 92 115 123 149 213 223
  269
WEBB George 148
WEBB Pete 54
WEBB Stan 71
WEBB Terry 91
WEBLEY Martin 91
WEBLEY Mick 37 212
WEST Mike 26 27
WESTWOOD Trevor 209
WHADDLEY Dave 63
WHEELAND Dave 'Wongy' 19
WHEELER Andy 283
WHITE Ian 28
WHITE Pete 61 139
WHITEHOUSE Paul 126 227
WILD CHERRY 88 113 114
WILDCATS 44
WILLIAM & THE CONQUERORS 36 37 130
  134 149 154 155 198
WILLIAMS Dave 126 179 239
WILLIAMS Frankie 35
WILLIAMS Keith 33 135
WILLIAMS Rick 36
WILLIAMS Roy 235
WILLIAMSON Grenville 51
WILLIAMSON Sonny Boy 106
WILLINGTON Paul 152
WILSON Bob 259 285
WINWOOD Muff 22 82 151 207
WINWOOD Steve 82 151 158 167 186 197 198
  207
WITHERS Tony 16 34 49 85
WIZZARD 115 282
WONDER Stevie 82
WOOD Chris 71 147 186 198 200 207
WOOD Colin 82 128
WOOD Fred 159
WOOD Kenny 168 211
WOOD Roy 85 88 127 145 154 155 159 182 188
  202 219 221 236 238 247 257 279 282
WOODROFFE Jack 40
WOODS Mick 235
WOODWARD Derek 'Pecker' 154
WOOLDRIDGE Alan 25
WORLD OF OZ 256
WORRALL Peter 25
WORTLEY Gary 236
WRIGHT Ken 210 229
WSJM 30
WYNSCHENK Howard 111
YARDBIRDS 241
YEATES Brian 78 138 177 275
YORK Pete 22 151 242
YOUNG BLOOD 274
YOUNG Jimmy 99
YUKON Billy 30 38
ZENITH Lee 30 69
ZEPPELIN Led 278 288
ZISSMAN Bernard 73
ZUIDER ZEE 144

PLACES

Back cover: Magic Roundabout's Chris Norton & Keith Evans